LATIN JOURNEY

LATIN JOURNEY

CUBAN AND MEXICAN IMMIGRANTS IN THE UNITED STATES

ALEJANDRO PORTES

ROBERT L. BACH

University of California Press
Berkeley • Los Angeles • London

University of California Press
Berkeley and Los Angeles, California

University of California Press, Ltd.
London, England

©1985 by
The Regents of the University of California

Library of Congress Cataloging in Publication Data

Portes, Alejandro, 1944–
Latin journey.

Bibliography: p.
Includes index.
1. Cubans—United States—Economic conditions.
2. Cubans—United States—Social conditions.
3. Mexicans—United States—Economic conditions.
4. Mexicans—United States—Social conditions.
5. United States—Foreign population.
I. Bach, Robert L.   II. Title.
E184.C97P67   1985   305.8′687291′073   83-9292
ISBN 0-520-05003-7
ISBN 0-520-05004-5 (pbk.)

Printed in the United States of America

To the Memory of Our Fathers

CONTENTS

10. CONCLUSION: IMMIGRATION THEORY AND ITS PRACTICAL IMPLICATIONS   334

TABLES

APPENDIX

FIGURES

ACKNOWLEDGMENTS

During the ten years that it took to plan, implement, and analyze the study on which this book is based, we accumulated debts to a number of people who provided financial, intellectual, and moral support for the project. The usual statement that such debts are "too numerous to acknowledge" has, in this case, a particularly appropriate meaning. We apologize in advance for any omission due to our faulty recall and the constraints of space.

The first steps of the study were to ascertain the possibility of interviewing newly arrived immigrants, determine the time and places in which they could be reached, and choose the range of questions that could be asked. The cooperation of the agencies that received, processed, and resettled immigrants was essential for initiating field research. This preliminary stage was supported by grants from the Hogg Foundation for Mental Health and the Institute of Latin American Studies, both at the University of Texas, Austin. The support of these agencies, at a time when there was no guarantee that even the first surveys could be initiated, is acknowledged with special gratitude.

The U.S. Immigration and Naturalization Service agreed to cooperate in identifying newly arrived Mexican immigrants; it also provided space for interviewing them in its border offices in Laredo and El Paso. In Miami, the Cuban Refugee Center, an agency of the Department of Health, Education, and Welfare, also agreed to help in locating recently arrived refugees. Manuel Rodriguez Fleitas, a senior officer of the center and later its director, provided invaluable assistance to the field team, both in the initial survey and in the two subsequent ones. Private agencies entrusted with resettlement of the refugees offered similarly generous support. Without them, it would have been impossible both to contact new arrivals and to follow them in time. In particular, we acknowledge the support of Hugh McLoone of the U.S. Catholic Conference and Silvia M. Gaudie of the International Rescue Committee.

The first surveys along the Texas border and in Miami were conducted under simultaneous grants from the National Science Foundation and the

National Institute of Mental Health. These grants also provided funds for tracing respondents during the first three years after their legal entry. The two follow-up surveys, in 1976 and 1979, as well as the operations connected with tracing respondents in this second interval, were supported by two subsequent joint grants from the same agencies: NSF (# SOC75-16151; SOC77-22089) and NIMH (# MH 27666/01-04).

From 1973 to 1975, a station responsible for locating and maintaining contact with respondents was operated at the Population Research Center of the University of Texas, Austin. We are grateful to its director, Harley L. Browning, for providing the necessary space as well as valuable advice during this stage. From 1976 to 1978, a similar station was based at the Sociology Department of Duke University. Charles Hirschman, then a faculty member at Duke, worked closely with the project's staff and helped organize both the tracing effort and the analysis of first-wave data. We are greatly indebted to him for his support in this phase of the study. Guillermina Jasso, who served as a special assistant to the director of the U.S. Immigration and Naturalization Service in 1978, enlisted the support of that agency in the effort to relocate lost respondents prior to the final follow-up survey. Her assistance at this stage proved most valuable.

Graduate assistants who worked in various aspects of the study were, at the University of Texas, Reynaldo Cue, Kenneth L. Wilson, and Jose A. Cobas, and at Duke, Madeline Haug and Robert N. Parker. The heavy administrative and secretarial duties associated with the project were competently handled by Lindsay Woodruff at the University of Texas and by Sally West and Fifi Gonzalez at Duke. They all have our gratitude for their ability and dedication.

The team of interviewers during the first and the two follow-up surveys in Miami was led by Juan Clark, a sociologist at Miami–Dade Community College. Field research for the first Mexican survey was directed by David Alvirez, then at the Sociology Department of the University of New Mexico. Alvirez also coordinated the 1976 Mexican follow-up from his new post at Pan-American University. The third Mexican survey was conducted by Operations and Marketing Research (OMAR), a Chicago private firm. Luis Salces, a sociologist with OMAR, directed this stage of data collection.

Manuel M. Lopez spent most of his year as an NSF postdoctoral fellow at Duke coordinating the 1979 surveys, serving as liaison with the Miami and Chicago stations, and preparing the data for analysis. This study owes its existence to the field teams under Clark, Alvirez, and Salces, and to the competent coordination of the last stage provided by Lopez. We are fortunate and thankful to have had their collaboration.

Immediately after completion of the last survey, the senior author received a timely fellowship at the Center for Advanced Study in the Behavioral Sciences, permitting him to engage full-time in data analysis. Support for this fellowship year was provided, in part, by a grant from the National Science Foundation (# BNS 76-22943). The assistance of the center staff, in particular that of Kay Wax, Deanna Dejan, and Lynn Gale, is hereby gratefully acknowledged. At about the same time, the junior author spent a year's leave of absence at the Brookings Institution and the Office of Research and Development (ORD), United States Department of Labor. Special recognition for their support is due Howard Rosen, then ORD Chief, and his assistant, Ellen Sehgal. The praises of the Center for Advanced Study and the Brookings Institution have been sung by many. We can only attest to their veracity. It is difficult to imagine environments more conducive to sustained scholarly work than those offered by these unique institutions.

As is often the case, the "book" meant to be written during a year's leave was never finished. Materials and data taken to the West Coast had to make the return trek back East. The final stage of data analysis and writing was conducted simultaneously at Johns Hopkins University and at SUNY–Binghamton. This last stage of the project was supported by a supplementary grant from the Ford Foundation (# 815-0620) and the National Institute of Child Health and Human Development (# RO1-HD-14281). The Center for Social Organization of Schools (CSOS) at Hopkins and the Graduate School at SUNY made available their computer facilities and support personnel. We are thankful to Jeff Puryear of the Ford Foundation; Earl Huyck of the Center for Population Research, NICHD; CSOS director, James McPartland; and the SUNY Provost for Graduate Studies, Arthur K. Smith, for their valuable support.

Our editor at the University of California, Grant Barnes, provided needed encouragement to complete the manuscript and to bring the endless revisions to closure. Joanne Hildebrandt and Shirley Sult retyped all chapters and prepared the final draft. We commend them for their skill and patience in confronting repeated versions of the same material and are indebted to them for their unfailing gracious assistance.

Finally, our colleagues Karl Alexander, Andrew Cherlin, James Fennessey, and Richard Rubinson read and commented on different parts of the manuscript. We received from them many valuable suggestions, but absolve them of any responsibility for the contents of this final version.

1

THEORETICAL OVERVIEW

The movement of human population across space represents one of the major recurrent themes in history. The causes of such movements have been very diverse: escape from hunger and political oppression, the search for economic opportunity, the lust for riches and conquest. The gradual constitution of a state system in the modern world has modified the character of many such movements, adding to them an explicitly political dimension. Contemporary migration movements occur both within the boundaries of particular states and across international borders. Although the causes of internal and international migrations are often similar, increasing state regulation and control separate them today into juridically distinct phenomena.

This book concerns contemporary international migration between Latin American countries and the United States. It presents results of a six-year longitudinal study in which immigrants from Mexico and Cuba were interviewed as they arrived in the United States and reinterviewed twice over that time span. These results help clarify the initial stages of the process of incorporation into a new society and bear directly on competing hypotheses about the role of immigrants in the modern world. In the first chapter, we examine the phenomenon of international migration, its types, and the theories advanced to explain its different aspects. This material serves as the theoretical context in which ensuing findings can be interpreted. Not all the hypotheses reviewed here can actually be tested with the available data. However, even those that are not tested elucidate the analysis and help delimit the scope of its results.

International migration is not an homogeneous process. It includes refugee movements forced by political repression and by dire economic conditions; colonizing movements bent on occupying territory in relatively less advanced countries and profiting from their land and labor; flows of skilled technicians and professionals in search of opportunities denied them in their home countries; and, finally, massive displacements of manual labor moving, permanently or temporarily, to meet labor needs in the receiving economy. Many contemporary treatises on international migration focus exclusively on one type of movement without explicitly recognizing its distinct character and its differences from other movements.

Under the mercantilist international system initiated in Europe in the sixteenth century, the dominant form of international migration was the colonizing movement flowing from the hegemonic powers to newly opened territories or to subordinate nations. As a theory of development, mercantilism itself opposed such out-migrations, for it equated the power and wealth of the home country with the size of resources within its boundaries, including its population.[1] This position was rejected by classic political economists, who demonstrated the advantages to the hegemonic nation of shifting excess population to the colonies. For one advocate of this position, emigration was "merely the application of the redundant capital and population of the United Kingdom to the redundant land of the colonies." For John Stuart Mill, it was "the best affair of business in which the capital of an old and wealthy country can engage," since, among other benefits, it slowed the tendency of profits to fall to a minimum.[2]

The consolidation of capitalism as the dominant economic system in the nineteenth century was accompanied by a gradual reversal of the international migratory flows. Colonizing movements from the European centers to the colonies and semicolonies were eclipsed by the migration of peripheral peoples to fill the demand for labor in the newly industrializing countries. Germany became a center of attraction for eastern European migrants, and the United States received millions of immigrants from southern and eastern Europe. Since the late nineteenth century, the dominant form of international migration has been that of manual labor, and its most consistent direction has been from peripheral regions to regional and world centers. This phenomenon should not lead us to neglect other flows occurring simultaneously: massive refugee movements, the international circulation of professionals, and labor migrations between relatively underdeveloped countries. Still, (manual) labor migrations toward the advanced economies have become increasingly important in terms of both their numbers and their functions for capitalist development.

1. Brinley Thomas, *Migration and Economic Growth*, chap. 1.
2. Both cited in ibid., pp. 5–6.

It is therefore not surprising that most theorizing about international migration has focused on the origins, uses, and effects of labor flows. Refugee movements, professional emigration, and the few remaining colonizing migrations tend to be conceptualized at present as variants of the models applied to labor migration. Existing theories do not generally attempt to encompass the process in its totality but concentrate on one of its specific aspects. Four major foci of theoretical interest can be identified at present: the origins of migrant flows, the determinants of their stability over time, the uses of immigrant labor, and the adaptation of immigrants to the host society. Although these topics overlap somewhat, each has served as a primary object of attention for a different theoretical perspective. In the following sections, we review all these aspects as a way of approaching the migration process in its totality and of placing specific findings from our study in an appropriate theoretical context.

THE ORIGINS OF LABOR MIGRATION

The most widely held approach to the causes of migration is that of *push–pull theories*. Generally, they consist of a compilation of economic, social, and political factors deemed to force individuals to leave their native region or country and of a similar list impelling them toward another. This approach is employed *mutatis mutandis* for explaining movements other than manual labor migrations. Thus, refugee flows are frequently contrasted with labor migrations by noting the greater importance of "push" factors in the former.[3] Students of professional emigration have compiled polar lists of incentives, often termed *differentials of advantage*, to explain the causes of the brain drain from certain countries.[4]

Orthodox economic theories of migration also emphasize the gap in wage incentives between sending and receiving regions. The notion of *unlimited supplies of labor*, employed in analysis of both internal and international migrations, is based on the existence of a permanent large differential in favor of receiving areas. A recent study of international migration notes, for example, that "unlimited supply," demonstrated by the ease with which new labor flows are initiated when older ones are cut off, is attributed to vast income advantages of advanced countries over all peripheral ones.[5] The existence of an unlimited labor supply suggests that the initiation of

3. Richard R. Fagen, Richard A. Brody, and Thomas J. O'Leary, *Cubans in Exile*; Sylvia Castellanos, "The Cuban Refugee Problem in Perspective, 1959–1980."

4. Enrique Oteiza, "Emigración de Profesionales, Técnicos y Obreros Calificados Argentinos a los Estados Unidos"; James A. Wilson, "Motivations Underlying the Brain Drain."

5. Michael J. Piore, *Birds of Passage*, chap. 2.

migrant flows depends almost exclusively on labor demand in receiving areas. When such demand exists, migration takes place. Thus, these economic theories shift emphasis from "push" factors to the "pull" exercised by receiving economies.

This position is a common one among analysts of immigration to the United States. In a study published in 1926, H. Jerome declared that "the pull was stronger than the 'push' since the size of the flow was almost always governed by labor conditions in the United States."[6] The same position was taken by Brinley Thomas in his study of trans-Atlantic migration. For Thomas, overseas migration from Europe in the nineteenth century was accompanied by substantial flows of capital in the same direction. A positive lagged correlation existed between the two movements: capital investments in North America gave rise to labor demand, which in turn stimulated migration from the old countries.[7]

Several problems exist with these theories on the origins of migration. Lists of push and pull factors are drawn almost invariably *post factum* to explain existing flows. Seldom are they used to predict the beginnings of such movements. The limitations of these theories boil down, ultimately, to their inability to explain why sizable migrations occur from certain countries and regions whereas others in similar or even worse conditions fail to generate them. Recent studies of undocumented labor migration from Mexico to the United States indicate, for example, that the bulk of this flow originates in a few Mexican states that are neither the most impoverished nor necessarily the closest to the U.S. border. Mexican immigrants frequently come from the urban working class rather than from the most impoverished sectors of the peasantry, where the gap with U.S. wages is largest.[8]

Similarly, analyses of professional emigration from Third World countries reveal that differentials of advantage measured in either economic or social terms are poor predictors of the origins of such flows. In South America, Argentina, the most developed country of the region, has been a major exporter of professionals during recent decades. In contrast, less developed countries, where economic and social gaps with the advanced world are greater, have registered insignificant flows both in absolute and in relative terms. In Central America, Panama, with a relatively more developed

6. Harry Jerome, *Migration and Business Cycles*, cited in Stanley Lebergott, *Manpower in Economic Growth*, p. 40.

7. Thomas, *Migration and Economic Growth*, Part III.

8. Wayne A. Cornelius, "Immigration, Mexican Development Policy, and the Future of U. S.–Mexican Relations"; Wayne A. Cornelius, "Illegal Immigration to the United States"; Francisco Alba, "Exodo Silencioso"; Alejandro Portes, "Illegal Immigration and the International System."

economy and higher income per capita, has exported a higher proportion of her professionals than Honduras, the least developed country.[9]

A United Nations–sponsored study of Third World university students in advanced countries reveals a most erratic relationship between level of economic development and emigration: among countries enjoying a per capita income of $1,000 U.S. dollars or more in the early 1970s, students committed to return to their home countries ranged from 63 percent for Venezuela to only 16 percent for Argentina. At the other extreme, among countries with a per capita Gross National Product of less than $250, commitment to stay or return varied from 89 percent for Ghana to only 15 percent for Egypt.[10]

Modern history is replete with instances in which the "pull" of higher wages has failed to attract migration from less developed regions. When labor has been needed, it has had to be coerced out of such places, as in the forced employment of native peoples from Africa and the Americas in mines and plantations. The failure of push–pull theories to explain migration flows adequately has led some scholars to propose an alternative interpretation, based on deliberate labor recruitment, according to which differentials of advantage between sending and receiving regions determine only the *potentiality* for migration. Actual flows begin with planned recruitment by the labor-scarce (and generally more advanced) country. Recruiters inform prospective migrants of the opportunities and advantages to be gained by the movement and facilitate it by providing free transportation and other inducements.

Thus, the vaunted "pull" of U.S. wages had to be actualized in the early years of European migration by organized recruitment. In the 1820s and 1830s, American migration agents were sent to Ireland and the Continent to apprise people of "the better meals and higher wages" available for work in the Hudson and other Canal companies.[11] Similarly, labor migration from Mexico, later attributed to the vast wage differences between that country and the United States, was initiated by recruiters sent by railroad companies into the interior of the country. Recent studies of Puerto Rican migration to New England also indicate that the apparently spontaneous flow started with the recruiting activities of large manufacturing concerns among the rural population of the island.[12]

While more persuasive than push–pull theories, an explanation of migra-

9. Alejandro Portes, "Determinants of the Brain Drain," 489–508.

10. Ibid.; William A. Glaser and Christopher Habers, "The Migration and Return of Professionals," 227–244.

11. Lebergott, *Manpower in Economic Growth*, p. 39.

12. Piore, *Birds of Passage*, pp. 23–24.

tion flows that is based on labor recruitment also runs into problems. First, not all early migrant flows were based on recruitment through economic incentives, since some required outright coercion. Second, recent labor migrations from several countries, especially involving undocumented workers, have been initiated without any apparent recruitment effort.

Migrant recruitment on the basis of economic inducement can be seen as the midpoint of a process that has ranged from forced labor extraction to the spontaneous initiation of a flow on the basis of labor demand in the receiving country. The central difficulty with push–pull and labor recruitment theories is not that they fail to identify important forces, but that they do not take into account the changing historical contexts of migration. For each of these theories, migration occurs between two distinct, autonomous social units: that which expels labor and that which receives it. The possibility that such flows may actually be internal to a broader system to which both units belong is not usually contemplated. An alternative conceptualization of the origins of migration requires a grasp of the character of this changing global system and of the mode of incorporation of different areas to it.

A point of departure for this alternative approach is the fairly obvious observation that the pull of high wages has meant nothing in areas external to the international capitalist economy, since such areas have possessed their own internal economic logic and integration. Hence, when dominant countries wanted to put the population of these outlying regions to work in mines or plantations, force, not economic incentives, had to be used. Labor recruitment worked only when the groups addressed were sufficiently integrated into the capitalist system to apprehend the significance of inducements in relation to their existing conditions.

More recently, networks of trade and information across the world, the homogenization of culture, and the extension of consumption expectations even to remote areas have resulted in the "inexhaustible supplies of labor" described in the economic literature. Countries at the center of the system are today in the enviable position of requiring neither force nor recruitment efforts to meet labor demands, but simply regulating a permanently available supply at their borders.

The gradual articulation of an international economic system has resulted in changing forces underlying labor migrations. The effects of this articulation on such flows have not been limited to the diffusion of new life standards and expectations. More generally, the penetration of outlying regions by capitalism has produced imbalances in their internal social and economic structures. Though first induced from the outside, such imbalances become internal to the incorporated societies and lead in time to migratory pressures.

Hence, the pull from advanced economies is based not primarily on invidious comparisons of advantage with the outside world, but on the solution that migration represents to otherwise insoluble problems *internal* to the sending countries. Recent studies of both manual and professional flows indicate that immigrants leave their countries not merely to increase their earnings by X amount, but to solve problems rooted in their own national situations. For immigrants, these problems seem internal ones, but in reality they have been induced by the expansion of a global economic system.

The imbalancing of peripheral areas ranges from the outright imposition of hut taxes among native African populations to create a need for ready cash, to the maintenance of wage scales bearing little relation to costs of consumption in contemporary Latin America. It includes as well the training of new Third World professionals for career expectations compatible with the advanced economies but divorced from actual conditions in their own labor markets.[13]

Labor recruitment was a device used at certain periods in the expansion of the world economy to make certain populations in backward areas aware of the advantages of out-migration. The pull of the advanced economies, insufficient to provoke migrant flows then, is today more than enough to permit routine control of an "inexhaustible supply." The changing character of push and pull, the obsolescence of labor recruitment, and the "spontaneous" origins of recent migrant flows are all consequences of the development of an international economy and of the shifting modes of incorporation of countries into it. This relational dynamics within a global order appears to offer the most adequate explanation of the origins of international migrations.

STABILITY OF MIGRATION

A second aspect discussed by current theories of migration concerns the directionality of these flows and their stability over time. Orthodox analyses tend to view migration in fairly simple terms: people leave their home country in response to economic or political conditions, move to another with the hope of a better life, and struggle for years or generations to attain equality within the new society. Once initiated, the movement can be expected to continue as long as push and pull factors remain and as long as the receiving nation permits it. Massive returns of immigrants to their home country only occur under conditions of deliberate repatriation or severe economic depression.

13. For supporting evidence on this general argument see, Alejandro Portes, "Migration and Underdevelopment," 1–48.

Classic studies of immigration to the United States such as those by Handlin, Thomas and Znaniecki, Child, Wittke, and others generally assumed this basic process and proceeded to analyze the mechanisms for survival among the different groups.[14] Such studies were concerned with European immigrants—the successive flows of Germans, Irish, Italians, Poles, Jews, and Scandinavians coming to meet labor demand in an expanding economy. While some references were made to returns to the home country, these reverse flows were generally attributed to individual circumstances or to periodic recessions in the United States.

The experience of massive immigrations from peripheral to advanced countries in the post-World War II period has given rise to a different theoretical emphasis. The bulk of labor migrations in this period has taken place under "guest worker" arrangements or as a surreptitious flow. These immigrants are labelled *target earners,* since they are assumed to be motivated by the accumulation of money with which to fulfill goals in the home country. It has been noted that a very high proportion of their earnings are sent home as remittances, either to subsidize consumption needs or for investment.[15]

This "economic man" characterization is accompanied by an emphasis on these immigrants' lack of integration and their general indifference to the institutions of the host society. Immigrants seldom speak the language of the receiving country and seldom take part in its associations or in intimate relationships with members of the majority. This divorce from the surrounding society enables them to concentrate exclusively on monetary rewards and to perform jobs that they would reject in their own country.

This new theory has accorded central importance to the phenomenon of return migration. Unlike earlier analyses, it views return to the home country as part of the normal, patterned sequence of labor displacements. While it acknowledges the settlement of vast numbers of European immigrants in the United States at an earlier period, it contends that permanence in the receiving country is not at present a sign of immigrant success:

It is absolutely essential to dispel the notion that seems to emerge in naive versions of this idea of settlement as *success* that the essential aspect of *success is income* . . . migrants tend to be target earners, and *the effect of rising incomes, all other things*

14. Oscar Handlin, *Boston's Immigrants*; Oscar Handlin, *The Uprooted*; William I. Thomas and Florian Znaniecki, *The Polish Peasant in Europe and America*; Irving L. Child, *Italian or American?*; Carl Wittke, *Refugees of Revolution.* A review of this literature is presented in Alejandro Portes, Robert N. Parker, and Jose A. Cobas, "Assimilation or Consciousness," 200–224.

15. Piore, chap. 3.

being equal, is to increase the rate at which they return home. This last effect occurs because, in terms of the original motivations of migrants, settlement is the product of failure.[16] [Emphasis in original.]

This ebb-and-flow characterization of immigration advances our understanding in comparison with earlier descriptions of a simple unidirectional movement. The emphasis on return migration also agrees with some aspects of contemporary Mexican and Dominican labor flows to the United States, as described by recent studies.[17] Still, this alternative theory also runs into difficulties. First, there is evidence that many immigrants do stay in the host country precisely because they have been economically successful. Second, the movement in many cases does not involve a single coming and going, but a series of displacements, frequently involving a seasonal pattern.[18]

More generally, this new theory, like earlier ones, is based on the perspective of the receiving country and, hence, fails to capture the process in its totality. It does not take into account for instance the actual nature of "return" migration, which may be either to the actual places of origin or to others. Similarly, it does not consider common patterns in which individuals alternate between internal and international migration or in which households "assign" some members to travel abroad and some to journey to cities within the country.[19] These omissions stem from the fact that this theory conceives of international migration as a process occurring between two separate national units. An alternative conceptualization would again be based on a definition of the flow as internal to the same economic system. Migration has a dual economic function: from the standpoint of capital, it is the means to fulfill labor demand at different points of the system; from the standpoint of labor, it is the means to take advantage of opportunities distributed unequally in space.

The complexity of international labor flows is a function not only of the shifting locations of opportunities, but of the fact that those locations

16. Ibid., p. 61.

17. Wayne A. Cornelius, "Mexican Migration to the United States"; Ina R. Dinerman, "Patterns of Adaptation Among Households of U. S.-Bound Migrants from Michoacan, Mexico," 485–501; Antonio Ugalde, Frank D. Bean, and Gilbert Cardenas, "International Migration from the Dominican Republic," 235–254; Saskia Sassen-Koob, "Formal and Informal Associations," 314–332.

18. Dinerman, "Patterns of Adaptation"; Cornelius, "Immigration, Mexican Development Policy"; Jorge Bustamante, "Espaldas Mojadas."

19. Robert E. Rhoades, "Intra-European Return Migration and Rural Development," 136–147; Dinerman, "Patterns of Adaptation"; Saskia Sassen-Koob, "The International Circulation of Resources and Development," 509–545.

sought by individuals and families change over time. Opportunities for wage earning are often better in national and international centers, while those for investment in land or small enterprises are often better in the places of origin.[20]

The progressive articulation of a global economic order allows individuals and families in remote areas to gain access to a much broader range of economic opportunities and to "map" their use. Villages in the interior of Mexico today maintain regular contact with ethnic communities in Chicago. Remote towns in the mountains of the Dominican Republic are accurately informed about labor market conditions in Queens and the Bronx.[21]

A full understanding of how these ties are established and how multiple displacements take place requires the introduction of the concept of social networks. Networks link populations distributed widely across the system. It is through networks that the economic opportunities of migration are often actualized. Numerous studies in the United States, Canada, Western Europe, and Latin America show that these linkages are crucial in regulating migrant flows, ensuring the early survival of migrants, finding jobs, and maintaining up-to-date information on economic conditions in the home countries.[22] Labor migration can thus be conceptualized as a process of network building, which depends on and, in turn, reinforces social relationships across space. The microstructures thus created not only permit the survival of migrants, but also constitute a significant undercurrent often running counter to dominant economic trends.

This alternative perspective helps explain a phenomenon that escapes earlier theories: the resilience of migrant flows after original push and pull forces have disappeared or after original opportunities for target earning have been removed. The fact that migrant flows do not respond automatically to such changes is related to their organization through social networks. Once in place, these structures stabilize such movements by adapting to shifting economic conditions and by generating new opportunities apart from the original incentives. While not indifferent to the broader context, the network structures of migration have frequently led to outcomes quite different from those anticipated by conventional economic hypotheses.

20. Robert E. Rhoades, 136–147; Bryan R. Roberts, "The Provincial Urban System and the Process of Dependency"; Cornelius, "Mexican Migration to the United States."

21. G. L. Hendricks, *The Dominican Diaspora*; Sassen-Koob, "Formal and Informal Associations"; Sherri Grasmuck and Patricia Pessar, "Undocumented Dominican Migration to the United States."

22. Charles Tilly, "Migration in Modern European History"; John S. MacDonald and Leatrice D. MacDonald, "Chain Migration, Ethnic Neighborhood Formation, and Social Networks"; Grace M. Anderson, *Networks of Contact*; Lourdes Arizpe, *Migración, Etnicismo y Cambio Económico*; Larissa Lomnitz, *Networks and Marginality*; Roberts, "The Provincial Urban System."

THE USES OF LABOR MIGRATION

Most contemporary theorizing on international migration has focused neither on its origins nor on its directionality and stability over time. Instead, the theories have dealt with the two remaining aspects—uses of migration for the receiving economy and the adaptation of new immigrants. The different theoretical positions on these issues are both more complex and more controversial than those reviewed above, since each lays claim to a supporting empirical literature. Since results from our study will bear on these two aspects of migration, the discussion here is limited to an outline of the major perspectives. An assessment of the relative adequacy of these perspectives is reserved for the book's conclusion.

The orthodox economic perspective views immigrant labor as a supplement to a scarce domestic labor force. Immigrants are recruited to fill jobs in an expanding economy that has run out of hands in its own population. This is the type of situation assumed since the time of classic political economy. John Stuart Mill, for example, defended labor emigration in those terms. He noted, however, that such labor could be profitably utilized by capital in the new countries only if immigrants were prevented from gaining access to land. In the latter case, immigrants would work only for themselves, denying their labor to employers. In the last chapter of *Principles of Political Economy*, Mill had no qualms in abandoning laissez faire doctrines to advocate government sponsorship of emigration. Only state power could prevent migrants from turning into colonists of little or no use to capital.[23]

The situation studied by Mill was obviously one in which land was plentiful. The actual mechanism by which labor scarcity and demand for new labor were created in nineteenth-century America has been described by Lebergott. The supply of cheap land then appeared inexhaustible. The availability of the western frontier enabled domestic workers to invest directly in land, abandoning wage labor for agricultural self-employment. The same could be done by immigrants after a few years:

> In 1820 when lands were worth $50 per acre in Massachusetts and one dollar in Ohio, the New England farmer improved his condition by emigrating to Ohio, and when in 1840 the best lands of Ohio were worth $50 per acre and those of Illinois one dollar and a quarter he could again move with profit to Illinois; and again in 1850 from lands worth $50 in Illinois to the cheap lands of Minnesota and Kansas.[24]

Westward emigration by natives and older immigrants maintained a downward pressure on labor supply, helping to keep wages high and attracting new immigrant flows. But why didn't new immigrants take imme-

23. John Stewart Mill, *Principles of Political Economy*, chap. XI.
24. Lebergott, *Manpower in Economic Growth*, p. 39.

diate advantage of frontier lands? The answer appears to be the combined lack of capital and lack of experience in the new country. Immigrants regarded themselves primarily as wage workers. They concentrated in eastern cities, and only after accumulating sufficient savings and experience did many start the trek westward. This pattern explains both the attractiveness of immigrant labor to eastern employers and the rapid fluctuations of the flow corresponding to the ups and downs of U.S. labor demand.[25]

Orthodox economic theory explains the gravitation of immigrants toward the worst jobs as a natural consequence of an expanding economy. In this view, native workers move upward toward better paid, more prestigious, or more autonomous positions. In the United States, the existence of a frontier played a central role in maintaining an "open" economic structure and abundant opportunities for advancement. This situation can occur, at least in theory, even in the absence of cheap land through the expansion of an industrial economy. Because labor scarcity occurs at the bottom, wages for unskilled and semiskilled workers tend to rise as a result of employer competition. The dual consequences are the attraction of prospective immigrants and the forcing of employers to seek new sources of labor as means of controlling or reducing wages. Both trends encourage further immigration.[26]

In this theory, immigrant workers are not qualitatively different from native ones except that they are newer entrants in the labor force and have less experience and perhaps less education. With time, immigrants can acquire the experience and qualifications to move upward as well, leaving the bottom of the occupational structure to new labor flows. The process helps maintain three "moving" equilibria over time: (1) between labor scarcity in some countries and labor abundance in others, (2) between the needs of employers and the needs and skills of workers, and (3) between workers' aspirations and mobility opportunities in the economic structure.

A second theoretical perspective has focused on the experience of those immigrant groups who have not come of their own free will or who have been made to work under conditions of slavery, servitude, or peonage. These *colonized minorities* also meet a labor demand, but one qualitatively distinct from that described by orthodox theory. They occupy positions at the bottom of the occupational structure—not, however, positions vacated by domestic workers but rather ones requiring a particular class of worker since no free domestic labor can be found to perform them.

In his classic analysis of plantation economies, Edgar Thompson noted the gradual development of this institution and its shift from white inden-

25. Ibid., chap. 2.
26. Ibid.; Barry R. Chiswick, *An Analysis of the Economic Progress and Impact of Immigrants.*

tured servants to black slave labor. In areas of open resources, where land was far more abundant than labor, it was easier to recruit a work force than to keep it. Indentured servants were not motivated to work for planters, since they were paid in advance, but they were highly motivated to escape and work for themselves. Natives were also difficult to control. In the land of their birth, they would rebel or escape to remote places rather than submit to the planter's yoke. It thus became necessary to locate a labor force fit for the hard work but so alien that it would become entirely dependent on the planter's providence. For such workers, the plantation would not be a workplace but a "total institution," where laborers spent their entire lives and without which they would lack the means of survival. Thus it was that the choice of African slaves and the transformation of plantations into social and political as well as economic organizations evolved together. Not until these developments had taken place did a racial ideology emerge as a means of legitimizing them.[27]

The incorporation of a colonized minority to the receiving economy has been marked in general by two central features. First, the group is employed in nonurban extractive tasks, primarily mining and agriculture. Second, production is organized along precapitalist lines, where labor is subject, under various legal arrangements, to the will of employers. The existence of labor under these circumstances gives rise, in turn, to ideologies that justify the situation in terms of racial or cultural differences and the need to educate and control the subordinate group.

Most analysts of the colonial situation have focused on its cultural and ideological aspects. For Blauner, for example, the colonization process is marked by five major events:

First, colonization begins with a forced, involuntary entrance into the dominant society. Second, the colonizing power acts on a policy to constrain, transform, or destroy the indigenous culture. Third, representatives of the dominant power administer the law and control the government bureaucracy. Fourth, there is a separation of labor status between the colonizers and the colonized. Fifth, racism develops as a principle through which people are seen as biologically inferior in order to justify their exploitation.[28]

The shift from precapitalist arrangements to fully capitalist relations of production is experienced only in partial form by colonized minorities. Though in theory the minorities come eventually to join the "free" labor force, they are still relegated to the worst menial jobs. This situation is strikingly different from that portrayed by orthodox theory: when em-

27. Edgar T. Thompson, "The Plantation."
28. James A. Geschwender, *Racial Stratification in America.*

ployed in wage labor, colonized minorities are not simply "new" entrants in the work force capable of moving upwards after a period of time. For colonized minorities that mobility is blocked by a variety of legal and informal mechanisms. Racial and cultural ideologies legitimize both their condition and the deliberate closure of opportunities to move out of it.

The central feature of the colonial perspective on immigration is that it regards the use of this labor as useful for the dominant racial/cultural group *as a whole*. The different classes of the dominant group benefit from the colonial situation in different ways. Employers gain because they have at their disposal a cheap and exploitable source of labor to which they can dictate their own terms. Dominant-group workers benefit in various ways. First, they gain symbolically by the existence of an inferior group with which they can compare their own lot. This allows them to entertain feelings of superiority and to identify vicariously with the dominant classes. Second, they stand to gain materially through three mechanisms: (1) the exclusion of the colonized from competition for the better-paid menial and supervisory jobs; (2) the lowering of the cost of goods and services produced with colonized labor, which cheapens their own consumption; (3) the redistribution of part of the surplus extracted from that labor by the employer class in the form of higher wages and other benefits for dominant-group workers.

The dominant group as a whole thus endeavors to stabilize its monopoly on economic and social advantages through mechanisms that reserve the best positions for its members. Hechter terms this situation the "cultural division of labor" and identifies two modes by which it is maintained:

It may be enforced *de jure* when the individual from the disadvantaged collectivity is denied certain roles by the active intervention of the state. This is the racist solution to the maintenance of the *status quo*. The cultural division of labor may alternatively be preserved *de facto* through policies providing differential access to institutions conferring status in the society at large . . . This is the institutional racist solution to the maintenance of the *status quo*.[29]

A third perspective on the uses of migrant labor also stresses the significance of racial/cultural differences and a racist ideology but interprets its effects differently. Employing migrants from culturally and racially distinct origins is identified here as a common strategy used by the employer class *against* organizations of domestic workers. Hence, the benefits brought about by a subordinate minority in the labor market accrue not to all members of the dominant group, but only to members of the employer class. Such benefits are extracted precisely against the interests

29. Michael Hechter, *Internal Colonialism*, pp. 39–40.

of the domestic proletariat, which is pitted against the new sources of labor. Immigrant workers, whether free or coerced, are generally in a weaker position to resist employer dictates than domestic ones. First, immigrants lack familiarity with economic and social conditions in places of destination, and do not have the means to resist exploitation. Second, they are separated from the domestic working class by linguistic and cultural barriers and by the all too common prejudices among the latter. Third, conditions in places of origin are frequently so desperate that immigrants willingly accept whatever kind of occupation is given them.

Fourth, an immigrant labor force is usually brought under legal constraints, which place it from the start in a vulnerable position. While the nature of these arrangements varies with the country or period, their common effect is to render immigrants subject to ready exclusion or deportation. Organizational efforts or protests among immigrants can thus be defined as a police matter, rather than one involving legitimate class revindications.[30]

This perspective on labor immigration does not necessarily contradict the colonialist one, since each is applicable to different historical periods. However, this last perspective calls attention to an important alternative outcome neglected by most analysts of colonialism: a "cultural division of labor," which works to the direct advantage of certain classes within the racially dominant group and to the direct disadvantage of others. In this view, ideology is employed less to legitimize the privileges of a race or cultural group over another than to sustain the separation between two segments of the working class and to fragment organizations based on class solidarity. The racism that is widespread among domestic workers is thus, ultimately, an ideology directed against themselves.

This analysis directly contradicts predictions stemming from the first-described orthodox perspective on labor immigration. If immigrant labor serves exclusively as a supplement to the domestic labor force, a strong inverse correlation should obtain between domestic levels of unemployment and size of the immigrant flow. Periods of economic recession that bring about higher unemployment should produce, within a relatively short time, decreases in immigration. On the other hand, if the function of immigration is not solely to supplement the domestic labor force but to weaken its organizational base, the result would be quite different. In this case, there should be a positive correlation over time between levels of unemployment and immigration. An organized and militant labor force becomes "useless" to capital, which opts in favor of hiring immigrant workers over

30. Manuel Castells, "Immigrant Workers and Class Struggles in Advanced Capitalism," 33–66; Edna Bonacich, "Advanced Capitalism and Black / White Relations," 34–41.

unemployed domestic ones. The presence of a new preferred source of labor has the effect of accelerating the displacement of domestic workers, thus leading to higher unemployment.

The most systematic version of this perspective has been presented by Edna Bonacich in her analysis of southern black migration to cities in the American North. Bonacich labels her thesis a *split-labor-market interpretation*. During the first three decades of this century, southern black migrants constituted a "preferred" labor force because of their willingness to work at menial jobs for low wages, their lack of organizational experience, and their deferential attitude toward bosses. The strategy through which employers targeted this migrant labor force against the organizational efforts of white workers took three forms: first, strikebreaking; second, replacement of white workers with lower-paid black labor; third, a policy of paternalism toward blacks and black organizations that cemented their alliance with employers against white unions.[31]

Free immigrants had been used before blacks to fill a similar role. In 1832, the directors of the Delaware and Hudson Canal, confronted with demands for higher wages, found that "against this evil the only effective remedy was the introduction of additional miners from abroad." Immigrant labor was imported as promptly as possible and to such an extent that a recurrence of the "evil" was not experienced for some time.[32] The use of European immigrants for strikebreaking and weakening native labor organizations later on in the century is documented in the study by Rosenblum. More recently, Galarza describes a similar process involving the use of Mexican labor against organizational efforts of domestic farm workers in California and throughout the Southwest.[33]

The fourth and last perspective on immigrant labor combines elements of the preceding two, though it focuses primarily on the contemporary situation. Different versions of this perspective exist but the most coherent one is that based on an analysis of the increasing segmentation of social relationships of production under advanced capitalism. The core of this *dual-economy thesis* is the observation that advanced economies have generated an oligopolistic segment in which control of the different facets of production and commercialization is far more extensive than among typical earlier capitalist firms.[34]

31. Bonacich, "Advanced Capitalism," 34–41.
32. Cited in Lebergott, *Manpower in Economic Growth*, p. 40.
33. Gerald Rosenblum, *Immigrant Workers*; Ernesto Galarza, *Farm Workers and Agribusiness in California, 1947–1960*.
34. This thesis has also been presented under the label *dual labor markets*. Certain versions of this formulation have evolved into quasi-psychological models that deflect attention

The emergence of oligopolies in different segments of the economy is a process common to all the industrialized capitalist countries. These firms control a significant portion of their respective markets, rely on capital intensive technology to enhance productivity, and are able to pass on part or all of the increases in the wage bill to consumers through their control of markets. Their social relationships of production have several distinct characteristics determined both by requirements of firms and by past struggles between management and labor for control of the production process.[35]

A prime goal of corporations in the oligopolistic sector is stability in labor relations, and the main strategy to accomplish it is bureaucratization of the production process and the creation of so-called internal markets. *Bureaucratization* means the substitution of a system of control based on direct personal command by one based on adherence to impersonal rules. *Internal markets* means the division of work into finely graded job ladders. Hiring is generally at the bottom, and access to higher positions is usually through internal promotion rather than external recruitment. Stability is promoted by the fact that workers confront not the arbitrary orders of a boss or foreman, but rather a set of explicitly laid-out rules. More importantly, job ladders offer the incentive to remain with a particular firm, since seniority and training are rewarded with increases in pay and status. Oligopolistic corporations are able to create internal markets because of their size and because they can compensate for increases in labor costs with increases in productivity, higher prices for the final product, or both. Wages in this sector of the economy are thus higher and fringe benefits and work conditions more desirable.[36]

A second segment of the economy is formed by those smaller competitive enterprises that more faithfully reflect the structural conditions under early industrial capitalism. Such firms operate in an environment of considerable economic uncertainty. Their markets are usually local or regional, they do not generate their own technology, and they often rely on labor-intensive processes of production. Firms in this sector do not have internal

---

from structural processes to focus on individual attitudes and traits. This description, in particular, applies to the work of Michael Piore. The mix of individual and structural variables in this analysis fails to differentiate it sufficiently from orthodox theories of individual mobility. For this reason, we employ the label *dual economy* to refer to this fourth theoretical perspective. Our outline follows closely the analysis presented by James O'Connor in *The Fiscal Crisis of the State*. A dual-labor-market formulation that reproduces this discussion in all its essentials appears in Richard C. Edwards, "The Social Relations of Production in the Firm and Labor Market Structure."

35. Ibid.; Katherine Stone, "The Origins of Job Structures in the Steel Industry."
36. O'Connor, *The Fiscal Crisis*, chaps. 1 and 2.

markets. Because they also lack a monopoly position, they face greater difficulties in passing on increases in their wage bill. The conditions of production in this sector thus lead to a downward pressure on wages. Control over workers cannot depend on the incentives attached to job ladders or be based on impersonal rules. Instead, discipline is imposed directly, and it is often harsh. Firing is a permanent threat and a common practice, since most labor employed by these firms can be easily replaced. Wages are not only lower than in the oligopolistic sector, but their distribution is flat over time. For workers in the secondary sector, seniority is not a guarantee of higher income or job security. High labor turnover in these firms is a joint consequence of employer dismissals and of worker dissatisfaction.[37] For competitive capital, the viability of these relationships of production depends on the presence of a labor force that is both abundant and powerless. Otherwise, labor costs would go up and the existence of firms, as presently structured, would be threatened. For labor, these conditions are acceptable only in the absence of any other alternative.

Differences in conditions of employment in a dual economy do not depend primarily on the requirements of the job or on the qualifications of the worker. Advantages in income and security enjoyed by those in the oligopolistic sector are the direct outcome of earlier class struggles which resulted in an eventual accommodation: organized labor gained its present advantages and security, while firms gained control over the work process in a manner that promoted stability and minimized disturbances in production. Hence, it is perfectly possible that *jobs* with equal requirements are unequally rewarded depending on the segment of the economy in which they are located.

Entrance into the oligopolistic labor market is primarily a function of the requirements of firms and not the qualifications of workers. As part of its control over the work process, management has systematically opted for capital-intensive technology that reduces labor demand. As many authors have noted, the adoption of technological innovations is determined not by their availability but by the fact that they represent a rational strategy for capital when confronted with an organized labor force. The supply of qualified workers for available positions in the oligopolistic sector consistently exceeds demand. Hence, it is perfectly possible that *individuals* with equal qualifications are also rewarded unequally depending on the segment of the economy in which they are located.[38]

37. Ibid.; David M. Gordon, *Theories of Poverty and Unemployment.*
38. Saskia Sassen-Koob, "Immigrant and Minority Workers in the Organization of the Labor Process."

The dual economy in the United States tends to coincide with preexisting racial and cultural divisions. However, as Sassen-Koob has pointed out, the existence of similar segmentation in European countries without sizable racial minorities shows that the process is a structural requirement of modern economies. The massive presence of white workers in the competitive sector of the U.S. economy also confirms this fact.[39]

The class struggles that led to present relationships of production in the oligopolistic sector were conducted when most workers were white. They involved both white Americans and older European immigrants. The final consolidation of a protected, unionized labor force in this segment of the economy took place only after the New Deal and World War II. Subsequent entrants into the labor market confronted a situation of progressive closure of the economy and employment restricted to the competitive sector. These new entrants were, for the most part, unorganized and hence vulnerable. They included white women, white teenagers, and white rural migrants, as well as black migrants and immigrants.[40]

Students of immigration in the United States have noted the increasing reliance of competitive firms on immigrants, primarily illegal ones, as a source of labor. This process accelerated in the mid-1960s and reached both numerical importance and notoriety during the 1970s. It coincided with the exhaustion of certain labor sources—teenagers and rural migrants—and the increasing resistance of others to accept conditions of employment in these firms. Women and blacks, previously available as pliant sources of labor, have increasingly refused to accept these jobs at those wages. The availability of protective social legislation ("welfare") and other devices have enabled them to withhold their labor from what they perceive as harsh and unfair working conditions.[41]

The analysis offered by dual-economy theory and its predictions concerning labor immigration are more complex than both the colonialist and split-labor-market theories. This complexity is not necessarily a function of shortcomings in the other perspectives, but rather derives from an emphasis on the recent transformation of advanced economies, itself a complex development.

The dual-economy thesis agrees with notions advanced by the two preceding perspectives, but in a modified form. It agrees with colonialist the-

39. Ibid.
40. Bonacich, "Advanced Capitalism"; Robert L. Bach, "Mexican immigration and the American State"; Americo Badillo-Veiga, Josh DeWind, and Julia Preston, "Undocumented Immigrant Workers in New York City."
41. Badillo-Veiga, DeWind, and Preston, "Undocumented Immigrant Workers"; Sassen-Koob, "Immigrant and Minority Workers"; Alejandro Portes, "Toward a Structural Analysis of Illegal (Undocumented) Immigration."

ory that the incorporation of a subordinate racial or cultural minority into the labor market can benefit both employers and workers among the dominant group. This prediction is valid *if* we limit the definition of domestic labor to those in the oligopolistic sector. Workers in these firms benefit from the labor of subordinate immigrant minorities for all the reasons advanced by colonialist theory: lower costs of goods and services, the possibility of sharing in the surplus extracted from immigrants, and the symbolic rewards of superior status.

The dual-economy analysis also agrees with split-labor-market theory in its characterization of immigrants as a "preferred" labor force used against the organizational efforts of domestic workers. This prediction is valid at present *if* we limit the definition of domestic labor to those in the competitive sector. The increase in illegal immigration during the last decade and its employment by competitive firms are developments targeted against the resistance of the domestic-minority work force to accept present conditions and their efforts to improve them.

The situation in this case is different from that described by Bonacich, for it does not pit vulnerable immigrant labor against an unionized working class in the forward sectors of the economy. Instead, immigrants are used to undercut domestic workers who are themselves weak and frequently unorganized and who are employed by the most backward firms. Oligopolistic labor, most of it white, is largely invulnerable to the competition of new immigrant workers and may actually profit from their existence. Competitive labor, most of it nonwhite, is pitted against the new workers and is frequently displaced by them. In this modified form, dual-economy theory supports the split-labor-market prediction concerning unemployment and immigration: there should be no inverse relationship between prior domestic unemployment and present immigration since immigrants are not a supplement to the domestic labor force; there *can* be a positive relationship between the two as immigrants displace workers in the competitive sector of the economy.

IMMIGRANT ADAPTATION

The last set of the theories deals with the social relationships between immigrants and members of the native majority and their cultural interactions. Different perspectives on immigrant adaptation correspond to different theories on the uses of immigrant labor. Thus, the theory that views immigrants essentially as a supplement to the domestic labor force is complemented by a first perspective on adaptation in terms of social and cultural assimilation. The *assimilationist school*, as these writings are collectively known, comprises most of the classic studies of immigrants in the

United States. These include the work of such sociologists and historians as Thomas and Znaniecki on Polish peasants, Handlin on the urban Irish, Child on the second-generation Italians, Wittke on the Germans, and Blegen on the Norwegians. It also includes an array of contemporary writers from Milton Gordon to Thomas Sowell.[42]

The assimilationist perspective defines the situation of immigrants as involving a clash between conflicting cultural values and norms. The native majority represents the "core" while immigrants are peripheral groups. Assimilation occurs by the diffusion of values and norms from core to periphery. By osmosis, as it were, these new cultural forms are gradually absorbed by immigrants bringing them closer to the majority. The process, sometimes called *acculturation,* is generally seen as irreversible though it may take different lengths of time for different groups.[43]

In the most extensive treatise on assimilation, Milton Gordon defines acculturation as a precondition for other forms of assimilation. Next in line comes structural assimilation, or extensive participation of immigrants in primary groups of the core society. This is followed, in a loose sequence, by amalgamation, or intermarriage, between immigrants and natives and by identificational assimilation, or the development of a common national identity based on the symbols of the core group. Attitudinal assimilation reflects the absence of prejudice toward immigrants while behavioral assimilation represents the absence of discrimination.[44]

According to Gordon, there is no necessary linear relationship between different types of assimilation past the stage of acculturation. Learning the norms and values of the society may lead to an immediate reduction of prejudice and discrimination, with both groups choosing to remain apart in terms of social interaction. Identificational assimilation might occur in the absence of amalgamation and even of extensive structural assimilation. Nevertheless, it is the latter process—extensive primary-level interaction between immigrants and members of the core group—that Gordon defines as central to assimilation.[45]

This view is shared by other sociologists of the same school such as Warner and Srole. For them, assimilation is a linear process, but the speed at which immigrants gain access to closer interaction with members of the core groups is affected by three variables: race, religion, and language. The more similar an immigrant group is to the white, Protestant, English-

---

42. Thomas and Znaniecki, *The Polish Peasant;* Handlin, *The Uprooted;* Child, *Italian or American?;* Wittke, *Refugees of Revolution;* Theodore Blegen, *Norwegian Migration to America;* Milton M. Gordon, *Assimilation in American Life;* Thomas Sowell, *Ethnic America.*
43. Hechter, *Internal Colonialism,* chap. 2.
44. Gordon, *Assimilation.*
45. Ibid.; Geschwender, chap. 3.

speaking majority, the faster they will be assimilated. The process may take many generations for immigrants different from the majority in all three variables. For Warner and Srole, race is the primary criterion and nonwhite groups are those whose assimilation is most difficult. The process in this case may take centuries.[46]

Gordon examines three alternative outcomes of the assimilation process labelled, respectively, Anglo conformity, the melting pot, and cultural pluralism. As the label indicates, *Anglo conformity* refers to the complete surrender of immigrants' symbols and values and their absorption by the core culture. The process culminates in identificational assimilation, though it may not lead to structural assimilation or to the total elimination of discrimination and prejudice.

The *melting pot* thesis holds that assimilation results in a blend of the values, norms, life styles, and institutions of the different groups, both core and peripheral. This is manifested, for example, in "American" food, in the incorporation into the language of a number of foreign expressions, and in the adoption of symbols and festivities brought by different immigrant groups.

Cultural pluralism refers to a situation in which immigrants are able to retain their own culture, modified by contact with the core but still preserved in its distinct character. Under pluralism, these differences do not result in prejudice and discrimination; each group is allowed to function in a plane of equality with limited structural assimilation and amalgamation among them. While cultural pluralism is the option favored by most immigrants, Gordon asserts that it has never really existed in the United States. In his view, the acculturation process has led to outcomes best reflected in the Anglo conformity thesis: basic values, norms, and symbols taught to immigrants and fully absorbed by their children correspond to those of the dominant culture.

Other assimilationists, such as Sowell, argue that the more benevolent melting-pot imagery is actually the more empirically accurate. American society and culture are a distillate of many national contributions, of which the Anglo-Protestant tradition is a most significant but by no means exclusive one. In words that parallel those of many others, Sowell asserts that,

the American culture is built on the food, the language, the attitudes, and the skills from numerous groups . . . features of American culture . . . are a common heritage, despite ethnic diversities that still exist. Budweiser is drunk in Harlem, Jews eat pizza, and Chinese restaurants are patronized by customers who are obviously not Chinese.[47]

While rejecting such statements as superficial, other writers believe,

46. W. Lloyd Warner and Leo Srole, *The Social Systems of American Ethnic Groups.*
47. Sowell, *Ethnic America*, p. 286.

nonetheless, that the melting-pot concept is useful as a description of more fundamental processes. Rebuffed in their attempts to translate acculturation into structural assimilation, second- and third-generation "immigrants" have developed their own melting pots, segmented along religious lines. Following earlier authors, Gordon proposes the notion of a *triple melting pot*, in which primary-level relations and intermarriages occur within broad groupings defined by religion: Protestants, Catholics, and Jews. While ethnic identities might persist within each of these broad segments, the general tendency is toward emergence of an undifferentiated "American" population within each of them. Anglo conformity in the culture and segmented melting pots in the social structure emerge from this analysis as basic tendencies of immigrant assimilation in the United States.[48] Other authors, particularly Glazer and Moynihan, have added to the triple melting pot a fourth segment separated from the others not by religious but by racial lines. Blacks and perhaps other nonwhites do not readily "melt" into the broader society or its subsegments, though they have also been acculturated in the dominant values.[49]

Despite the many qualifications and typologies that pervade this literature, its basic insight is that contact between a new foreign minority and an established majority will lead, through a series of stages, to an eventual merging of values, symbols, and identities. This integration into a single society and culture, or perhaps into several major subsegments, is held to be a good thing. For the majority, such a merging represents a guarantee of social stability and the enrichment provided by elements of new cultures. For the minority, it offers the possibility of access to positions of higher prestige and power and the promise of a better future for their children.

The assimilation perspective reflects a view of society as a consensual structure. Social change consists of attempts to restore equilibrium disrupted by external forces. The massive arrival of individuals with a foreign culture represents such a disruption. Assimilation is the process by which equilibrium is restored. As immigrants come to learn the new culture and language, they shed traditional preconceptions and early feelings of alienation. As they come to know and understand members of the core majority, they adopt a more positive attitude toward them. This process of apprenticeship is rewarded, in turn, by greater openness of the host society and greater opportunities for economic and social advancement.

The colonialist, split-labor-market, and dual-economy perspectives on immigrant labor correspond to a very different analysis of immigrant adaptation. From this alternative viewpoint, greater knowledge of the core lan-

---

48. Gordon, *Assimilation*; Geschwender, *Racial Stratification*.
49. Nathan Glazer and Daniel P. Moynihan, *Beyond the Melting Pot*.

guage and culture by new immigrants and greater familiarity with members of the dominant group do not necessarily lead to more positive attitudes and more rapid assimilation. Such conditions can lead precisely to the opposite, as immigrants learn their true economic position and are exposed to racist ideologies directed against them as instruments of domination. This perspective on immigrant adaptation emphasizes ethnic consciousness and the resilience of ethnic culture as instruments of political resistance by exploited minorities.

Studies of ethnicity typically begin by noting the persistence of distinct cultural traits among groups formed by immigration despite extensive periods of time in the host country. This situation can only be explained, from an assimilationist perspective, by the insufficient diffusion of the culture of the core to peripheral groups. However, this kind of explanation runs contrary to the actual experience of many immigrant groups that have been in the receiving country for several generations. These groups have learned the language, are thoroughly familiar with values and life styles of the majority, and are completely integrated into the economic structure. Still, they have not abandoned their distinct cultural traits and self-identities and often resist further assimilation.

At this point, the ethnicity literature splits into two currents. One notes the functional advantages of ethnicity, ranging from the moral and material support provided by ethnic networks to political gains made through ethnic bloc voting. It "pays" to preserve ethnic solidarity, which is often the only edge that immigrants and their descendants have for advance in the broader society. This line of argument is associated in the United States with the works of Greeley, Suttles, and Glazer and Moynihan. Research supporting this position has dealt primarily with the experience of "white ethnics," descendants of European immigrant groups, though it has been extended to nonwhite minorities.

For Greeley, in particular, ethnic resilience is not a cultural "lag" from premodern times but rather the communal basis on which modern social structures rest. Far from constituting a "social problem," ethnic bonds represent one of the few sources of emotional support and social solidarity left in the modern urban context:

The ethnic group . . . came into existence so that the primordial ties of the peasant commune could somehow or other be salvaged. . . . But because the primordial ties have been transmitted does not mean that they have been eliminated. . . . They are every bit as decisive for human relationships as they were in the past.[50]

50. Andrew Greeley, *Why Can't They Be Like Us?* See also Gerald D. Suttles, *The Social Order of the Slum.*

A second current generally agrees with these statements but focuses on the origins of ethnic solidarity. It emphasizes the experience of immigrant groups, which, though acculturated to dominant values and norms, have been rebuffed in their attempts to seek entrance into the core society. As seen above, assimilation theorists have also noted these experiences but do not draw from them any implications beyond the "triple segmentation" of the melting pot. In this second current of the literature, such rejection is a necessary consequence of the subordinate position of immigrant minorities in the labor market and of the ideologies employed to legitimize it. Blacks and Mexicans, like Chinese and Japanese or Poles and Italians before them, have been kept "in their place" because they have formed, each in their time, the mainstay of a segmented labor market. As colonized minorities or fresh labor supplies for the competitive sector, they constitute an indispensable component of the economic structure. Granting such groups admittance into the core society on the basis of merit would jeopardize their utility to employers and to the entire dominant group. Learning the "right" values and behavior patterns is thus not usually enough to gain entrance into the core.[51]

The rejection experienced by immigrants and their descendants in their attempts to become fully assimilated constitutes a central element in the reconstitution of ethnic culture. As several authors have noted, this culture is not a mere continuation of that originally brought by immigrants, but is a distinct emergent product. It is forged in the interaction of the group with the dominant majority, incorporating some aspects of the core culture, and lending privilege to those from the past who appear most suited in the struggle for self-worth and mobility. "Nationalities" thus emerge among immigrants who shared only the most tenuous linkages in the old country. They are brought together by the imputation of a common ethnicity by the core society and its use to justify their exploitation.[52]

The central insight of the ethnic-resilience perspective is that the same ideology employed to justify the condition of colonized and other immigrant groups is eventually turned around as an instrument of solidarity and struggle. As they discover assimilation to be a deceptive path, immigrant minorities come to rely on in-group cohesiveness and cultural reassertion as the only effective means to break out of their situation. The emergence of ethnicity as *the* central identity among peripheral minorities is aided by their common fate both inside and outside the workplace. Minorities tend to work in the same industries and jobs and to live in the same areas. In both

51. Hechter, *Internal Colonialism*, chaps. 2, 10, and 11.

52. Ibid.; Robert Blauner, *Racial Oppression in America*; Oliver C. Cox, *Caste, Class, and Race*.

spheres, they suffer the pervading effects of discrimination. This unity of work and life, of production and consumption, greatly facilitates intragroup interaction. It also increases the significance of ethnic over class identity, the latter being based primarily on relationships in the workplace. For this reason, when discontent finally turns into mobilization, the rallying symbols for these minorities are those of race and culture rather than those of a universal proletarian class.[53]

CONCLUSION

The apparent theoretical fragmentation of the field of immigration actually conceals a certain affinity among the different theories. Analyses of the origins of immigration in terms of push–pull forces generally correspond to a portrayal of the flow as a one-way escape from hunger, want, or persecution. If this analysis is extended to the uses of migrant labor, it tends to emphasize the role of immigrants as a supplement to the domestic labor force. This leads, in turn, to a view of the adaptation process as a gradual series of stages culminating in assimilation into the core society or at least into one of its subsegments. Underlying these theories is a view of society as a structure supported by value consensus and of social change as an equilibrium-restoring mechanism.

On the other hand, an analysis of the origin of labor immigration in terms of an expanding capitalist economy is consonant with a view of the process as part of a series of multiple displacements in space. The articulation of internal and international migrations is better understood within a framework that does not sharply separate "national" from "international" phenomena but that sees both as part of the same economic system. From this perspective, migration can also be readily analyzed as a means to cope with labor "rigidities" in different parts of the system: the impossibility of securing suitable domestic labor for colonial plantations and mines; organizational efforts by domestic workers; and the need to limit the expansion of a unionized and protected labor force. Immigration emerges from this analysis as an integral component of the struggle between labor and capital and as evidence that this struggle is not confined by national borders.

This perspective on uses of immigrant labor is, in turn, congruent with the ethnic-resilience hypothesis on immigrant adaptation. The process entails not a gradual assimilation into the core but the gradual awareness of exploitation and an increasing dissatisfaction with a subordinate role in the cultural division of labor. The eventual reaction to this situation is framed

---

53. Blauner, *Racial Oppression*; Geschwender, *Racial Stratification*, chaps. 4 and 5.

by cultural solidarity and mobilization around the symbols of a common ethnicity. Underlying this second set of theories is a view of society as a structure of material interests supported by different amounts of power and intertwined with ideological justifications. Social change occurs as the outcome of conflict between classes and class segments. The scene of these struggles transcends regions and countries and at present encompasses the entire world.

The interplay between these two general theoretical perspectives provides the background for this study. From them and from the specific theories reviewed, we derive hypotheses to account for different aspects of the immigrant experience as reflected in the data. In several instances, our efforts are directed less at choosing between consensus and conflict theories than at determining whether existing explanations indeed capture the entire reality of the process. In particular, we focus on the phenomenon of economic *enclaves*, created by certain immigrant groups as their distinct mode of incorporation to the receiving society. The nature of this phenomenon and its effects is examined in the next and subsequent chapters.

As stated above, results to be presented bear primarily on the last two aspects discussed above—uses of labor immigration and immigrant adaptation. This analysis is organized into nine additional chapters. A brief synopsis of each is in order. Chapter 2 examines more closely the history of modern immigration to the United States in the context of theories reviewed above. It assembles numerical and qualitative data on the changing origins, labor-market incorporation, and social adaptation of immigrants over time.

Chapter 3 introduces the two immigrant groups that are the subject of empirical study, Cubans and Mexicans. It reviews the history of each flow and its different stages, from the perspective of the process of adaptation to the receiving country. This review provides, in turn, a background for discussion of the design of the study and the characteristics of the final data set. Chapter 4 presents a statistical profile of the two immigrant groups as they were at the time of arrival in the United States. This description is set in the context of changing conditions in the sending countries, Mexico and Cuba. The analysis interrelates survey results with national-level data to show how individual characteristics correspond to the structural course of development in the immigrants' country of origin. Chapter 5 presents similar profiles of both samples after three and six years in the United States. The longitudinal data enables us to compare present characteristics of immigrants with those at arrival and with the latter's original attitudes and aspirations. Together these chapters provide an overview of the basic results of the study concerning social adaptation and position of immigrants in the U. S. labor market.

The next four chapters are devoted to more complex analyses of significant variables. Each draws on theories reviewed in this chapter to derive a series of testable hypotheses, which are then evaluated through bivariate and multivariate statistical techniques. Chapters 6 and 7 examine occupation and earnings of Cubans and Mexicans, respectively. They bring together individual-level variables, suggested by neoclassical economic theory and sociological models of status attainment, and structural-level predictors, derived from theories of segmented labor markets.

Chapter 8 turns to the immigrants' social psychological orientations, including their perceptions of discrimination against their own group in the United States. The analysis is guided by predictions stemming from assimilation and ethnic-resilience theories of adaptation. It results in a multivariate model that incorporates the most significant effects over time. Basic similarities, as well as systematic differences, emerge between Cuban and Mexican orientations toward American society.

Chapter 9 examines the social relationships of immigrants, both in face-to-face interactions and in secondary organizations. The incidence of out-group relationships, primarily with Anglos, is modelled on a series of exogenous variables suggested by various theories. Several reliable but counterintuitive results emerge that challenge conventional wisdom concerning social relations outside the ethnic community.

The concluding chapter summarizes results of the study, highlighting major trends and the manner in which they bear on theoretical and policy debates in the field of immigration. It discusses probable future trends and their relationships with other processes in an evolving international system.

2

IMMIGRATION TO THE
UNITED STATES, 1890–1979

By 1890, immigration to the United States had lost the characteristics of a colonizing movement from the metropolis and acquired those of a labor movement from peripheral countries to a new industrial center. During the three preceding decades, immigration had brought close to 10 million people to the country. From 1881 to 1890 alone, more than 5 million new immigrants arrived. The overwhelming majority of these came from "traditional" emigration countries—England, Ireland, Germany, France, and the Scandinavian countries. During the last decade of the nineteenth century, however, there was a marked shift toward new sources of immigration at the European periphery. The rural populations of Italy, Greece, Poland, the eastern reaches of the Austro-Hungarian empire, and Russia became the major purveyors of immigrant labor.[1]

The mid-decade depression of the 1890s slowed this flow, which amounted to about 2 million for the decade. The movement literally exploded during the following decade and continued unabated until the start of World War I. From 1901 to 1910, close to 9 million new immigrants arrived; two-thirds of these came from East Central and Southern Europe. Immigration surpassed the 1 million mark for the first time in 1904 and continued at this or higher levels for all the years before World War I except 1907–1908.[2]

The turn toward new sources of immigration and the rapid increase of this movement by the turn of the century coincided with shifts in the struc-

1. U. S. Immigration and Naturalization Service, *1977 Annual Report*, Table 13.
2. Ibid.

ture of the American economy. The powerful drive toward industrial consolidation and monopoly displaced agriculture as the dominant sector of the economy and reduced the demand for a permanent, settler-oriented immigration. New, urban-based industries generated a strong demand for manual labor. Skills became less necessary as technological innovation and large-scale methods of production reduced many jobs to routine, machine-tending tasks.

What the new industries required was a mass of unskilled workers who could be hired cheaply and dismissed freely during economic downturns. The demand was augmented by large railroad and canal construction projects. Domestic labor supplies proved insufficient from the start for two reasons: first, they were relatively scarce in relation to the emerging demand; second, cheap land was still available and this factor, plus other economic opportunities, freed domestic workers from dependence on factory labor, allowing them to demand higher wages. The same reasons applied *mutatis mutandis* to the "old" immigration, oriented as it was toward colonization and permanent settlement on the land.[3]

The shift toward new peripheral sources of labor did not just "happen"; rather, it originated in the deliberate efforts of American industry to find new and suitable supplies. The push and pull forces, which were to be described *a posteriori* by analysts of immigration, could not have been actualized without the activities of labor recruiters paid by the companies. The task was actually divided between steamship lines, which promoted emigration to fill their vessels, and labor recruiters at home ports, which channeled newly arrived immigrants to their final destinations.

By the end of the nineteenth century, even people of remote rural regions in Eastern Europe were sufficiently integrated into the world economy to grasp the significance of a daily wage of $1.23, paid to common laborers in New York City. Still, they had to be informed of that fact. Because these regions were not sufficiently integrated to generate a "spontaneous" flow, deliberate recruitment, at times involving economic incentives for the passage, had to be employed.[4]

The stability, uses, and adaptation of this turn-of-the-century immigration are discussed in the following sections. The analysis of pre-World War I immigration as a whole serves as a point of comparison for present trends, starting after World War II. Stability, uses, and adaptation of recent immigrants are then examined in this general context with special emphasis on the distinct experiences of legal, undocumented, and contract labor immigration.

3. Stanley Lebergott, *Manpower in Economic Growth,* chap. 2.
4. Michael J. Piore, *Birds of Passage,* chap. 6; Rudolph Vecoli, "The Italian Americans."

IMMIGRANT LABOR, 1890–1914

The currents of Eastern and Southern European immigrants coming to American cities during this period were composed of individuals whose motivations were, for the most part, exclusively monetary and guided by conditions in the native country. There was a natural fit between the willingness of immigrants to return home and the fluctuating labor needs of the industries that employed them. Thus, unlike the earlier British and Northern European immigrants, the new arrivals generated a significant return flow.

The U.S. Immigration (Dillingham Commission) Report of 1911 estimated that two-fifths of the "new" immigrants returned to Europe and that the bulk of returnees did so after a relatively short period. The commission also estimated that about four-fifths of those who returned did so after five years or less in the United States.[5] The portrait of these immigrants as target earners and of their movement as a two-way flow is thus generally accurate, though it is subject to two important qualifications.

First, in the short span of two and one-half decades, Eastern and Southern European immigration left a sizable "sediment" in the receiving country. In 1910, immigrants represented 21 percent of the labor force; by 1920, half of the urban population of the United States was either foreign born or second generation. The immigrants' concentration in particular geographical areas and occupations made their presence even more visible. Of the 875,000 Polish immigrants who came to the United States between 1870 and 1924, about 70 percent were estimated to have remained in the country. By the turn of the century, Polish colonies in Pittsburgh, Buffalo, Detroit, and other cities were larger than many cities in Poland. Chicago, with 360,000 Poles, ranked only behind Warsaw and Lodz as the third largest Polish city in the world.[6]

Second, the very cheapness of third-class passage to and from Europe promoted the beginnings of cyclical, or multiple-displacement, migration. While this outcome was certainly less common than among contemporary immigrants, it did not seem numerically insignificant. The same 1911 Immigration Commission that emphasized the importance of return migration estimated that one-third of those who returned to Europe came back eventually to the United States.[7]

European immigrants were in demand during this period to fill the bot-

5. Immigration Commission, *Reports*.

6. Saskia Sassen-Koob, "Immigrant and Minority Workers in the Organization of the Labor Process"; William I. Thomas and Florian Znaniecki, *The Polish Peasant in Europe and America*.

7. Immigration Commission, *Reports*, p. 24.

Table 1. Unemployment, Immigration, and
the Labor Force, 1890-1914

Year	Labor Force Unemployed %	Immigrant Arrivals, Age 16-44 (in thousands)	Immigrants as Percent of the Labor Force
1890	4.0	315	1.4
1891	5.4	406	1.9
1892	3.0	492	2.3
1893	11.7	420	1.9
1894	18.4	258	1.2
1895	13.7	233	1.1
1896	14.4	255	1.2
1897	14.5	165	0.8
1898	12.4	165	0.8
1899	6.5	248	1.1
1900	5.0	370	1.3
1901	4.0	396	1.4
1902	3.7	539	1.9
1903	3.9	714	2.6
1904	5.4	657	2.4
1905	4.3	855	3.1
1906	1.7	914	3.3
1907	2.8	1,101	4.0
1908	8.0	631	2.3
1909	5.1	625	2.3
1910	5.9	868	2.6
1911	6.7	715	2.1
1912	4.6	678	2.0
1913	4.3	986	2.9
1914	7.9	982	2.9

Source: U.S. Bureau of the Census, Historical Statistics of the United States, Colonial Times to 1970, Bicentennial Edition (Washington, D.C.: U.S. Government Printing Office, 1976).

tom positions of the industrial labor market. There is evidence of an incipient division at the time between small competitive firms and large ones bent on monopoly. Still, a dual-economic structure had not yet emerged. Among other factors, the labor struggles that eventually gave rise to segmentation of the labor market had not yet run their course. Similarly, as Rosenblum points out, immigrant workers were used repeatedly as strikebreakers during the period and their presence was a powerful tool against the American Federation of Labor and other organizations of the domestic working class.[8]

It is undeniable that Eastern and Southern European immigrants functioned as a source of cheap labor and that they frequently constituted a "preferred" labor force in the sense described by dual-labor-market theory. Still, their primary role in the unified industrial labor market of the time

8. Gerald Rosenblum, Immigrant Workers, chaps. 1 and 6.

Fig. 1.   Unemployment and Immigration, 1890 – 1914

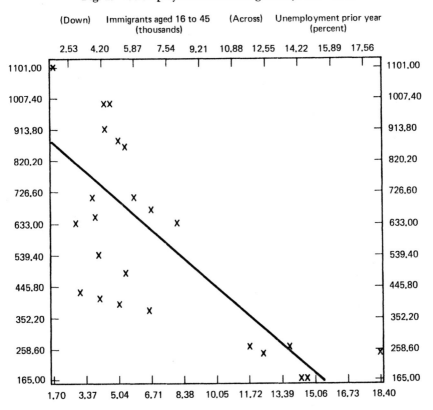

(Down)   Immigrants aged 16 to 45   (Across)   Unemployment prior year
(thousands)   (percent)

was to supplement a scarce domestic labor force. Native workers and older immigrants could take advantage of opportunities opened by an expanding economy, abandoning the bottom of the labor market to the newcomers. There were no instances at the national level in which sustained high unemployment coexisted with high levels of immigration. The relationship between the two variables corresponded during the period to the predictions of conventional economic theory.

Table 1 presents time-series data for immigration, its size relative to the domestic labor force, and unemployment rates between 1890 and 1914. The figures for immigration are the number of immigrants of working age, 16 to 44, arriving in a given year. The ups and downs of the immigration flow closely follow economic conditions, as reflected in the percentage of the labor force unemployed. As predicted, the higher the unemployment for a given year, the lower the immigration. The correlation of these variables over the 25-year period is – .61.

Table 2.   Economic Determinants of
Immigration, 1890-1914

Endogenous Variable Year t	Exogenous Variables[a] Year t - 1			R	R²
Immigration, ages 16-44	Immigration, 16-44	Unemployment	Gross National Product		
--	.649* (.148)	-19.43* (8.94)	--	.87	.75
--	.450* (.181)	--	48.96* (17.52)	.88	.78

[a]Figures are linear regression slopes; standard errors in parentheses.

*Significant at the .01 level.

Perhaps a more appropriate indicator is the lagged correlation between immigration and unemployment in the prior year. Figure 1 presents this relationship. It shows a strong inverse association corresponding to a correlation of $-.71$. The same pattern is reflected in the proportions of the labor force represented by yearly immigration. This figure tended to increase over time but was lowest during unemployment peaks, increasing again when unemployment declined.

Economic determinants of immigration are reflected in results presented in Table 2. Immigration in year t is regressed there on unemployment in $t - 1$ and then on GNP, both controlling for autocorrelation effects. After we take the latter into account, the effect of economic variables remains highly significant. During this period, a 1 percent increase in unemployment reduced working-age immigration in the ensuing year by an average of 19,000 people. Similarly, a 1 percent increase in Gross National Product (1958 = 100) led to a net increase of 49,000 immigrants on the average in the following year. These results indicate that labor market conditions not only had a long-term association with the size of immigration but also decisively affected year-to-year changes. These effects are consistent, in every case, with conventional economic predictions.

The fact that European immigration constituted primarily a supplement to the domestic labor force suggests, in turn, that its adaptation to the new country would follow the gradual stages described by assimilation theory. However, this was not the case. Most historical evidence indicates that immigrants from peripheral Europe suffered heavily from prejudice and discrimination in the United States. They and their children acculturated rapidly, but the rejection by the native majority forced them to fall back on their own resources for social and economic support. The ethnic communities that they created in all major cities have lasted to our day.

Since these groups were neither colonized minorities nor suppliers of labor for a split-labor market, the virulence of the racial stereotyping against them requires explanation. Italians, the single largest immigrant group arriving during the period, were subjected to particularly harsh forms of attack. They were accused of being "the most vicious, ignorant, degraded, and filthy paupers, with something more of an admixture of the criminal element."[9] Italians were lynched by mobs in the South and made the target of vigilante justice justified, in every case, by their "patent criminal" inclinations. Other large immigrant groups, such as the Poles, did not fare much better in escaping racism.

The ideological attack on the new European immigrants had its structural base in two convergent forces. First, it was in the interest of employers to keep the immigrant population as weak, vulnerable, and socially distant from domestic workers as possible. Though formally part of a "free" labor market, the new immigrants were confined to the worst jobs, and were often made to work under incredibly harsh conditions. Between 1880 and 1920, about 4 million Italians arrived in the United States. Their work conditions were described as follows:

These were the legendary dago ditchdiggers who built the nation's railroads, dams, subways, and cities. . . . living in boxcars and shanties, eating wretched food, killed and maimed by explosions and accidents, the immigrants labored twelve or more hours a day in all kinds of weather. Most endured this purgatory so that of the $1.50 daily wage they might save fifty cents.[10]

Justification for these conditions was provided by racism and the degradation of the immigrants' culture. Such efforts obviously did not conflict with employers' goals: the longer immigrants could be maintained as an atomized work force, and the more their participation in domestic unions could be retarded, the longer the problem of recruiting new sources of low-wage labor could be postponed.

Second, by the turn of the century and particularly in the years preceding World War I, native workers and older immigrants came to view the new immigration as a growing threat to their own well-being. From the point of view of domestic workers, there were three serious causes of concern: first, the sheer numbers of the newcomers; second, the progressive closure of the frontier and of opportunities outside the factory system;

9. Leonard Dinnerstein and Frederick Cole Jaher, *Uncertain Americans*, p. 201.
10. Vecoli, "The Italian Americans," p. 202.

third, the experiences, scattered but growing in number, of immigrant strikebreakers in mines and factories. The defense of the interests of native labor by established unions did not take the course of solidarity with oppressed immigrants. Instead, there was widespread rejection of the newcomers and repeated demands for exclusion based on a racist ideology.

The extremes of discrimination and prejudice suffered by the new European immigrants thus had their ultimate cause in the fact that such attitudes were deemed appropriate by the two classes with which the immigrant population interacted in the labor market. Denied support by their employers and by their native co-workers, the new groups reacted predictably by banding together under the symbols of a common ethnicity. The path followed since then by the Italian, Polish, Slovak, and other immigrant communities conforms, in all its essentials, to the predictions of ethnic-resilience theory.

This course of action followed two main channels: first, territorial concentration and emphasis on ethnic control of designated patches of urban land; second, the emergence of protective social organizations. Italian immigrants came together in numerous "Little Italies," sometimes divided in blocks by the provinces or even villages of origin. Social clubs, bars, and shops provided the necessary atmosphere where immigrants could retrieve their sense of self-worth and brace themselves for confronting the outside society. According to Thomas and Znaniecki, the process of territorial concentration among Polish immigrants took place in a more deliberate manner. It began with the construction of a church as near as possible to where Poles lived and worked. At a later stage, a Polish real estate agency or building association initiated a campaign to transfer land and houses in the area to Polish hands. The resulting homogenous communities proved remarkably resilient to subsequent social and economic changes.[11]

Even after prosperous descendants of the first generation had moved to the suburbs, the old ethnic neighborhoods continued to exist, remaining the centers of community life. The pattern of spatial adaptation of Eastern and Southern European immigrants thus followed a direction precisely opposite that predicted by assimilation theory: from dispersal to deliberate ethnic concentration. Rather than joining any particular melting pot, immigrants created their own "reception centers" from which they could defend themselves against discrimination and through which they could seek avenues for economic mobility.

This process was complemented by the emergence of a number of ethnic organizations and institutions. These ranged from local mutual aid societies providing help in family emergencies to large insurance and savings

11. Thomas and Znaniecki, *The Polish Peasant.*

and loan institutions. At the national level, such organizations as the Italy–America Society or the Polish–American Alliance defended immigrants against racist campaigns and made sustained efforts to preserve the national culture. Among the organizations created by immigrants, perhaps none was more important than the parish school. For the Poles, in particular, this institution had a unique place, being established immediately after the foundation of the parish itself. As told by Thomas and Znaniecki,

The most essential point . . . is the function of the parochial school as a factor of the social unity of the immigrant colony and of its continuity through successive generations. . . . Whereas children who go to public school become completely estranged from their parents, if these are immigrants, the parish school . . . prevents this estrangement . . . because it inculcates respect for these traditional values and for the nation from which they came.[12]

A recent study by Ralph and Rubinson confirms this relationship between Eastern and Southern European immigration and the educational system. The study models school expansion as a linear function of a series of variables including the eligible school-age population and the size of the immigrant flow, lagged five and ten years. Regression slopes for the 1890–1924 period show that immigration had a consistently negative effect on the expansion of *public* schools, but a consistently positive one on the growth of *private* (mainly parochial) education.[13] The creation of a parallel school system, sometimes going all the way to high school and college, was one of the central elements in the immigrants' response to the prejudice and hostility with which society confronted them.

The pattern of adaptation after the first generation is a tale of economic progress within the context of persistent ethnic identification. Second-generation Italians, Poles, and Greeks were torn between demands of loyalty by their parents and the desire to escape the all-too-obvious stigma of their ethnicity among Americans of their generation. While many became more or less "assimilated," the trend for most appears to have been an eventual return to the ethnic community. For some, this might have been an outcome of the rejection experienced in their attempts to "melt" into the broader society. For others, especially those of the third generation, it was a conscious attempt to recover a lost identity and to make use of the social and economic advantages derived from ethnic networks and solidarity.[14]

12. Ibid., pp. 241–242.

13. John H. Ralph and Richard Rubinson, "Immigration and the Expansion of Schooling, 1890–1970."

14. Vecoli, "The Italian Americans"; Andrew Greeley, *Why Can't They Be Like Us?*

JAPANESE AND JEWS

Two immigrant groups arriving during the 1890–1914 period differed markedly from other minorities both in the way their labor was utilized and in their mode of adaptation. The similarity between these two groups after their arrival in the United States could not have been anticipated on the basis of their background, for it is difficult to imagine more different national origins. One of these groups came to the United States to escape the brutal persecutions of their own country's government; the other came as part of an officially sponsored and monitored flow. One came to fill industrial and service jobs in an urban economy; the other came to meet labor demands in agriculture. One was committed from the start to permanent settlement in the country; the other viewed its sojourn as a temporary stay until debts could be settled or land bought in the mother country.

Both groups were non-Christian, but they were different in religion, language, and race. They disembarked at opposite ends of the continent and never met in sizable numbers at any point. Yet, Jews and Japanese developed patterns of economic and social adaptation that were remarkably similar. What both groups had in common was their collective resistance to serving as a mere source of labor power. From the start, their economic conduct was oriented toward two goals: (1) the acquisition of property, and (2) the search for entrepreneurial opportunities that would give them an "edge" in the American market.

In coastal cities at both ends of the land, Jews and Japanese created tightly knit communities that in appearance resembled the ethnic neighborhoods of many other immigrant groups but differed from these neighborhoods in their social and economic organization. These communities were not exclusively residential—places where an immigrant working class could find comfort and sociability. They were instead economic *enclaves*, areas where a substantial proportion of immigrants were engaged in business activities and where a still larger proportion worked in firms owned by other immigrants.

To overcome the lack of capital, the absence of connections in the general economy, and the patent hostility surrounding them, Jewish and Japanese entrepreneurs made use of the resources made available by their own communities. For the entrepreneurially inclined, networks based on ethnic solidarity had clear economic potential. The community was (1) a source of labor, which could be made to work at lower wages; (2) a controlled market; and (3) a source of capital, through rotating credit associations and similar institutions.

Starting from very humble beginnings, many immigrant enterprises reached a modicum of success, and some expanded into major firms. Characteristically, these immigrant groups experienced significant economic mobility *in the first generation* and this progress frequently preceded, not followed, acculturation. There were immigrant millionaires who spoke broken English and whose cultural allegiance was still to the home country. This pattern contradicted the typical assimilation saga, whereby economic advancement was supposed to involve a long and difficult acculturation process. The pattern also earned for these groups the enmity of the surrounding population and a series of attacks more venomous perhaps than those suffered by other minorities.

The content of anti-Japanese and anti-Jewish sentiment differed, however, from that directed against other immigrants. Whereas Italians and Poles were labelled shiftless, ignorant, and otherwise inferior, the qualities most frequently imputed to Japanese and Jews were a lack of national loyalty and slyness. The combination of cultural distinctness and economic success provoked in both cases a number of racist campaigns. Quotas were established for keeping Jewish students out of the best universities. Increasing in frequency and intensity, anti-Semitic campaigns forced the creation of the Jewish Anti-Defamation League and other ethnic defense organizations. On the West Coast, continuous attacks against the Japanese culminated in confiscation of their property and their mass internment in camps during World War II.[15]

The first major wave of Jewish immigration took place roughly between 1840 and 1870, when about 50,000 Jews of German origin arrived in the United States. These immigrants engaged almost exclusively in commerce. Starting as street peddlers and small merchants, they managed to reach significant economic prosperity in the course of a single generation. By 1890, the German Jewish community in the United States was better off economically than the average native population. Merchants specializing in the sale of "dry and fancy goods" pioneered in the creation of the modern department store, laying the basis for such firms as Macy's and Sears Roebuck. In banking, Jewish companies such as Kuhn and Loeb, Speyer, and the Seligmans reached significant size. In 1870, about 10 percent of Jewish firms were capitalized at or above $100,000; in 1890, almost 25 percent reported a minimum capital of $125,000.[16]

Starting in 1870, a new wave of Jewish immigration overtook the original one. Between 1870 and 1914, more than 2 million Jews abandoned Russia, where the Jewish population had been confined to the "Pale of Settlement," a belt of land extending from the Baltic to the Black seas. After the

15. Leonard Dinnerstein, "The East European Jewish Migration"; William Petersen, *Japanese Americans*, chaps. 3 and 4.

16. Moses Rischin, *The Promised City*, p. 52.

onset of industrialization, the Russian government pursued a policy of systematic discrimination destined to keep ownership out of Jewish hands. In addition to economic and geographic restrictions, Jews suffered increasing political persecution. After the assassination of Tsar Alexander II in 1881, a wave of major pogroms against the Jewish population occurred with the connivance of the government. Major pogroms took place in 1881, 1882, 1903, and 1906.[17]

To escape such conditions, Eastern European Jews moved en masse to the United States. They arrived and remained, for the most part, in New York City. Within it, they concentrated heavily in a small section of Manhattan, the Lower East Side. In the heart of this district, the 10th Ward, population density reached 523.6 people per acre by the turn of the century. Efforts to disperse this population met with very limited success. Despite the initially harsh conditions, few Jewish immigrants abandoned their community. Thousands took to street peddling, others opened small shops, and many went to work in factories owned by German Jews.[18]

The German Jewish community viewed the arrival of these impoverished masses with alarm, fearing that they would stigmatize the whole group in American eyes and jeopardize its own position. It promptly realized, however, that the best strategy lay not in rejecting the newcomers but in integrating them. Louis D. Brandeis, a prominent member of the Jewish community, put it as follows:

a single though inconspicuous instance of dishonorable conduct on the part of a Jew in any trade or profession has far reaching evil effects extending to the many innocent members of the race. . . . Since the act of each becomes thus the concern of all, we are perforce our brothers' keepers.[19]

Organizations such as the Hebrew American Aid Society, the United Hebrew Charities, the Independent Order of B'nai B'rith, the Baron de Hirsch Fund, and others ministered to the needs of the immigrants. They attended both to their material welfare and to the imperative need of teaching them the language and the ways of the new country. Though charity was often administered in an impersonal and even condescending manner, the Jewish organizations proceeded with such efficiency as to prompt outsiders to note that no other immigrant group had "proved so generous to their own kind."[20]

The newcomers, however, lost little time in emulating the earlier German immigrants. As they improved their economic position, German aid

17. Dinnerstein, "The East European Jewish Migration."
18. Ibid.
19. Cited in ibid., p. 226.
20. Rischin, *The Promised City*, chap. 6.

societies were replaced by Russian, Hungarian, and Galician ones. The Yiddish language, regarded by the Germans as a symbol of the patent inferiority of the new arrivals, became increasingly acceptable. In industry, the pattern of German-owned firms and Russian Jewish labor rapidly changed as more Eastern Europeans became contractors and entrepreneurs. Jewish industry proliferated in the building and metal trades, in jewelry and printing, and in tobacco and cigar making. It was, however, the clothing industry that became "the great Jewish metier."[21] In 1920, of 23,479 factories in the borough of Manhattan, almost half, 11,172, were engaged in clothing production and employed more than 200,000 people. Except for the larger firms, employers were no longer German Jews, but overwhelmingly East Europeans.[22]

The Jewish entrepreneurial drive led to significant economic mobility among first-generation immigrants. The ascent along the economic and social ladders was to be completed by the second and third generations. The original immigrants lacked the resources and time to take advantage of the public higher-education system in New York City. Their children, however, were able to do so and literally monopolized facilities at City College. By the third generation, Jewish students were attending top-rated schools, including those created by their own minority. Thus, despite anti-Semitism, quota systems, and other restrictions, the remarkable progress of this immigrant group continued unabated. At the end of the 1930s, two-thirds of all Jewish workers were in white-collar positions. By the early 1940s, Jews comprised 65.7 percent of New York City's lawyers and judges, 55.7 percent of its physicians, and 64 percent of its dentists. Today, Jewish family income is the highest of any ethnic group, exceeding by 72 percent the national average.[23]

From the start, Jewish adaptation to America proceeded along two simultaneous lines. First, rapid *instrumental* acculturation, with an emphasis on learning the language, business and occupational skills, and the general "ways" of the new society. Second, defense of traditional Jewish values and maintenance of collective solidarity. What is distinctive about this adaptation process is that geographic concentration in an economic enclave, resistance to dispersal efforts, and the proliferation of mutual aid and ethnic organizations did not occur as a reaction to outside hostility, but emerged *from the start* as part of a collective survival strategy. Through it, Jewish immigrants endeavored to carve for themselves an autonomous place in the receiving country. Processes of assimilation—geographic displacement,

21. Ibid., p. 61.
22. Ibid., p. 67.
23. Dinnerstein, "The East European Jewish Migration"; Thomas Sowell, *Ethnic America*, chap. 4.

intermarriage, and so on—took place much later and in terms governed by minority interests and evolving needs, rather than by majority decisions.

Under very different circumstances, Japanese immigration to the West Coast followed a similar adaptation pattern. Significant Japanese immigration to the mainland did not start until 1890. From that year until 1908, about 150,000 male immigrants came. After the Gentlemen's Agreement of 1908, Japanese arrivals were predominantly the spouses of earlier immigrants, until the 1924 Immigration Act banned all further Asiatic immigration. During the entire period, there were fewer than 300,000 Japanese recorded as entering the United States.[24] This figure does not take into account the return flow and, hence, overestimates the actual size of net immigration. From 1908 to 1924, for example, the 160,000 Japanese immigrants resulted in a net inflow of only 90,000. The 1920 census counted 111,010 Japanese in the United States out of a total population of 106,000,000.[25]

Several authors have commented on the discrepancy between the tiny size of this group and the magnitude of the public reaction to it. Repeatedly, the California press and the labor movement engaged in virulent campaigns against the "Japanese invasion." In 1905, both houses of the California legislature passed a resolution asking Congress to limit further Japanese immigration. Included in a long bill of particulars was the following statement:

Japanese laborers, by reason of race habits, mode of living, disposition, and general characteristics, are undesirable. . . . They contribute nothing to the growth of the state. They add nothing to its wealth, and they are a blight on the prosperity of it, and a great impending danger to its welfare.[26]

For the next forty years, not a single session of the California legislature ended without at least an attempt to pass one more piece of anti-Japanese legislation.[27] One reason for such hostility was that, like Jews back East, the Japanese were highly concentrated and resisted efforts at dispersal. The vast majority lived in the three West Coast states, with the greatest number in California. Of the 111,010 Japanese counted by the 1920 census, 71,952 were in California. Even within this state, there was heavy concentration: one-third of Japanese residents of California in 1940 lived in Los Angeles County; six other counties accounted for another third.[28] Given their distinct racial features, concentration in limited geographic areas increased the immigrants' visibility.

24. Roger Daniels, "The Japanese-American Experience: 1890–1940."
25. Petersen, *Japanese Americans*, p. 16.
26. Cited in Daniels, "The Japanese-American Experience," p. 257.
27. Ibid.
28. Ibid., p. 251.

But this was not the only reason for hostility, as the Japanese continued to be a tiny minority even in the areas of highest concentration. More basic problems had to do with their role in the economy:

So long as the Japanese remained willing to perform agricultural labor at low wages, they remained popular with California ranchers. But even before 1910, the Japanese farmhands began to demand higher wages. . . . Worse, many Japanese began to lease and buy agricultural land for farming on their own account. This enterprise had the two-fold result of creating Japanese competition in the produce field and decreasing the number of Japanese farmhands available.[29]

In 1900, there were in the United States about 40 Japanese farmers who combined held less than 5,000 acres of land. By 1909, according to official estimates, about 6,000 Japanese were farming under all sorts of tenancy and controlling more than 210,000 acres.[30] Faced with such "unfair" competition, California ranchers turned to the ever sympathetic state legislature. In 1913, the first Alien Land Law was passed, restricting the free acquisition of land by the Japanese. This legal instrument was perfected in 1920, when Japanese nationals were forbidden to lease agricultural land or to act as guardians of native-born minors in matters of property, which they themselves could not own.[31]

Restrictions in agriculture drove many Japanese into urban enterprise. Already in 1909, the Immigration Commission had found a total of about 3,000 small shops owned by Japanese in many Western cities. By 1919, 47 percent of hotels and 25 percent of grocery stores in Seattle were Japanese-owned. Forty percent of Japanese men in Los Angeles were self-employed, operating dry-cleaning establishments, fisheries, and lunch counters. A large percentage of Japanese urban businesses were produce stands that marketed the production of Japanese farms.[32]

Two recurrent questions at the time about the emergence of Japanese enterprise in agriculture and services were these: (1) How could they compete with larger and better-capitalized American farms? and (2) Where did common laborers find the capital to start even small firms? Answers to both questions were found primarily in the strength of economic networks within the ethnic community. Japanese farms could compete with large agricultural corporations not only because of the legendary efficiency of individual growers, but also because of their collective organizations. These associations aided their members in finding ranches, served to limit the competition for land . . . assisted in marketing the crops and obtaining supplies, interested themselves where

29. Ivan H. Light, *Ethnic Enterprise in America*, p. 9.
30. Petersen, *Japanese Americans*, p. 10.
31. Ibid., p. 52.
32. Light, *Ethnic Enterprise in America*, p. 29.

disputes arose between a landlord and tenant, and disseminated scientific knowledge through publications of their own.[33]

Rotating credit associations, variously known as *ko, tanomoshi,* or *mujin*, provided capital for urban businesses and farms where banks would offer none. Such associations depended heavily on mutual trust, and this was found within the immigrant community to an extent that effectively counterbalanced discrimination by the banks. Even relatively large undertakings, requiring sums close to $100,000, were financed on the basis of *tanomoshi.*[34]

Despite the many political restrictions and the continuous hostility, Japanese immigrants continued to improve their economic positions. Every effort to return the first generation *Issei* to the status of common laborers seemed to strengthen their resolve to move out of it. As with the Jews, the final climb up the economic and social ladders was left to the following generations, the *Nisei* and *Sansei*.

The major blows of wholesale confiscations and camp internments during World War II seriously disrupted the ethnic economy, but did not entirely eliminate it. Aging *Issei* and many of their children came out of the camps to create or reestablish small businesses. In addition, the end of the war brought about a rapid growth of labor demand, along with a reduction of hostility toward the Japanese. The *Nisei* were thus able to explore alternative mobility paths. As second-generation Jews before them, the *Nisei* moved en masse toward higher education. Between 1940 and 1950, the number of professionals among the Japanese increased by 142 percent, while farmers and proprietors decreased by 14 percent and 29 percent, respectively. The third generation, *Sansei*, followed a similar course, with a remarkable 88 percent attending college. Still, a number of them continued the entrepreneurial tradition of their parents, though along new lines. In addition, there has been a significant movement toward ethnic reaffirmation and pride in the third generation.

There are at present about 600,000 Japanese Americans. Since 1940, they have had more schooling than any other group in America, including native whites. The average in 1960 for both males and females was 12.5 years. Average occupational attainment trailed that of native whites in 1950, but exceeded it in 1960, being the highest for any ethnic group. In 1959, Japanese-American males on the mainland earned 99 percent of the income of whites. By 1969, the average Japanese family income exceeded

33. Masakuzu Iwata, "The Japanese Immigrants in California Agriculture," cited in Petersen, *Japanese Americans*, p. 54.
34. Light, *Ethnic Enterprise in America*, chap. 2.

the national average by 32 percent, second only to the Jews among all American ethnic groups.[35]

Several theories have been advanced to explain the success of ethnic enterprise in the United States. Kinzer and Sagarin explained the entrepreneurial activity of some immigrant minorities by the availability of a protected ethnic market, which immigrant firms could monopolize. The existence of particular cultural preferences in food and clothing, of religious precepts governing consumption of these items, and other unique cultural demands created business opportunities "protected" from outside competition.[36] Clearly, the existence of ethnic markets that could be monopolized by entrepreneurs of the same minority was important in the development of *some* businesses among Jews, Japanese, and other groups.

However, this explanation is insufficient. First, not all immigrant minorities that generated ethnic markets gave rise to economic enclaves. Other European immigrants also brought with them a series of culturally dictated preferences. But apart from a few grocery shops, restaurants, and other small retail outlets, these immigrants never made the transition to the complex network of enterprises characteristic of an enclave. Second, the experience of Jewish and Japanese businesses makes clear that while some firms were oriented to provisioning the ethnic market, many others produced for and sold outside of it. As Light noted, the value of Japanese crops around 1920 was about 10 percent of the total for California. The Japanese themselves, who were less than 1 percent of the population, could hardly have consumed all that produce. In fact, many retail outlets did their business exclusively with non-Japanese.[37]

A second common explanation is based on the particular "ethic," or value, syndrome found in the religion of certain immigrant groups. This argument has its roots in Weber's classic writings on religion and economic behavior and in other prominent works, such as Werner Sombart's study of Judaism and Marion Levy's analysis of the role of religion in China and Japan.[38] Despite its authoritative underpinnings, the religious thesis on immigrant entrepreneurship is also inadequate, since it fails to explain why groups of very different religions converged on similar patterns of economic behavior.

35. Daniels, "The Japanese-American Experience"; Sowell, *Ethnic America*, chap. 7; Edna Bonacich and John Modell, *The Economic Basis of Ethnic Solidarity*, chaps. 7 and 15.

36. Robert H. Kinzer and Edward Sagarin, *The Negro in American Business*.

37. Light, *Ethnic Enterprise in America*.

38. Max Weber, *The Protestant Ethic and the Spirit of Capitalism* and *The Religion of China*; Werner Sombart, *The Jews and Modern Capitalism*; Marion J. Levy, *Modernization and the Structure of Societies* and *Modernization: Latecomers and Survivors*.

Jewish and Japanese immigrants brought with them very different religious traditions. Apart from them, other modern immigrant groups, such as the Koreans, have given rise to enclave-like formations. Their religion is Christian for the most part, but includes both Protestantism and Catholicism, as well as some Eastern rites. If such very different religions can give rise to similar economic patterns, the exercise of finding unique "value themes" in each loses theoretical significance. The historical record strongly suggests that immigrant groups of the same religion can experience very different modes of economic incorporation and, conversely, that groups of different religion can follow similar economic paths.

Other explanations of ethnic enterprise have emphasized a number of contextual and situational factors. For some authors, immigrants engage in small businesses because society forces them by blocking alternative mobility paths. Others attribute primary importance to the fact that some immigrant groups are sojourners—that is, they come as target earners with every intention of returning to their home country. Sojourning is said to encourage thrift and hard work and to favor risk taking over job security. Sojourning also tends to promote ethnic solidarity, which in turn supports entrepreneurial ventures.[39]

None of these explanations provides a very satisfactory account of actual historical experiences. The argument that Jews and Japanese were compelled to engage in small businesses is an improbable one. If anything, they were compelled to engage in wage labor, as other immigrant groups were doing at the same time. The mobility path charted by dominant classes for new immigrants prescribed at least one generation of low-paid wage labor, followed perhaps by a slow climb along the educational and occupational ladders. First-generation economic progress among Jews, Japanese, and a few other immigrant groups was due precisely to their deviating from this charted path. Nor does the sojourning argument stand up to empirical challenge. If Japanese farmers came to the United States with the intention of returning, that was certainly not the case among Russian peddlers and merchants. For if there was a firm decision among Jews as they left the Pale, it was that of never coming back.

A final and more satisfactory explanation has its roots in what E. Franklin Frazier called a "tradition of enterprise" based primarily on experience in "buying and selling."[40] The central difference here is between those immigrant groups containing a substantial proportion of individuals with en-

<hr>

39. For a review of these and other theories, see Edna Bonacich and John Modell, *The Economic Basis of Ethnic Solidarity*, chap. 2.

40. E. Franklin Frazier, *The Negro in the United States*.

trepreneurial backgrounds *in the country of origin*, and those made up exclusively of peasants or urban workers. Immigrants who have been merchants and factory owners in their country of origin are better prepared to find economic opportunities, put available capital to productive use, and even to generate it through pooled savings and rotating credit. This class of immigrants is not content to live off wages. They search for opportunities to establish their own businesses, through partnerships or self-employment, and to apply the know-how brought from their own country.

The impact of a class of entrepreneurs among immigrants goes well beyond that class itself. Ethnic firms tend to hire workers of the same national origin. While owners frequently employ paternalistic arrangements to extract more labor and pay lower wages, they also provide an apprenticeship opportunity for other immigrants. The principle of ethnic solidarity cuts both ways: if owners can exploit fellow immigrants to make their firms succeed, they are also obliged, when their businesses expand, to make the new opportunities available to members of the minority. Jewish entrepreneurs hired and promoted other Jews; Japanese merchants did so with other Japanese.

The presence of a strong "tradition of enterprise" among turn-of-the-century Jewish immigrants is well-known. In the Pale of Settlement, Russian Jews, forced in part by laws restricting their ownership of land, had actively engaged in trade and commerce. An 1898 survey of the area found that one-third of all the factories were Jewish-owned. Upon arrival in New York, Jewish immigrants with commercial, craft, and entrepreneurial skills easily surpassed comparable numbers among other immigrant groups. By 1914, they ranked first among printers, bakers, and cigar packers. They made up 80 percent of the immigrant hatmakers, 68 percent of the tailors, and 60 percent of the watchmakers. They were up to half of the jewelers, photographers, dressmakers, and butchers. In total, Jews ranked first in 26 out of 47 trades recorded by the 1911 Immigration Commission.[41]

Japanese immigrants came, for the most part, from rural areas. They were not, however, part of an impoverished subsistence peasantry, but members of a commercial farming class. They frequently sojourned to America to buy additional lands or retire loans incurred for commercial production. Among Japanese requesting passports to travel to the United States between 1886 and 1908, 20 percent were designated as merchants and an additional 20 percent were classified as "students." Evidence of class origins is also found in their average educational attainment. Among a sample of wage earners surveyed by the Immigration Commission, 97.8 percent could read and write Japanese. This proficiency in their original lan-

41. Rischin, *The Promised City*, p. 59.

guage allowed them to "acquire the use of the English language more quickly and more eagerly than . . . some of the European races."[42]

The origins of Jewish and Japanese immigration to the United States before 1914 contrast markedly with the bulk of European immigrants coming during that period. The Italian industrial and commercial classes did not join the flow of impoverished Southern *contadini*. The Polish peasant was not accompanied in his journey by his landowner or by members of the Warsaw and Lodz bourgeoisie . . . these remained at home. It was neither ethnic markets nor religion, but the class composition of the different immigrant flows, that played a decisive role in determining their modes of incorporation and subsequent economic destiny in the United States.

THE INTERIM PERIOD

World War I and its aftermath significantly altered the structure of the American economy and the role of immigrants in it. In essence, European immigration ceased to be the prime supplier of low-wage labor and had to be replaced by other, primarily domestic sources. The war itself drastically reduced immigration, but the flow picked up again in its aftermath. The event that decisively restricted labor immigration and eventually reduced it to insignificance was the passage of the Immigration Act of 1924.

Prior to passage of the act, the Quota Law of 1921 had already established the first numerical constraints on European immigration by limiting it to a total of approximately 355,000. Immigration from any one country was restricted to 3 percent of the foreign born of that nationality living in the United States in 1910. This reduced Southern and Eastern European immigration to less than 50 percent of the total quota.

The act of 1924 further tightened immigration. Since most Asians had been barred from the United States by earlier laws, the new restrictions effectively applied to the European flow. The act reduced immigration from any country to 2 percent of the foreign born of that nationality, as reported by the earlier census of 1880. The total annual quota was drastically reduced to 165,000. This number was further cut by the 1929 National Origins system, which modified the earlier act by basing limits on the national origins of persons living in the United States in 1920. This again had the effect of reducing immigration from peripheral Europe.[43]

In effect, delays in the implementation of the law and a number of exceptions permitted immigration to continue at levels considerably above

42. Cited in Petersen, *Japanese Americans*, p. 14.
43. Robert L. Bach, "Mexican Immigration and the American State"; Sassen-Koob, "Immigrant and Minority Workers."

Table 3.   Immigration in the
Interim Period, 1920-1939

Year	Immigrant Arrivals, Age 16-44 (in thousands)	Immigrants as Percent of the Labor Force
1920	308	0.8
1921	588	1.5
1922	210	0.5
1923	384	1.0
1924	514	1.3
1925	214	0.5
1926	228	0.6
1927	255	0.6
1928	231	0.6
1929	208	0.5
1930	177	0.4
1931	67	0.1
1932	22	0.0
1933	15	0.0
1934	19	0.0
1935	22	0.0
1936	23	0.0
1937	33	0.1
1938	47	0.1
1939	54	0.1

Source: U.S. Bureau of the Census, *Historical Statistics of the United States, Colonial Times to 1970*, Bicentennial Edition (Washington, D.C.: U.S. Government Printing Office, 1976).

the formal limits. As seen in Table 3, even figures for immigrants in working-age years exceeded during the 1920s those established by law. However, immigration never reached the absolute numbers of prewar years, and the proportion of the total labor force represented by annual inflows became insignificant. The sharp drop in immigration during the 1930s can be attributed primarily to the Depression and secondarily to the final implementation of the National Origins system.[44]

The causes of legal restrictions to immigration during the 1920s are commonly identified with growing public alarm at de-Americanization of the society and the presumed genetic and cultural inferiority of the newcomers. While, on the surface, antiforeign agitation was a key determinant of the new laws, the real causes must be sought in more basic factors. Antiforeign sentiment and ethnocentric campaigns had occurred throughout the period of mass immigration without ever achieving such a drastic shift

44. Ibid.; Piore, *Birds of Passage*, chap. 6.

in public policy. Thus, the *timing* of these measures cannot be explained by preexisting events.

The first significant factor leading to this decision was the growing number and power of labor organizations. The force behind increasing working-class organization and militance was the rapid disappearance of opportunities for self-employment for workers outside the industrial system. This process had two underlying determinants: first, the exhaustion of cheap frontier lands, which closed opportunities for rural self-employment; second, the absorption of demand previously met by artisans and household industries by the rising industrial monopolies.

As opportunities for leaving the factory system decreased, workers had to seek security and economic advancement within it. These efforts naturally conflicted with employers' goals of preserving elasticity of the labor supply. They also directly conflicted with mass immigration, which continuously undercut wages and work conditions. Working-class struggles became more virulent and unions grew in numbers. In 1920, there were more than 5 million unionized workers. The AFL and affiliated unions were able to organize huge strikes, which, like the Steel Strike of 1919, took tens of thousands of workers out of the mills. Organized labor was strongly anti-immigration and did not hesitate to resort to racist agitation and xenophobic campaigns to reach its goals. This attitude carried, surprisingly perhaps, into its allies in the Socialist party.[45]

The National Origins Act can thus be counted as a victory to labor in its efforts to eliminate foreign competition. But while the interests of the domestic working class were certainly a major force in bringing about this legislation, they were not the only ones. During and after the war, large firms in the emerging oligopolistic sector had begun to make use of an alternative labor supply that, from their point of view, had three major advantages: first, it was subject at both origin and destination to domestic political controls; second, it was unorganized and "docile"; third, it was less likely in the long-run to join existing organizations of the white working class.[46]

As early as 1916, major firms were embarking on a systematic policy of replacing white with black labor. During the 1920s, important industrial sectors such as meat packing, coal mining, and auto making followed suit. The Ford Motor Company proved notably adept at using blacks to avoid

45. In his campaign for Asiatic exclusion, AFL President Samuel Gompers frequently denounced these workers as scabs but refused to admit them even into segregated locals. If exclusion was impossible legally, he argued, it should be done "by force of arms." The same sentiment was echoed by Socialist Party theoreticians, one of whom noted that "no amount of proletarian solidarity or International Unity can ignore racial incompatibility." See Petersen, *Japanese-Americans*, chap. 2.

46. Edna Bonacich, "Advanced Capitalism and Black/White Relations."

unionization of its plants. Negro workers were systematically employed for strikebreaking, as was the case with the Steel Strike of 1919.

Because their labor was mostly unskilled, the policy of encouraging Southern black migration was accompanied by the adoption of capital-intensive techniques that displaced white skilled labor. With this two-pronged strategy, employers attempted and largely succeeded in breaking the power of the unions. From 1920 to 1929, union membership dropped by almost 2 million. In 1933, it stood at 2,973,000, a precipitous decline from the peak years after World War I.[47]

The enactment of restrictive immigration legislation during the 1920s was, therefore, the outcome of the withdrawal of support for it by one of the major contenders in the domestic class struggle. The demands of organized labor could be satisfied; the closing of the immigration door could be made part of the "historic pact" between conservative unions and capital, because the latter could and had indeed turned to an alternative source of low-wage labor. Southern black migration was channelled toward the same northeastern industrial regions that had previously received European immigrants. This was the area where demand for unskilled industrial and service labor concentrated:

Between 1900 and 1910, for every 15 foreigners that were added to the population of this region, there was one black added, a ratio which not only contracted, but actually reversed in the next decade, when for every new immigrant there were three new blacks.[48]

By 1930, more than 50 percent of the blacks living in the North were southern born, a proportion that held until the 1950s. As a "preferred" labor force, southern blacks experienced consistently lower unemployment rates than whites. This relationship lasted for two decades and was to be reversed only in the aftermath of World War II.[49]

Since the 1930s, black migration to the North took place in the context of a massive rural displacement to the cities. White rural migrants came to join blacks at the bottom of the labor market. The supply of low-wage workers was further augmented by the mass entrance of women into the labor force in the 1950s. While these developments were to be important later on, it was the migration of southern black workers that played the decisive role in the two major labor events of the interwar period: (1) the effective end of labor immigration; and (2) the change in the nature of the class struggle culminating in the emergence of a dual economy.

47. Ibid.
48. Sassen-Koob, "Immigrant and Minority Workers," p. 3
49. Bonacich, "Advanced Capitalism."

CONTEMPORARY IMMIGRATION, 1946–1979

Legal Immigration

Since the end of World War II, immigration to the United States has been characterized by two major traits: increasing numbers and increasing segmentation. There are at present at least three major flows arriving in the country: legal immigrants, illegal or undocumented immigrants, and temporary workers.

Legal immigration to the United States has been decisively affected by a series of changes in immigration laws and, in particular, by the 1965 Immigration Act. Its principal effect was to change the basis for preferential admission from national origin to, first, family reunification and, second, occupational skills. Though this act and subsequent modifications established an annual world quota of 290,000, in practice immigration has been running above this figure, since immigrants coming under family reunification provisions are generally excluded from the quota.

The end of the national origins system has shifted the sources of immigration toward Third World countries and away from traditional European ones. From 1955 to 1965, one-half of the new immigrants were born in Europe, but in the next decade the figure declined to less than one-third. Immigration from Asia, which was less than 2 percent in 1950, now accounts for about one-third. African immigration, insignificant to begin with, has been expanding rapidly. Immigration from Canada is down sharply while that from Latin America and the Caribbean is on the increase.[50]

In terms of geographical destination, the new immigration follows the tendency of the old to concentrate in a few locations. Six states accounted for almost 75 percent of the intended places of residence of immigrants during the 1966–1975 decade. California and New York alone received more than 40 percent. Four cities—New York, Los Angeles, Miami, and San Francisco—received more than a third of all new immigrants in 1975. New York City alone accounted for 19.1 percent.[51]

The family-reunification clauses of the act have also resulted in a very different demographic composition of new immigrants as compared with those arriving at the turn of the century. The immigrants' demographic profile now resembles that of the native population as a whole. The proportion of women is slightly higher among immigrants, and the proportion of children under 14 slightly lower. Persons aged 45 and older continue to represent a smaller percentage of immigrants than natives. Partly as a result

50. National Commission for Manpower Policy, *Manpower and Immigration Policies in the United States.*
51. Ibid., exhibits 7 and 8.

of these changes, the rates of labor-force participation among recent immigrants have dropped sharply.

Records from the Immigration and Naturalization Service (INS) indicate that between 1970 and 1975, only 40 percent of new immigrants reported having an occupation, while 60 percent declared themselves to be out of the labor market. These figures have been criticized by several authors, who note that they represent an undercount of those who actually go to work in the United States. Women, for example, who declare their occupation to be housewives might find themselves forced to join the labor market because of economic necessity. According to the 1970 census, labor-force participation of foreign-born adult males was 76 percent, as compared to 77 percent among the native-born of native parentage; the proportions among women were 44 percent and 42 percent, respectively.[52]

The relative contribution made by recent legal immigration to the U.S. labor force is much smaller than at the turn of the century. As shown in Table 4, even if *all* adult immigrants aged 16 to 44 were considered to have joined the labor force (instead of the 59.3 percent estimated by the INS), their contribution to the labor force would not exceed three-tenths of 1 percent for any given year. This proportion represents about one-tenth of the annual average between 1900 and 1914 and is even lower than during the 1920s.[53]

Owing to geographic concentration, the impact of immigrant workers is higher in certain cities. Estimates of the 1978 National Commission for Manpower Policy put the potential loss in the civilian labor force of New York City at 416,000 instead of the 186,000 actual decrease between 1970 and 1975. The difference was due to immigration. For the ten largest cities in the country, the potential additional reductions in their labor force during those years would have been 400,000.[54]

There is no evidence that present legal immigration has its origins in systematic employer recruitment. Instead, the process has become a self-propelled flow in which agencies of the state are used to regulate an ever-present supply of immigrants. There is also no evidence of extensive return migration among legal immigrants. Visas are granted on the assumption of permanent residence in the United States, and all indications are that recipients do indeed establish permanent residency. Despite minuscule annual increments, the foreign born already represented 5.5 percent of the civilian labor force in 1970 and 6.5 percent of native workers of native parentage. Because of modest out-migration rates, the contribution being made by

52. Ibid., exhibit 11.

53. U. S. Bureau of the Census, *Historical Statistics of the United States—Colonial Times to 1970,* vol. 2.

54. National Commission, *Manpower and Immigration,* exhibit 12.

Table 4.   Unemployment, Immigration,
and the Labor Force, 1946-1979

Year	Labor Force Unemployed, %	Immigrant Arrivals, Age 16-44 (in thousands)	Immigrants as Percentage of the Labor Force
1946	3.9	86	0.1
1947	3.9	101	0.2
1948	3.8	112	0.2
1949	5.9	123	0.2
1950	5.3	152	0.2
1951	3.3	121	0.2
1952	3.0	160	0.2
1953	2.9	110	0.2
1954	5.5	136	0.2
1955	4.4	156	0.2
1956	4.1	207	0.3
1957	4.3	208	0.3
1958	6.8	162	0.2
1959	5.5	165	0.2
1960	5.5	170	0.2
1961	6.7	171	0.2
1962	5.5	182	0.2
1963	5.7	197	0.3
1964	5.2	187	0.2
1965	4.5	189	0.2
1966	3.8	190	0.2
1967	3.8	207	0.3
1968	3.6	263	0.3
1969	3.5	211	0.3
1970	4.9	222	0.3
1971	5.9	216	0.2
1972	5.6	225	0.2
1973	4.9	237	0.3
1974	5.6	234	0.2
1975	8.5	226	0.2
1976	7.7	234	0.2
1977	7.0	267	0.3
1978	6.0	363	0.4
1979	5.8	277	0.3

Source: U.S. Bureau of the Census, *Historical Statistics of the United States, Colonial Times to 1970*, Bicentennial Edition (Washington, D.C.: U.S. Government Printing Office, 1976); U.S. Bureau of the Census, *Statistical Abstract of the United States, 1978* (Washington, D.C.: U.S. Government Printing Office, 1982), Tables 121, 645, 667, 708; *USA Statistics in Brief 1981; Economic Report of the President, 1980*, Tables B27, B29; Immigration and Naturalization Service, *1979 Statistical Yearbook* (Washington, D.C.: U.S. Government Printing Office, 1980).

Table 5.   Occupational Distribution of the U.S. Civilian Labor Force,
Sixteen Years of Age and Over in 1977 and
Fiscal Years 1974 and 1977 Immigrants

Category	U.S.-1977, %	FY 74 Immigrants, %[a]	FY 77 Immigrants, %[a]
Professional, technical and kindred	15.2	23.5	23.8
Managers and proprietors	10.6	6.1	9.0
Farmers and farm managers	1.5	--	--
Clerical and sales	24.1	10.7	13.9
Craftsmen and kindred	13.2	13.2	11.2
Operatives	15.2	11.9	18.6
Service workers, including private household	13.6	18.4	13.3
Laborers, except farm	5.2	12.1	6.4
Farm laborers	1.4	4.1	3.8
Total[b]	100.0	100.0	100.0

Source: U.S. Bureau of the Census, Statistical Abstract of the United States
1978 (Washington, D.C.: U.S. Government Printing Office, 1978), pp. 419–21;
Immigration and Naturalization Service, Annual Reports, 1974 and 1977
(Washington, D.C.: U.S. Government Printing Office, 1975, 1978).

[a]As percentage of immigrants declaring an occupation at arrival.

[b]Rounded percentages.

recent adult immigrants and their children to the labor force is projected to
be as high as 13 percent of the total increase by 1985.[55] Contemporary legal
immigration is, for the most part, a movement of permanent residents
rather than a two-way flow of target earners.

There is little evidence as well that legal immigrants concentrate in the
bottom occupational categories. In 1970, the proportion of "professional,
technical, and kindred" workers among the foreign born, 15.5 percent, was
slightly higher than that for the native born of native parentage. Compared
to the proportion among native blacks and Hispanics, 8.1 percent and 9.4
percent, the foreign born had a decisive occupational advantage. Nor were

55. Ibid., p. 102.

immigrants found to cluster at the opposite end of the spectrum: the proportion of nonfarm laborers among the foreign born, 4.0 percent, was smaller than the figure for the native-born of native parentage; it was also less than half the proportion among native blacks.[56]

Table 5 presents the occupational distribution of the U.S. labor force and of legal immigrants declaring an occupation at arrival in two recent years. The proportion of immigrants in the highest occupational category—professionals and technicians—compares very favorably with that in the labor force as a whole. There is evidence of some downward mobility as immigrants enter the U.S. labor market and as many of those declaring no occupation at arrival become employed. Even then, however, the occupational distribution of recent immigrant cohorts remains similar to that of the native labor force.[57] Additional evidence of this trend is provided by average educational attainment and earnings figures. In 1970, the average education of the foreign born, native born of foreign parentage, and native born of native parentage was essentially the same, ranging from 12.2 to 12.6 years. Median earnings among foreign-born workers were slightly below those of the labor force as a whole but were, in turn, substantially higher than among native-born minorities.[58]

The fact that legal immigration is heterogeneous in terms of occupational background and actual employment precludes its playing a role similar to that of southern black migrants during the interwar period. Legal immigration today is clearly not the mainstay of a dual-labor market. The alternative interpretation provided by orthodox economic theory is that it functions primarily as a supplement to the domestic labor force. This interpretation does not accord, however, with the evidence.

Figure 2 presents the relationship between prior-year unemployment and legal immigration. There is a moderate *positive* relationship corresponding to a correlation of .37. Thus, the higher the rate of unemployment in a given year, the higher the level of immigration the next. If figures for unemployment and immigration for the same year are considered, the result is the same. Table 4 presents the relevant time series that yield a correlation of .37: in recent years, legal immigration and unemployment have thus tended to increase together.

This result is, of course, the opposite of that found for 1890–1914 immigrants. So are the results of regressing legal immigration in the year t on rate of unemployment and immigration in $t - 1$. These results are presented in Table 6. Net of autocorrelation effects, unemployment has no effect on

56. Ibid., exhibit 13.
57. Ibid., exhibits 13 and 14.
58. Ibid., p. 110; Sassen-Koob, "Immigrant and Minority Workers," p. 8.

Fig. 2.   Unemployment and Immigration, 1946 – 1978

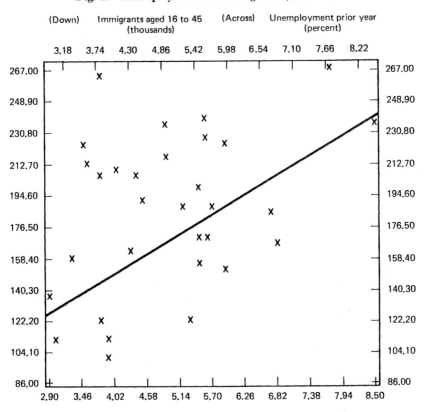

year-to-year changes in levels of immigration. Table 6 also shows, however, that GNP continues to be a significant predictor of changes in immigration.

The most appropriate interpretation of these findings is that levels of legal immigration continue to be governed by U.S. labor demand but that this demand is not conditioned by the sheer availability of domestic workers. Immigrant labor is no longer a simple supplement to the domestic labor force. This situation can have three causes: (1) legal immigrants are mostly employed in the public sector and by large firms. Labor demand in this sector is not governed by global rates of unemployment, which tend to reflect primarily the situation of the competitive sector; (2) legal immigrants are employed by competitive firms primarily to counteract organization and protests by domestic workers. Hence, demand for immigrant workers goes together with growing domestic unemployment; (3) legal immigrants are mostly employed in economic enclaves created by earlier ar-

Table 6. Economic Determinants of
Immigration, 1946-1978

Endogenous Variable Year t	Exogenous Variables[a] Year t - 1			R	R^2
Immigration, ages 16-44	Immigration, 16-44	Unemployment	Gross National Product		
--	.848* (.109)	4.30** (3.71)	--	.85	.73
--	.346* (.172)	--	1.015* (.282)	.90	.80

[a]Figures are linear regression slopes; standard errors in parentheses.

*Significant at the .01 level.

**Not significant.

rivals. The economic conditions in these protected enclaves are not af-fected by the global unemployment rate.

The analysis of total legal immigration, conducted previously, and the image of the "advantaged" foreign worker that emerges from it might sug-gest that the first interpretation is correct. An in-depth analysis of the evi-dence indicates, however, that all three causes operate. The main limita-tion of existing studies of legal immigration is that they tend to neglect its internal structural diversity. Under the same formal label coexist very dif-ferent phenomena. As an illustration, Table 7 compares the occupational distribution of the 1977 immigrant cohort as a whole with four of its main subcomponents: Mexican, Dominican, Philippine, and Korean flows. These nationalities were selected because they all made sizable contribu-tions to total immigration and because they all represent Third World coun-tries, a condition that eliminates known differences with the more devel-oped European nations. Even then, there are vast differences in the occupational distribution of these four immigrant groups.

Mexican and Dominican legal immigration represents the "upper crust" of a much larger movement composed primarily of undocumented workers. The articulation between the two occurs through family-reuni-fication provisions of the immigration law. Korean and Philippine immigra-tions, on the other hand, are primarily suppliers of professional and skilled labor, many coming under the occupational-preference categories of the

Table 7. Occupational Distribution of Total,
Mexican, Dominican, Philippine,
and Korean Immigration, 1977

Categories[a]	Total, %	Mexican, %	Dominican, %	Philippine, %	Korean, %
Professional, technical, and kindred	23.8	3.6	6.8	38.6	36.3
Managers and proprietors	9.0	3.0	6.3	8.2	14.4
Farmers and farm managers	--	--	0.1	0.1	--
Clerical and sales	13.9	5.0	6.9	16.3	15.3
Crafts and kindred	11.2	12.7	10.5	5.9	12.8
Operatives	18.6	29.2	25.4	6.2	12.6
Service workers, including private household	13.3	13.5	19.8	16.6	6.6
Laborers, except farm	6.4	25.4	10.5	2.0	1.6
Farm laborers	3.8	7.6	13.7	6.1	1.0
Total	100.0	100.0	100.0	100.0	100.0

Source: Immigration and Naturalization Service, Annual Report (Washington, D.C.: U.S. Government Printing Office, 1978).

[a]As percentage of immigrants declaring an occupation at arrival. Rounded figures.

law. Aside from employment in the general economy, Korean immigration is also targeted on a rapidly growing ethnic enclave in Los Angeles.[59]

The existing literature on the adaptation of recent immigrants points to a series of similar outcomes. Some groups, primarily from Europe but also from several Asian countries, appear to "melt" readily into American society. These groups are composed primarily of professional and skilled workers. Others, such as the "new" Chinese immigration from Hong Kong and Taiwan and Korean immigration, are involved to a large extent in enclave

59. Edna Bonacich, "U. S. Capitalism and Korean Immigrant Small Business."

economies. Other minorities seem to retreat into ethnic neighborhoods and exhibit patterns of resistance reminiscent of earlier European working-class immigrations. This is especially the case among those linked to larger, undocumented labor flows.[60] This diversity attests to the impossibility of subsuming all legal immigration under the same general rubric. To a greater extent than among earlier cohorts, it suggests the central importance of different modes of incorporation for the subsequent adaptation of different immigrant groups.

Contract and Undocumented Immigrants

The bulk of contemporary labor immigration to the United States occurs not through legal channels but through surreptitious ones. This activity is known as illegal, or undocumented, immigration. In addition, there has been in the last thirty years a sizable inflow of contract workers coming under various temporary arrangements. Undocumented and contract immigrations are similar in several respects and they both contrast markedly with legal immigration. Unlike the latter, the proportion of labor force participation is very high in both flows.

The available data indicate that the two movements are composed overwhelmingly of adult men. While both were originally confined to agricultural labor in the South and Southwest, there is growing evidence of a northbound drift of the undocumented toward urban industrial and service employment. A survey of 47,947 undocumented immigrants apprehended by the INS in 1975 showed that about half, 53 percent, were employed in agriculture, but that 27.5 percent were in light and heavy industry, and 19.4 percent in construction and services. These figures probably underestimate the proportions in urban employment, since the resource deployment by the INS tends to concentrate in the agricultural regions of the Southwest.[61]

Like legal immigration, current contract and undocumented inflows do not require extensive recruitment. Recruitment for contract immigration, carried on predominantly in the West Indies, is limited to screening a ready supply of laborers. For undocumented immigration, recruitment seems to occur through informal communications, indicating that jobs are available in a certain industry or area. In both cases, immigration takes the form of a "spontaneous" flow motivated by the prospect of economic gain. Undocumented immigrants usually bear the full cost of the journey; among contract

---

60. Sassen-Koob, "Formal and Informal Associations: Dominicans and Colombians in New York."

61. National Commission, *Manpower and Immigration*, p. 136.

workers, these costs are usually discounted from their first weeks' pay.[62]

Unlike legal immigration, undocumented and contract flows are usually temporary. For the latter, the period of residence in the United States is regulated by employers and the government, and it usually ends with the harvest. The available data on undocumented immigration point to a cyclical pattern, in which periods of work in the United States alternate with periods of residence in the home country.

The pattern varies, however, with the means of entry. The relative openness of the United States–Mexico border in recent years has allowed Mexican undocumented immigrants to trek back and forth with relative ease. The result is shorter but more numerous stays in the United States. Among immigrants from other countries, the costs and hazards of illegal entry dictate longer periods of residence. In the North–Houstoun survey of apprehended illegals, for example, Mexicans reported an average of 4.5 trips before apprehension (or about one every six months), while Eastern Hemisphere and non-Mexican Western Hemisphere immigrants reported an average of 1.8 and 1.4 trips, respectively.[63]

Contract and undocumented workers cluster at the lower end of the occupational and income hierarchies. There is little controversy over the fact that they represent primarily sources of low-wage labor. Sugar cane cutters brought from the West Indies under contract are paid an "adverse effect" wage, or the minimum hourly wage set by the Department of Labor. In 1977, this wage averaged $2.74 for one of the harshest forms of agricultural labor. In 1975, the previously mentioned INS survey of 47,947 apprehended illegals found that 65 percent earned less than $2.50 an hour and a further 30 percent earned between $2.50 and $4.49. The North–Houstoun study reported that 24 percent of surveyed undocumented workers were paid less than the minimum wage. At a time when the minimum wage for nonfarm labor was $2.10, the average for Mexicans in this survey was only $2.34.[64]

The best known of the programs under which temporary contract labor has been brought into the United States is, without doubt, the bracero program, initiated by an executive agreement between the United States and Mexico in 1942. Under this agreement, Mexican workers were hired for fixed periods to perform agricultural labor in the United States. U.S. government-paid agents were sent into the interior of Mexico, and public

62. Ina Dinerman, "Patterns of Adaptation Among Households of U. S.-Bound Migrants from Michoacan, Mexico"; Jorge A. Bustamante, "The Historical Context of Undocumented Mexican Immigration to the United States"; Josh DeWind, Tom Seidl, and Janet Shenk, "Contract Labor in U. S. Agriculture," NACLA Report on the Americas.

63. National Commission, Manpower and Immigration, pp. 126–127.

64. Ibid., p. 137.

funds were spent in setting up and expanding the program's operations. Such public expenditures provided a direct subsidy to the growers who employed this labor. The agreement was conceived as a wartime expedient, but growers managed to extend it repeatedly during the postwar years. In 1951, the program was institutionalized by Congress as Public Law 78. By 1964 when it was officially terminated, the bracero program had brought to the United States close to 5 million workers.[65]

A less well-known but on-going program is the one bringing West Indian laborers, primarily Jamaicans, to work in the cane fields of southern Florida and to tend fruit harvests throughout the Eastern seaboard states. Section H-2 of the Immigration and Nationality Act of 1952 (or Public Law 414) authorizes the issuance of temporary visas to foreign workers to fill jobs in U.S. agriculture. Since 1952, the number of temporary workers imported under this program has ranged from 11,775 to 44,952. In recent years, the average has been close to 25,000. H-2 workers have been employed in all major agricultural regions of the United States, but the primary beneficiaries have been East Coast growers.[66]

Despite mechanization, a number of agricultural tasks such as cane cutting, shade tobacco harvesting, and apple picking still require intensive labor. The primary function of the H-2 program is to provide employers with this labor at low wages and under their direct control. Workers are contracted to a specific employer; protests over work conditions or wages can easily lead to dismissal, which means, in turn, deportation. While employers are obliged by law to offer the available jobs to domestic workers first, the *adverse wage rate* is so low and the work so hard that few domestic workers apply.

Contract workers also lack control of the terms under which they labor. These terms are set by agreement between growers' associations and the British West Indies Central Labor Organization (BWICLO). The agreement allows employers to deduct the cost of transportation during the first weeks of employment. In addition, 3 percent of the workers' wages are kept by BWICLO to buy insurance or pay "for expenses reasonably incurred on behalf of the worker." In general, contract workers are very much at the mercy of their employers after arriving in the United States. In the Florida sugar industry, this kind of discretion has been used to extract more production from workers. According to a U.S. Department of Agriculture study, it took 2.4 labor hours to produce a ton of Florida sugar cane in 1963; in 1973, it took only 1.6 hours, a productivity increase of 30 percent.[67]

65. Alejandro Portes, "Migration and Underdevelopment," p. 29.
66. U. S. Immigration and Naturalization Service, *1977 Annual Report*; DeWind, Seidl, and Shenk, "Contract Labor."
67. Ibid., pp. 13–15.

Undocumented immigration covertly permits a massive labor flow to fulfill the labor needs of a large number of employers in both urban and rural areas. While there are no reliable figures, it is widely agreed that the level of undocumented immigration in recent years far exceeds that of legal immigration. The only estimates of the annual level of undocumented im-

Table 8. Nonwhite Unemployment, Contract and
Undocumented Immigration: 1946-1979

Year	Nonwhite Unemployment, %	Braceros (in thousands)	H-2 Workers (in thousands)	Apprehensions ("Deportable Aliens") (in thousands)
1946	5.9	32	--	100
1947	5.9	20	--	194
1948	5.9	35	--	193
1949	8.9	107	--	288
1950	9.0	68	--	468
1951	5.3	192	--	509
1952	5.4	234	12	529
1953	4.5	179	14	886
1954	9.9	214	8	1089
1955	8.7	338	13	254
1956	8.3	417	15	88
1957	7.9	450	16	60
1958	12.6	419	15	53
1959	10.7	448	17	45
1960	10.2	427	20	71
1961	12.4	294	19	89
1962	10.9	283	21	93
1963	10.8	195	48	89
1964	9.6	182	56	87
1965	8.1	104	52	110
1966	7.3	9	46	139
1967	7.4	8	50	162
1968	6.7	6	45	212
1969	6.4	--	44	284
1970	8.2	--	47	345
1971	9.9	--	42	420
1972	10.0	--	39	506
1973	8.9	--	37	656
1974	9.9	--	34	788
1975	13.9	--	25	767
1976[a]	13.1	--	22	876
1977	13.1	--	22	1042
1978	11.9	--	19	1058
1979	11.3	--	18	1076

Sources: Leo Grebler, Joan W. Moore, and Ralph C. Guzman, The Mexican-American People (New York: The Free Press, 1970), p. 68; Immigration and Naturalization Service Annual Report (Washington, D.C.: U.S. Government Printing Office), 1979, 1977, 1970, 1960, Table 18; 1979, p. 56; 1977, pp. 85, 92. David S. North, Nonimmigrant Workers in the U.S.: Current Trends and Future Implications (Washington, D.C.: Report for the U.S. Department of Labor, 1980), p. 68.

[a]Excludes 1976 Transition Quarter in INS Reports.

migration are apprehension figures published by the INS. These figures have been criticized on two counts: first, they reflect the deployment practices of the INS rather than the actual nature of the flow; second, they are workload figures rather than actual counts.[68]

The latter problem inflates the total estimate, since the same individual may be apprehended several times in a year. This is counterbalanced by the known fact that the efforts of the INS are less than successful and that a great many illegals manage to slip by. The extent to which the two factors cancel each other is unknown. Still, over the long term and with exceptions for specific years, the curve of apprehensions may well reflect the overall magnitude of the flow. In that sense, this curve remains a flawed but necessary gauge and is superior to other estimates based on questionable assumptions.

Until recently, undocumented immigration was equated with undocumented *Mexican* immigration, since the vast majority of apprehended illegals came from that country. The inverse relationship between temporary contract labor from Mexico and annual apprehension figures has been noted by a number of authors. As Table 8 shows, the number of "deportable aliens" decreased sharply from 1955 to 1960, while the bracero program was in full swing, and began climbing again as the number of braceros decreased and the program was brought to an end. Interestingly, the category of H-2 contract workers followed, from 1955 to 1966, a pattern similar to that of annual apprehensions, suggesting that both undocumented and H-2 workers functioned at the time as a complement to braceros.

Recently, undocumented immigration seems to have greatly expanded its presence in the labor market. As seen above, existing studies suggest that undocumented workers are now employed in industry and urban services as well as agriculture. The weight of undocumented workers is now felt not only in rural labor markets of the Southwest, but in large industrialized cities of the North as well. Simultaneously, the national origins of this flow appear to be diversifying as contingents from countries other than Mexico arrive through various means. There are now an estimated 300,000 Dominicans in New York City, making it the second largest Dominican city. Other Caribbean and South American countries are also becoming significant contributors to the inflow.[69]

Most non-Mexican undocumented immigrants appear to enter the United States not by crossing the border surreptitiously, but by securing a tourist or student visa and overstaying it. Since this procedure requires ob-

68. National Commission, *Manpower and Immigration*, p. 121; Portes, "Migration and Underdevelopment," p. 36.

69. Sassen-Koob, "Formal and Informal Associations"; Sherri Grasmuck, "International Stair-Step Migration: Dominican Labor in the United States and Haitian Labor in the Dominican Republic."

taining a visa from a U. S. consulate and then covering the costs of airfare or other expensive transportation, non-Mexican illegals tend to come from higher socioeconomic strata than Mexican illegals.[70]

Over time, large flows of undocumented immigrants have produced a stratum of legal immigrants. The primary mechanisms for this conversion are the family-reunification procedures, which allow spouses, children, parents, and siblings of U.S. citizens and permanent residents to obtain entry as legal residents. While the available data indicate that undocumented immigration tends to be of the target earning or cyclical type, another sizable group remains in the country and eventually legalizes its situation. The linkage between undocumented and legal immigration is reflected in the occupational distributions of immigrants from such countries as Mexico and the Dominican Republic, examined above. As will be seen in a subsequent chapter, most contemporary legal immigrants from Mexico are formerly undocumented immigrants who have managed to regularize their situation.

As Table 8 showed, the steady climb of apprehensions during the 1970s reached 1 million for the first time in 1977 and stayed at that level in the two following years. Only in one previous year, 1954, had the 1 million mark been surpassed, and this was the consequence of a forced repatriation campaign known as Operation Wetback.[71] In the absence of large increases in the INS enforcement budget, the apprehension figures for recent years seem to reflect not increasing efficiency, but rather the continuous growth of the undocumented inflow.

It is generally accepted that contract and undocumented immigrants resemble turn-of-the-century European immigration in that both are channelled toward low-wage positions at the bottom of the labor market. It is also generally acknowledged that, more than legal immigrants, contract and undocumented workers represent *the* significant labor inflow to the United States at present. Consequently, it is these groups that theories concerning the uses of immigrant labor should address. The labor-supplement argument should lead to a strong negative correlation between domestic unemployment and the size of menial-labor immigration, as it did during the 1890–1914 period.

We first examine this prediction by adding up the recorded number of contract immigrants (braceros and H-2 workers) to that of apprehensions for a given year and correlating this figure with the prior-year rate of unem-

70. David S. North and Marion F. Houstoun, *The Characteristics and Role of Illegal Aliens in the U. S. Labor Market*, chaps. 4 and 5.

71. Leo Grebler, Joan W. Moore, and Ralph C. Guzman, *The Mexican-American People*, chap. 4.

Fig. 3.   Nonwhite Unemployment, Contract, and Undocumented Immigration, 1946–1979

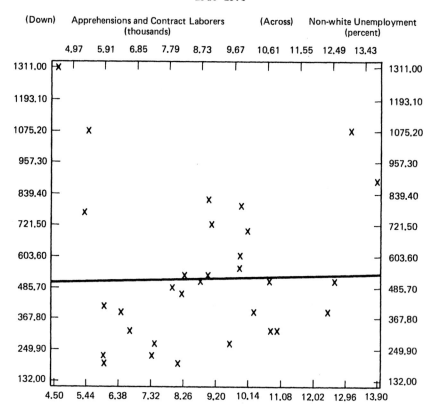

ployment. The correlation is weaker than that for legal immigration, but still positive, .14. Since this coefficient is insignificant, it can be best interpreted as indicating that there has been no relationship between these variables over time.

This result can be challenged on several counts. First, it can be argued that the overall rate of unemployment is too insensitive a measure. Contract and undocumented workers fill low-paid menial occupations where only a segment of domestic workers concentrates. This segment is characterized by the heavy representation of domestic minorities, particularly nonwhites. It is *their* labor-market situation that should vary inversely with undocumented and contract immigration.

Figure 3 presents the relationship between nonwhite unemployment and combined contract immigration and apprehensions the following year.

As the figure shows, there is no association between these variables; the corresponding correlation (.05) is insignificant. Contract and undocumented immigrations, as measured, are thus indifferent to rates of unemployment among both total and nonwhite domestic labor. Other modifications of the analysis, such as removing the "exceptional" year, 1954, do not alter this conclusion.

A second challenge is based on the fact that apprehension figures are only a proxy for the actual size of the undocumented immigration. Despite the fact that apprehensions appear to reflect long-term variations in the underlying flow, we heed this challenge by removing apprehension figures altogether from the analysis. The relationship between recorded contract labor immigration and prior-year unemployment can then be considered. Since immigrant contract labor has been employed overwhelmingly in agriculture, the appropriate independent variable in this case is the rate of unemployment among domestic agricultural workers. The correlation is again positive and insignificant, .12. The size of the contract labor flow is also unrelated over time to prior-year agricultural unemployment.

These last results can be challenged, in turn, by noting that the bracero program terminated in 1964 and that this decision introduces a "break" in the time series. To eliminate this problem, we replicate the analysis only on that series corresponding to the years in which the bracero program was being fully implemented, 1954 to 1965. The correlation in this case is significant in the *positive* direction, .31. Agricultural unemployment and the number of braceros imported ran parallel courses over those years, rather than varying inversely.

Table 9 presents the results of regressing the various indicators of contract and undocumented immigration on the different measures of domestic unemployment, controlling for autocorrelation. The table shows that unemployment, however measured, has nothing to do with year-to-year variations in contract and/or undocumented immigration. As a whole, these results provide convincing evidence against the labor-scarcity argument and its definition of immigration as a supplement to the domestic labor force.

Having rejected this theory as it applies to present labor immigration, we must turn to other theoretical perspectives for interpretation. Among them, the internal-colonialist thesis may be rejected out of hand. Though the situation of contract labor workers in agriculture has approached, at times, that of an "unfree" labor force, this occurs only under exceptional conditions. The temporary stay of these immigrants, as well as undocumented ones, runs against the concept of colonialism, which denotes a situation of permanent subjugation. Above all, contract and undocumented

Table 9.   Unemployment, Contract Labor, and
Undocumented Immigration, 1946-1978

Endogenous Variables Year t	Exogenous Variables[a] Year t - 1			R	R^2
	(A+C)	Total Unemployment	Nonwhite Unemployment		
A. Apprehensions and contract labor immigration (A+C)	.865* (.117)	-11.181** (23.810)	--	.82	.67
	.878* (.115)	--	-13.744** (12.879)	.82	.68
B. Contract labor immigration (CLI)	(CLI)	--	Unemployment-Agricultural Labor Force		
	.931* (.074)	--	-.325** (6.731)	.93	.86
C. Contract labor immigration, 1946-1965	.760* (.139)	--	3.494** (10.456)	.84	.71

[a]Figures are linear-regression slopes; standard errors are in parentheses.

*Significant at the .01 level.

**Not significant.

workers do not represent an homogeneous group forced to perform labor for the benefit of the domestic majority as a whole. There is abundant evidence that both groups have been employed in jobs previously held by domestic workers and against the economic interests of the latter.

Nor does the split-labor-market hypothesis seem to apply to the present situation. In no known instance have contract or undocumented workers been employed to break strikes or to undercut the wages or work conditions of the organized industrial labor force. Unions in large industries are still too powerful to be challenged by immigrant workers. There is abundant evidence, however, that braceros and undocumented laborers have been employed against incipient labor organization among domestic farm workers throughout the South and Southwest.[72]

Among alternative theoretical perspectives, it is the dual-labor-market hypothesis that seems to fit best contemporary immigration patterns. Con-

72. For a vivid account of these practices see Ernesto Galarza, *Farm Workers and Agribusiness in California, 1947–1960.*

tract and undocumented workers are simply not found in the monopoly sector. The labor force in this sector, primarily white, is protected by trade unions, which enforce existing labor legislation. Employment of the two immigrant flows is thus limited to the competitive sector in agriculture, industry, and services. As seen above, they do not merely supplement the domestic labor force there. Instead, they are used to strengthen the hand of employers against incipient labor organization and demand making.

Immigrants benefit employers directly by helping to perpetuate wages and work conditions that domestic labor finds increasingly unacceptable. They also benefit the monopoly sector indirectly by reducing the costs of goods and services produced by competitive firms. Cheaper food and clothing, restaurants, lodgings, and places of entertainment are among such benefits. Along with these benefits are these negative effects: an average income among U.S. farm workers that until recently did not exceed $3,000 a year; a life expectancy among this group of scarcely 50 years; the maintenance of minimum and subminimum wages among workers in the garment industry; and the vigorous "revival" of the sweatshop in New York, Los Angeles, and other large American cities.[73]

The dual-economy thesis provides an integrated interpretation of present patterns of labor immigration, since, as seen above, it also helps explain the initially puzzling differences within the legal flow. Legal immigrants coming under occupational preferences and established admission procedures are often channelled toward the primary labor market associated with the monopoly sector; those who have legalized a previously undocumented entry tend to continue filling roles in the competitive sector. Employment chances for either group are not affected by domestic unemployment, though for different reasons. Global unemployment rates, primarily reflecting conditions in the competitive sector, do not directly affect immigrant professionals and skilled workers employed by large firms. In the competitive sector, immigrants are hired as a "preferred" labor force, even in the face of high domestic unemployment.

To the extent that contract and undocumented immigrants return to their home country, the issue of later adaptation ceases to exist. A study by Wayne Cornelius on a sample of undocumented Mexican immigrants living in the United States suggests that the situation of this group is governed by two major considerations: plans for an eventual return to Mexico and the vulnerability and insecurity attached to their illegal status. A study by the North American Congress for Latin America (NACLA) in New York City notes the situation of "entrapment" in which many undocumented immi-

73. Subcommittee on Migratory Labor, U. S. Senate, "Migrant and Seasonal Farmworker Powerlessness"; Americo Badillo-Veiga, Josh DeWind, and Julia Preston, "Undocumented Immigrant Workers in New York City"; Jay Mazur, "The Return of the Sweatshop."

grants find themselves. They cannot return to their home countries because of the absence of an open border and the difficulty of reentry. Yet their attempts at adaptation to American society are consistently blocked by their illegal status.[74]

The available evidence suggests that the undocumented lead lives confined, almost exclusively, to the ethnic areas where most of their compatriots live. Mexican, Dominican, and West Indian communities fulfill not only the "classic" functions of economic assistance and emotional support but, in addition, offer protection against detection by police and immigration officials. In general, however, there is remarkably little information about adaptation processes in this segment of the immigrant population. Orientations toward the host society and patterns of social relationships among the undocumented and formerly undocumented have not, to our knowledge, been systematically explored so far.

SUMMARY

This overview of recent immigration to the United States covers those mainstream processes identified by the existing research literature. Its most significant conclusion is that immigration is segmented into several subflows qualitatively distinct from each other. Legal immigration not only differs from contract and undocumented flows, but is itself heterogeneous. Immigration in the post-World War II era is also different in origins, patterns of settlement, and modes of incorporation from that coming to the United States at the turn of the century. Unlike the latter, the arrival of legal, undocumented, and contract labor immigrants cannot be satisfactorily explained by classic theories of labor scarcity. The internal divisions within contemporary immigration seem to reproduce and mirror the structural segmentation of the American economy. This process has given rise to patterned differences in modes of labor-market incorporation, which in turn can lead to markedly different outcomes in the social-adaptation process.

This overview also identifies areas about which we need additional information. The adaptation of undocumented and formerly undocumented immigrants from major national groups is one such area. Another is the situation of those minorities who, though numerically less significant, follow patterns of economic behavior similar to those of earlier Jewish and

74. Wayne A. Cornelius, "Mexican and Caribbean Migration to the United States," chap. 5; Badillo-Veiga, DeWind, and Preston, "Undocumented Immigrant Workers in New York City."

Japanese immigrants. Immigrant entrepreneurship and the emergence of economic enclaves are among the least-studied topics in this area.

The analysis of Mexican and Cuban immigration presented in the following chapters bears on these questions. It will focus primarily on two issues: the immigrants' role in the U.S. labor market and their social-adaptation patterns. Mexican and Cuban immigrants are among the most numerous national contingents to have arrived in recent years, and they reflect, in addition, many of the disjunctions and contradictions of all contemporary immigrations. The analysis of their experiences should provide answers to a series of important questions concerning the condition and prospects of immigrants in American society.

3

CONTRASTING HISTORIES: CUBAN AND MEXICAN IMMIGRANTS IN THE UNITED STATES

The two immigrant groups that furnish the primary data for the study are described in this chapter. Both are numerically important, ranking consistently among the top five national contingents of legal immigrants in recent years. Both come from similar cultural contexts and from the same world region—Latin America. Yet the specific origins of the two flows and the history of their incorporation into American society differ sharply. The combination of these characteristics is the main justification for a comparative research design: by comparing two large inflows, similar in cultural background but different in a series of structural variables, it may be possible to arrive at novel insights concerning different aspects of immigration.

A brief analysis of the differences between refugees and immigrants, a topic of increasing significance in the literature, follows. Next is an overview of the history of Mexican and Cuban immigration to the United States. Finally, the plan for the study and the difficulties encountered during its implementation are discussed.

POLITICAL AND ECONOMIC IMMIGRANTS

Cuban and Mexican migrations to the United States are representative of a distinction made with increasing frequency in journalistic and official circles. The difference between political refugees and economic immigrants is held to affect every major aspect of the immigration experience—from its social origins to patterns of adaptation in the receiving country.

The more conventional perspective on immigration portrays refugees and economic immigrants as characterized by a different "mix" of push and pull factors. Immigrants are mostly pulled by the attractions of high wages and the promise of long-term economic progress. Their move is deliberate and voluntary and frequently involves careful planning. Refugees, on the other hand, are mostly pushed by an immediate threat to basic personal rights, such as life and liberty. The decision to emigrate is not motivated by the promise of gain, but by the need to escape an intolerable situation. Refugee flight is thus depicted as an unplanned, often desperate venture.

On the basis of this analysis, inferences are made about the course of adaptation of migrants, chances for return to their home country, and probabilities of social and economic advancement in the receiving society. These predictions, based on the imputation of personal characteristics derived from an assumed "mix" of motivations, are frequently contradictory. Three examples may be cited.

First, refugees have been described as internally homogenous groups, since reasons for their flight are often linked to a common class origin, religion, or political ideology. Jewishness or the "wrong" kind of Christian sect, membership in the nobility or the bourgeoisie, and opposition to those in control of the state have been common reasons for persecution and exile in the past. On the contrary, other views stress the relatively diverse composition of refugee flows as opposed to the homogenous class origins of economic immigrants. The Cuban exodus and its diverse class origins have been used in support of this argument.[1]

Second, refugee flows have been characterized as mostly temporary. Since people are pushed out of their country without desiring to leave it except to escape persecution and possible harm, it follows that they will return once these conditions disappear. According to one author,

An exile is a person compelled to leave or remain outside his country of origin on account of well-founded fear of persecution . . . a person considers his exile temporary (even though it may last a lifetime), hoping to return to his fatherland when circumstances permit.[2]

Other authors have chosen, however, to stress the *permanent* nature of refugee migrations in contrast with the target-earning behavior of economic immigrants. According to this view, immigrants are free to go back and forth in pursuit of different economic objectives, but refugees are confined to the country of destination and unable to contemplate the return option.[3]

Assumed characteristics of refugees and immigrants lead to a third contradiction concerning their chances for economic success. The image of political exile as sudden and unplanned escape in contrast to the deliberate

1. Silvia Pedraza-Bailey, "Cubans and Mexicans in the United States."
2. Paul Tabori, *The Anatomy of Exile.*
3. George Borjas, "The Earnings of Male Hispanic Immigrants in the United States."

planning characteristic of economic immigration suggests that the latter would be more conducive to success in the receiving country. Immigrants ought to do better because their move is part of a rational strategy of economic advancement; refugees, on the other hand, are completely at the mercy of post-escape circumstances.[4]

On the contrary, other authors have viewed the "no return" situation of refugees as one likely to produce strong motivations toward economic mobility. Refugees are more aggressive in the marketplace precisely because they know that going back is impossible and, hence, that they must make a life in the new country. In one of the few empirical comparisons of refugees and migrants, Miriam Gaertner concluded that

Puerto Ricans [economic migrants] did not have the strong psychological motivation to make a place for themselves and to get ahead which the European refugees had developed out of oppression and persecution.[5]

To these contradictions must be added the difficulties of identifying concrete immigration flows as *political* or *economic*. Individuals labelled *political refugees* have been found, on closer inspection, to have very definite economic motivations to leave their home country. Flows that at the start were clearly political may devolve in time into *de facto* economic migrations, as others learn of the advantages conferred by refugee status in the receiving country.[6]

Conversely, movements that on the surface appear to be economic may turn out to have direct political roots. The political decisions of national states have frequent and major consequences for the socioeconomic context in which individual decisions are made. Political processes may turn out to induce migration, directly or indirectly, as they constrain the economic opportunities available to the general population or particular segments of it.

In the case of the Cuban exodus to the United States, Jorge and Moncarz attribute the political motivations of refugees to the failure of the redistributive policies of the revolutionary government.[7] Such may be the case. But if such failure is the basis of classification as political or economic, then the entire history of Mexican emigration would be fundamentally political. For, as one Mexican writer notes, the political problems of Mexico are unquestionable:

---

4. Barry R. Chiswick, *An Analysis of the Economic Progress and Impact of Immigrants,* chap. 3.

5. Miriam L. Gaertner, "A Comparison of Refugee and Non-refugee Immigrants to New York City," p. 110.

6. Astri Suhrke, "Global Refugee Movements and Strategies."

7. Antonio Jorge and Raul Moncarz, "Cubans in South Florida."

Political manifestos, discussions of diverse professional and interest groups, conclusions of students and the press, all attest to the prevalence of economic injustice [and] monopoly of power. . . .[8]

These contradictions and empirical difficulties reflect the limitations of an analysis based exclusively on individual motivations and traits. At this point we propose an alternative interpretation of alleged differences between these two types of migrations. In contrast to conventional push–pull accounts, this alternative framework is based on the historical context in which individual-level variables are embedded. As a point of departure, we return to the structural perspective on the origins of migration, outlined in Chapter 1.

The articulation of an economic system on a world scale is the historical context in which contemporary migrations occur. As components of this system, national states interact to maximize different goals. The nature of these interrelationships has a decisive impact not only on the origins of migrant flows, but in the manner in which they are defined. The characteristics and motivations of individual migrants do not determine *ipso facto* the label applied to them. It has been a common occurrence that receiving states insist on labelling particular migrations "economic" even when, from a subjective standpoint, they have clearly political origins.[9] Conversely, the status of political refugees has been routinely conferred on individuals whose motivation to leave their home country has been economic.

Recently an author has defined refugee migrations to the United States as follows:

Refugees are aliens for whom the U.S. feels a special obligation. Most are admitted because they are fleeing the forces of international communism. . . .[10]

The definition bestowed on particular international flows is ultimately a *political* decision in the hands of the receiving state. A structural perspective on migration suggests two related hypotheses on this point: (1) that such a decision has major consequences for the incorporation of immigrants in the host society and their ensuing patterns of adaptation, and (2) that this decision is affected, but not determined, by migrants' self-definitions. Equally if not more important is the history of economic and political interrelationships between sending and receiving nations and the functions that the migration stream plays with respect to each of them.

Large-scale migrations always reflect the internal structure and politi-

8. Francisco Alba, *La Población de México*, p. 156.
9. Suhrke, "Global Refugee Movements and Strategies."
10. David S. North, "The Impact of Illegal and Refugee Migrations on U.S. Social Service Programs," pp. 2, 7.

cal and economic dynamics of the sending nations. Such internal processes do not occur in isolation, however, but are themselves influenced by the position of the country in an overarching world system. Both the internal origins of migrations and the countries to which they are directed are deeply conditioned by such global relations. Chances of individual economic success are similarly dependent on the migrants' correct assessment of these relations as they determine changing modes of reception in the host societies.

Following this general perspective, the background of Mexican and Cuban immigrations to the United States will be presented in two parts. The next two sections outline the history of these immigrations as they reflect changing "stages" in the relationships between the United States, Cuba, and Mexico. Following a description of the empirical study, Chapter 4 presents data on the social origins of the two immigrant samples as they interact with the recent history of the sending countries. Through this strategy, the resulting "profiles" of individual migrants are placed in the context of broader processes, internal and international, conditioning the characteristics of each flow.

MEXICAN IMMIGRATION

The heavy presence of a population of Mexican descent throughout the American Southwest is a phenomenon that did not predate the conquest of the region by the United States, but that followed it. Mexican immigration is unique in that it came to populate a region that belonged previously to the immigrants' country of origin. Several writers have referred to this inflow as a "late" chapter in American immigration history, since the first significant numbers of legal Mexican immigrants were recorded around 1910.[11] This view confuses actual population movements with the administrative enforcement of a political border.

Mexican labor immigration to the United States is a century-old phenomenon, coming hard on the heels of the Texan war and the subsequent annexation of Texas by the United States. Until the beginning of the twentieth century, this flow took place outside of administrative controls as a gradual drift northwards of agricultural laborers in search of temporary employment. Construction of the national railroads in Mexico facilitated this movement, while the economic devastation wrought by continuous political instability stimulated it.[12]

11. Leo Grebler, Joan W. Moore, and Ralph C. Guzman, *The Mexican-American People*, p. 62.

12. Enrique Santibañez, *Ensayo acerca de la Inmigración Mexicana en los Estados Unidos*, pp. 39–41.

Even before 1910, substantial numbers of peasants from central Mexico were found in the mines of Arizona and in the cotton fields of Texas. They settled close to the border, for the most part, and Mexican towns and labor encampments grew alongside Anglo settlements. Traffic across the border was free, a situation that was to change dramatically in the course of a few years:

Until 1907, Mexicans only had to pay five cents for boat transportation across the Rio Bravo and they did so whenever they wished. . . . After 1917 they needed: two birth certificates, two marriage certificates, a certificate of good conduct, another of good health, proof that they would not be a public charge; a fee of ten dollars for the visa and another eight for entry tax.[13]

The progressive enforcement of the border reflected major events taking place at the center of the American political economy. As seen in Chapter 2, these events had to do with the growing opposition of organized labor to European and Asiatic immigration and with the shift of industrial capital to new sources of low-wage labor in the South. The restrictions on immigration imposed by the national origins legislation had different consequences in the industrial North, where European and Asiatic labor was being replaced by southern black migrants, than in the agricultural Southwest, where no such alternative was available.

One of the consequences of this legislation along the Mexican border was to create the category of *illegal* immigrant out of a preexisting, established flow, since many migrants simply chose to bypass the increasingly cumbersome regulations. Another consequence was the dilemma confronted by the American state of enforcing the "historic pact" between industrial capital and labor, and responding to the clamor for Mexican workers among southwestern agricultural and railroad employers.[14]

The upsurge of Mexican immigration in the national statistics after 1910 is thus, in part, a consequence of the imposition of administrative controls on a preexisting inflow. Authors such as Grebler, Moore, and Guzman have placed great emphasis on the upheavals caused by the Mexican Revolution as a primary force leading to increasing immigration at this time.[15] But this interpretation neglects economic processes taking place simultaneously on the other side of the border.

By 1910, the massive importation of Asian immigrants for agriculture and the railroads had all but ceased. As seen in the last chapter, the campaign for exclusion, especially in the case of the Japanese, was fueled by the propensity of these immigrants to deny their labor to U.S. growers and to

13. Ibid., p. 45.
14. Robert L. Bach, "Mexican Immigration and the American State."
15. Grebler, Moore, and Guzman, *The Mexican-American People*, pp. 63–66.

acquire property and go into business by themselves. At a time of rapid economic expansion, southwestern employers had only Mexico to turn to as a convenient source of low-wage labor.

The pull of labor demand and higher wages in the United States had to be activated, however, by direct recruitment. Paid labor agents were sent by growers' associations and railroad companies into the interior of Mexico. By 1916, the *Los Angeles Times* reported that five or six weekly trains full of Mexican workers hired by the agents were being run from Laredo. According to another author, the competition in El Paso became so aggressive that recruiting agencies stationed their Mexican employees at the Santa Fe bridge, where they literally pounced on the immigrants as they crossed the border.[16]

Access to Mexican labor in the Southwest obviously conflicted with the increasingly exclusionary mood in the rest of the country. The history of immigration laws and regulations from the end of World War I to the Great Depression is a case study of state efforts to conciliate incompatible demands through legislative compromise and administrative regulation. Direct attempts by southwestern growers to repeal increasingly restrictive immigration laws were defeated. However, in 1918, an exception to the ban on illiterates was granted by Congress in favor of immigrants from Mexico, Canada, and the West Indies. In addition, President Wilson authorized the Food Administration and the U.S. Employment Service to actually serve as contractors and employers of Mexican immigrant workers.[17]

The 1924 National Origins Act imposed a quota restricting immigration from most countries. Exempted again were Mexico, Canada, and other Western Hemisphere countries. The same legislation created the Border Patrol, which was instituted to restrict surreptitious European and Asian immigration but was also to have a profound effect along the Mexican border. In 1929, however, a Supreme Court decision upheld an earlier administrative decree declaring individuals who commuted between residences in Mexico and their work in the United States to be legal immigrants. In effect, after enforcing the border to prevent undesired immigrant flows, the state reversed itself to accommodate the demands of a regionally powerful segment of capital.[18]

Table 10 presents figures on Mexican immigration to the United States by decades. The sharp increase in absolute numbers and in the relative proportion of this inflow during the 1920s can be defined as a consequence

16. Mario Garcia, *Obreros: The Mexican Workers of El Paso.*
17. Bach, "Mexican Immigration," p. 547; Santibañez, *Ensayo acerca de la Inmigración Mexicana*, p. 44.
18. Bach, "Mexican Immigration," p. 548.

Table 10. Mexican Immigration to the
United States, 1881-1978

Decade or Year	Number (in thousands)	As Percent of Total Immigration
1881-1890	2	.04
1891-1900	1	.02
1901-1910	50	.6
1911-1920	219	3.8
1921-1930	459	11.2
1931-1940	22	4.2
1941-1950	61	5.9
1951-1960	300	11.9
1961-1970	454	13.7
1971	50	13.5
1972	64	16.6
1973	70	17.5
1974	72	18.2
1975	62	16.1
1976	58	14.5
1977[a]	44	9.5
1978	92	15.3

Source: Compiled from U.S. Immigration and Naturalization
Service, Annual Report, 1978 (Washington, D.C.: U.S.
Government Printing Office, 1979), pp. 36-37.

[a]Excludes transition quarter of 1976.

of the consolidation of Mexico as the chief supplier of low-wage labor for southwestern agriculture and the parallel replacement of European immigrants by blacks in similar roles in northern industry.

If the origins of mass Mexican immigration are found in political conquest and direct labor recruitment, its stability and directionality in time correspond quite closely to the predictions of cyclical theory. More than any other movement, Mexican immigration has followed an ebb-and-flow pattern, both at the aggregate and individual levels. At the level of aggregate processes, high demand for Mexican workers in agriculture, mines, and railroad construction gave way to a post-Depression period in which this demand not only disappeared, but Mexicans were actually blamed for domestic unemployment. A campaign of forced repatriation followed in which not only immigrants, but U.S.-born Mexican-Americans were returned to Mexico.[19]

Labelling Mexicans as a source of grief for American workers was quickly abandoned, however, with the onset of World War II and the re-

19. Jorge A. Bustamante, "Espaldas Mojadas."

emergence of labor scarcity. The bracero program corresponded to this new stage. It continued providing low-wage labor for southwestern agriculture long after the end of the war. By 1954, however, there was renewed concern with the increasing number of illegal workers coming alongside the braceros. Hence, a new repatriation campaign was initiated, which, in one year, sent back to Mexico more than a million "wetbacks." [20]

Since that time, every economic recession has produced renewed denunciations of the "alien invasion" and the harm meted on American society by waves of illegal immigrants. As the evidence presented in Chapter 2 suggests, however, demand for Mexican and other low-wage immigrant workers has continued to rise even in the face of high domestic unemployment.

At the level of individual behavior, Mexican immigration has been characterized by a strong return orientation and a cyclical pattern, in which periods of work in the United States alternate with periods of residence in Mexico. This pattern was already recognized in the 1911 (Dillingham Commission) Report on Immigration, which spoke, in no uncertain terms, about the undesirability of permanent settlement and the convenience of temporary labor immigration. For the commission, Mexican immigrants were not easily "assimilable," but this was unimportant provided that they returned home after a short period. [21]

The trend continued with the bracero program and extends to present-day undocumented immigration. Temporal labor migration to the United States is deeply embedded in the social and economic fabric of remote Mexican rural communities. Remittances sent by migrants provide means both of consumption and resources for investment in agricultural land and even industry. But if remittances are central to the economic life of these communities, so too is the eventual return of its migrants.

In his study of the Los Altos de Jalisco region, for example, Cornelius found that the average stay of migrants in the United States was about six to eight months, with most leaving in March and returning in early December. A study conducted by the Mexican Labor Department among 5,271 apprehended illegals returned to Mexico found that 70.6 percent of those employed in nonagricultural occupations had spent less than six months in the United States. Among those employed in agriculture, the corresponding figure was still higher, 89.8 percent. [22]

The pattern of cyclical Mexican immigration over time has been sustained by the fact that neither employers nor migrants are generally inter-

20. Bustamante, "Espaldas Mojadas"; Grebler, Moore, and Guzman, *The Mexican-American People*, pp. 68–69.
21. Immigration Commission, *Reports*, pp. 690–791.
22. Wayne A. Cornelius, "Mexican Migration to the United States"; Jorge A. Bustamante and Geronimo Martinez, "La Emigración a la Frontera Norte del País y a Estados Unidos."

ested in permanent settlement. For Southwestern growers, Mexican migration has been a reliable source of migrants, and this labor has been a source of relatively high wages with which to meet social and economic needs back home. Because of this cyclical pattern, undocumented immigrants today are often the offspring of braceros and earlier immigrants. Their decision to leave is not the desperate escape frequently portrayed in the journalistic literature, but a deliberate move embedded in a well-established pattern of career mobility.

After World War II, and especially since the bracero program ended, the uses made of Mexican immigrant labor have become more diversified. The evidence points to a sustained move toward urban employment responding to labor demand in the competitive sector of the American economy. Undocumented and legal Mexican immigrants now find jobs in such enterprises as plant nurseries, construction firms, foundries, shipyards, cement companies, furniture factories, rubber factories, paper factories, restaurants, hotels and motels, car washes, and butcher shops. Immigrants with more experience in the United States and those who come legally ("with papers") appear to move into better-paid urban jobs, while undocumented newcomers tend to continue seeking employment in agriculture.[23]

The shift in labor-market incorporation—from a temporary rural labor force to a lower-tier urban proletariat—has been accompanied by changes in the geographic distribution of Mexican immigrants. Though the immigrants have always been widely scattered throughout the Southwest, the trend at present seems to be toward even greater dispersal, as migrants follow jobs in services and industry into new regions. Immigrants from a single rural town in Jalisco were reported to be living in 1975 in 285 different U.S. localities. Together with the more familiar Southwest locations, there were immigrants from this town in such places as Detroit, Atlantic City, and Toledo, Ohio.[24]

The move toward cities and toward areas other than the Southwest makes it likely that Mexican immigration will become a national rather than regional phenomenon in the future. The magnitude of the present inflow also points in this direction: for the last two decades, the Mexican contingent has been the single largest among both legal and undocumented (apprehended) immigrants to the United States.

As noted in Chapter 2, family-reunification provisions of the 1965 Immigration Act have facilitated conversion of part of the undocumented flow into legal immigration. During the 1970s, Mexicans represented increasing proportions of total legal immigrants, a trend that peaked in 1974 when

23. Cornelius, "Mexican Migration to the United States."
24. Ibid.

they amounted to 18 percent. In the following three years, the trend was reversed by new legislation extending to the Western Hemisphere the quota system already applied to Eastern Hemisphere nations. While most Mexican immigrants continued to come outside the quota as relatives of U.S. citizens, the imposition of the 20,000-per-year limit reduced the legal inflow by almost half. In fiscal 1978, however, the absolute number of legal Mexican immigrants climbed back to its highest level since the end of World War II and represented again more than 15 percent of total immigration. This new upturn was due to the massive use of nonquota family-reunification visas as well as new modifications in entry rules.

Concerning individual characteristics, the available evidence points to a profile of undocumented immigrants as young (under 30), male, with low levels of education, and born predominantly in rural communities. However, other studies also indicate that the flow does not originate primarily in the most impoverished Mexican states nor among the poorest sectors of the peasantry.

The study conducted by the Mexican Labor Department found, for example, that four states—Michoacan, Jalisco, Chihuahua, and Guanajuato—jointly accounted for 54.1 percent of undocumented immigration. These states do not represent, as a whole, the poorest regions of Mexico. At least three studies provide additional evidence indicating that undocumented immigrants have average levels of education that are higher than among the total population and do not come from the lowest income strata in their respective communities. The most destitute seldom have the means to finance a trip to the United States. The border-crossing enterprise is thus one undertaken primarily by a "middling" stratum with some land or other economic resources.[25]

Because of many restrictions to legal immigration, the sex–age distributions of the legal inflow do not fully reflect the characteristics of the underlying undocumented movement. Family-reunification provisions favor entry of spouses and older persons, such as parents of U.S. citizens and residents. These groups thus come to represent larger proportions among legal immigrants. However, as shown in Table 11, Mexicans are still younger on the average and more likely to be male than legal immigrants from other countries. Seventy-three percent of Mexican immigrants in 1977 were under twenty-nine years of age, as compared with 59 percent for all immigrants. Females are overrepresented in the total, while they continue to be underrepresented among Mexicans.

25. Bustamante and Martinez, "La Emigración"; Joshua S. Reichert, "The Migrant Syndrome"; Bustamante, "Espaldas Mojadas."

Table 11. Mexican and Total Immigration
by Sex and Age, 1977

Individuals	Mexican Immigration		Total Immigration	
	Numbers (in thousands)	%	Numbers (in thousands)	%
By Sex				
Female	21	47.7	246	53.2
Male	23	52.3	216	46.8
		100.0		100.0
By Age				
Under age 20	16	36.4	145	31.4
20-29	16	36.4	126	27.3
30-39	7	15.9	79	17.1
40-49	2	4.5	43	9.3
50-59	2	4.5	32	6.9
60 or more	1	2.3	37	8.0
Total	44	100.0	462	100.0

Source: Adapted from U.S. Immigration and Naturalization Service, *1977 Annual Report* (Washington, D.C.: U.S. Government Printing Office, 1978).

Despite the strong tendency toward return migration, Mexican immigration has left a sizable "sediment" in many U.S. communities. It is also likely that displacement toward more distant northern locations and toward more stable urban employment will further stimulate permanent settlement.

Mexican immigration has been studied in the past primarily on the basis of returnees to places of origin, apprehended illegals, or even established Mexican-American communities. Excluded from these alternatives is the situation of the most recent additions to the permanent Mexican-origin population of the United States: first-generation immigrants. Their modes of economic incorporation and their adaptation patterns, as compared with return migrants or the U.S.-born Chicano population, are not well known at present. This subject is covered in the following chapters.

CUBAN IMMIGRATION

Unlike Mexican immigration, most of the Cuban inflow to the United States has occurred relatively recently. This flow has its roots not in a system of labor recruitment but in a major revolutionary upheaval. For this reason, and unlike Mexican immigrants, the vast majority of Cubans in the United States arrived during the span of a single government in their home country. Prior to the advent of Fidel Castro to power in January, 1959, the Cuban immigrant population in the United States was relatively insignificant. The 1960 census reported 79,156 Cuban-born persons living in the United States; if the refugees who arrived during 1959 are subtracted from these, the prerevolutionary Cuban population in the country can be estimated at no more than 30,000.[26]

Between 1959 and 1980, more than 800,000 Cubans, or about one-tenth of the island population, left. Of these, at least 85 percent went to live in the U.S. mainland and Puerto Rico. The origins of the Cuban inflow and its evolution over time furnish a prime example of the difficulty of distinguishing "political" from "economic" migrations. Though the American government defined the movement from the start as a political exodus, it is clear that individual determinants of emigration were frequently economic. At the very least, it would be hard to prove that the movement out of Cuba was significantly less "economic" than that out of Mexico or that the latter was much less "political." In both cases, state decisions and international relations interacted to limit economic opportunities for particular segments of the population or to induce these people to leave in search of a better life abroad. For Cuban refugees, the general politicoeconomic determinants of emigration have remained a constant, though their particular manifestations have changed over time.

For the propertied classes, emigration followed the loss of wealth and economic power. The wealthy left early, either to organize the overthrow of Castro from exile or to rebuild fortunes and position abroad. For Cubans of more modest origins, who left in subsequent waves, dissatisfaction with lack of personal freedom was mixed with the incentive of higher standards of living in the United States. In this sense, the motivations of recent emigrés come very close to those generally imputed to "economic" immigrants.

Unlike Mexican immigration, however, the movement out of Cuba has been, by and large, a one-way flow. Earlier exile waves regarded their stay in the United States as temporary, pending the overthrow of the Castro government. More recent groups have arrived, however, with the expectation of permanent settlement. Despite a political rhetoric that continues to promise

26. Jorge and Moncarz, "Cubans in South Florida."

Table 12. Cuban Immigration to
the United States, 1959-1980

Year[a]	Number	Year[a]	Number
1959	26,527	1970	49,545
1960	60,224	1971	50,001
1961	49,661	1972	23,977
1962	78,611	1973	12,579
1963	42,929	1974	13,670
1964	15,616	1975	8,488
1965	16,447	1976	4,515
1966	46,688	1977	4,548
1967	52,147	1978	4,108
1968	55,945	1979	2,644
1969	52,625	1980	122,061

Source: U.S. Immigration and Naturalization Service, "Cubans
Arrived in the United States by Class of Admission: January 1,
1959-September 30, 1980," Washington, D.C., October 1980
(mimeo).

[a]Definition of "year" is as follows: 1959=January 1 to June 30;
1960-1976, year ends June 30; 1977-1980, year ends September 30.

a triumphal return "next year," most members of the Cuban emigré community have either resigned themselves to or indeed planned from the start a
new life in America. In this sense, the movement lacks the short-term orientation and cyclical pattern characteristic of Mexican labor immigration.

Table 12 presents figures on Cuban immigration by year. The very erratic pattern of the flow over two decades reflects the changing political
relationship between the United States and Cuba and the various forms
through which this movement has been channelled. Cuban immigration to
the United States can be divided into five main stages:

1. *From January 1959 to October 1962.* The flight of dictator Fulgencio
   Batista and his supporters was followed by the departure of an increasing number of landowners, industrialists, and managers of ex-
   propriated U.S. enterprises. As the revolution fueled the transformation of the Cuban class structure, these groups were joined by

sizeable contingents of professionals and smaller merchants. Most came via commercial flights, which continued even after the Bay of Pigs invasion in April, 1961. In the United States, these immigrants received the status of parolees—exiles from a communist government—and were admitted outside of immigration quotas. Approximately 215,000 Cubans came during this period.[27]

2. *November 1962 to November 1965.* The confrontation between the United States and the Soviet Union over Russian missiles in Cuba brought to an end all direct flights between the island and the United States. The number of refugees dwindled rapidly during the next three years, as it was possible to leave the island only through clandestine means or through restricted flights to third countries, such as Mexico. In September 1965, however, the Cuban government announced that it would permit the departure through the fishing port of Camarioca of relatives of exiles living in the United States. The boatlift that followed brought in about 5,000 new exiles. In total, close to 74,000 refugees arrived during this period.[28]

3. *December 1965 to April 1973.* Three months after the start of the Camarioca boatlift, the governments of Cuba and the United States signed a "memorandum of understanding" that launched an airlift from Varadero Beach in Cuba to Miami. The two daily flights that operated during this period brought in more than 340,000 new refugees, or about half the total inflow. Studies conducted during these years noted the declining socioeconomic origins of the new arrivals, who encompassed increasing proportions of the lower-middle and urban working classes. Even then, average educational and occupational attainments of the new exiles continued to be above those of the Cuban population. Exiles were also disproportionately urban in origin, while the proportion of blacks and mulattoes continued to be much lower than in the island's population.[29]

4. *May 1973 to April 1980.* In April 1973, the Cuban government unilaterally terminated the airlift, returning to the *status quo ante.* Clandestine escapes and travel to third countries, mainly Spain, again became the only means of leaving Cuba. Emigration decreased rapidly, and by 1979 the number of refugees arriving on U.S. shores had dwindled to fewer than 3,000.

5. *May to September, 1980.* By 1980, many considered the exodus and resettlement of Cubans in the United States to be a closed chapter.

27. Sergio Diaz-Briquets and Lisandro Perez, "Cuba"; Max Azicri, "The Politics of Exile."
28. Diaz-Briquets and Perez, "Cuba," p. 26; Azicri, "The Politics of Exile."
29. Alejandro Portes, Juan M. Clark, and Robert L. Bach, "The New Wave"; Diaz-Briquets and Perez, "Cuba," pp. 26–30.

Their predictions proved wrong. The occupation of the Peruvian embassy in Havana in April 1980 jolted the emigré Cuban community and triggered the largest ever Cuban emigration in a single year. Announcing first that it would authorize an airlift only to Peru and Costa Rica, the Cuban government reversed itself and declared the port of Mariel open to anyone who wished to leave. Exiles who went to pick up their relatives, often at great financial cost, were frequently forced to return with a boatload of strangers. The Cuban government publicly declared that it was using the opportunity to get rid of "undesirables," a claim widely echoed in the American press.

The Carter administration first announced that it would admit only 3,500 refugees, but then shifted to an "open hearts, open arms" policy and started setting up camps to receive the exiles. Just ten days later, on May 14, the administration ordered the Coast Guard to set up a blockade to prevent boats from going to Mariel. The Coast Guard and Navy continued, however, aiding returning craft and accepting new refugees. In the course of five months, 124,769 new Cubans arrived, more than the combined total for the preceding eight years. In one month alone, May, more refugees arrived than during all of 1962, previously the record year of Cuban immigration.[30]

This last massive stage of Cuban immigration received wide coverage by the press and has been the object of much public debate. An analysis based on a representative sample of the camp population and other official data sources indicates that a significant split developed within the Mariel exodus. The 62,000 persons processed in and released directly into the Miami community were, on the average, not too different from earlier exile cohorts. Their occupational profile was similar to that of refugees arriving in the early seventies. There was a high proportion of family groups and of individuals with relatives already living in the United States. Declared unemployment in Cuba and previous criminal offenses were uncommon.

On the other hand, refugees going to the camps established by the U.S. government were, for the most part, single men. They were also younger than earlier cohorts, with the largest share found in the 25–29 age category. This age profile is markedly different from that of the Cuban exile community as a whole, which is older than both the U.S. and Cuban populations. Few of the camp exiles had relatives in the country. In addition, 16 percent had been incarcerated in Cuba. However, the occupational distribution of the remainder of this population again resembled that of pre-Mariel cohorts. Most workers were drawn from urban manufacturing, construction, and service sectors; very few of the entrants were farmers or farm laborers.[31]

30. Diaz-Briquets and Perez, "Cuba," pp. 26–30.
31. Robert L. Bach, Jennifer B. Bach, and Timothy Triplett, "The Flotilla 'Entrants.'"

The differences between the two segments of the Mariel inflow cannot be attributed to a deliberate effort to separate, from the start, the more from the less assimilable. Instead, the split developed as part of the sequence of events during the exodus. Earlier arrivals, processed and released into Miami, were, for the most part, individuals rejoining families in the city. The proportion of unattached men increased in subsequent waves. There is also evidence that the number of criminals and other "undesirables" grew as the boatlift progressed. These later waves arrived when processing had been shifted from Miami to military camps in the North.[32]

The proportion of nonwhites among Mariel exiles is significantly higher than among earlier emigré cohorts, approaching the figure in the Cuban population. Nonwhite Cuban refugees before the new inflow numbered less than 5 percent, a figure that held constant for those arriving during the early seventies. The proportion among Mariel exiles has been estimated at 30 percent.[33]

Since December 1960, the processing and resettlement of Cubans in the United States has been coordinated by the Cuban Refugee Program (CRP) under the Secretary of Health, Education, and Welfare. In the early sixties, the arrival of Cuban refugees in Miami was viewed as a source of strain aggravating the depressed economy of the area. Thus, efforts of the Cuban Refugee Emergency Center, established by the CRP in Miami, concentrated in relocating the exiles away from the area and throughout communities in the United States. Cuban lawyers were transformed into language teachers and sent to high schools and colleges in the North. Others found widely varied occupations, often with the support of private charity organizations.

The existence of the refugee center gave Cubans access to resources seldom available to other immigrant groups. On the other hand, it restricted their adaptation process to a pattern of close conformity with government directives. For example, to ensure that relocation proceeded smoothly, the center made emergency welfare aid contingent on acceptance of job offers elsewhere when available. By 1978, 469,435 had been resettled away from Miami.[34] Overall, the policy of government aid, benevolent reception, and constrained resettlement amounted to a unique entry and early adaptation process to American society. Regardless of whether motivations of particular individuals were "political" or "economic," the reception accorded to all Cuban refugees was markedly different from that awaiting other groups.

32. Ibid.; Juan M. Clark, José I. Lasaga, and Rose Reque, *The Mariel Exodus*, pp. 13–16.
33. Azicri, "The Politics of Exile," p. 4.
34. Juan M. Clark, "Los Cubanos de Miami"; Diaz-Briquets and Perez, "Cuba," p. 33.

Since the early seventies, there has been evidence of a significant return drift to Miami. In 1973, a survey estimated that more than 27.4 percent of the Cubans residing in the Miami metropolitan area were returnees from other U.S. localities. A survey conducted by the *Miami Herald* in 1978 raised that proportion to 40 percent. In 1970, 40 percent of the Cuban-born population of the U.S. lived in Miami. All indications are that the 1980 census will show a significant increase in this figure. Indeed, preliminary estimates indicate that more than 60 percent of the Cuban-American population now live in the Miami metropolitan area. The total Cuban-born population in the city is six times larger than the next largest refugee concentration, the West New York / Union City area in New Jersey.[35]

Cultural and climatic reasons have obviously much to do with return decisions. There is evidence, however, that relocated exiles used their time in northern communities much as other migrants have used their stay in high-wage regions: as an opportunity for accumulating capital. Small-scale investments by returnees from the North were added to those made with capital brought from Cuba to stimulate the emergence of an economic enclave.

Cuban-owned enterprises in the Miami area increased from 919 in 1967 to about 8,000 in 1978 and to an estimated 13,000 at present. Most of these are small, with the average number of employees per firm being only 8.1 in 1977. However, some enterprises, especially in manufacturing, employ hundreds of workers. Enclave firms concentrate in services (35 percent), retail (28 percent), manufacturing (11 percent), and construction (9 percent). From 1969 to 1977, the number of manufacturing firms almost doubled and that of construction enterprises tripled. Refugee-owned industries included textiles, leather, footwear, furniture, and cigar making. Common enterprises in the service sector are restaurants (a favorite investment for small entrepreneurs), supermarkets, private clinics, realty offices, legal firms, funeral parlors, and private schools. Cuban-owned firms have increased not only in numbers, but in size as well. In 1969, for example, gross receipts of Cuban manufacturing firms averaged only $59,633; eight years later the figure was $639,817, a 1,067 percent increase. Though Miami ranks second to Los Angeles in the number of Hispanic businesses, the size of the Miami firms is much larger. By 1972, average gross receipts of Miami Hispanic-owned firms (overwhelmingly Cuban) were $75,000, exceeding the corresponding Los Angeles figure by 70 percent.[36]

The pattern of initial dispersion followed by increasing spatial concen-

35. Juan M. Clark, *The Cuban Exodus*; *Time*, "Spanish Americans"; Thomas D. Boswell, "Cuban Americans."

36. Antonio Jorge and Raul Moncarz, "The Cuban Entrepreneur and the Economic Development of the Miami SMSA."

tration seems to have paid off economically. In 1979, the median income of Cuban-origin families in the United States was $17,538, higher than the figure for all Spanish-origin families ($14,569), though still lower than that for the native white population ($19,965). About 19 percent of all Cuban-origin employed persons were professionals or managers, a proportion also intermediate between those for the Spanish-origin employed population and the rest of the labor force.[37]

In general, cohorts of exiles arriving during the sixties experienced significant economic and occupational advancement after a period of initial downward mobility. It cannot be assumed, however, that subsequent waves, especially the Mariel refugees, will be able to replicate this pattern. Average educational and occupational levels have declined in each successive period of emigration. To the extent that such "human capital" variables determine opportunities of immigrants in the American labor market, prospects for later exiles appear less promising.

For this reason, it is important to examine effects of a preexisting enclave economy on the occupational and economic prospects of recent arrivals. It is possible that the economic and social structures created by earlier exile cohorts may modify the conditions faced by later ones, providing them with opportunities in the labor market unavailable to other immigrants. The existence and significance of these contextual effects will be explored in ensuing chapters.

THE RESEARCH DESIGN

Immigrant adaptation and immigrant workers' incorporation into the labor market are highly dynamic processes. For the most part, however, recent studies of immigration are based on static cross-sectional designs. For example, the issue of illegal or undocumented immigrants is one that has received a great deal of attention in the past. Most studies on the topic are based on one-time interviews with specific segments of this population—apprehended illegals, undocumented workers in places of destination, or returnees to the source countries. Though valuable, such studies face the problem of establishing causal order among significant variables and of ascertaining whether results are a function of particular circumstances at the time of data collection.[38]

---

37. Boswell, "Cuban Americans."

38. See, for example, David S. North and Marion F. Houstoun, *The Characteristics and Role of Illegal Aliens in the U. S. Labor Market*; Vic Villalpando, *A Study of the Socioeconomic Impact of Illegal Aliens on the County of San Diego*; Joshua Reichert and Douglas S. Massey, "History and Trends in U. S. Bound Migration from a Mexican Town."

The highly dynamic quality of immigration and immigrant adaptation is reflected in a complex interrelationship between different variables, which makes it difficult to determine *a priori* which ones are causes and which effects. For example, studies of undocumented immigration have found a relationship between out-migration from rural localities and a pattern of economic development characterized by the disappearance of subsistence agriculture and rapid increases in the price of land. In the absence of a time-extended design, it is not clear whether such economic conditions force peasants to migrate or whether a preexisting migrant flow and the remittances it sends force changes in the local economic structure.

Similarly, a positive relationship has been detected between immigrant economic success and changes of values, lifestyles, and language in a direction congruent with the host culture. It is not clear, however, which comes first. Early acculturation may lead to advantages in the occupational marketplace, as suggested by assimilation theorists. On the other hand, it is also plausible that immigrants consent to sacrifice their cultural preferences only after experiencing a measure of material success, thus making acculturation a function of economic mobility.[39]

The principal methodological feature of this study is its longitudinal character, which constitutes an attempt to tailor research design to the actual dynamic quality of the phenomenon to be studied. By following immigrants over time, it is possible to untangle the sequence of events leading to specific results, and to compare effects of what immigrants "bring with them" with those stemming from the social and economic context that receives them.

As already noted, the study is also comparative. During the early seventies, Mexican immigration to the United States received a great deal of attention from scholars and the press. Even if one were only interested in this particular group, the analysis would profit greatly from systematic comparison with another minority of similar cultural origins. In the wake of the recent Mariel exodus, greater attention has been paid to Cuban immigration and its impact on American communities. Exactly the same argument can now be made in reverse: knowledge of this group will improve through a comparison of its experiences with those of another immigrant minority.

In the study, samples of Cuban and Mexican immigrants were interviewed at the moment of arrival in 1973–1974, reinterviewed in 1976, and again in 1979. The plan of the original survey called for samples of 500 from each immigrant group. Cubans were interviewed in Miami; Mexicans were interviewed at the two major entry points along the Texas–Mexico border:

39. Alejandro Portes, "Dilemmas of a Golden Exile."

Laredo and El Paso. The final number of interviews exceeded the original plan. In total, 1,412 immigrants were interviewed: 822 Mexicans and 590 Cubans.

The original Mexican survey required the collaboration of the U.S. Immigration and Naturalization Service. Immigrants were escorted to the interview station immediately after completing official formalities. This was the only feasible way of locating legal arrivals, but had the disadvantage of establishing a link between the project and the INS. Three strategies were used to avoid a possible biasing effect: first, interviewers were Mexican-American students who addressed immigrants in their own language and in a manner different from that of government officials; second, respondents were told at the start that their participation was voluntary and confidential and that the project was not sponsored by the INS; third, all questions that could possibly have had a biasing effect, such as those concerning the Border Patrol, the U.S. government, and so on, were deleted.

It was possible to check the representativeness of this sample against INS data for the universe of Mexican immigrants in 1973–1974. Comparative figures for the sample and universe do not differ significantly in education and occupation, age, or marital status. Predictably, the sample overestimated immigration originating in eastern and central Mexico and going to Texas, Arizona, New Mexico, Illinois, and the rest of the Midwest. Laredo and El Paso serve as the main gateways for these flows. On the other hand, the sample underestimated immigration originating in western Mexico and going to California, which tends to be channelled through another entry point in Tijuana/San Isidro. With this exception, the sample appears representative of Mexican immigration during fiscal year 1973.

One of the variables for which sample results coincided with those in the universe was the proportion of immigrants arriving with family-reunification visas. Fully 43.7 percent of the sample came outside immigration quota limits as spouses of U.S. citizens (with IR-1 visas). An additional 4.7 percent came as children of U.S. citizens (IR-2 visas). The INS did not break down figures on quota immigrants from the Western Hemisphere (SA-1 visas) by specific categories. It is likely, however, that most of the 46.5 percent of quota immigrants in the sample received visas as spouses or immediate relatives of U.S. permanent residents.

These results are important because they suggest the extent to which prior Mexican immigration became legal immigration through use of the family-reunification provisions of the Immigration Act. When asked, 61.5 percent of our respondents said that they had resided previously in the United States. This figure seems an underestimate, since some respondents appeared reluctant to report prior undocumented entries. By collating responses to several other questions, we arrived at an estimate of 69.9

percent of the sample, which could reliably be assumed to have resided in the United States for extended periods prior to legal entry.

This figure suggests that the study of contemporary legal Mexican immigration is, to a large extent, the study of prior (mostly undocumented) immigration. While former illegal immigrants identified in this manner cannot be said to be representative of the total illegal population, they still constitute a significant and so far understudied segment.

Another characteristic of our Mexican sample is the wide dispersal of intended places of destination. Table 13 presents intended first addresses of Mexican respondents by city and state. As shown here, there was considerable dispersal even within states, with the exception of Illinois. Apart from its substantive importance, this residential pattern was significant because it created major problems for locating and reinterviewing respondents in subsequent surveys. Compounding this problem was the high geographic mobility of immigrants. Among those reinterviewed in 1976, 65.7 percent had moved at least once since their arrival and 30.8 percent had done so twice or more.

The survey of Cuban exiles met with greater initial obstacles. Just prior to the start of data collection, the airlift ferrying emigrés from Varadero Beach to Miami was terminated. Cubans continued to leave via Spain, but they were blocked from coming to the United States by the need to obtain a permanent resident's visa. However, in the fall of 1973, Secretary of State Kissinger signed an executive resolution authorizing Cuban exiles with families in the United States to come into the country as parolees.

Family-reunification flights were organized by private charities, principally the United States Catholic Conference and the International Rescue Committee. Most of these flights had Miami as their point of destination. After obtaining the cooperation of these agencies and of the Cuban Refugee Center in Miami, we contacted and interviewed exiles shortly after their arrival. There are no comparable published data on the universe of 1973–1974 Cuban exiles against which to assess the representativeness of this sample. However, almost all new arrivals within predefined sample categories were contacted. Discounting refusals (6 percent), the sample can be considered equivalent to the universe of Cuban exiles arriving in Miami during the fall of 1973 and early spring of 1974.

The pattern of residential destinations of this sample contrasts sharply with that of Mexican immigrants. Fully 98.8 percent of Cuban respondents intended to remain in Miami. The follow-up surveys confirmed this extreme residential concentration. In 1976, all but one of the reinterviewed Cubans lived in the Greater Miami area; in 1979, 97 percent did so. There was, however, considerable intraurban residential mobility: in 1976, 78.7 percent of reinterviewed immigrants had changed addresses at least once.

Table 13.   Intended U.S. Addresses of Respondents:
Mexican Survey, 1973-1974

State and Principal Localities of Destination		Number	%
Texas		407	49.6
El Paso	(149)		
San Antonio	(60)		
Houston	(39)		
Laredo	(38)		
Dallas	(34)		
Austin	(7)		
Corpus Christi	(6)		
Ysleta	(5)		
Odessa	(4)		
Others	(65)		
Illinois		128	15.6
Chicago	(107)		
Others	(21)		
California		108	13.2
Los Angeles	(37)		
San Jose	(4)		
Others	(67)		
New Mexico		40	4.9
Las Cruces	(6)		
Others	(34)		
Colorado		33	4.0
Arizona		21	2.6
New York		13	1.6
Michigan		12	1.5
Indiana, Missouri, Nebraska, Wisconsin		5 each	2.4
Nevada, Oklahoma, Utah		4 each	1.5
Florida, Kansas, Oregon		3 each	1.2
Georgia, Idaho, Iowa, Louisiana, Minnesota, Pennsylvania, Maryland, Massachusetts, Montana, New Jersey, Washington, Wyoming		1 each	0.6
N.D.		1	.01
		822	100.00

More than 98 percent of these moves and of those reported in 1979 were within the Greater Miami area.

Both samples are composed of males aged 18 to 60 and not dependent for their livelihood on others. Restriction of the sample to male family heads was necessary because of the many difficulties and time constraints of the initial interviews. We felt at the time that an exploratory study, directed at comparison of two immigrant groups over time, would become excessively complex were it to encompass all categories of immigrants. In subsequent interviews, however, respondents were also used as informants about major characteristics of other family members, in particular, their wives.

The main difficulty faced by the project was to maintain contact with respondents in the intersurvey periods. Most longitudinal studies to date have been based on samples of native-born respondents. Unlike them, immigrants do not have strong roots in receiving communities and do not leave as many traces in local record-keeping mechanisms. Difficulties are compounded by the tendency of recent immigrants to change addresses frequently.

The first survey included questions on the respondent's intended address and place of employment and on the names, addresses, and phone numbers of two relatives or friends who would know his place of residence at all times. These persons were labelled *anchors*. On the basis of this information, tracing stations were established after the first and second surveys to maintain regular contact with respondents and locate those who moved.

This effort entailed mailing letters of appreciation, requests for new addresses, and progress reports on the project. This work was intensified immediately before each survey. In 1975–1976, responsibility for locating lost Mexican respondents was assigned to a tracing station at Duke University. The series of basic steps involved in the process are summarized in flowchart form in Figure 4. A similar procedure was followed for both samples in 1979.

The first follow-up survey was based on personal interviews. Since almost all Cuban respondents had remained in Miami, a single field station was established there under the direction of a Cuban-American sociologist and staffed by Spanish-speaking interviewers. This station reinterviewed 427 cases, or 72.3 percent of the original sample.

For the 1976 survey, four field stations were established in the areas of greater Mexican sample concentration. Stations were located as follows: University of Texas at Austin covering Laredo, San Antonio, Dallas, Houston, Corpus Christi, and other cities in central and eastern Texas; University of Texas at El Paso covering El Paso, Albuquerque, Las Cruces, Denver, and other cities in west Texas, Arizona, New Mexico, and Colorado;

Fig. 4.   Basic Sequence of Tracing Operations for Locating Mexican
Respondents, 1976

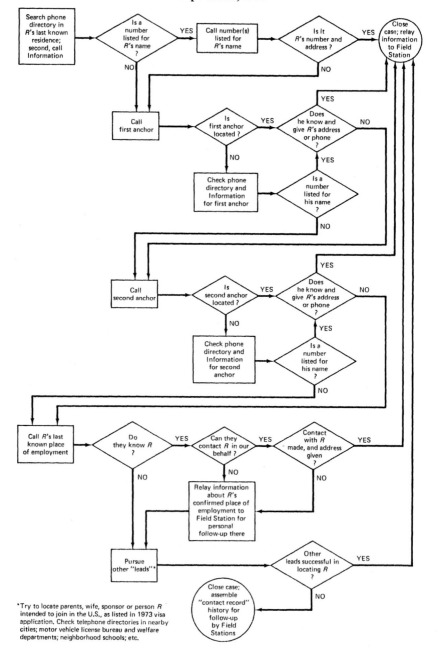

* Try to locate parents, wife, sponsor or person R
intended to join in the U.S., as listed in 1973 visa
application. Check telephone directories in nearby
cities; motor vehicle license bureau and welfare
departments; neighborhood schools; etc.

Juarez Associates, a private Los Angeles firm, covering all locations in California; Operations and Marketing Research, another private research firm, covering Chicago and the Midwest. Interviewers in all four stations were Spanish speaking. The coordinator of the entire survey was a Mexican-American sociologist. A total of 439 respondents, or 53.4 percent of the original sample, were reinterviewed.

Telephone interviews were used during the 1976 survey to reach respondents who were too distant from the field stations. Contrary to our earlier expectations, these interviews proved to be of equal quality to those conducted in person. Based on this experience and after a series of additional tests, we decided to conduct the final survey on the basis of phone interviews. This procedure reduced costs and facilitated closer supervision of interviewers. As an incentive to respondents, a reward of $10 and a certificate of appreciation were promised and sent to those who took part in the survey.

The third survey took place in 1979. Interviews were conducted in two field stations: Miami for the Cuban sample and Chicago (offices of Operations and Marketing Research) for the Mexican. A total of 413 cases, or exactly 70 percent of the original Cuban sample, were retrieved; among Mexicans there were 455 reinterviews, or 55.4 percent of the original.

The high mortality rates in both follow-ups are a result of the many difficulties involved in tracing and reinterviewing immigrant samples. During each survey, every effort was made to locate respondents, including contacting neighbors and persons of similar surnames, churches, and school officials. Cases were not closed until all possible leads had been exhausted.

Because cases retrieved during each follow-up do not completely overlap, the actual number of first-wave respondents who were never reinterviewed is significantly lower than the separate surveys suggest. Thus, the proportion of Mexican respondents reinterviewed during the second or third waves is 67 percent; the corresponding figure for Cubans is 82 percent. Still, these results give reason for concern about the extent of bias in follow-up subsamples. The greater this bias, the smaller the possibility of generalizing to the original samples and, hence, to the universes from which they came.

An initial test for sample mortality bias was conducted by comparing mean scores of respondents and nonrespondents in each follow-up survey over a series of first-wave variables. Results from this analysis are presented in Tables 14 and 15. Mean differences for each follow-up survey in each sample are small and, for the most part, insignificant. The few significant differences do not follow a consistent pattern except for two variables.

Immigrants with a higher number of children in 1973 were significantly more likely to be reinterviewed in 1976 and again in 1979. This result held

Table 14. Comparison of Second- and Third-Wave Respondents
and Nonrespondents on Wave 1 Variables--Cuban Sample

Variables, 1973	Wave 2			Wave 3		
	Respondents $\bar{X}$	Nonrespondents $\bar{X}$	t-Statistic for Difference	Respondents $\bar{X}$	Nonrespondents $\bar{X}$	t-Statistic for Difference
Age	41.20	39.59	2.35*	40.83	40.52	0.44 (n.s.)
Length of previous residence in U.S. (collapsed scale)	0.19	0.20	-0.17 (n.s.)	0.20	0.19	0.05 (n.s.)
Education (years)	8.57	8.77	-0.58 (n.s.)	8.67	8.52	0.42 (n.s.)
Prestige of main occupation (Duncan SEI scores)	38.11	38.99	-0.43 (n.s.)	38.59	37.81	0.39 (n.s.)
Prestige of last occupation (Duncan SEI scores)	34.12	34.50	-0.20 (n.s.)	34.01	34.78	-0.38 (n.s.)
Income, last occupation (dollars per month)	251.93	205.13	2.00*	248.78	216.55	1.41 (n.s.)
Unemployment during past 5 years (months)	5.61	5.44	0.88 (n.s.)	5.63	5.42	1.07 (n.s.)

Number of children	1.54	1.28	2.26*	1.58	1.20	3.43**
Number of relatives and friends in U.S.	10.65	9.02	2.64**	10.65	9.17	2.45**
Father's education (years)	6.10	6.11	-0.01 (n.s.)	5.97	6.45	-1.53 (n.s.)
Mother's education (years)	5.60	5.73	-0.54 (n.s.)	5.57	5.78	-0.86 (n.s.)
Prestige of father's occupation (Duncan SEI scores)	27.56	31.27	-1.89 (n.s.)	27.25	31.70	-2.33*
Prestige of aspired occupation in U.S. (Duncan SEI scores)	32.21	31.59	0.24 (n.s.)	31.88	32.40	-0.20 (n.s.)
Income aspirations (collapsed scale)	7.09	7.26	-0.43 (n.s.)	7.39	6.42	2.68**
Expected income in first U.S. occupation (dollars per month)	495.31	553.67	-1.37 (n.s.)	519.76	486.80	0.80 (n.s.)
Modernity (index)	0.01	0.05	-0.56 (n.s.)	0.04	-0.02	0.86 (n.s.)
Knowledge of English (index)	0.01	-0.02	0.31 (n.s.)	0.02	-0.04	0.61 (n.s.)

*p=.05.   **p=.01.

n.s.=difference not significant.

Table 15. Comparison of Second- and Third-Wave Respondents and Nonrespondents on Wave 1 Variables--Mexican Sample

Variables, 1973	Wave 2			Wave 3		
	Respondents $\overline{X}$	Nonrespondents $\overline{X}$	t-Statistic for Difference	Respondents $\overline{X}$	Nonrespondents $\overline{X}$	t-Statistic for Difference
Age	28.22	27.60	1.09 (n.s.)	28.08	27.74	0.62 (n.s.)
Length of previous residence in U.S. (collapsed scale)	1.72	1.59	1.07 (n.s.)	1.69	1.63	0.46 (n.s.)
Number of times R has been in U.S. before	2.24	2.18	0.33 (n.s.)	2.26	2.16	0.53 (n.s.)
Education (years)	6.48	6.43	0.23 (n.s.)	6.46	6.46	0.02 (n.s.)
Prestige of main occupation (Duncan SEI scores)	20.30	20.65	-0.31 (n.s.)	20.17	20.84	-0.60 (n.s.)
Prestige of last occupation (Duncan SEI scores)	19.91	20.10	-0.17 (n.s.)	19.78	20.27	-0.43 (n.s.)
Income in last occupation (dollars per month)	312.88	282.54	1.44 (n.s.)	292.68	307.91	-0.72 (n.s.)

Unemployment during past 5 years (months)	0.18	0.23	1.64 (n.s.)	7.48	7.43	0.46 (n.s.)
Number of children	1.61	1.33	2.86**	1.61	1.20	3.10**
Number of relatives and friends in U.S.	3.91	3.99	-0.43 (n.s.)	4.05	3.82	1.11 (n.s.)
Father's education (years)	3.59	3.61	-0.08 (n.s.)	3.51	3.72	-0.72 (n.s.)
Mother's education (years)	3.36	3.79	-1.90 (n.s.)	3.43	3.74	-1.36 (n.s.)
Prestige of father's occupation (Duncan SEI scores)	19.40	17.67	1.44 (n.s.)	18.48	18.74	-0.21 (n.s.)
Income aspirations (collapsed scale)	5.07	4.84	1.30 (n.s.)	4.98	4.97	0.07 (n.s.)
Expected income in first U.S. occupation (dollars per month)	481.66	460.23	1.35 (n.s.)	469.45	474.58	-0.32 (n.s.)
Modernity (index)	0.07	0.05	0.31 (n.s.)	0.08	0.04	0.54 (n.s.)
Knowledge of English (index)	0.06	-0.07	1.95 (n.s.)	0.08	-0.09	2.51*

n.s.=difference not significant. $*p=.05$ $**p=.01$.

for both samples. Among Cuban respondents, those with more relatives and friends in the country at the time of arrival proved more likely to appear in subsequent surveys. These results are congruent with the experiences of field research and suggest that tracing efforts were more successful among the less isolated and more family-attached immigrants.

With this exception, the overall pattern of results does not reveal a consistent bias in any follow-up sample. Mean differences in important variables such as education, occupation, unemployment, parental education, and prior residence in the United States are all insignificant. In three out of four comparisons, differences in age, knowledge of English, father's occupation, last income, and income aspirations are also insignificant. Other significant differences follow a random rather than cumulative pattern.

A second approach to sample mortality consists of examining the effect on nonresponse in subsequent surveys of a series of first-wave predictors. Following Astin and Panos, we regressed a "missing" dummy variable on a number of first-wave variables for each sample and each follow-up.[40] Representative results are presented in Table 16.

As seen in the table, all zero-order correlations and beta weights are small, and only those associated with income aspirations in the Cuban third survey are statistically significant. The presence of one significant coefficient among 36 is explainable on the basis of chance alone. "Variance" accounted for in the attrition variable does not exceed 6 percent in any single regression.

These results do not support the hypothesis of large or consistent mortality biases in the follow-up samples. It is still possible that nonrespondents differ in ways not reflected in analyses based on the first survey. While this alternative cannot be tested with the available data, the evidence at hand points strongly in the direction of relatively minor and unsystematic effects due to attrition. We interpret the ensuing results accordingly.

SAMPLE-TO-POPULATION COMPARISONS

The analysis of sample mortality effects above is complemented in this section by a comparison of results from our follow-up surveys with those of a representative study of the Mexican- and Cuban-born populations in the United States. The data for this comparison come from the Survey of Income and Education (SIE), a large study of U.S. households conducted by the Bureau of the Census in 1975. The sampling design used in the SIE generated a sufficient number of Hispanic households and, in particular,

40. A. Astin and R. J. Panos, "The Educational and Vocational Development of College Students."

Table 16. Regressions of Second and Third Waves
Attrition Variables on Wave 1 Predictors

Predictors--Wave 1	Endogenous Variable: "Missing"							
	Cubans				Mexicans			
	Wave 2		Wave 3		Wave 2		Wave 3	
	r	β	r	β	r	β	r	β
Father's occupation	.078[a]	.086	.096	.131	-.051	-.040	.008	.021
Father's education	.000	.056	.068	.067	.009	.016	-.020	.055
Mother's education	.024	.022	.040	-.025	.012	-.009	-.079	-.109
Education	.024	.016	-.017	.018	.056	.071	.051	-.030
Main occupation	.008	.000	-.034	-.023	-.017	.008	.027	.040
Age	.097	-.086	-.018	-.039	-.039	-.036	-.022	-.035
Size-place of community of origin	.055	.050	.083	.036	-.023	.013	-.018	-.014
Income aspirations	.028	.009	-.170*	-.217*	-.059	-.041	-.003	.017
Knowledge of English	.011	-.053	-.012	-.016	-.060	-.054	-.080	-.089
R		.140		.240		.115		.147
R^2		.020		.057		.013		.022

[a]Figures are zero-order correlations and standardized partial regression
coefficients (beta weights).

*$p=.01$.

Cuban and Mexican ones to allow detailed analyses of occupational characteristics. In this section, we compare the occupational and industrial distribution of Cuban and Mexican immigrants obtained by the last follow-up
survey with those for the parent populations, as reported by SIE.

Table 17 presents the industrial sector distributions of each group.
Given the different timing of the two studies and the different populations
sampled, one would expect only a distant similarity between both sets of
results. Yet the striking feature of this table is how well represented the
samples of 1973 immigrants are in the major sectors occupied by their respective foreign-born populations. For example, according to the SIE, the
largest single concentration of foreign-born Mexicans is in firms that manu-
facture durable goods (19.8 percent). Six years after legal entry, the 1973
arrivals also concentrated in this sector (23.8 percent). Similar comparisons

Table 17. Industrial Sector of Foreign-Born
Male Workers, Mexicans and Cubans

Industry	Survey of Income and Education, 1975		Longitudinal Samples, 1979	
	Mexican, %	Cuban, %	Mexican, %	Cuban, %
Agriculture	18.4	0.7	6.2	1.8
Mining	0.4	1.1	1.9	0.5
Construction	9.5	7.6	10.9	11.3
Manufacturing--durable goods	19.8	11.9	23.8	14.8
Manufacturing--nondurable goods	12.9	13.2	16.9	16.9
Transportation, communication and public utilities	4.9	5.4	4.8	5.4
Wholesale trade	1.9	5.3	3.8	5.4
Retail trade	15.0	20.1	11.6	14.8
Finance, insurance, and real estate	1.5	6.1	0.7	2.8
Business and repair services	4.3	8.9	10.7	11.3
Personal services	2.8	2.1	2.8	3.8
Entertainment and recreation services	1.3	4.1	0.5	0.5
Professional and related services	5.0	10.2	2.6	9.7
Public administration	2.4	3.2	2.8	1.0
Total			100.0	100.0
N	649	176	421[a]	391[b]

Source: Adapted from Patricia Guhleman, Marta Tienda, and Marion Bowman, "An Employment and Earnings Profile of Hispanic Origins Workers in the U.S.," In Marta Tienda (ed.), Hispanic Origin Workers in the U.S. Labor Market: Comparative Analyses of Employment and Earnings, Final Report to the U.S. Department of Labor, 1981, pp. 1-91. Table 1A-4.

[a]Excludes 29 persons unemployed in 1979 and 5 missing observations.

[b]Excludes 21 persons unemployed in 1979 and 15 missing observations.

Table 18. Occupation of Foreign-Born Male Workers,
Mexicans and Cubans

Occupation	Survey of Income and Education, 1975		Longitudinal Samples, 1979	
	Mexican, %	Cuban, %	Mexican, %	Cuban, %
Professional and technical	3.3	13.0	1.7	10.0
Managers and administrators	4.6	13.0	1.7	9.2
Sales	1.6	8.4	0.5	3.6
Clerical	1.9	6.0	2.8	6.1
Craft	15.5	25.1	26.2	30.7
Operators, nontransport	21.5	13.3	30.7	18.2
Operators, transport	6.6	6.3	3.5	5.4
Laborers, nonfarm	15.5	7.7	17.3	8.7
Farm laborers	12.8	0.7	5.7	0.5
Farmers and farm managers	1.6	0.0	0.0	0.2
Service workers	15.0	6.6	9.9	7.4
Total	*100.0*	*100.0*	*100.0*	*100.0*
N	*649*	*176*	*423*[a]	*391*[b]

Source: Adapted from Patricia Guhleman, Marta Tienda, and Marion Bowman, "An Employment and Earnings Profile of Hispanic Origin Workers in the U.S.," in Marta Tienda (ed.), *Hispanic Origin Workers in the U.S. Labor Market: Comparative Analyses of Employment and Earnings,* Final Report to the U.S. Department of Labor, 1981, pp. 1-91, Table 1A-3.

[a]Excludes 29 persons unemployed in 1979 and 3 missing observations.

[b]Excludes 21 persons unemployed in 1979 and 15 missing observations.

include substantial clusters in construction, nondurable manufacturing, and retail trade. The largest difference is in agriculture, where the 1973 immigrants were much less likely to have found a job than the total Mexican-born population. This result is congruent with the known drift of recent Mexican immigrants away from agriculture and into urban jobs.

The 1973 wave of Cuban refugees also moved into the same industrial sectors occupied by the rest of the exile community. Primary differences include a larger proportion of the immigrant cohort finding jobs in the construction industry and in manufacturing. A somewhat smaller proportion than in the parent population was employed in retail trade and financial institutions.

Table 18 completes this profile with the occupational distributions of both groups. Following their industrial concentration, the sample of 1973 Mexican immigrants had more craftworkers and operatives than found in the general Mexican-born population. The largest difference, however, is again in agriculture: nearly 13 percent of the Mexican population worked in these jobs, compared to only 6 percent among the recent immigrants. Despite these differences, an inspection of results in Table 17 shows a consistent similarity between the two distributions. Both the longitudinal survey and the SIE figures indicate that Mexican-born workers are underrepresented in the categories of professionals and technicians, managers and administrators, sales and clerical workers. In both cases, the largest concentrations are in the operative and craftwork categories, followed by laborers and service workers.

A similar trend is apparent in the Cuban distributions, except that, in this case, the convergence between immigrant sample and population occupations is more striking. Reflecting their more recent entry and their occupational backgrounds, 1973 refugees are somewhat less represented among professionals and technicians, managers, and sales personnel. Very similar proportions are found, however, in the categories of clerical work, operatives (transport and nontransport), laborers, and service workers.

Added to the apparent absence of mortality biases over time, the present results offer additional evidence of the generalizability of findings derived from these longitudinal surveys. The similar occupational distributions obtained from the final immigrant surveys and from a nationwide study of the respective populations add to our confidence that results stemming from these samples are not unique, but can be generalized to Cuban and Mexican immigrant cohorts arriving in recent years.

INDICES

This final section introduces two multivariate indices developed in the course of the study. They will be used in subsequent chapters, but are presented here because of their general significance and possible utility in future research. A third index, designed to measure immigrants' attitudes toward American society, will be presented in Chapter 8. These measures were developed through questionnaires applied to both immigrant samples on at least two occasions. They tap dimensions not generally measured in general population surveys, but important for the study of new immigrant groups. Standardized measures of these variables, applicable to recent immigrants, have not been available so far.

Knowledge of English

The Knowledge of English Index (KEI) is the unit-weighted sum of correct responses to a series of items asking respondents to translate into Spanish a series of simple sentences and words read to them in English. For the initial survey in 1973, items were six sentences at an elementary level of reading comprehension and two words at a seventh- to ninth-grade level. In each follow-up, items were introduced at higher proficiency levels. However, variance in the latter items was close to zero, since very few respondents could translate them. The final indices, constructed in 1976 and again in 1979, thus reproduce the original one. Only one additional item was added. Table 19 presents item components of KEI, first-factor loadings, item-to-total correlations, and indicators of reliability and validity for each sample.

Factor analysis reveals a clear unidimensional structure, with the first factor accounting for almost all common variance. Internal consistency reliability is very high, whether measured by the alpha or omega reliability coefficients.[41] Correlations of KEI with theoretically related variables, such as education and occupational status which serve as indicators of construct validity, are consistently significant and in the predicted direction.

Results presented in Table 19 are based on 1979 data; similar patterns were obtained in the two earlier surveys. Alpha coefficients, which estimate a theoretical lower-bound of reliability, were .951 (Mexicans) and .967 (Cubans) in the original survey and again exceeded .95 in the 1976 follow-up. Factor analyses in 1973–1974 and again in 1976 produced exactly the same unidimensional structure.

Originally, we estimated that more difficult items would be required in subsequent surveys so as to gauge increasing English proficiency in both samples. Results proved us wrong. On the basis of the above findings, the original KEI scale, composed of relatively simple items, can be offered as a suitable measure of knowledge of English among recent immigrants from Latin America.

Information about U.S. Society

The U.S. Information Index (USIN) is designed to measure the individual's knowledge of American social and political institutions, as well as practical economic matters. Immigrants' information about the host society is an important dimension, since it may affect occupational and economic mobility and different outcomes of the adaptation process. The index was developed during the 1976 follow-up and reapplied in 1979.

USIN is the unit-weighted sum of correct answers to nine factual

---

41. David R. Heise and George W. Bohrnstedt, "Validity, Invalidity, and Reliability."

Table 19. The Knowledge-of-English Index

Item	Mexicans		Cubans	
	Loading[a]	r_{it}[b]	Loading[a]	r_{it}[b]
1. "He raises his hands."	.804	.754	.761	.722
2. "It is very cold."	.630	.580	.788	.742
3. "The door is not open."	.583	.537	.700	.661
4. "She is playing with her doll."	.807	.756	.802	.772
5. "She writes with chalk."	.787	.742	.808	.778
6. "There is a horse near the church."	.825	.775	.821	.790
7. "Guilt."	.772	.719	.609	.711
8. "Surplus."	.377	.342	.549	.518
9. "Glance."	.281	.258	.594	.494

First Factor:	Eigenvalue	4.152	4.844
	% of variance explained	86.8	92.2
	α[c]	.875	.908
	Ω UWML[d]	.906	.935

Validity coefficients[e]	(1) $r_{KEI.EDUC}$	.489	.636
	(2) $r_{KEI.OCC}$	.304	.531
	(3) $r_{KEI.EARN}$	.142	.243
	(4) $r_{KEI.NEWS}$	.464	.467

[a]Unrotated first factor loadings.
     Principal factors extraction with iteration.

[b]Item-to-total correlations corrected for autocorrelation.

[c]Cronbach's alpha.

[d]Heise and Bohrnstedt's unit-weighted maximum likelihood omega.

[e]Indicators of construct validity:
     Correlations of knowledge of English with
     (1) Education (years);
     (2) Present occupation (Duncan SEI scores);
     (3) Monthly earnings (natural logarithm);
     (4) Language of newspapers read (Spanish/English).

Table 20. The U.S. Information Index

Item	Mexicans Loading[a]	Mexicans r_{it}[b]	Cubans Loading[a]	Cubans r_{it}[b]
1. Name of U.S. vice president.	.511	.342	.615	.468
2. Name of state governor.	.402	.274	.530	.434
3. Definition of *Social Security*.	.472	.363	.204	.190
4. Definition of *inflation*.	.413	.330	.206	.181
5. Relationship between home mortgage interest and income tax.	.433	.330	.412	.352
6. Definition of AFL-CIO.	.314	.228	.390	.335
7. Interest rate charged by common credit cards (Master Charge, Visa).	.441	.354	.662	.481
8. Credit card interest rates higher/lower than those charged by banks.	.454	.328	.750	.546
9. Credit card interest rates higher/lower than those charged by finance companies.	.271	.210	.378	.320

First Factor:		Mexicans	Cubans
	Eigenvalue	1.576	2.207
	% of variance explained	64.1	67.2
	α_c	.619	.698
	Ω UWML[d]	.673	.773

Validity coefficients[e]		Mexicans	Cubans
	(1) $r_{USIN.EDUC}$	.362	.447
	(2) $r_{USIN.OCC}$	.283	.338
	(3) $r_{USIN.EARN}$	.462	.444
	(4) $r_{USIN.NEWSFREQ}$	.263	.337

[a]Unrotated first factor loadings.
   Principal factors extraction with iteration.

[b]Item-to-total correlations corrected for autocorrelation.

[c]Cronbach's alpha.

[d]Heise and Bohnrstedt's omega.

[e]Indicators of construct validity:
   Correlations of information about U.S. society with
   (1) Education (years);
   (2) Present occupation (Duncan SEI scores);
   (3) Knowledge of English (KEI);
   (4) Frequency of newspaper reading.

questions. Table 20 presents the item components, factor loadings, and indicators of reliability and validity based on 1979 data. Actual wording of questions in Spanish and literal translations are presented in appendix Table A.

As seen in the table, factor analysis yields an unidimensional structure, with the first factor accounting for more than 60 percent of common variance in both samples. No secondary eigenvalue exceeds 1.00. Estimates of internal consistency reliability are lower than for KEI, but remain acceptable. In the 1976 survey, coefficients were .60 (Mexicans) and .71 (Cubans); in 1979, they increased to .67 and .77, respectively. To assess construct validity, we correlated USIN with a series of related variables, including level of education, present occupation, knowledge of English (KEI), and frequency of newspaper reading. Coefficients are consistently significant and in the expected direction for both samples.

Items forming the USIN scale converged at two different points in time and for two independent samples into the same dimension. This offers strong evidence of the scale's potential usefulness. As will be seen in future chapters, information about American society is a consistently significant predictor of different aspects of economic and social adaptation. Several of these effects are counterintuitive, running in a direction unanticipated by most existing theories.

4

PRELUDE TO IMMIGRATION:
THE SOCIAL ORIGINS OF
CUBAN AND MEXICAN IMMIGRANTS

This chapter initiates the analysis of our two immigrant samples by focusing upon two of the four principal subfields identified in Chapter 1: the social origins of immigrants and the stability and direction of migrant flows over time. Our primary purpose here is to describe the immigrants' backgrounds, identifying in particular those personal attributes likely to be most important to their subsequent incorporation in the United States. To accomplish this goal, we must take the reader through a fairly lengthy excursion among findings produced by the first survey. The material presented consists of a tabular overview of results, with more complex causal analyses left for subsequent chapters. The task is not merely descriptive, however, for we attempt to locate the sampled migrants within the stratification system of their country of origin and in the context of relationships and activities that accompanied the process of migration at its source.

In previous chapters we have identified three sets of stratifying relationships that organize or structure migrant flows. These account for the social composition of the individuals that compose each movement. The first set includes the obvious and direct economic linkages between origin and destination, foreign firms and capital employed in the sending country, trade relations, and cultural and consumption expectations. These linkages, however, form only part of the less apparent but more important overall organization of the origin population around a development strategy integrated with similar activities in the receiving country. The structure of national development in the country of origin shapes the unequal distribution of resources and opportunities across sectors and social groups, and gives rise to both migratory labor and refugee flows.

A second set consists of diverse political relationships, in the sense both of formal connections between governments of sending and receiving countries and of informal ties or shared interests among social groups that arise from their access to sources of economic power. Obviously, tied to the particular pattern of national development, the influence of these political relationships on the social composition of migrants is expressed most clearly through migration policies. On the side of the country of origin, this influence may be direct, as when certain groups are allowed to leave while others are not. The influence may also be indirect, as in situations where policies of income distribution or land reform make it essential for workers to seek alternatives to local employment. The policies of the receiving country also determine in large part not only who leaves, but more importantly, who is allowed to enter. For example, the emphasis in U.S. immigration policy on family reunification provides a clear criterion for selecting among potential emigrants.

The third set consists of the numerous social ties that bind the migrant to family, kin, and friends abroad. As noted in Chapter 1, these social networks account for both the directionality and stability of the migration. They help explain, for instance, the geographical origins of the emigrants as well as their expectations regarding the location of their future residence. These networks also provide the resources that allow certain individuals to emigrate while others are unable to do so. And, finally, it is access to these resources that facilitates and reinforces the circulation of migrant workers across international borders.

These three sets of relationships form the context for the following discussion of the social backgrounds of the sampled Mexicans and Cubans. The discussion documents for each group the social and economic histories of each respondent and his family. The characteristics discussed include those that locate the individual in the origins of the migrant flow and that may contribute to the explanation of his subsequent experiences in the United States.

MEXICAN DEVELOPMENT AND THE ORIGINS OF EMIGRATION

Conventional models of Mexican emigration typically divided the country into a modern-urban and a traditional-rural Mexico, and assigned the origins of the outflow to the latter. Under this analysis, individual emigrants are economic outcasts, peasants surpassed by progress in the cities, left with migration alone as a means of self-advancement. The implication is that as modernity overcomes tradition and progress conquers backwardness, the sources of the migration will be progressively eliminated.[1]

Alternatively, the argument may be advanced that the sources of Mexican emigration are to be found neither in the backward, rural economy nor among the traditional attributes of the individual migrants. Rather, Mexican migration is propelled by the successful and rapid development of Mexico. Individual migrants are not members of a homogeneous, illiterate peasantry being pushed off the land, but rather originate in sectors of the economy and society that are fully exposed to and incorporated in the nation's progress. Their origins are diverse, indicative of the larger social divisions within the Mexican population as a whole. Indeed, the sources of Mexican emigration lie in the mainstream of their origin society.

Mexico's strategy of national development, which defines the contours of mainstream society, creates and reproduces four fundamental contradictions that influence emigration. The first is rooted in the success of the Mexican Revolution, which was fought largely over the "agrarian question," and the strategy of agricultural development pursued afterwards. Both factors mobilized the rural population and brought a previously isolated peasantry into contact with modern society.[2] Because this rural transformation cut the traditional ties to the land without creating alternative opportunities for local employment, it contributed to the persistence of strikingly high levels of disguised unemployment and underemployment. By 1970, for instance, about half of the nation's total labor force consisted of persons who were either minimally remunerated or infrequently employed.[3]

Second, the surpluses accumulated through rapid agricultural expansion fueled an import-substitution industrialization program that successfully produced and sustained a high rate of aggregate economic growth. From the late 1940s to the 1970s the Mexican GNP rose approximately 6 percent annually. Yet during this time the distribution of income became more unequal. By 1973 the richest 5 percent of the population shared 29 percent of the national income, while the poorest 20 percent split a meager 4 percent of the income. That same year, even though Mexico had a per capita GNP of (U.S.) $774, a full 18 percent of the population still had annual incomes of less than $75.[4]

The third contradiction is perhaps the most important for understanding the precise determinants of individual outmigration. Simply stated, it is

1. Alejandro Portes, "Illegal Immigration and the International System."

2. See John Womack, Jr., *Zapata and the Mexican Revolution*; also Lourdes Arizpe, *Migración, Etnicismo y Cambio Económico*.

3. Victor L. Urquidi, "Empleo y Explosión Demográfica"; Francisco Alba, "Mexico's International Migration as a Manifestation of Its Development Pattern."

4. Portes, "Illegal Immigration," p. 433.

the profound clash between the absorption of an increasingly modern culture, with its strong attachment to the cult of advanced consumption, and material conditions that deny most Mexicans the means of participating even minimally within it. Mass media advertising has penetrated most sectors of the Mexican population with the attractions and promises of modern consumerism. But despite this desire to consume, underemployment and vastly unequal incomes deny access to these goods.[5]

Fourth, Mexico faces the paradox of a formally nationalistic government policy and an international reality of increased dependence upon foreign economic sources, especially those based in the United States. The United States, for example, entirely dominates Mexico's foreign trade; in the mid-1970s it accounted for 62 percent of imports and 56 percent of exports. Moreover, foreign corporations own half of the four hundred largest industries in Mexico and are acquiring interests in more at an ever increasing rate. Taken as a whole, the foreign sector accounts for more than 25 percent of Mexican national production.

This extensive external dependence has two major effects on labor emigration. First, the foreign-sector participation in Mexican industrialization has been largely capital intensive. This situation has resulted in an impressive level of manufacturing output, but relatively few new jobs have been created. Manufacturing absorbs roughly one-fifth of the economically active population, but has increased its share only 5 percent since the revolution.[6] In its place, the urban service sector has become the leading employer, expanding its share of the workforce between 1950 and the early 1970s from 28.3 percent to 38.3 percent.[7] Urban service jobs, however, are very heterogeneous and typically do not approach the stability *of regular employment opportunities* or wages found among the other high-growth sectors. Consequently, employment in this sector restricts the widening of the local consumer market that is needed to match the expanded production of domestic-consumption items.

Second, the presence and influence of the United States have accelerated the modernization of Mexican culture. For the individual, the North has come to symbolize the land where problems in Mexico may be solved. In the eyes of the Mexican worker, the United States is the place in which the benefits of an advanced economy, promised but not delivered by the Mexican development plan, can be turned into reality. It is only natural that so many should go North in search of the means to acquire that which transnational firms and mass media have advertised insistently for years,

5. Alba, "Mexico's International Migration"; Susan Eckstein, *The Poverty of Revolution*.
6. Charles Cumberland, *Mexico*.
7. Wouter Van Ginneken, *Socio-economic Groups and Income Distribution in Mexico*, p. 68.

and that which a high-growth, fully monetized economy has required from its modern labor force.

The lives of the immigrants in our sample, most of whom were born between the mid-1930s and early 1950s, have been dramatically shaped by these contradictory dimensions of Mexican social and economic progress. Most of the men in our sample lived as adults in Mexico between 1960 and 1970, when the economy was growing at an even faster rate than its postwar average. They also witnessed and were absorbed in the processes that have produced the familiar characteristics of modern Mexico: rapid urbanization, rural outmigration, spreading unemployment and underemployment, and widening income inequality. Their position within each major dimension of the Mexican social structure is described below.

Residential Histories

The family histories of our sampled men reflect the spatial shifts of the total Mexican population as industrialization and rural transformation moved many to larger urban areas. Between 1940 and 1970, the proportion of all Mexicans living in places of 2,500 inhabitants or more increased from 28 percent to 53 percent.[8] Mexico City, the nation's capital, attracted most of the internal migrants and alone accounted for 22 percent of the national population. But it was the northern states, especially border towns such as Tijuana, Ciudad Juarez, and Nuevo Laredo, that experienced the highest growth rates.[9]

When the men of our sample were born, most of their families, like most Mexicans, still resided in either rural areas or small market towns. More than half (53.2 percent) lived in places that had fewer than 10,000 inhabitants, while only one-fifth (19.2 percent) resided in the larger cities of more than 100,000 persons. Yet even by this early date, their families had already been affected by the processes encouraging urbanization. Between the time of their parents' births, which for most was only a decade or two after the Mexican Revolution, and their own births, nearly one in every five of the men's fathers who had lived in a rural area had come to reside in a much larger town.

This cityward push continued, either by migration or the pressure of rapid growth of the local area's population. In the late fifties and early sixties, when most of the sampled men were sixteen years old, the proportion living in the larger cities (more than 100,000 persons) had nearly doubled.

8. John S. Nagel, "Mexico's Population Policy Turnaround." This change represents a clear shift toward urban concentration even though the 2,500-person definition of an urban place is hardly appropriate for the Mexican population. See Jorge Balan, Harley L. Browning, and Elizabeth Jelin, *Men in a Developing Society.*

9. Luis Unikel, "El Proceso de Urbanización en México."

And as their sons entered the United States in 1973–1974, only a third (34.3 percent) of the sampled immigrants' fathers remained in the countryside. Fully half lived in large cities.

The immigrants' family histories also correspond to the increasing demographic importance of the northern states and, especially, of the border. The families' rural origins were primarily, though not exclusively, in these states: nearly three-quarters (73.9 percent) of the sampled men were born in this area. Chihuahua, with its burgeoning urban center, Ciudad Juarez, was the state of birth for 30 percent of the sampled men. Another 26 percent were born along the border in Nuevo Leon (11.9 percent), Tamaulipas (7.1 percent), and Coahuila (6.9 percent). Still in the North but removed from the border, Durango accounted for 11 percent, San Luis Potosi almost 5 percent, and together, Aguascalientes and Sinaloa 1 percent. The remainder were born in the central states, the traditional regional sources of Mexican emigrants,[10] while only a few persons in the sample had come from the South.

These states of birth were merely temporary stops in a series of steps destined to take the migrants' families to the cities of the North. Table 21 summarizes this lifetime geographical distribution, showing the states of residence at three major periods of the families' histories, the fathers' birth, the migrants' sixteenth birthday, and at the time of legal immigration, 1973–1974. Column 1 shows that the immigrants' fathers were born much farther from the border than were their sons; in fact, places of birth were equally distributed among the central, northern nonborder, and border states. Yet, by the sons' sixteenth birthday, more than 65 percent of the families lived along the border. This figure compares to the roughly 56 percent of the sons who were born in these states. Finally, column 3 shows that by the time of their sons' emigration to the United States, 90 percent of the families had moved either to the border states in Mexico or beyond to the southwestern states of the United States.

Of course, strong social, economic, and political forces encouraged these overall population shifts. Stimulated by the nation's import-substitution strategies, the northern states benefitted from the intensive efforts at irrigation farming in the Northwest and the growth of industry-related activities in the cities. Regional inequality increased throughout the post-1940 period and vast differences developed in wage rates and in the concentration of wealth between northern and southern Mexico.[11]

10. Manuel Gamio, *Mexican Immigration to the United States*; cited in Reynaldo A. Cue, *Men from an Underdeveloped Society*, p. 74.

11. For example, in 1974 the official minimum-wage scale varied between the southern level of 34.75 pesos in Oaxaca to the northern level of 99.75 pesos in Baja California.

Table 21. States of Residence in the Family Histories
of Mexican Immigrants

State	Father's Birth		Son's Sixteenth Birthday		Son's Last Before Entry	
	N	%	N	%	N	%
Border	*324*	*42.6*	*533*	*65.6*	*411*	*50.1*
Chihuahua	158	20.8	315	38.9	251	30.6
Nuevo Leon	85	11.2	98	12.1	64	7.8
Tamaulipas	22	2.9	91	11.2	92	11.2
Coahuila	57	7.4	28	3.5	4	0.5
Sonora	2	0.3	0	0.0	0	0.0
Baja California	0	0.0	1	0.1	0	0.0
Northern Nonborder	*153*	*20.1*	*114*	*14.0*	*19*	*2.3*
San Luis Potosi	45	5.9	34	4.2	8	1.0
Sinaloa	3	0.4	1	0.1	0	0.0
Durango	93	12.2	73	9.0	11	1.3
Aguascalientes	12	1.2	6	0.7	0	0.0
Baja Cal. Sur	0	0.0	0	0.0	0	0.0
Southern[a]	*5*	*0.7*	*3*	*0.4*	*2*	*0.2*
Central	*242*	*31.9*	*163*	*20.0*	*58*	*7.1*
Federal District and Mexico	17	2.2	27	3.3	15	1.9
Zacatecas	59	7.8	33	4.1	10	1.2
Guanajuato	53	7.0	27	3.3	10	1.2
Michoacan	34	4.5	22	2.7	3	0.4
Jalisco	54	7.1	34	4.2	14	1.7
Veracruz	6	0.8	5	0.6	1	0.1
Puebla	5	0.6	5	0.6	1	0.1
Others[b]	14	1.9	10	1.1	4	0.5
United States	*36*[c]	*4.7*	*0*	*0.0*	*330*	*40.3*
Texas	0	0.0	0	0.0	118	14.4
New Mexico	0	0.0	0	0.0	16	1.9
Arizona	0	0.0	0	0.0	14	1.7
California	0	0.0	0	0.0	59	7.2
Colorado	0	0.0	0	0.0	21	2.6
Illinois	0	0.0	0	0.0	74	9.0
Other	0	0.0	0	0.0	28	3.4
Total	*760*[d]	*100.0*	*813*[e]	*100.0*	*820*[f]	*100.0*

[a] The southern states include Oaxaca, Chiapas, Campeche, Yucatan, and Quintana Roo. The frequencies are too small to be of use.

[b] Other central states include Guerrero, Hidalgo, Nayarit, Morelos, Queritaro, and Tlaxcala.

[c] State of father's birth not available when in the United States.

[d] Missing observations = 62.   [e] Missing observations: 9.   [f] Missing observations: 2.

Nonetheless, the most revealing outcomes of this mode of development were the nature and extent of the social inequalities it created.

Social Locations

The social and political foundations of the post-1940 industrialization program were organized by and around a "development alliance," which included foreign and national capital, government bureaucrats, and workers of the most advanced, often state-run, enterprises.[12] Each of these groups benefitted substantially from the industrialization drive and maintained a disproportionate share of Mexico's expanding wealth. The highly skewed distribution of national income, however, obscures the significant diversity among groups formed around particular growth sectors. It also hides the differential participation of each group in what have become multiple streams of internal and international migration. The wealthier groups, for example, consist of owners of large-scale agricultural and industrial capital, some smaller scale employers in the commercial and service sectors, and even a segment of the working class employed in strategic industries. By all accounts, few of these groups contribute their members to the migratory flows destined for the United States.

The heterogeneity of the social origins of the outmigration is most evident in the countryside, where historically most emigrants to the United States began their migratory careers. But rather than the conventional portrait of undifferentiated peasants emerging from rural stagnation, the primary social relations out of which these flows developed were formed by the accelerated growth of agriculture following the 1940s. Adoption of capital-intensive, Green Revolution technologies raised productivity and profits, but at the same time sharply increased the concentration of land and wealth.[13] Formerly labor-intensive sectors such as cotton and wheat lost their capacity to absorb additional workers, with the result that the agricultural sector became a contributor to the rise in unemployment and underemployment.[14] The persons most affected were the agricultural day laborers. Although they represented one-fifth of the economically active population by 1970, they were among the lowest paid workers in Mexico and were almost completely unprotected by federal social legislation or national organizations.

12. Van Ginneken, *Socio-economic Groups*, p. 140.
13. For example, the proportion of the rural population who owned their own land dropped from 42 percent in 1940 to 33 percent in 1970.
14. For instance, throughout the 1950s the average number of days in a year in which an agricultural wage earner could find work fell from 190 to 100. See Van Ginneken, *Socio-economic Groups*, and Lourdes Arizpe, "The Rural Exodus in Mexico and Mexican Migration to the United States."

A key determinant of emigration from this agricultural sector became an individual's relationship to the land. Private landholders, for instance, were themselves unlikely to migrate, but they often employed others who did. On the larger private farms, those above five hectares, circulating day laborers, small-scale farmers, and *ejidatarios* working part-time away from their own land provided roughly two-thirds of the necessary farm labor.[15] The remainder consisted of full-time, nonremunerated family laborers.[16] Other small private farmers also employed rather than joined the migrants, especially if they had more productive land to cultivate or livestock to raise, which helped them diversify their income and subsistence base. Consequently, it has been the agricultural wage worker and part-time farmer who migrated both within Mexico and to the United States.

The characteristics and motivations of these two groups, however, are actually quite different. The agricultural day laborer is typically younger than the average age of the national labor force. For some, the move north exemplifies the traditional portrait of the subsistence farmer driven off the land. Many more, however, migrate to the United States as an extension of entrenched circulation patterns, in which full dependence on a wage income requires constant movement between residence in the Mexican countryside and locations in which jobs are available. In contrast, the *ejidatarios* and small farmers often move not to abandon their attachments to the land, but actually to maintain them. On the average, they are older than the day laborers and, of course, have access to land ownership, however small. Rather than be fully dependent on wages, these two groups maintain a considerable mix of subsistence, wage, and rental income.

Outside the agricultural sector, the wealthier merchants have little pressure to migrate. This is not the case, however, for smaller, self-employed merchants such as carpenters and barbers. They share a precarious dependence on the uncertain fluctuations in the larger markets and, when faced with periodic drops in demand, temporarily migrate north.

Within the nonagricultural segment of the working class, those who have benefitted as shareholders in the "development alliance" have been least likely to emigrate. This segment includes the regular wage earners and salaried employees of strategic industrial sectors and the government. By 1970, 30 percent of Mexico's economically active population consisted of regular wage earners, the majority of whom worked in manufacturing, mining, construction, transport, and the electrical and petroleum industries. Average incomes were the highest for those employed in large-scale manufacturing, where annual wages were often between 14,000 and 18,000

15. Van Ginneken, *Socio-economic Groups*, p. 56.
16. Ibid., p. 57.

pesos, almost three times that of the day laborer. Moreover, salaried employees, of whom one-third were government employees or those working
in the largest enterprises, banks, and insurance companies, had incomes
nearly two to three times higher than those in the above industrial sectors.

Those most susceptible to emigration from Mexico's cities have originated in the service sectors. Such persons were often employed, but more
often than not they were vastly underemployed. They move to the United
States, as do their rural counterparts, both to supplement their own income and to maintain their homes in Mexico. The average minimum
yearly income for many of these jobs, when the minimum is paid, is
around 10,000 pesos per year, which is calculated to cover seven days of
work each week. In many areas, particularly in the informal sectors,
wages are even lower, often as low as the 6,000 pesos per year earned by
the agricultural day laborers.

The social backgrounds of our sampled men tell only part of this national story, since they are among those already selected to emigrate. Still,
their family histories share many of the characteristics of the Mexican population throughout this period of industrialization.

Education

Table 22 presents the educational backgrounds of the sampled men and
their fathers. The *fathers'* years of formal schooling is clearly a reflection of
their rural origins. Since most were eligible for school before the national
drive to expand educational opportunities in the 1950s and 1960s, their
exposure to schools was minimal. A full third had received no formal
schooling and another third (35.7 percent) had attended primary school but
had not completed it. One in five (21.6 percent) had finished primary
school. Still, with an average of three or four years of formal education, the
fathers had obtained more formal schooling than the majority of the Mexican population of comparable age.

The families' lifetime residential shifts to the northern border towns
parallel an expansion of the educational opportunities available to the sons.
Like their fathers, nearly one-third of the sampled men had attended but
not completed primary school. But unlike their parents, this was the least
educated group: virtually no one (2.4 percent) had failed to receive at least
some formal education. Instead, one in four (27 percent) had completed
primary school, and a full 17 percent had attended secondary school; 6 percent completed it. The sons' access to universities, though still minimal,
was four times that of their fathers (up to 4 percent), and another small
group (9 percent) had completed training in postsecondary business or
technical schools. On average, the immigrants' six years of education was
not only substantially above that of their parents, but just as their fathers

Table 22. Educational Background of
Sampled Men and Their Fathers

Highest Grade	Fathers		Sons	
	N	%	N	%
No formal education	178	33.5	19	2.4
Primary incomplete	190	35.7	264	32.3
Primary complete	115	21.6	222	27.1
Secondary incomplete	5	0.9	93	11.4
Secondary complete	13	2.5	47	5.7
Business or vocational incomplete	6	1.1	62	7.6
Business or vocational complete	12	2.3	72	8.8
University incomplete	6	1.1	19	2.3
University complete	5	0.9	11	1.3
Other	2	0.4	9	1.1
Total	*532*[a]	*100.0*	*818*	*100.0*

[a]In this and subsequent tables, some absolute totals do not
equal total sample size owing to missing observations.

had received more education than their comparable nonimmigrant age group, these interviewed men had twice the number of years in school as the national average.

Occupation

Well before these men were old enough to migrate to the United States, their parents' backgrounds had placed them among the groups most likely to become emigrants. In terms of their fathers' principal lifetime occupation, rural family beginnings meant that many of the sampled men had early roots in agriculture: more than one-third (37.4 percent) of the fathers spent most of their working time in this sector. The majority were farm laborers, although 8 percent within this group were small proprietors, and 5 percent managed a medium or large farm. Those primarily employed in the urban sectors came to the cities in the late 1950s and early 1960s, in the midst of the industrialization drive. Once there, most of the fathers were employed in the service sector (32.3 percent), split nearly evenly between commercial and personal services. These jobs included, but were not limited to, bus and taxi drivers, bakers, small retail merchants, cooks, street vendors, gardeners, and domestic servants. The remainder of the fathers were spread among the construction (9.4 percent), manufacturing (8.8 percent), and transportation (5.0 percent) sectors.

Twenty percent of all those employed outside agriculture were skilled or semiskilled workers. The skilled workers included industrial or construction foremen, plumbers, electricians, and machine operatives with formal training. Those classified as semiskilled were construction carpenters, butchers, bakers, and operatives who had some, but not necessarily formal, training. Only 8 percent were unskilled apprentices or helpers in construction or industrial jobs. Yet this concentration in agriculture and urban services left few of the fathers with experience in the comparatively privileged sectors of the working class. Only 4 percent could be considered white-collar workers, which of course includes a wide range of jobs, from bookkeepers and clerical workers to key punch operators. Another 2 percent were managers of small firms. In addition, the low level of formal education enabled less than one percent to become professionals.

Comparison of columns 1 and 2 of Table 23 reveals that intergenerational occupational changes were clearly away from agricultural employment. Compared to 34 percent of their fathers, only one in ten (11.5 percent) of the immigrants worked as agricultural laborers. None of the sons of the small- or even medium- and large-scale farmers had followed their fathers' attachments to the land. Instead, their move to the cities placed them in the service sector, where most were in personal (25.7 percent) or collective (5.8 percent) services, respectively. Manufacturing had also become a more important employer, increasing its share from 9 percent of the fathers to roughly one-fourth (23.4 percent) of the sons. Construction work employed 15 percent, while commerce (7.6 percent) and transportation became relatively insignificant (3.1 percent).

The intergenerational shift to urban service, manufacturing, and construction sectors had its expected impact on the skill levels of the migrants. As column 2 of Table 23 shows, almost half (46.2 percent) spent most of their working lives in Mexico as skilled workers and artisans or as semiskilled urban laborers, and the proportion in white-collar work doubled. Fourteen percent were unskilled urban laborers, which is significantly greater than the concentration of their fathers in these jobs but substantially less than the overall percentage shift out of agriculture. Consequently, there is little doubt that the sons' employment in the cities of the northern border had significantly increased the status and skill levels of

Table 23. Principal Lifetime Occupations of
Sampled Men and Their Fathers

Occupation	Fathers		Sons	
	N	%	N	%
Out of labor market	3	0.4	53	6.6
Agricultural laborer	259	34.4	93	11.5
Minor urban service worker	61	8.1	60	7.4
Unskilled urban laborer	57	7.6	113	14.0
Semiskilled urban worker	74	9.8	181	22.4
Small rural proprietor	24	3.2	0	0.0
Skilled worker	77	10.2	192	23.8
Intermediate service worker	133	17.7	49	6.1
White collar and minor professional	28	3.7	53	6.5
Medium or large agricultural proprietor	16	2.1	0	0.0
Manager of firm	15	2.0	5	0.6
Professional	5	0.7	8	1.0
Other	1	0.1	1	0.1
Total	*753*	*100.0*	*808*	*100.0*

their occupational backgrounds. Of course, given their average levels of education, still very few became professionals.

Although the most dramatic occupational changes were those taking place over the generations, part of the contrast discussed above was because of shifts during the immigrants' own working lives. The timing of these sectoral shifts can be clarified if, instead of the sampled men's last or principal occupation in Mexico, we examine their next-to-last occupation before emigrating. For example, a few of the sons initially followed their fathers' footsteps as agricultural proprietors, but then abandoned that path. The proportion that first worked in agriculture as laborers is also higher (19 percent) than that represented by the men's last or principal job. Fewer were skilled or semiskilled workers earlier in their careers, and not as many were in the urban manufacturing and service sectors.

Table 24.   Average Monthly Income Prior to
Legal Immigration

Monthly Income (in U.S. dollars)	Respondents	
	N	%
0-99	197	29.1
100-199	131	19.3
200-299	59	8.7
300-399	70	10.3
400-499	76	11.2
500-599	54	8.0
600-699	38	5.6
700-799	19	2.8
800 or more	34	5.0
Total	*678*	*100.0*

Wages

The processes that brought the immigrants' families to the cities clearly transformed the educational and employment opportunities available to them. They also exposed the sons to jobs in the higher wage areas of the northern border towns. On average, the immigrants said they earned the equivalent of $300 per month in the year immediately prior to their legal entry to the United States. Although this is a reasonably substantial Mexican income, it hardly places them among the privileged sectors at home. Of course, those in the group who earned large monthly salaries affected this average. As Table 24 reports, the distribution of earned income shows that one in every three (29.1 percent) made less than $100 per month, which is quite low. Another 19 percent earned between $100 and $199 per month. At the other extreme, 3 percent made between $700 and $800 per month, while a full 5 percent made over $800.

It is clear from this family-history profile that the sampled immigrants were greatly affected by the major transformations of the Mexican economy and society. The immigrants tended to come neither from the rural back-washes nor from the extremely poor segments of the urban population. Instead, their family histories had brought them to the North and to major cities, where they enjoyed a relatively superior economic position.

THE STABILITY AND DIRECTIONALITY
OF MEXICAN MIGRATION

At least as early as 1972, there was evidence that Mexican legal immigration to the United States was inextricably connected with the illegal movement of workers across the border.[17] This interrelationship took two forms. First, illegal migrants could use their time in the United States to obtain the economic or social connections that enabled them to meet the certification requirements of United States immigration law. Second, with substantial visa backlogs, those who were otherwise qualified for legal entry could enter the United States illegally and spend the waiting period with their families or at their jobs. In either case, it is clear that illegal entry for many was merely the first step to achieving legal residence.

The social networks established by multiple moves across the border are extensive and pervasive, and literally form international kinship communities that extend across generations.[18] One study, for example, reports that 49 percent of the Mexicans interviewed that had migrated since 1969 had fathers who were former migrant workers in the United States.[19] Indeed, for many families and communities, migration to the United States had become a tradition, one that circumscribes expectations, plans, and opportunities. Reciprocity relations, including remittance income, mobilize the resources and contacts on both sides of the border that are needed for a successful move. Access to these resources also becomes a primary source of differentiation among both the origin population and the migrant subgroup.[20] The special character of Mexican immigration to the United States is precisely a function of the importance of these social networks.

Paths of Legal Entry

In Chapter 3 we compared the occupational backgrounds of our sampled men with those of all legal immigrants into the United States during 1974. These aggregate figures, however, obscured the influence of illegal migration in determining, through established informal social networks, who becomes a legal Mexican immigrant. Since illegal workers are generally believed to originate in and be destined for low-status jobs, their contribution to the legal pool is likely to account for the Mexican group's occupational concentration.[21] The characteristics of our sampled men actually un-

17. Alejandro Portes, "Return of the Wetback."
18. Joshua Reichart and Douglas Massey, "Guestworker Programs."
19. Wayne A. Cornelius, "Mexican Migration to the United States: Causes, Consequences, and U. S. Responses," p. 17.
20. Richard Mines, "'Las Animas, California.'"
21. Cornelius, "Mexican Migration," p. 21.

Table 25. Length of Prior Residence and
Total Length of Time in the United States

Years	Length of Residence		Total Time Abroad	
	N	%	N	%
No previous residence	313	38.5	228	29.9
Less than one year	111	13.6	215	28.2
One to three years	142	17.4	150	19.7
Three to five years	121	14.9	91	11.9
Five to seven years	82	10.1	47	6.1
Seven to nine years	25	3.1	17	2.2
Nine to eleven years	6	0.7	6	0.8
Eleven to fifteen years	5	0.6	6	0.8
Fifteen years or more	9	1.1	3	0.4
Total	*814*	*100.0*	*763*	*100.0*

cover the extent to which illegal immigrants influence the legal profile, and identify the specific manner in which family and kinship networks differentiate the Mexican flow.

The character of this influence can be documented by examining the 70 percent of the sample whom we identified in Chapter 3 as having previously resided in the United States. When asked for the total length of time they had lived north of the border, well over half said one year or more. Although a full 6 percent reported significant periods of residence (six to twenty-four years), the large majority had lived in the United States previously for one to three years. Even these striking figures, however, underestimate the direct, prior contact these migrants had had with the United States. Table 25 reports their answers when asked both how long they had lived in the United States and, simply, the total length of time they had spent in the United States. Fewer than 30 percent had never been to the United States. At the other extreme, one in five said they had previously held a multicross card that allowed them to commute across the border virtually at will. Clearly, most of the men in our sample did not face legal entry into the United States as strangers or newcomers. Instead, the vast majority were "return immigrants," coming back to places and people that had long before become established parts of their lives.[22]

22. Mines, "'Las Animas, California.'"

Table 25 actually identifies two groups of legal Mexican immigrants, those entering the United States for the first time (without prior experience north of the border) and those returning. Presumably the 30 percent who waited in Mexico until they could gain legal access to the United States differed from the return immigrant group in that (1) they did not need the experiences abroad to acquire the social ties necessary for meeting United States immigration requirements and (2) they had sufficient resources to sustain themselves at home to await their turn for a legal visa. Both characteristics, of course, may still be related to a binational kinship network, the resources of which would allow them to enter under the family-reunification preference system and provide the remittance income to maintain them in the Mexican economy.

This peculiar intermingling of prior or illegal residence and legal immigration means that the characteristics of our group should be similar to the profile of illegal immigrants to the United States, for they too were once part of that undocumented flow. But the Mexican immigrants will also be different from the majority of the undocumented migrants, because only a fraction of that larger flow is able to adjust its status to that of permanent legal immigrant.[23] In fact, the success of our sampled men in gaining legal access is very different from the success of the illegal migrant. Success for most undocumented workers is unfettered circulation between work in the United States and residence in Mexico, rather than permanent resettlement in the United States.[24] On the other hand, those who are entering without this prior experience, the first-time group, should resemble more closely the typical profile of international migrants.

Age and Education of the Two Subgroups

Although studies of Mexican illegal immigrants are fraught with methodological difficulties, a series of detailed field studies has provided a relatively consistent profile.[25] The characteristic demographic feature of these illegal immigrants is that most are young men, usually between ages 22 and 32. The youngest cohorts have educational backgrounds that are much higher than the national average: the average varies from 4.9 to 6 years.[26] Older illegal migrants have considerably less education, having spent only three years in school.[27]

23. U. S. Immigration and Naturalization Service, *Annual Reports.*
24. David S. North and Marion F. Houstoun, *The Characteristics and Role of Illegal Aliens in the U. S. Labor Market.*
25. Cornelius, "Mexican Migration."
26. Jorge A. Bustamante and Geronimo G. Martinez, "Undocumented Immigration from Mexico."
27. Ibid., p. 282.

A first glance at the age differences between the two groups of migrants in our sample is somewhat surprising. Overall, the men are young at the time of their legal entry: fully half were between ages 25 and 35, and another 32 percent were between 16 and 24 years old. But unlike the general profile of illegal migrants, the former illegal or return immigrants of our sample are on average 29 years old. This is roughly two years older than the average age of the first-time arrivals. The reason for this higher average age is simply that the illegal migrants in this sample are at a later or advanced stage of their migratory careers. Since most have already spent one to three years in the United States, and a substantial proportion even longer, upon initial entry they were in their early twenties. Consequently, their age profile is comparable to that developed by the many field studies of illegal migrants.

The educational background of the return immigrants also corresponds to the general portrayal of the Mexican illegal migrant population. As part of the younger cohorts of illegals, the sampled men's average of six years of formal schooling lies within the range of estimates derived from other surveys. The return immigrants were also less educated than the men arriving for the first time. This latter group had on average one full year of additional schooling—that is, seven years of schooling. Yet, this slight but significant educational advantage of the first-time arrivals merely suggests a more important status difference between their families' origins and those of the longer-term migrants.

Occupation and Path of Entry

The occupational backgrounds reported for the general population of illegal Mexican immigrants depends to a large extent upon where the particular study was conducted. Field research undertaken within the villages of the Mexican Central Plateau has documented that many were farmworkers before they emigrated.[28] A study of illegals conducted in the United States, however, found that only half had worked on farms.[29] As such, most were unskilled laborers.[30] Still, there is some agreement that the occupational backgrounds of undocumented workers actually cover a wide range of jobs, especially as over the last decade more of the migrants have originated from Mexican cities. The same United States-based research that found farm origins among half of those interviewed also reported that roughly one-quarter were skilled craft workers, managers, or professionals, and another quarter were salespersons, clerical workers, or operatives.

28. Cornelius, "Mexican Migration." Also see Joshua Reichart and Douglas S. Massey, "Patterns of U. S. Migration From a Mexican Sending Community."
29. North and Houstoun, *The Characteristics and Role of Illegal Aliens*, p. 103.
30. Ibid., p. 102.

Table 26. Principal Lifetime Occupation for
First-time and Return Immigrants

Occupation	First-time		Return	
	N	%	N	%
Out of labor market	30	13.3	18	3.4
Agricultural laborer	23	10.2	65	12.3
Minor urban service worker	16	7.1	41	7.8
Unskilled urban laborer	20	8.9	86	16.3
Semiskilled urban worker	29	12.9	141	26.8
Skilled urban worker	50	22.2	125	23.8
Intermediate service worker	26	11.6	21	4.0
White collar and minor professional	23	10.2	23	4.4
Manager of firm	2	0.9	3	0.6
Professional	5	2.2	3	0.6
Other	1	0.5	0	0.0
Total	*225*	*100.0*	*526*	*100.0*

As previously noted, a significant proportion of the fathers of our sample's respondents had their primary lifetime occupation in agricultural work, with almost 37 percent listing agriculture as their main sector of employment. The fathers of the illegal migrants, however, were more likely to have worked in agriculture: the difference between the groups is approximately 10 percentage points. Conversely, the fathers of those who were immigrating for the first time held semiskilled and skilled urban jobs much more frequently than their counterparts. Yet there were no differences in the degree of concentration in the urban service or white-collar sectors. The latter would be expected from the minimal exposure of both groups to higher education.

The contrasts among their fathers, however, are virtually the reverse of those found among the sampled men. Table 26 reports the occupations held by both the return and first-time respondents. Unlike their fathers, both groups share nearly the same proportion coming from a primarily agricultural background, although at a much lower frequency. Also unlike their fathers, the former illegal migrants listed skilled work as their principal job in Mexico as often as did the first-time group. Most of these jobs were in the manufacturing sector.

The men arriving for the first time, however, were almost three times as likely as the returnees to have held higher status occupations—that is, intermediate service work, white-collar jobs, and professional positions. On the other hand, the men returning to the United States were twice as likely to have worked as a semiskilled or unskilled urban laborer. Finally, the first-time arrivals reported they were not actively engaged in the labor market at a significantly higher rate than the circulating migrants: 13.3 percent compared with 3.4 percent. The reason was simply that the first-time migrants had spent their earlier years in which they were eligible for employment in school, or had sufficient support to defer their job-related activity.

Admissions Status and Family Networks

As a sample of legal Mexican immigrants, this group reflects the emphasis in United States immigration law upon family reunification. It also establishes that contacts achieved through multiple illegal moves provide the means for meeting the requirements of this preference system. For instance, the return immigrant group was significantly more likely to enter legally through the family-reunion preference categories than were the first-timers. Indeed, well over half (56.1 percent) of the former group successfully adjusted their status to that of a legal immigrant through a claim to a close familial tie to a United States citizen. Ninety percent of these men had wives who were United States citizens. Of course, a substantial proportion (44 percent) of first-time immigrants also used these family-network provisions, but not nearly to the extent indicated above. Only about 70 percent gained admission because their wives were United States citizens.

Although most of the men in both groups were married, the groups made very different use of these family connections. Table 27 shows the wives' participation in the actual move, whether they were accompanying their husbands and, if not, where they were residing at the time. The proportion of the men whose wives were travelling with them was essentially equal for both groups: 23 percent of all the married men entered with their wives. But the wives' locations if they were not with their husbands were quite different. Almost two-thirds (63.2 percent) of the returning immigrant group had wives waiting for them in the United States, compared to 48 percent of the first-time arrivals. This figure may underestimate the proportion of returnees who were rejoining their wives, for when the men were asked who the first person would be to meet them in the United States, more than 67 percent said it would be their wives.

Table 27. Location of Respondents' Wives
at Time of Legal Entry

Location	First-time		Return		Total	
	N	%	N	%	N	%
Not married[a]	84	38.4	51	10.4	135	19.0
Married, wife accompanying	29	21.5	103	23.4	132	23.0
Married, wife in Mexico	41	30.4	59	13.4	100	17.4
Married, wife in U.S.	65	48.1	278	63.2	343	59.6
Total	*135*	*100.0*	*440*	*100.0*	*575*	*100.0*

[a]Except where respondents are not currently married, all percentages are based only on persons who were married at the time of legal entry.

The geographical location of the men's children at the time of their legal entry also provides evidence of the differential transnational organization of their families. Within the return group, more than half (53.8 percent) of those who were married and had children reported that their children already lived in the United States. This porportion compares to only 28 percent of their counterparts among first-time arrivals. Evidently, most of the first-time migrants who had children were venturing into the United States without them, presumably leaving them behind with their wives or families.

Geographical Circuits of Illegal and Legal Migration

The geographical origins of both groups were also quite distinct. Although both groups had substantial roots in Mexico's smallest rural communities, the fathers of the first-time immigrants were more likely to have been born in large towns and cities. Well over two-thirds (69.5 percent) of the fathers of the future illegal migrants lived in areas with fewer than 10,000 inhabitants, compared with only one half (56.7 percent) of the fathers of the first-time group.

An important shift in these differential geographical origins, however, was already evident by the time most of the sampled men were teenagers. As both groups became a part of the transformation of the Mexican economy in the 1950s and 1960s, the differences between the size of their places of residence narrowed. This was primarily a result of the movement of the families of the eventual illegal migrants to the larger towns and cities. Between the ages of 16 and 25, the illegal subgroup moved in large numbers to cities of 1 million persons or more. In fact, one in every three reported such a large city as their last place of permanent residence before reentering the United States as a legal immigrant. This number compares to just 3 percent of the first-time group. The latter had joined the overall national shift toward more populated places of residence, but their targeted locations were primarily intermediate-size cities of one hundred to five hundred thousand people.

The groups' diverse geographical origins were actually more evident in the location of these cities than in their mere size. Table 28 lists the ten most common states of origin for a group of Mexican migrants expelled from the United States. These figures form part of the large-scale study of the migration system commissioned by the Mexican government. [31] Also provided are the comparable proportions of our sample's first-time and return legal immigrants from these states. The striking feature of this comparison is the similar proportion of the expelled undocumented workers and return legal immigrants that originated in these ten states: 80.4 percent of the expelled migrants compared with 74.6 percent of the return, legal migrants. In contrast, only about half of the more conventional migrants, the first-time arrivals, came from these states. On the other hand, the returning legal migrants had origins located in the northern border cities to a much greater extent than did the expelled illegals. Chihuahua accounted for a full 43 percent of the legal migrants, compared to only 11 percent of the Mexican government's sample of "unsuccessful" undocumented workers. Conversely, the states of the Central Plateau, especially Michoacan, Jalisco, and Guanajuato, had produced a much greater share of the undocumented migrants than the return legal group.

Despite the differences between these two groups of undocumented workers, the Mexican sample and ours, their contrast is much less sharp than that among the return and first-time legal immigrants. For instance, while Chihuahua was the state of origin for 40 percent of the former group, at age 16 only about 30 percent (27.6 percent) of the first-time group resided there. And in the common Central Plateau source states for illegal immigrants, the group of return immigrants outnumbered the first-timers almost two to one: Michoacan and Jalisco, 7.6 percent compared to 5.7 percent, respectively; Zacatecas, 5.3 percent to 1.8 percent; and Guanajuato, 3.8 percent to 2.2 percent. The largest difference, however, was the frequency with which the men in our sample reported Nuevo Leon and Ta-

31. Bustamante and Martinez, "Undocumented Immigration," p. 268.

Table 28.   States of Origin for Expelled Mexican Migrants and
First-time and Return Legal Immigrants

States	Expelled, %	Return, %	First-time, %
Michoacan	17.6	3.0	1.8
Jalisco	14.5	4.6	3.9
Chihuahua	11.2	42.9	27.6
Guanajuato	10.8	3.8	2.2
Zacatecas	6.9	5.3	1.8
Durango	4.9	9.3	8.3
San Luis Potosi	3.9	4.7	2.2
Baja California Norte	3.8	0.2	0.0
Sinaloa	3.5	0.2	0.0
Guerrero	3.3	0.6	0.0
Total	*80.4*	*74.6*	*47.8*

Source: Jorge A. Bustamante and Geronimo G. Martinez, "Undocumented Immigration from Mexico: Beyond Borders but Within
Systems," *Journal of International Affairs* 33 (Fall/Winter
1979): 268.

maulipas as their state of origin. Together these states represented only 2 percent of the Mexican study's sample of expelled undocumented workers. Within our sample, 16 percent of the illegal group listed the two states as their place of residence at age 16, compared with fully 40 percent of the first-time, legal group.

Finally, the geographical locations and moves of the two groups had parted even more dramatically by the time the men were preparing for legal entry. Among the men in the return immigrant group that originated in the traditional source states of undocumented migrants, a substantial share had already moved to the United States before they reentered officially. For example, the proportion from Jalisco and Michoacan dropped from 7 to 1 percent, and Chihuahua lost about half of its share. Many of the large cities listed by these men as their last place of residence were actually their former homes in the United States. These prior journeys had taken them to six principal states: Texas (20.4 percent), Illinois (13.5 percent), California (10.5 percent), Colorado (3.9 percent), New Mexico (3.0 percent), and Arizona (2.4 percent). Another 4 percent had lived in other states north of the border. Yet, over this same period of time and family history, those men who would later enter the United States for the first time moved in large proportions to the border states. Reflecting the distribution trends of Mexico's internal population, the proportion of first-timers residing in Chihuahua, for example, rose from 28 percent to 37 percent. And the concentration in Nuevo Leon and Tamaulipas increased from 41 to 48 percent.

Plans and Aspirations

Intended Residence

Contrary to the conventional arguments that predict Mexican migrants will join the agricultural labor force in the rural areas of the southwestern United States, most of these sampled men, whether they had been prior illegal migrants or not, intended to resettle in the largest communities. Only 15 percent of all the men planned to live in a town with fewer than 10,000 inhabitants, and just 20 percent planned to live in cities of up to 50,000 residents. On the other hand, fully 73 percent said they were moving to cities with more than 100,000 persons. In fact, the largest number planned to live in the largest cities, those with more than 1 million residents.

Table 29 also shows that most of the men in both groups intended to resettle in the southwestern states, with the additional commonly men-

Table 29. State of Intended Residence
in the United States

State	First-time		Return		Total	
	N	%	N	%	N	%
Texas	155	68.0	226	42.2	381	49.9
Illinois	24	10.5	95	17.8	119	15.6
California	15	6.6	85	15.9	100	13.1
New Mexico	6	2.6	31	5.8	37	4.8
Colorado	2	0.9	30	5.6	32	4.2
Arizona	2	0.9	18	3.4	20	2.6
All others[a]	24	10.5	50	9.3	74	9.8
Total	228	100.0	535	100.0	763	100.0

[a]Includes 21 of the remaining 44 states.

tioned destination of Illinois. Not surprisingly, the former illegal migrants expected to move to the same areas where they had lived previously. The overwhelming majority (68.0 percent) of the first-timers, however, planned to move from their border communities in Mexico to their "twin cities" on the United States side, or just north to the larger Texan cities such as San Antonio, Houston, and Dallas. Outside Texas, Chicago and Los Angeles were popular urban attractions for both groups.

Social Support

The men also expected to continue to utilize the resources available from family and kinship networks. Only about 2 percent said they had no family members or friends to meet them upon arrival as legal immigrants. More than half (56.6 percent) of the others who had family and friends in the United States expected some form of aid. A significantly greater proportion of the first-time arrivals planned to receive "lots of help" from these supporters than did those returning to the North: 31.0 percent of the first-timers compared with 17.0 percent of the return immigrants. Conversely, almost half the return migrants expected no aid at all, while only one out of three of the first-timers intended to resettle on his own.

The primary person who would meet and provide aid to these men was also quite different for each group. Table 30 reports that three-fourths (74.0 percent) of the returning men were greeted by their wives or children, compared with just 46 percent of the more conventional, first-time migrants. Compared with the return migrants, these latter men were

Table 30. First Person Respondent Will
Meet in the United States

Relationship	First-time		Return		Total	
	N	%	N	%	N	%
None	1	0.5	14	2.7	15	2.1
Parent	70	32.6	46	8.9	116	15.9
Brother or sister	19	8.8	17	3.3	36	4.9
Wife	91	42.3	347	67.2	438	59.9
Children	7	3.3	35	6.8	42	5.7
Other relatives	20	9.2	51	9.9	71	9.7
Friends	7	3.3	6	1.2	13	1.8
Total	215	100.0	516	100.0	731	100.0

Table 31. Occupational Aspirations
in the United States

Occupation	First-time		Return		Total	
	N	%	N	%	N	%
Agricultural labor	4	2.9	16	4.6	20	4.1
Minor urban service	4	2.9	6	1.7	10	2.0
Unskilled urban labor	4	2.9	22	6.3	26	5.3
Semiskilled labor	23	16.7	50	14.3	73	15.0
Skilled urban labor	48	34.8	148	42.3	196	40.2
Intermediate service	12	8.7	42	12.0	54	11.1
White-collar	16	11.6	25	7.1	41	8.4
Medium or large agricultural proprietor	0	0.0	3	0.9	3	0.6
Manager of firm	9	6.5	19	5.4	28	5.7
Professional	17	12.3	18	5.1	35	7.2
Other	1	0.7	1	0.3	2	0.4
Total	*138*	*100.0*	*350*	*100.0*	*488*[a]	*100.0*

[a]Missing observations or persons without clear aspirations: 334.

rejoining their parents or brothers and sisters at a rate almost three to one. The groups shared a small but significant proportion (roughly 9 percent) who expected to meet and receive aid first from more distant relatives. Friends rather than family were to be the initial hosts for only 2 percent of both groups.

Economic Aspirations

Finally, Tables 31 and 32 show that these men aspired to significant levels of economic stability and reward in the United States. Clearly, few found farmwork desirable enough to list as a goal of their economic efforts, nor did they aspire to minor service or unskilled labor. In Mexico about one-third of these men had worked in these jobs. In the place of such employment, the men desired jobs that involved substantial skills—40 percent, skilled urban labor, and 15 percent, semiskilled work. Probably as a reflection of the commitment to professionalism imposed by the educa-

Table 32. Salary Expected in First Job and
Highest Aspirations in the United States

Monthly Salary	Expected						Highest Aspirations					
	First-time		Return		Total		First-time		Return		Total	
	N	%	N	%	N	%	N	%	N	%	N	%
Less than $400	94	60.6	154	32.1	248	49.1	11	10.2	11	3.2	22	4.9
$400-499	31	20.0	86	17.9	117	18.4	16	15.0	21	6.1	37	8.2
$500-599	14	9.0	89	18.5	103	16.2	10	9.3	37	10.8	47	10.4
$600-699	12	7.7	78	16.3	90	14.2	22	20.6	65	19.0	87	19.3
$700-799	2	1.3	31	6.5	33	5.2	3	2.8	17	5.0	20	4.4
$800-899	1	0.6	21	4.4	22	3.5	24	22.4	80	23.3	104	23.1
$900 or more	1	0.6	21	4.4	22	3.5	21	19.6	112	32.7	133	29.6
Total	155	100.0	480	100.0	635	100.0	107	100.0	343	100.0	450	100.0

tional background and certification requirements of the job, roughly the same number of men aspired to a university professional position as had held one in Mexico.

Table 31 also shows that status levels of the jobs aspired to by the two groups differed. Although the largest number of men in both groups hoped to acquire a skilled urban job, the generally higher status origins of the first-time group were reflected again in the types of jobs to which they aspired. They were less likely to desire a skilled urban job but more likely to have set their goals on white-collar work. This difference is most evident in the proportions planning, if things went well, to obtain a professional job: 12.3 percent of the first-timers compared with 5.1 percent of former illegal migrants.

The groups' income expectations and longer-range aspirations, however, do not follow this pattern based on the men's social status backgrounds. Table 32 demonstrates strikingly that the lower status and only slightly older return migrants expected and aspired to a much larger salary than the men arriving for the first time. For instance, in their first job in the United States, only one-third (32.1 percent) of the returning men expected to earn less than $400 per month, compared to well over half of the first-time migrants. Although substantially fewer aspired to such a low monthly wage, the group difference is actually three to one: 3.2 percent of the return migrants prized less than $400, as opposed to 10.2 percent of their counterparts. At the other extreme, a much larger share of the return group anticipated in the short-term and eventually to earn more than $900 per month.

Regardless of these differences, however, both groups expected to earn more in the United States than they reported making before legal entry. Overall, more than two-thirds of the sampled men had a monthly salary before this latest migration of less than $400. But only half the men expected to earn as little as this in their first United States job. And only 5 percent were content to have this amount as their highest monetary goal. Instead, a large proportion of the men aspired to an income level that, while modest by United States standards, would represent a substantial salary gain. For while a mere 5 percent reported a previous monthly income of more than $800, nearly one in three (29.6 percent) aimed for this level. If these men achieve their aspirations in the United States, as a group they will have virtually doubled their wages.

Summary

In synthesis, the social origins of these Mexican immigrants were quite diverse and, in general, much different from those typically claimed by conventional profiles. Rather than being illiterate peasants from the countryside, these men originated from the most dynamic sectors of Mexican life. Their individual histories paralleled that of the Mexican economy and society since World War II, with large-scale urbanization and industrialization pressures pushing the men into the larger cities of northern Mexico and beyond into the United States.

Residence in the northern cities accounts for many of the men's personal characteristics. It was in these cities that the men acquired an average of six years of schooling, substantially above the national average. Most of these men found jobs in the growing urban service and manufacturing sectors and were able to gain substantial experience as skilled workers and artisans and semiskilled laborers. And because of the inflated wage scales of the border region, the men received a monthly income that surpassed the Mexican national average.

Their diverse social origins also included substantial prior experience in the United States. Seventy percent of the men had lived in the United States before their legal immigration, and more than half stayed there for at least a year. This previous access to the United States divided the entire sample into two subgroups: the 70 percent who were return immigrants, and the remaining 30 percent who were entering the United States for the first time. The return immigrants were from lower social origins than the first-time immigrants and resembled the general characteristics of many illegal Mexican migrants. Compared with the first-time group, the return immigrants had less education and were less likely to have worked as skilled laborers. But they were more likely to use preestablished social ties to gain access to the United States through family reunification. For example, two-thirds of these returnees had wives already waiting for them in the United States. This figure compares with only 48 percent of the first-time arrivals.

Finally, the industrialization and urbanization drives that began influencing these men's lives in Mexico continued to shape their experiences as they entered the United States. Few of the men sought rural, agricultural jobs. Instead, they selected as their destinations the largest cities of the Southwest, where the manufacturing and service jobs they hoped to obtain would provide them higher status and greater skill than those they had held in Mexico. The men also expected that the result of their migration would be a substantial increase in their salaries. In fact, many aspired to jobs in the United States that would pay two or three times the income they could have earned if they had stayed in Mexico.

THE CUBAN REVOLUTION AND THE ORIGINS OF ITS REFUGEES

Contrary to conventional wisdom, the seeds of the post-1959 Cuban emigration did not sprout suddenly with the victory of the Castro-led guerilla forces in the Sierra Maestra. Although the revolution may be appropriately claimed as the "first cause" [32] of the refugee flight, the origins of that flow, and those of the outmigration as well, lie in the sweep of prerevolutionary history. For this history structured economic and social relations in a manner that made particular groups the direct and indirect targets of subsequent revolutionary reforms. Yet this process of political-economic selection in no way suggests that the cause of an individual's migration was simply his or her class location. Too many theses on the Cuban refugee flow have been plagued by a judgmental "worms or heroes" approach. Nor can the outflow be reduced to a series of spasmodic eruptions of spontaneous dissent. Rather, as with the Mexican emigration, the determination and composition of the Cuban outflow are complex and heterogeneous. Moreover, these factors have changed considerably over time as long-term, recurring social, economic, and political pressures have themselves changed in character and intensity.

Before the Revolution

On the eve of the revolution, Cuba had achieved in aggregate terms impressive signs of economic development. But just as Mexico's "economic miracle" had given it a glow of prosperity and a reality of despair, Cuba's growth had left many promises unfulfilled. Vast disparities existed throughout the population, and poverty was particularly acute in the countryside.

Even more than in the case of Mexico, we cannot understand the roots of Cuba's emigration without considering the long-term, foreign domination of its economy. One author aptly described the prerevolutionary situation as follows:

The Cuban economy was so wedded to the U.S. economy that the country was in many ways an appendage of it—though without enjoying [the benefits] a poor state in the United States does.[33]

In the mid-1950s, for instance, United States capital controlled 40 percent of Cuba's raw sugar production, 50 percent of the public railways, and 90 percent of public services such as telephone and electricity. The United States dominated petroleum refining and distribution, manufacturing, and retail merchandising. U.S. interests also ran the highly acclaimed tourist attractions in Havana, serving some two hundred thousand United States visitors annually.

This foreign domination had three important effects on the structure of class relations. First, dependence on sugar exports restricted industrialization. One result was that the industrial sector was able to employ only about

---

32. Richard R. Fagen, Richard A. Brody, and Thomas J. O'Leary, *Cubans in Exile.*

33. Dudley Seers, *Cuba: The Economic and Social Revolution*, p. 4, quoted in Nita R. Manitzas, "The Setting of the Cuban Revolution," p. 6.

20 percent of the nation's workforce, well under half the proportion engaged in agriculture. In addition, because foreign capital controlled even this relatively small industrial sector, domestic Cuban capital moved readily into real estate and investment abroad. In 1955 Cuban citizens had already invested an estimated $150 million in Florida real estate alone.

Second, with roots dating to the nineteenth century, United States involvement on the island promoted the thorough penetration of capitalist principles of economic and social organization. Money as a commodity formed the basis of most transactions and, more critical to the later emigration, the source of social status differences.[34] Rather than maintaining its wealth primarily through land inheritance and other familiar seigneurial rights, Cuba's upper class held claim to its privileged position through cash profits and large salaries. Both meant that this group needed close contact to the more dynamic, foreign-controlled activities.

Third, United States lifestyles had a profound effect upon the population of Cuba, especially among the wealthier groups, and tied them even more tightly to the North.[35] At rates virtually unheard of throughout Latin America at the time, the Cuban people had direct access to United States consumer goods and mass communication. One pair of authors has even argued that this northward orientation was so pervasive that large sections of the Cuban population became psychologically dependent upon the United States.[36]

In short, the legacy of prerevolutionary Cuba to the subsequent emigration not only was one of extensive poverty with substantial wealth, but also represented an alignment of diverse groups alongside United States activities and interests. The futures of the Cuban bourgeoisie and upper-middle-income groups were clearly dependent upon the progress of relations with the United States. But these groups were not alone in this dependence. Those of lower social rank who benefitted least from the contact were also tied to similar United States-influenced activities. From sugar producers adjusting production schedules to United States quotas to neighborhood shopkeepers selling imported goods, few from the middle class or above could have avoided the United States presence.

After the Revolution

A key to understanding the social transformation after 1959 is an understanding of the enormity of the political-economic project under way at that time: to turn a dependent, capitalist society into a socialist state whose goals were independence from the United States, accelerated economic

34. Richard R. Fagen, *The Transformation of Political Culture in Cuba.*
35. Sergio Diaz-Briquets and Lisandro Perez, "Cuba," p. 6.
36. Antonio Jorge and Raul Moncarz, "Cubans in South Florida."

growth, and elimination of the class, region, racial, and sex inequalities formed before the revolution.[37] As one group of authors has noted,

The Mexican Revolution brought much more death, destruction, and disorganization in its early years, but the Cuban Revolution stands alone as the most far-reaching and rapidly paced social transformation in the history of Latin America.[38]

The direction of this transformation was evident even before the revolution. Fidel Castro's famous Moncada speech of July 26, 1953, provided a simple and unambiguous catalogue of the groups that he expected to become supporters and beneficiaries of the revolution. These included the unemployed; farm laborers; industrial laborers and stevedores; small farmers who did not own their lands; a conglomerate of poorly paid teachers, disaffected doctors, engineers, and lawyers; and small business people overburdened by debts. Even at this early date the projected ranks of the new society excluded the bourgeoisie, landowners, bankers, rentiers, and industrialists. Of course, the revolution did not reward all those listed as planned beneficiaries; indeed, many of these favored groups contributed heavily to the subsequent exodus. Yet it is clear that in this list, the specific aim of the revolution was to transform the pattern of development that had been forged with United States support before 1959.

Revolutionary reform transformed the nature of class relations in Cuba in three ways that shaped the social composition of the groups that left the island and, over time, formed the demarcating features of the stages of the emigration highlighted in Chapter 3. First, during the earliest period, there was a clear and thorough attempt to redistribute national wealth. The Agrarian Reform Law of 1959, for example, nationalized the island's *latifundia* and sugar *centrales*, taking from the landowners and administrators their primary source of wealth. There were also attempts to redistribute real income from the cities to the countryside. Collective stores, guaranteed prices, and higher rural wages raised the living standard of the rural population, while in the cities rents for the poor were limited to 10 percent of the family's income.[39]

Second, although the redistributive policies clearly cost the new government some support, especially among middle-class supporters, it was the clash with the United States, the confiscation of United States holdings, and the subsequent nationalization of all domestic property related to the Batista government that progressively pressured and eliminated many groups and individuals from the government's constituency. Groups particularly affected during this second stage included domestic business people,

---

37. Diaz-Briquets and Perez, "Cuba."
38. Fagen, Brody, and O'Leary, *Cubans in Exile*, p. 100.
39. David Barkin, "The Redistribution of Consumption in Cuba."

professionals, and some labor groups tied to work in the foreign sector.[40]

The third major transformation, which developed primarily after 1965, resulted from the adoption of a "turnpike" development strategy emphasizing expanded production. This push seriously restricted the production and consumption of consumer goods. But rather than allow the distribution of such goods to become "self-regulating" through prices, the government initiated a rationing program. It began with meat and spread to include almost all food items, clothing, and consumer durables. This situation brought more pressure to bear on the middle class.[41]

Favorable world-market prices for sugar permitted an increase in real terms of the national income by about 11 percent between 1962 and 1965, with a similar rise in per capita consumption. In 1966, however, both dropped, falling back to the 1962 levels. Gross National Product also dropped by 4 percent. That same year marked the beginning of a period of radicalization in the government's policies. Until that time, a considerable private sector had survived, especially among small farmers and merchants. But it had also become an increasingly serious *competitor* with the government for the control and use of scarce resources and labor, and with severe shortages in consumer goods, offered an alternative, even if illegal, source for such items. A revolutionary offensive was launched in March, 1968, to eliminate this sector, cautiously first in agriculture, but aggressively in urban services and retail trade.[42]

By 1969, the end of the first decade of the revolution, Cuba faced aggregate economic problems, an extremely ambitious sugar-production goal, and a drive to socialize the remaining private sector. That combination resulted in additional attempts to freeze or even lower personal-consumption levels and to direct more investment sources into production and collective consumption. It became clear in 1969 and 1970 that consumption possibilities for rationed goods were likely to become more restricted or, at least, that the prevailing levels would persist for some time in the future.

As is well-known, these changes in postrevolutionary Cuba produced a refugee outflow that was actually a series of emigrations. First, the moves in the early 1960s against United States interests and activities on the island, particularly those involving the nationalization of land and enterprise, uprooted persons who had either direct ties with United States affairs or a relatively privileged position in the old order. As noted, however, this also involved many in the middle sectors of the society, who in one way or another had jobs or lifestyles connected to the formerly foreign-controlled activities.

40. Ibid., pp. 91–92.
41. Ibid., pp. 92–93.
42. Bertram Silverman, "Economic Organization and Social Conscience."

Second, after the early crises with the United States, the Cuban government's accelerated economic drive and its deepening revolutionary changes drew the opposition of groups who had been affected only marginally by previous reforms: for example, private shopkeepers and lower level government officials. Consumption limitations intensified this disaffection.

Third, the fluctuating character of the outflows has been directly linked to the action of the Cuban government in restricting its citizens' ability to leave the island for the United States. Except at the very beginning of the outflow, registration to leave and prior screening were required. Registration was difficult because it was considered an open declaration of the registrant's opposition to the revolutionary government. Many took this risk, but still could not leave until the government initiated a departure program, whether it involved simply opening a harbor to those who wished to leave, agreeing to aerial flights, or accepting an orderly departure program. To a large extent, therefore, it has been this pattern of state regulation, rather than sudden or radical shifts in economic or social pressures, that has made the emigration appear spasmodic.

Like the Mexican emigration, the nature of the Cuban refugee flow reproduced pressures to emigrate. The most important was the cumulative formation of binational family networks, with members of the same family becoming divided between Cuba and, primarily, South Florida. Under the United States legal preference for family reunification, each wave of Cuban refugees created another pool of potential exiles. It added an intensive personal desire for family reunion to the list of reasons for emigrating.

The individual and family histories of our sampled men reflect this profound restructuring of Cuban society brought about by the revolution and, in relation to other Cuban refugees, the type of changes occurring well after 1959. Virtually all the men in the sample (96.4 percent) were at least 18 years of age at the time of the revolution. The positions their families occupied in prerevolutionary Cuba were, consequently, a strong influence upon the character of the personal attributes they brought to the United States. But all of the men also experienced most of the first decade of revolutionary changes.

Residential Histories

The geographical origins of our sampled men clearly reflect Cuba's major ecological characteristic, the overwhelming predominance of Havana, both as a city and a province. According to the 1953 census, the last taken before the revolution, roughly one in every five Cubans lived in metropolitan Havana. It was the only city of 1 million or more inhabitants, and its population outnumbered the nearest rival, Santiago, nearly seven to one.[43]

43. Diaz-Briquets and Perez, "Cuba," p. 11.

Table 33. Province of Residence in the
Family Histories, Cuban Refugees

Province	Father's Birth		Son's Birth		Son's Sixteenth Birthday		Last Residence	
	N	%	N	%	N	%	N	%
Havana	124	21.9	244	41.5	258	43.7	377	63.9
Pinar del Rio	60	10.6	48	8.2	43	7.3	20	3.4
Matanzas	62	10.9	68	11.6	65	11.0	46	7.8
Las Villas	94	16.6	106	18.0	95	16.1	53	9.0
Camaguey	21	3.7	47	8.0	48	8.1	41	6.9
Oriente	41	7.2	60	10.2	60	10.2	53	9.0
Spain	146	25.7	0	0.0	20	3.4	0	0.0
Another country	19	3.4	15	2.5	1	3.2	0	0.0
Total	*567*	*100.0*	*588*	*100.0*	*590*	*100.0*	*590*	*100.0*

When combined with Havana, other cities spread throughout the country contained a majority of the national population. But most of these secondary cities held only twenty to fifty thousand people, and around them lived a large rural population.

Cuban refugees generally are more likely than the national population to have been born and raised in the largest cities. Eighty-seven percent of those who left before 1963 were born in a city with more than fifty thousand inhabitants, as were roughly 56 percent of those leaving in the mid-1960s.[44] Fifty-two percent of our sampled men were born in similarly sized cities. But these figures actually understate the extent to which the men spent most of their lives in the largest cities. By the age of sixteen, for instance, 60 percent lived in places with more than fifty thousand persons, and before they left the island a full 80 percent had come to live in these cities. More than half (53.4 percent) left from Havana alone.

Whether in the city or not, as Table 33 shows, most of the sampled men had lived in the province of Havana. There was a steady increase over the men's family histories in the proportion living in the province. One in five

44. Fagen, Brody, and O'Leary, *Cubans in Exile*. Also see Eleanor Meyer Rogg, *The Assimilation of Cuban Exiles*.

(21.9 percent) of their fathers were born there, compared with 42 percent of the sampled men. Havana was also the last province of residence in Cuba for 64 percent, with the departure points for the remainder of the men equally spread over the rest of the island.

By birthplace, Las Villas was the second largest provincial contributor, but along with Pinar del Rio and Matanzas, it had steadily lost its share of the group during the men's lifetimes. On the other hand, the men born in Oriente and Camaguey tended to have remained there. However, it is perhaps more interesting that almost one-third (29.1 percent) of their fathers had been born outside Cuba, many of them having immigrated from Spain. This finding reflects the fact that for many years before the revolution Cuba had been a country of net immigration, becoming a large-scale nation of emigration only after 1959.

The concentration of both the national and refugee population in Havana reflects the city's overwhelming importance as the center of economic, social, and cultural activities. "Although Cuba had a one-crop, rural economy," writes Jorge Hardoy about prerevolutionary Cuba, "it poured its earnings into Havana, to the detriment of the rest of the economy."[45] After the revolution, Havana was the center and target of many of the reforms. To a large extent, therefore, the refugees' regional backgrounds are merely indications of their social positions before and after the revolution.

Social Locations

The national focus on Havana can hardly be overstated, for located within it were the following: 90 percent of the nation's shipping, the principal fishing port, the bulk of government offices, the best-equipped hospitals, the sole facilities for university education, and the largest department stores and shops.[46] Life in general was more advanced in the city. For example, before the revolution only 9 percent of its inhabitants were illiterate, compared with more than 35 percent in Oriente province.

In the countryside, land use was organized around *latifundia* owned or controlled by large landowners or administrators representing foreign (United States) interests. Sugar production alone shaped many of the social and economic relationships embedded there. As one author notes,

when Batista fled the country, the twenty-eight largest sugar-cane producers together owned or rented more than 20 percent of all farmland—thus controlling in effect almost one-fifth of the national land area.[47]

45. Jorge E. Hardoy, "Spatial Structure and Society in Revolutionary Cuba," p. 6.
46. Maruja Acosta and Jorge E. Hardoy, *Urban Reform in Revolutionary Cuba*, p. 35.
47. Manitzas, "The Setting of the Cuban Revolution," p. 3.

Rural workers in general received low incomes and were badly housed and largely uneducated. In 1956, for instance, they earned roughly $91 for a year's labor, well under one-third of the national average.[48]

The middle class was substantial, but compared with the upper class and working class, poorly defined. Included in its ranks were small-scale business people, local shopkeepers, salaried managers, and even semi-skilled technicians who received a comparatively substantial wage by working for a United States firm. Educational facilities were relatively advanced and available, but produced many professionals whose skills were related directly to the presence of United States business rather than the local economy.[49]

Both the urban and rural working class fell at the very bottom of the economy. In 1951, for instance, more than half of the nation's families (53.8 percent) had incomes that were either below poverty levels (less than $70 per month) or minimal ($70 to $149 a month).[50] Unemployment was an equally important problem, especially among the rural agricultural workers, whose dependence upon wages and the cycles of sugar production offered only periodic employment and few alternative, subsistence resources.

The reflection of these stratifying relations in the social origins of successive waves of Cuban refugees has been strongly affected by the Cuban government's selective refusal of permission to leave. For example, when the government opened the fishing port of Camarioca in Matanzas province on September 28, 1965, professionals and men between ages 16 and 27 were barred from leaving.[51] Nonetheless, the origins of the series of outflows generally indicate two trends in the social composition of the individual refugees. First, as noted in Chapter 3, there is a secular decline in the social-status origins, beginning with landowners and professionals in the first waves and reaching into the lower ranks as the revolutionary reforms involved wider sectors of the economy. Second, despite the first trend there was significant heterogeneity from the very beginning. Our sampled men mirror both trends.

Education

Since most of the sampled men were over age 18 at the time of the revolution, both they and their fathers were most likely to have attended school well before the new government's push to expand access to educa-

48. David Barkin, "Cuban Agriculture."
49. For example, in the 1950s there were only about 300 agricultural engineers on the entire island. By comparison there were more than 6,500 lawyers.
50. H. T. Oshima, "A New Estimate of the National Income and Product of Cuba in 1953."
51. Juan M. Clark, José I. Lasaga, and Rose S. Reque, *The 1980 Mariel Exodus.*

Table 34. Educational Backgrounds of
Sampled Men and Their Fathers

Type of Schooling and Highest Grade	Fathers		Sons	
	N	%	N	%
No schooling	26	5.3	2	0.3
Primary, not complete	149	30.1	84	14.3
Primary, complete	236	47.6	194	33.1
Secondary, not complete	23	4.6	82	14.0
Secondary, complete	17	3.4	23	3.9
Business and vocational, not complete	8	1.6	50	8.5
Business and vocational, complete	19	3.8	70	11.9
University, not complete	3	0.6	30	5.1
University, complete	15	3.0	48	8.2
Other	0	0.0	4	0.7
Total	*496*	*100.0*	*587*	*100.0*

tion. As a result, that the average number of years of formal schooling was high for these refugees highlights their relatively privileged social status. The sampled men had attended on the average almost nine (8.6) years of school, which surpassed both their fathers' education and the average for the total Cuban population. Table 34 reports that the sons were well over three times more likely than their fathers to have received some university education and nearly four times as likely to be trained in a business or vocational school. Both fathers and sons, however, had many more years in school than the comparable national average. Roughly 8 percent of the fathers and 22 percent of the sons had twelve or more years of school, which compared to 4 percent in the national population enumerated in the 1953 census. Nevertheless, Table 34 also reveals the group's heterogeneity. Although the levels of formal schooling are substantial for the surveyed men, one in three had fathers who had either no formal schooling or had not completed primary school, and roughly 15 percent of the refugees themselves had been unable to obtain more than this amount.

These educational levels contribute to the observation that each successive wave of Cuban refugees had originated in lower social-status origins than those who left before.[52] Compared with previous cohorts, the 78 percent who had not completed twelve years of school is low. Studies of groups who came to the United States in the early and mid-1960s report that 64 percent and 62 percent, respectively, had not finished twelfth grade.

Occupation

The earliest defectors from the new government's project were the wealthier, more privileged groups, including the landowners, those who administered large commercial enterprises, and professionals. For example, Fagen, Brody, and O'Leary report that among those who arrived in the United States between 1960 and 1962, 37 percent of the heads of households were proprietors, managers, and professionals.[53] Only 10 percent of the prerevolutionary Cuban population had similar jobs. These figures, however, may even understate the proportion of the earliest arrivals who were from the wealthiest sectors. The data used for that early study were derived from the files of the Cuban Refugee Program in Coral Gables, Florida, which did not begin registering arrivals until 1961. Yet it was only in that year that Cuban regulations governing the removal of money and possessions were first applied stringently. Many of the wealthiest business people or landowners probably left before then.

Still, with only one-third of the early arrivals originating within the highest social ranks, a large number represented a wide variety of groups. Throughout these early years there was a relatively constant proportion of persons from the middle sectors: professionals, clerical and sales workers, and skilled and semiskilled craft workers. Among the professionals, there occurred short, intensive outbursts of specific types, reflecting the specific reform being pushed. The three largest were lawyers, judges, and doctors. There was also a large-scale outflow of government workers. One author characterized its scale and significance as follows:

This process of permitting the free emigration of old civil servants, and the managerial and administrative strata, is a distinctive feature of the Cuban Revolution. It permitted a relatively peaceful transformation of the social structure and at the same time avoided the dominance of the State by the old bureaucracy.[54]

By 1962, the general occupational levels had begun to shift, encompassing more diverse sectors and reducing the concentration in any single occupation.

The occupational histories of our sampled men and their fathers were characteristic of both the positive selectivity of Cuban refugees relative to

52. Lourdes Casal and Andres R. Hernandez, "Cubans in the U. S."
53. Fagen, Brody, and O'Leary, p. 65.
54. Silverman, "Economic Organization and Social Conscience," p. 407.

Table 35. Sector of Principal Lifetime Occupation
for Interviewed Men and Their Fathers

Sector	Father's Main Occupation		Son's Main Occupation		Son's Last Occupation	
	N	%	N	%	N	%
Out of labor market	7	1.2	4	0.7	17	2.9
Agriculture	149	25.9	28	4.7	34	5.8
Mining	1	0.2	0	0.0	0	0.0
Industry	77	13.4	83	14.1	93	15.8
Construction	23	4.0	26	4.4	39	6.6
Transportation, communication	51	8.9	43	7.3	50	8.5
Commerce, wholesale, retail	135	23.4	125	21.2	81	13.8
Collective service	85	14.8	192	32.5	194	32.9
Personal service	47	8.2	89	15.1	81	13.7
Total	*575*	*100.0*	*590*	*100.0*	*589*	*100.0*

the entire national population, and the declining status trends between successive waves of refugees. But they also highlight the nature of the reforms in Cuba that had produced these refugees.

Table 35 shows the sector of principal lifetime occupation for the refugees and their fathers as well as the refugees' last jobs in Cuba before emigration. The fathers' rural backgrounds meant that about one in every four families had origins in agriculture. Their subsequent shifts to the cities, however, brought their sons well into the urban economy: only 5 percent of the sons still worked on farms. This comparison also reveals that the fathers were able to pass on to their sons the family's social status. Fathers shared with their sons a high concentration in commercial and collective services, comparatively privileged sectors in an economy without significant industrial capacity. These were also sectors that had not been reached on a large scale by the earliest reforms.

The refugees' occupational backgrounds further describe a family social position that was situated in the middle of the Cuban economy. Table 36 shows that most of the fathers and sons held jobs in three general categories. The single largest number were concentrated among white-collar or minor professional jobs. But the most revealing occupational origins were

Table 36. Principal Lifetime Occupation
of Sampled Men and Their Fathers

Occupation	Father's		Son's		Son's Last	
	N	%	N	%	N	%
Out of the labor market	7	1.2	4	0.7	17	2.9
Agricultural laborer	104	18.1	14	2.4	19	3.2
Minor urban service worker	33	5.7	39	6.6	38	6.5
Unskilled urban laborer	21	3.7	28	4.7	49	8.3
Semiskilled urban laborer	52	9.0	44	7.5	58	9.9
Small rural proprietor	35	6.1	11	1.9	14	2.4
Skilled worker	86	15.0	131	22.2	132	22.5
Intermediate service worker	154	26.8	116	19.6	90	15.3
White-collar and minor professional	46	8.0	144	24.4	124	21.1
Medium or large agricultural proprietor	15	2.6	5	0.8	3	0.5
Manager of firm	8	1.4	4	0.7	2	0.3
Professional	14	2.4	50	8.5	42	7.1
Total	*575*	*100.0*	*590*	*100.0*	*588*	*100.0*

those among intermediate service jobs and those requiring skilled labor. Nearly half of each group listed their main occupation in those jobs that, by the late 1960s, were hardest pressed by the reorganization and socialization of small private businesses and by consumption limitations. Encompassing work that could easily be performed on a private, individual service basis, intermediate service jobs included barbers, taxi drivers, small retail merchants, and hairdressers, while most of the skilled urban jobs were plumbers, electricians, and carpenters. Many of these latter jobs also required the formal training reflected in these men's high education origins, especially, for example, the machine operatives. Of course the 9 percent who were professionals also benefitted from their educational training.

The refugees' last job before leaving also highlights the particular sectoral origins of the group. For despite the profound changes in the Cuban economy since 1959, most of the refugees held as their last job the same one they and their fathers reported as their main lifetime occupation. As a group, roughly 11 percent who mentioned the above jobs as their lifetime occupation had been unable to hold them up to their departure. It seems likely that it was the post-1966 reforms that reached into these sectors on a major scale for the first time and produced the circumstances that led to these men's emigration.

Income

The refugees' income in Cuba also identifies their backgrounds as belonging to the middle sectors of the urban population. A full third of the men earned an average of less than $100 per month. Most made between $100 and $200 monthly. At the other extreme, very few (4 percent) made more than $400 per month. These modest earnings were still considerably more than those reported for all employed Cuban males in 1958. Roughly 60 percent of this latter population earned only $75 per month, while only 30 percent in the sampled group earned so little. In postrevolutionary Cuba, where top government functionaries rarely earned more than $600 per month in the early 1970s, the sampled men's $150 monthly was still relatively privileged.

A significant share of these men also benefitted from their wives' work. Although the wives of urban middle-sector workers do not usually work in Cuba, more than 27 percent of these men's wives earned wages from jobs outside the home. The women worked in sectors similar to those of their husbands, especially in public institutions or in the commercial sectors.

THE STABILITY AND DIRECTIONALITY
OF THE REFUGEE OUTFLOW

Just as the activating mechanism of Mexican migration to the United States has been the extensive transnational family networks, so the Cuban emigration has been similarly propelled by the "prevailing strong ties among Cuban families."[55] Even among the exiles who left before 1963, family reunification had become a "self-sustaining dynamic." A full 67 percent of these sampled men had relatives already in the United States, and 70 percent had friends here. In a later sample, Eleanor Rogg [56] reports that almost 93 percent had family members in the United States when they entered. Most were parents or brothers and sisters. More importantly, however, 75 percent said they also had family still in Cuba who were hoping to come eventually to the United States.

The policies and agreements between the Cuban and United States gov-

55. Clark, Lasaga, Reque, *The 1980 Mariel Exodus*, p. 3.
56. Rogg, *The Assimilation of Cuban Exiles*, p. 28.

ernments contributed to this process. For example, the series of airlifts that began in 1965 brought a disproportionate number of children, homemakers, and students. And the screening procedures performed by the United States government gave priority to relatives of those already abroad, parents of un-married children under age 21, spouses, unmarried children below age 16, and brothers and sisters under age 21. The effect of these regulations is evi-dent in the characteristics of those who leave Cuba illegally, using either boats or passing through a third country. These "unconventional" exiles have been more representative of the Cuban population.[57]

Despite this pervasive influence of family reunion, the refugees' actual decisions to emigrate have been complex and heterogeneous. Fagen, Brody, and O'Leary found among the early exiles that personal experiences mattered the most. Ideological considerations often inspired an initial thought of leaving, but pragmatic concerns carried greater weight in the end. Of course, as the nature of the reforms changed, so did the content of the issues that these persons were forced to decide. One study, designed primarily to distinguish between those who left for political reasons as com-pared to more "traditional" reasons, observed the following:

> The Cuban migration to the U. S. is not an entirely political phenomenon but rather a significant number of the migrants are traditional immigrants who come to this country in search of a higher standard of living.[58]

Another recurrent motivation was the extent to which particular groups and individuals ran afoul of governmental directives and were subsequently imprisoned. There were, of course, cases of persons jailed in direct connec-tion with counterrevolutionary political activity. But there were also those who violated the new laws passed to support the social and economic re-forms. For instance, 15 percent of the pre-1963 arrivals reported that they had been imprisoned (unjustly, they said) by the new government.

The Context and Decision to Emigrate

There is some indication that these sampled men and their families had experienced economic problems in the few years before they decided to emigrate. Table 37 shows, for example, that a much greater proportion had been unemployed in postrevolutionary Cuba than before 1959. Indeed, generally supportive of their relatively privileged social status before the revolution, a full 96 percent of these men said they had never been unem-ployed in the years 1955 to 1960. But in the five years before emigration 27

---

57. Juan M. Clark, "Selected Types of Cuban Exiles Used as a Sample of the Cuban Popu-lation," cited in Casal and Hernandez, "Cubans in the U. S.," p. 28.

58. Casal and Hernandez, "Cubans in the U. S.," p. 27.

Table 37. Length of Unemployment in Cuba

Time Unemployed	1955-1960		Last Five Years Before Emigration	
	N	%	N	%
Never	567	96.1	161	27.4
Less than one month	7	1.2	78	13.3
One to six months	2	0.3	160	27.2
Six months to one year	2	0.3	74	12.6
One to two years	8	1.4	68	11.5
Two years or more	4	0.7	47	8.0
Total	*590*	*100.0*	*588*	*100.0*

percent had been unemployed. And most of this time the length of unemployment was significant: nearly one in four had been without work for at least one year.

The period after the decision to emigrate was also one of hardship. To leave Cuba, many had to perform compulsory agricultural labor, often extensive periods of difficult work in the sugar cane fields. Eighty-three percent of the men claimed this tax on their labor in order to gain permission to leave. Of this number, the largest group (44.8 percent) reported spending from nineteen to twenty-four months in these activities: 11.5 percent and 14.8 percent said their work lasted less than one year and more than two years, respectively. Roughly 16 percent did not specify the duration of their compulsory work.

Our sampled men's reasons for leaving were not only heterogeneous, but also often apparently contradictory. Although nearly one in every three (28 percent) said they had intended to emigrate even before the revolution, when asked to identify their principal reason for coming to the United States, an overwhelming 83 percent claimed political reasons. Family reunion was mentioned by only 6 percent and a mere 4 percent listed strictly work-related reasons such as income.

The question, however, restricted them to only one response, and as Table 38 reveals, the decision was not unidimensional. The table ranks the degree of importance attached to three very different types of influences on the decision to emigrate. Column 2 again shows the pervasive disaffection from the government that Cuban refugees in general have demonstrated since the early 1960s. But columns 1 and 3 suggest an equally strong con-

Table 38. Factors Affecting the Decision to Emigrate

Rank	Lack of Food and Other Goods		Lack of Liberty		Lack of Future for Self/Children	
	N	%	N	%	N	%
Very important	150	25.7	563	96.2	554	94.7
Somewhat important	139	23.8	12	2.1	18	3.1
Not very important	294	50.5	10	1.7	13	2.2
Total	*583*	*100.0*	*585*	*100.0*	*585*	*100.0*

cern over economic and social conditions. Virtually the same number of persons who listed "lack of liberty" as a major reason for leaving also indicated that the "lack of a future," in terms of aspirations for themselves and their children, was very important. Half of the men recalled as important the constraints on the availability of food and other consumer goods. The men seemed concerned with the long-term continuation of political and economic limitations, and only secondarily with the immediate shortages.

Social Networks

Clearly unlike the factors involved in the Mexican migration, the social networks fueling and organizing the Cuban flow could not have provided the migrant with a series of temporary, introductory periods of residence in the United States. Consequently, more than 90 percent of the sampled men arrived in Miami with no previous experience in the United States. Those who had travelled there had only stayed for less than a month. Also very different from the share of the Mexican flow is the proportion of the Cuban refugees migrating with their wives and children. Although 21 percent were not married at the time of their arrival in the United States, nearly 90 percent of the husbands were accompanied by their wives. The remainder (10.8 percent) had left their wives in Cuba. This was the pattern for the men with children also. Only 8 percent of these men had left their children on the island.

Yet, contrary to the image these figures may create, the men and their immediate families rarely faced an unknown world in Miami. Like Mexican migrants, the majority were reunited with family and friends. Table 39 documents the extensive, close contacts awaiting these Cubans. Only six men in the entire sample said they had neither a relative nor a friend in the United States. At the other extreme, fully one in every four had more than

Table 39. Relatives and Friends in the United States

Number of Relatives and Friends	Frequency	Percentage
None	6	1.0
One to four	132	22.5
Five to nine	172	29.4
Ten to fourteen	91	15.5
Fifteen to nineteen	62	10.6
Twenty or more	123	21.0
Total	*586*	*100.0*

twenty persons waiting for them. The median number of these relatives and friends was 8.5.

Since most of the men had their wives and children with them, the relationship they had to those awaiting their arrival was quite different than for the Mexican migrants. When asked who was the person in the United States to whom they were closest, 26 percent named a brother or sister. Another 22 percent were to meet their in-laws. Aunts, uncles, and cousins composed a third type of family relation, which greeted about 21 percent. In part because fully 99 percent of these relatives and friends lived in Florida, the amount of aid expected from them was significant. Twenty-three percent expected substantial assistance, with 42 percent expecting some, and 10 percent only a little. Twenty-three percent, however, expected no help at all.

Plans and Expectations

Where these men planned to resettle in the United States was affected by two primary characteristics of the history of the Cuban refugee resettlement program.[59] The first was the concentration in South Florida of relatives, friends, and those who had left Cuba earlier. The second was the only limited success of past United States government programs to redistribute Cuban exiles away from that area. As we mentioned in the preceding chapter, many of these former refugees had returned to Miami, and the programs had been discontinued by the time our sampled men arrived. Re-

59. This discussion is adapted from an earlier report on these migrants. See Alejandro Portes, Juan M. Clark, and Robert L. Bach, "The New Wave."

Table 40. Principal Occupation in Cuba and
Occupational Aspirations in the United States

Occupation	Principal Occupation in Cuba		Occupational Aspiration in U.S.	
	N	%	N	%
Out of the labor market/ no clear aspirations	4	0.7	124	24.0
Agricultural laborer	14	2.4	2	0.4
Minor urban service worker	39	6.6	8	1.6
Unskilled urban laborer	28	4.7	10	1.9
Semiskilled urban laborer	44	7.5	24	4.7
Small rural proprietor	11	1.9	3	0.6
Skilled worker	131	22.2	100	19.4
Intermediate service worker	116	19.6	124	24.1
White-collar and minor professional	144	24.4	57	11.0
Medium or large agricultural proprietor	5	0.8	1	0.2
Manager of firm	4	0.7	8	1.6
Professional	50	8.5	54	10.5
Total	*590*	*100.0*	*515*	*100.0*

gardless of the reason, however, the projected concentration was striking: 576 of 590 men interviewed planned to remain in Miami.

The men's personal goals could also have made the availability of a supportive community overwhelmingly attractive. For when asked to identify their most important goal in the United States, most gave answers that suggested security and the desire to regain their lost social status. Twenty-four percent said their first goal was to find employment. The remainder stressed education for themselves and their children (22 percent) and a general improvement in their current status (20 percent).

Both security and advancement were also reflected in the men's desire to acquire jobs that were similar to those held in Cuba. Table 40 shows the extent to which this was a general concern. The large proportion without an expressed occupational aspiration is not surprising, since many had just

Table 41.   Salary Aspirations in the United States

Monthly Salary, $	Frequency	Percentage
$399	6	1.1
$400-599	6	1.1
$600-799	27	5.0
$800-999	51	9.4
$1000-1299	74	13.7
$1300-1499	19	3.5
$1500-1999	23	4.3
$2000-2499	8	1.5
$2500-2999	3	0.5
$3000+	25	4.6
Does not know	299	55.3
Total	*541*	*100.0*

arrived in Miami. Nevertheless, among those with clear plans, skilled laborer jobs and white-collar work were favored. These two jobs were also frequently held in Cuba. However, many who held white-collar or minor professional jobs in Cuba, actually the largest occupational category for these men, did not desire to return to similar jobs in the United States. One possibility is that many within this group had worked for the Cuban government and may have perceived an inability or felt an unwillingness to reobtain public service employment in South Florida.

Like refugees in general, these Cuban men believed that their new home offered sufficient opportunities to reach their goals: 93.2 percent believed so. Specifically in terms of occupational aspirations, a similarly high proportion, 90 percent, foresaw opportunities to regain their lost status. The reality facing them, however, was much less optimistic. Their high expectations contradicted the modest levels of upward mobility experienced by their countrymen who had arrived previously.

Finally, the income to which these men aspired in the United States would reestablish them in the middle sectors of the local population. Table 41 shows that when these men had clear income aspirations, the majority desired a monthly salary of between $800 and $1,300. The largest share in the group, however, did not have any clear aspirations. This figure corresponds to a substantial proportion who also did not know what salary level to expect in the United States. When the refugees reported their expectations, the income levels were less than half those to which the men aspired.

Summary

In synthesis, the social origins of these Cuban refugees reflected the two principal characteristics of the trends formed by the successive waves of emigrants since 1959. First, although their social-status backgrounds were still above the national average, they were lower than those of each previous wave of refugees. Second, like each former cohort, there was a significant amount of social heterogeneity within the group. These characteristics, indeed entire individual histories, were tied closely to the series of economic and political reforms that initially transformed Cuban society after 1959 and subsequently reshaped the economy as the revolution matured.

The dominant presence of Havana accounted for many of these emigrants' experiences before leaving the island. In Havana most of the men attained nine years of formal schooling. Since nearly all of the men were educated before the revolution, their access to schools was significantly greater than that of the national population. Yet in comparison with the education of earlier waves of Cuban refugees, these nine years were relatively modest.

The men's occupational origins placed them well within the sectors that were the targets of post-1966 economic and political reforms. A large proportion were intermediate service workers or skilled craftsmen and artisans who could work as private, individual contractors. The single largest share were white-collar and professional workers. Few worked on farms. Their income also reflected these middle-level occupations. The majority earned between $100 and $200 per month and only 4 percent received more than $400 per month.

Part of the men's decision to leave the island may have included a spell of unemployment, which often lasted for more than a year. Roughly 25 percent of the men had such an encounter with joblessness some time after 1959, while very few were unemployed before the revolution. Yet nearly all the men listed as their last job in Cuba that which they also considered their primary job throughout their working lives. Consequently, it appears that the various reforms undertaken before the late 1960s, when the men took steps to leave, had not substantially altered their relationship to the economy.

The men also had other diverse reasons for leaving. Almost one in three said they had intended to emigrate even before the revolution. But after they had finally left, 83 percent reported political reasons for their departure. Overall, it seems that the long-term continuation of both political and economic limitations, rather than immediate shortages, gave the impetus for this wave of emigration.

Finally, upon arrival in the United States, most of these refugees had been able to bring their wives and children. They faced in South Florida neither a strange nor an unsupportive environment. Only six men in the entire sample did not have a relative or friend already in the United States, and usually there were many such potential supporters. Nearly everyone in the sample planned to resettle in South Florida, where they could use these social-network resources to help obtain their primary goals: to acquire security and regain their lost social status. They aspired to jobs similar to those they had held in Cuba and were generally optimistic about the possibilities of obtaining them. Indeed, if they had achieved the jobs and income to which they aspired, the men would have reestablished their lost middle-level social positions.

DISCUSSION

The primary purpose of this chapter has been to identify those personal attributes of our sampled immigrants likely to influence the incorporation of these men in the United States. To accomplish this task, we proposed that three sets of stratifying relationships in the countries of origin accounted for the social composition of each wave of emigration. We argued that, rather than pointing to marginal groups or rare events, the characteristics of our sampled men revealed that these individuals had emerged from the center of the principal economic and political transformations experienced by each country since World War II. The task still remains, however, to explain how similar stratifying relationships relate to the migrants' social backgrounds once they have moved outside their country of origin and into the United States.

There is, of course, substantial controversy over the theoretical importance of migrants' individual traits, especially their skills and values, as explanations for social and economic progress in the United States. We reviewed this debate in Chapter 1 and shall pursue it in detail in subsequent chapters. For the present purposes, it is sufficient merely to highlight the principal similarities and differences among the social origins of the two groups and to provide a brief introduction to the social mechanisms through which these background characteristics affect their incorporation into the United States.

We propose two comparative features of the social backgrounds of our sampled migrants as principal clues to the possibly diverse paths of incorporation that each group will follow in the United States. The first involves class and social-status differences. Table 42 reports the principal lifetime occupation for both the Mexican and Cuban migrants. These occupations

Table 42. Principal Lifetime Occupation
in Mexico and Cuba

Occupation	Mexicans		Cubans	
	N	%	N	%
Agricultural laborer	93	12.3	14	2.4
Minor urban service worker	60	8.0	39	6.6
Unskilled urban laborer	113	15.0	28	4.8
Semiskilled urban laborer	181	24.0	44	7.5
Small rural proprietor	0	0.0	11	1.9
Skilled worker	192	25.4	131	22.4
Intermediate service worker	49	6.5	116	19.8
White-collar and minor professional	53	7.0	144	24.6
Medium or large agricultural proprietor	0	0.0	5	0.8
Manager of firm	5	0.7	4	0.7
Professional	8	1.0	50	8.5
Other	1	0.1	0	0.0
Total	755	100.0[a]	586	100.0[b]

[a]Excludes 14 missing observations and 53 persons who were out of the labor market.

[b]Excludes 4 persons who were out of the labor market.

reveal not only the place each migratory flow holds in the political economy of the source country, but also clearly show the divergent class positions each group brings to the United States.

The long-term labor-migrant origins of the Mexican migration are clearly reflected in our sample and stand in contrast to that of the Cubans. First, more than 12 percent of the Mexicans had been farmworkers at home before emigrating to the United States, compared with only 2 percent of the Cubans. Second, a full 47 percent of the Mexicans had originated in urban service or laboring jobs, as opposed to only 19 percent of the Cubans.

The occupational origins of the Cubans, on the other hand, reveal their former positions in the middle-level, petty-commercial sectors of the Cuban economy. Fully one in every four (24.6 percent) worked in white-collar

or minor professional positions, while another 20 percent worked in intermediate service jobs. Taken together, only 14 percent of the Mexicans
worked in such jobs. This contrast is even greater at the level of professional
or proprietary occupations. Eleven percent of the Cubans held these jobs,
compared with a mere 1 percent of the Mexicans.

Similar status differences can be traced through educational backgrounds. On the average, the Cubans received formal schooling three years
longer than the Mexicans: nine years for the Cubans compared with six for
the Mexicans. Both groups, however, were better educated than the average person in their respective homelands.

One particularly noteworthy feature of the social-background comparison is, as we have emphasized throughout this chapter, the degree of occupational heterogeneity within each group. Contrary to conventional theory, the simple description of the Mexican and Cuban migrations according
to "economic" and "political" labels reveals little of the complexity of each
outflow. For example, both groups contain a substantial share of persons
from solid blue-collar backgrounds. Well over a third of each group may be
described this way even if we liberally assign most of the skilled workers to
a middle stratum. Perhaps more significant, however, is that each group
also has a similar proportion of skilled workers, mainly craftsmen, and that
nearly one in every four Mexicans or Cubans arrives in the United States
with this occupational experience. Consequently, even in the midst of distinctive migratory flows, the individuals within each group share, to some
degree, a common social background.

One reason for this similarity is the importance of social networks in
each migration. These networks, founded in and perpetuated through the
emphasis of United States immigration law on family reunification, provide
sufficient resources to allow persons who otherwise could not emigrate to
join the outflow. As we have noted, these resources are not necessarily restricted to the place of origin but are transnational in form. Indeed, the
most significant resource is perhaps the availability of aid once the migrant
enters the United States.

Through these transnational social-support mechanisms the social composition of the migrants becomes directly linked to their subsequent pattern of incorporation. The migrants' personal attributes reveal the individual's location in and access to the network's resources. Class and status
backgrounds represent not only an occupational skill or educational knowledge that may be put to use abroad, but also expose the position the person
will occupy in the stratification system of the United States. Indeed, since
each of our sampled groups is tied closely through these networks to previous waves of migration, the former progress of those who migrated earlier
within this stratification system may largely determine the selection of mi-

grants at the place of origin. Consequently, there is a similar set of stratifying relationships that both makes emigration possible for select persons and determines the boundaries of opportunities for the migrants in the United States. Migrants' personal traits become meaningful at both the place of origin and destination within the context of these social-support mechanisms.

It is likely, however, that the distinct patterns of migration involving our sampled Mexican and Cuban men mean that similar personal attributes may be valued very differently once they are embedded in the different communities of the United States. The historical pattern of low-wage migrant workers circulating between Mexico and the United States has produced extensive social networks tied to characteristically working class Mexican-American communities. As we have seen, many of our sampled men have themselves participated in this circulatory movement, enabling them to spend considerable time in the United States before gaining legal immigration status. Many expected to return to the same communities where they had lived before, many had wives who were United States citizens, and, for many, employers waited for their return.

The social-support networks awaiting the Cubans were just as extensive but of a very different character and form. The history of the Cuban flow, as we pointed out in Chapter 3, has involved a substantial recomposition of part of the Cuban bourgeoisie in South Florida. One principal mechanism has been the reestablishment of Cuban-owned private business. Our sampled migrants enter this context with an occupational profile that complements rather than supplements or competes with those already resettled. And they enter with sufficient anticipated support that the cooperation of these earlier, established Cuban refugees is virtually assured.

Taken together, the class composition of each group and the character of the social networks that each has developed through its respective history only begin to identify the parameters of the highly structured context through which these migrations have occurred. They also merely suggest the possible ways in which personal attributes of the migrants may interact with social resources to form distinctive patterns of incorporation. Yet, by highlighting the importance of larger structural factors in understanding the selection of these two groups of migrants with such varied histories and social characteristics, we have initiated the theme we shall pursue throughout the remaining chapters: the significance of community resources and labor market structure for migrants' social and economic progress in the United States. We shall examine this process of incorporation, which begins in the stratification system of the source countries, as it unfolds within the hierarchically-structured environment faced by Mexican and Cuban Americans in the United States.

5

THE FIRST SIX YEARS

The purpose of this chapter is to begin to address the two most popular classical subfields of immigration research: uses of immigrant labor and social adaptation in the country of destination. Our task is to describe the continuities and changes that the sampled Mexican and Cuban men experienced during their first six years as legal immigrants in the United States. As with the previous chapter, the intent is to lay the groundwork for subsequent, more complex analyses of the processes that account for the immigrants' social and economic positions after this initial period of residence. To this end, we must again take the reader through a lengthy descriptive discourse, relying frequently on tabular data to provide as much information about these men as possible. And yet, as with Chapter 4, our aim here is more than documentary. Although we must leave to later chapters the task of detailed cross-examination of opposing theories, this chapter will identify the principal stratifying relationships formed during the period of initial residence. This analysis will clarify the broad outlines of structurally distinct modes of incorporation.

To guide our story of these first six years, two comparisons will be emphasized. The first and most fundamental concerns time; perhaps more than most fields of social enquiry, the process of immigrant incorporation is known only as it unfolds over the years. Our basic comparison, therefore, involves the immigrants' personal attributes and social positions in 1973–1974, 1976, and 1979, the years of each interview. The second comparison focuses on the divergent experiences of the two groups. While the discussion highlights on occasion direct contrasts between particularly revealing group attributes, the emphasis for now is still on the overall experiences of each group and how, as a group, the Mexicans and Cubans follow different paths into the United States.

The story about to be told is primarily one of the intertwining of class and ethnicity, a theme carried forward in each of the major subsections. The first section describes the geographical distribution of each group after entry into the United States, their arrival in the large cities, and their resettlement into their respective ethnic neighborhoods. Following this, we construct a composite portrait of the men's households and their range of social activity. The focus of this second section is the migrants' social relations, including their access to education in the United States, information about the society, and use of the English language. The final section looks at the immigrants as workers. We concentrate here on their jobs and earnings as well as their social relations in the workplace.

RESIDENTIAL LOCATIONS

Mexicans

The Mexican-born population living in the United States has long been concentrated in five southwestern states: California, Texas, Arizona, New Mexico, and Colorado. For much of the nineteenth century, the proportion living in this territory exceeded 90 percent, reaching a maximum of 97 percent in the last decade. After 1900, and in the wake of increased immigration from Mexico, the concentration in these states declined. By 1970, just three years before our sampled men entered the United States, 86 percent of the Mexican-born population lived in the Southwest.[1]

Obscured by this regional stability, however, was a radical redistribution of the Mexican population among the five states. In 1850, just after much of this territory had become part of the United States and in the midst of the Gold Rush, nearly 50 percent of the Mexican-born residents of the United States lived in California. Another third lived in Texas. But by the beginning of the revolution in Mexico, California contained less than 10 percent of the group. Texas had increased its share to 69 percent, and Arizona, Colorado, and New Mexico approached their historical maximum with 20 percent of the total.

Our sampled men arrived in the United States at a time when, according to the 1970 U. S. census, California had regained its majority share of Mexican immigrants (54.1 percent), and the proportion in Texas had slipped to around a fourth (25.5 percent). Illinois, which in 1900 held less than 1 percent of the Mexican-born population, had gained almost 7 per-

---

1. A. J. Jaffee, Ruth M. Cullen, and Thomas D. Boswell, *The Changing Demography of Spanish Americans*, Table 6.2, p. 124.

cent by 1970. The states outside the Southwest held roughly 10 percent throughout most of the twentieth century.

Historically, this interstate redistribution parallels the changing locations of the economic sectors that employed substantial numbers of Mexican immigrant labor. In particular, the concentration of the Mexican-born in Texas during the late nineteenth and twentieth centuries reflects the area's heavy reliance on Mexican labor during its expansion into large-scale agricultural production. An even clearer correspondence is found in the distribution of the Mexican-born population among rural and urban areas. The twin processes of urbanization and industrialization, similar to those unleashed south of the border that were discussed in Chapter 4, initiated pressures that brought the U. S. resident Mexican population into neighboring cities. In 1910, for instance, only about one-third of this group lived in cities; by 1970, 85 percent lived there. Compared with the total U. S. population, this regional shift meant crossing over from a rural population in 1910 to a more urbanized group in 1970.[2] The cities that received them were among the largest: Los Angeles, Chicago, and Houston.[3]

The extensive transnational social networks identified in Chapter 4 brought and deposited most of our sampled men in these regions of heavy Mexican concentration. Table 43 shows that, when these men entered the United States they evidently had, as a group, a clear perception of where they would resettle. The table demonstrates a remarkable fulfillment of their residential intentions. Since our sample highlights that part of the migratory stream entering and spreading out from Texas, it is not surprising that a substantial proportion (roughly 50 percent) both intended to settle in Texas and, after six years, had done so. The same proportion of men who, upon arrival, intended to move to Illinois (15.6 percent) had also resettled in their chosen location by 1979 (16.0 percent). Indeed, the match of intentions and subsequent behavior is strikingly close for each of the major six states highlighted in the table.

As we mentioned in the description of the sampling procedures in Chapter 3, these men scattered among a relatively large number of cities. Of those who lived in Texas after the six years, more than half (53.1 percent) lived along the border with Mexico: 41.8 percent in El Paso and 11.3 percent in Laredo. El Paso, which was the entry point for most of the men, also represented the single largest concentration for the total sample, with almost one in every four (23.7 percent) still living there. Elsewhere in Texas, the immigrants moved on a much smaller scale into San Antonio (10.5 percent), Houston (8.4 percent), and Dallas (5.4 percent). Next to El

2. Ibid., Table 6.3, p. 132.
3. Ibid., p. 131.

Table 43. States of Residence in
the United States: Mexicans

State	Intended Residence at Entry, 1973-1974		Residence after Three Years, 1976		Residence after Six Years	
	N	%	N	%	N	%
Texas	407	49.6	209	47.6	239	52.5
Illinois	128	15.6	76	17.3	73	16.1
California	108	13.1	69	15.7	62	13.6
New Mexico	40	4.9	15	3.4	19	4.2
Colorado	33	4.0	14	3.2	13	2.9
Arizona	21	2.6	10	2.3	11	2.4
Other U.S. states	84[a]	10.2	27[b]	6.2	32[c]	7.0
Chihuahua	--	--	10	2.3	5	1.1
Other Mexican states	--	--	9	2.0	1	0.2
Total	*821*	*100.0*	*439*[d]	*100.0*	*455*[d]	*100.0*

[a]Includes 30 states in the United States.

[b]Includes 16 states in the United States.

[c]Includes 21 states in the United States.

[d]The figures for 1976 and 1979 in all the tables of this chapter are based on the total number of respondents interviewed at that time.

Paso, however, the city where the largest number relocated was Chicago. Representing 13 percent of all the men, Chicago contained more than three-quarters of those who had travelled as far north as Illinois. Los Angeles, Denver, and Phoenix were also among the major cities of destination.

Once resettled, the men did not change residences very often in the first three years: roughly 50 percent remained at the same address. But this pattern changed considerably after three years, when two of every three men moved to at least one other location. The number of moves increased as well. Between 1973–1974 and 1976, 32 percent changed their residence once, while only 11 percent had moved twice. After 1976 the proportion moving once rose to 35 percent, and those moving two and three times nearly doubled. Throughout the entire six years, less than one fourth (24.0 percent) of

Table 44. Residence in a Central City,
Mexican Immigrants in 1976 and 1979

Location	1976		1979	
	N	%	N	%
In Central City	292	70.3	311	69.4
In SMSA,[a] but not in Central City	70	16.9	43	9.6
In U.S., but outside SMSA	53	12.8	94	21.0
Total	*415*	*100.0*	*448*	*100.0*

[a]Standard Metropolitan Statistical Area.

the group remained at the same residence, while about a third (30.9 percent) had recently moved into their 1979 address (within the last year).

The majority of these moves were within or between the large cities. Table 44 reveals that these men settled and remained inside the central cities of the largest metropolitan areas from the very beginning of their U. S. residence: 70.3 percent lived in the central cities in 1976 compared with 69.4 percent in 1979. This relatively stable urban concentration, however, was accompanied by a much smaller move to the suburbs. In 1976, 17 percent lived within a Standard Metropolitan Statistical Area (SMSA) but outside its central city. This proportion declined by 1979 as half of these suburbanites then resided outside the SMSA. This may reflect on a small scale the apparent nationwide geographical decentralization that took place throughout the 1970s.

The heterogeneity that existed with this group at the time of legal entry continued as the men reached their destinations. The immigrants who had been in the United States prior to their legal entry dispersed throughout the region on a wider scale than those who entered for the first time. And while a similar share of both groups settled in the largest SMSAs, the return immigrants were more than twice as likely to have moved outside the central cities. First-time immigrants showed few signs during these six years of dispersing as widely as these return migrants. Indeed, between 1976 and 1979 they actually become more geographically concentrated.

Given the importance of social networks in directing these men across the border and into the United States, it was hardly unexpected that the overwhelming majority of the immigrants both moved to neighborhoods

Table 45. Ethnic Composition of Neighborhood of
Residence, 1976 and 1979: Mexicans

Predominant Ethnicity	1976		1979	
	N	%	N	%
Anglo	92	21.2	115	25.6
Mexican national, Mexican-American	257	59.4	274	60.9
Mixed	35	8.1	24	5.3
Other	49	11.3	37	8.2
Total	*433*	*100.0*	*450*	*100.0*

whose residents were either other Mexican nationals or Mexican-Americans and remained there throughout the six years. Table 45 shows that nearly 60 percent resettled in these Mexican communities. Twenty-one percent moved into predominantly Anglo neighborhoods in the first three years, with another 4.4 percent joining them by 1979.

An apparent split emerged within the Mexican group, with one subgroup moving to exclusively Mexican neighborhoods while the other concentrated in Anglo areas. This division overlapped the heterogeneity created by the immigrants' paths of entry. The men who had been in the United States the longest actually increased their concentration in Mexican neighborhoods: the proportion rose from 48.5 percent in 1976 to 54.4 percent in 1979. Those living in Anglo communities also increased, but only marginally, from 29 percent to 32 percent. The first-time immigrants, on the other hand, while maintaining an even stronger attachment to the Mexican communities (71 percent in both 1976 and 1979), also experienced a clear movement out of mixed neighborhoods and into predominantly Anglo ones.

The Mexicans also changed from apartment renters to home owners. In 1976, three-quarters (75.5 percent) said they rented; three years later, 40 percent owned their homes. Once again, the two subgroups diverged with time in the United States. In 1976, the first-time and return immigrants were equally likely to be renting their homes. By 1979, the return immigrants had moved ahead as home owners by more than ten percentage points.

In synthesis, these Mexican immigrants dispersed themselves rather widely from their ports of entry in Texas throughout the Southwest and northward into Illinois. They moved into the largest metropolitan areas, where they concentrated in predominantly Mexican neighborhoods of the central cities. Most rented apartments there. The majority remained in these areas, but a smaller group seemed to split off into virtually exclusive Anglo communities. In 1979, there were few living in ethnically mixed neighborhoods. The two subgroups formed by residence in the United States before legal entry moved along quite diverse geographical paths. Compared with first-time arrivals, return immigrants dispersed more widely both among the principal receiving states and away from the metropolitan areas' central cities.

Cubans

The 1970 U.S. census reports that 87 percent of the Cuban-American population, most of whom had arrived since 1960, lived in five states: Florida (45.5 percent), New York (16.4 percent), New Jersey (12.7 percent), California (9.1 percent), and Illinois (3.6 percent).[4] This fairly wide geographical distribution, however, only partially reflects the areas in which Cuban refugees after 1970 were likely to resettle. These figures conceal the overwhelming importance of the Miami area for these later refugees and our sampled men in at least two ways. First, the U.S. government had been trying for a number of years to induce previous waves of Cuban refugees to resettle outside South Florida. This effort largely failed and with time a significant number of those who had settled elsewhere returned to the Miami area. Second, as noted in Chapter 4, the family, relatives, and friends awaiting post-1970 Cuban refugees were themselves concentrated almost completely in South Florida.

Our sampled men followed these social ties closely. As first mentioned in Chapter 3, the migrants intended upon arrival to stay in the Miami area and did so for at least these first six years. By 1979 a full 97 percent lived in this one area and, even when they moved or planned to move to a new address, 95 percent stayed within the same city.[5] Unlike the sampled Mexican immigrants, therefore, the lives of the Cuban men revolved around the changing character of one area of heavy ethnic concentration, the Miami Cuban community.

Within this singular but heterogeneous community, there was a significant shift towards decentralization following the immigrants' initial relocation. Table 46 shows that immediately after arrival more than half of the men (51.7 percent) found homes in downtown Miami. Another quarter (28.1 percent) lived not far away in Hialeah. In 1979, the proportion in the downtown area had dropped to 39 percent, while a roughly equivalent share (34.9 percent) resided in Hialeah. There was also a corresponding increase in the proportion who lived outside the metropolitan area.

---

4. Ibid., p. 248.
5. Alejandro Portes, Juan M. Clark, and Manuel M. Lopez, "Six Years Later," p. 5.

Table 46. City of Residence of
Cuban Immigrants, 1973-1979

City	1973		1979	
	N	%	N	%
Miami, central	305	51.7	160	38.8
Hialeah	166	28.1	144	34.9
In Miami SMSA but outside Central City	40	6.7	24	5.8
Unincorporated Dade County	77	13.1	73	17.7
Other	2	.4	12	2.8
Total	*590*	*100.0*	*413*	*100.0*

Table 47. Ethnic Composition of Neighborhood of
Residence, 1976 and 1979: Cubans

Ethnicity	1976		1979	
	N	%	N	%
Anglo	55	13.0	55	13.4
Cuban	314	74.0	246	59.8
Mixed/other ethnic	55	13.0	110	26.8
Total	*424*	*100.0*	*411*	*100.0*

The neighborhoods in which these men first settled were almost exclusively Cuban, but as more moved away from the downtown area the overall level of ethnic concentration declined. Table 47 shows that three out of every four of these men relocated initially in the Cuban neighborhoods of Miami (primarily Little Havana) and that, by 1979, the proportion had dropped to roughly 60 percent. Unlike the Mexican group, however, the net redistribution resulted in a significant spread into mixed neighborhoods. In 1979, one-quarter of the men lived in heterogeneous communities. The 13 percent who lived in virtually exclusive Anglo communities in 1976 stayed there through 1979.

The Cuban men also differed from the Mexican group in their rate of residential mobility. In the first three years, slightly more than one in every four Cubans remained at their first address; 45 percent moved once. During the same period, the Mexicans showed greater stability: fully half did not move and only 32 percent moved once. After 1976, however, the mobility of the Cubans declined and dramatically shifted in relation to the Mexicans. In this second three-year period, the median number of residences among the Cubans fell from 2.1 in 1976 to 1.5 in 1979. Forty-nine percent stayed at the same residence and another 39 percent moved once. As noted previously, the Mexicans' rate of residential change increased, leaving just a third at the same address in 1979 as three years before.

Like their Mexican counterparts, many Cubans were able to purchase homes in the United States. In 1976, the Cubans started with only 14 percent of the group as home owners (compared with roughly 25 percent of the Mexicans). By 1979, a full 40 percent of the Cubans owned their homes, virtually the same proportion as in the Mexican sample. This increase in home ownership corresponds to the residential shift out of rental housing in Little Havana and into homes in the suburbs.

Overall, the pattern of geographical resettlement for the Cubans is quite different from the wide dispersal experienced by the Mexicans. The Cubans concentrated from the beginning in the principal Cuban city in the United States and remained there for all six years. But within this closely defined area there was a clear trend toward ethnic decentralization, with a significant proportion moving out of Little Havana and into suburbs of mixed ethnicity. This contrasts sharply with the Mexican's polarization into two communities, the majority remaining in ethnic neighborhoods, while those who started out in mixed areas shifted toward virtually exclusive Anglo communities. Finally, reflecting their wider dispersal, with time the Mexicans moved their residence more frequently than their Cuban counterparts.

SOCIAL ADAPTATION

Mexicans

The contribution of social networks to organizing the Mexican immigrants' journeys into American cities manifests itself again in the composition of households constructed after their arrival. Since many of our sampled men gained entry to the United States as spouses of American citizens, it is hardly surprising that the reunion of husband and wife should form the basis of these family groupings. In 1973–1974, more than 80 percent of the men (81.8 percent) were married; in 1976 the proportion had increased marginally to 86 percent, and three years later reached 87 percent. Yet a sizeable proportion of family separations accompanied this household formation: the share of those who were divorced or separated increased from less than 1 percent in 1973–1974 to nearly 6 percent in 1976, where it remained until 1979.

Although the composition of the households changed little throughout the six years, the size of the households increased steadily. Only 5 percent of the Mexican sample lived alone, while the typical household contained just the nuclear family, husband, wife, and children. When others were included, the men's parents, brothers, and sisters were the most frequent residents. Far fewer households contained the wives' parents or more distant relatives. And virtually no one had friends living in his household.

During the first three years, the birth of an additional child enlarged nearly two of every three households (63.4 percent). In 1976 the average household size was slightly greater than 4 persons (4.2) and it increased further over the next three years to almost 5 persons (4.8). According to the 1970 U.S. census, the Mexican family in the United States averaged a similar 4.6 individuals.

Outside their immediate household, however, these men and their wives had a significant number of relatives living in the same area. Roughly two-thirds of the men had at least one relative in the neighborhood and their wives had even more. In fact, the wives had an average of twice the number of relatives in the area as their husbands, obviously reflecting their longer residence in the city and, for some, their birth in the United States. The number of family connections to persons living in other U.S. cities was also substantial, with the men and their wives sharing a similar number.

One of the immigrants' principal activities in the earliest years of resettlement was the pursuit of additional formal education. As the men entered the United States, 82 percent planned to seek more schooling. By 1976, 36 percent had actually attended classes and, between that year and 1979, 25 percent received additional instruction. Language courses were the most popular in the first three years, attracting roughly 22 percent of the sample. Between 1976 and 1979, however, the proportion declined to only 8 percent. One person in every ten (9.6 percent) gained access in the early years to vocational-technical training; by 1979 these classes surpassed English-language instruction, with 13 percent of the men enrolled. Vocational and language courses may have been popular because they were either part-time or lasted only a short while. Throughout the six years, however, the average class was only six months in duration.

The immigrants' wives were much less likely than their husbands to obtain additional education. Only about 10 percent enrolled in courses, which even during the first three years were vocation-oriented. At least part of the reason for this apparently lower educational participation was the wives' superior knowledge of English, evidently resulting from their

Table 48.   Knowledge of English, 1979: Mexicans

Knowledge of English	N	%
No English (0-1 correct answers)	157	34.7
Some English (2-5 correct answers)	171	37.9
Moderate English (6-7 correct answers)	105	23.2
Fluent English (8-9 correct answers)	19	4.2
Total	*452*	*100.0*

much longer residence in the United States. The interviewers rated more than a third of the women (37.9 percent) as fluent in English.

Despite the men's instruction in English and their amount of time in the United States, they did not show a marked improvement in their English-speaking performance. The interviewers judged their speaking ability to be about the same in 1976 and 1979. And in 1979 an objective test of English knowledge, consisting of a series of single phrases and words at elementary, junior, and senior high school levels of reading comprehension, shows a very low level of performance (these items were aggregated to form the Knowledge of English Index—KEI—described in Chapter 3). Table 48 lists the number of items these men were able to translate correctly. Using very liberal cutting points, fully a third (34.7 percent) had essentially no knowledge of English (one or no correct translations), another third (37.9 percent) had only minimal language skills (2 to 5 correct answers), and 27 percent translated at least half the items correctly. Only 4 percent answered most of them successfully.

The immigrants' continued reliance on Spanish after six years (and many more years for the return immigrants) found support in several diverse social contexts. The principal context for reinforcing this language orientation was within the household and among family members. Table 49 compares the primary language used to communicate with relatives in the immigrants' homes between 1976 and 1979. Clearly, Spanish dominates: 83.1 percent used it in 1976 and 72.1 percent in 1979. The decline in exclusive dependence on Spanish within the home is distributed fairly equally among those using English and those who became bilingual. In absolute terms, however, bilingual conversation in the household was more frequent than an exclusive use of English.

Table 49. Language Spoken at Home and to
Relatives, 1976 and 1979: Mexicans

Language	1976 N	1976 %	1979 N	1979 %
English	28	6.4	43	10.8
Spanish	365	83.1	286	72.1
Both	44	10.0	62	15.6
Other	2	0.5	6	1.5
Total	439[a]	100.0	397	100.0

[a]Single persons or persons married but with no children at home: 58.

Table 50. Language of Mass Communication,
1976 and 1979: Mexicans

Language	Newspapers 1976 N	1976 %	1979 N	1979 %	Radio 1976 N	1976 %	1979 N	1979 %	Television 1976 N	1976 %	1979 N	1979 %
English	129	41.7	148	42.8	107	26.1	113	27.5	223	51.7	283	65.8
Spanish	123	39.8	148	42.8	173	42.2	204	49.6	70	16.3	69	16.1
Both	57	18.5	50	14.4	130	31.7	94	22.9	138	32.0	78	18.1
Total	309	100.0	346	100.0	410	100.0	411	100.0	431	100.0	430	100.0

Outside the household, especially when the men were confronted with various forms of mass media, the exigencies of living in a predominantly English-speaking country became evident. Table 50 documents the extent to which the immigrants encountered situations for which, according to the previous indicators at least, they were ill-prepared. In 1976, about half the men (51.7 percent) who watched television, and nearly all did, tuned into English-language programs. By 1979 that proportion had increased to 66 percent. A core of watchers, however, continued to depend primarily on Spanish programs, of which, during these years, there could have only been a few. Most of the increase in those watching English programs came from the group who, in the earlier years, had watched programs in both languages.

Table 51. Ethnicity of Primary Social Relations,
1976 and 1979: Mexicans

Ethnicity	1976				1979			
	Respondent		Wife		Respondent		Wife	
	N	%	N	%	N	%	N	%
Mexican nationals and/or Mexican-Americans	323	76.3	278	75.1	253	55.8	232	58.9
Anglos	7	1.7	9	2.4	32	7.0	36	9.1
Mixed	84	19.9	78	21.1	163	35.9	125	31.8
Other	9	2.1	5	1.4	6	1.3	1	0.2
Total	*423*	*100.0*	*370*	*100.0*	*454*	*100.0*	*394*	*100.0*

Among the media listed in Table 50, television was the least likely to have programs routinely available in Spanish. Consequently, it was the medium in which the largest proportion of the immigrants relied on English transmissions. When Spanish communications were more readily available, not only did more turn to them, but the proportion who did so increased marginally over time. Forty percent of the men read a Spanish-language newspaper in 1976; 43 percent did so in 1979. Similarly, 42 percent listened to Spanish radio programs in 1976 and, by 1979, the share had increased to 50 percent. The expanded use of Spanish-language mass media, however, was not at the expense of the English-language audience. Instead, the tendency was to turn to either an exclusively Spanish or completely English program or newspaper. That is, there was a progressive bifurcation with a marked decline in bilingualism in all three media.

The immigrants were also able to use their Spanish in fairly wide social circles. The previously mentioned concentration in ethnic neighborhoods undoubtedly provided a source of language support. In addition, Table 51 documents the fact that many of the men's primary social acquaintances were also potential Spanish-speakers. In 1976, only 2 percent of the men listed Anglo-Americans as involved in their key social relationships. Instead, three out of four of both the immigrants and their wives circulated socially only with other Mexican nationals or Mexican-Americans. This tendency still existed by 1979 even though the proportion had declined markedly to around 56 percent. During this time, a corresponding increase occurred in bicultural social relations, where Anglos and Mexican-Americans were fairly equally involved. Those with Anglo acquaintances also increased, but the proportion

Table 52.   Knowledge of U.S. Society,
1979: Mexicans

Number of Correct Answers[a]	N	%
No knowledge (0-1)	98	21.5
Some knowledge (2-5)	299	65.8
Moderate knowledge (6-7)	50	11.0
Extensive knowledge (8-9)	8	1.7
Total	*455*	*100.0*

[a]Answers are to items composing the U.S. Information
Index, described in Chapter 3.

remained low—less than 10 percent. While these results demonstrate a strong shift toward interethnic relationships, they also suggest continuing widespread support for use of the Spanish language.

The men's participation in local organizations also reflected their strong ethnic attachment. Although throughout the six years roughly two-thirds of the men did not belong to a local organization, when they did participate most of the members of the group were Mexican (70 percent). For a minority, however, these organizations may have offered the only opportunity outside the workplace to come into contact with Anglo-Americans, since 30 percent of their membership belonged to this latter group.

An additional important dimension of social adaptation is the immigrants' level of information about the receiving society. Language loyalty and strong ethnic attachments might suggest that information levels among these Mexican men were probably low. This possibility can be empirically examined. In 1979, a battery of items was included in the questionnaire to measure the immigrants' objective information about American society. These questions included recognition of political figures at the state and national levels, knowledge of American institutions and economic conditions, and a number of practical concerns in everyday life. A subset of these items converged into a unidimensional scale—the U.S. Information Index (USIN), described in Chapter 3. Of interest here are the distributions of correct answers to these questions and their differences across samples.

Table 52 reports the number of correct answers. Only 8 respondents were able to answer eight or more of the ten items correctly. Fully 87 percent were unable to respond to half of the questions and one in every five

(21.5 percent) could not even answer two items. These results support the above expectation of low levels of information among Mexican immigrants. Knowledge of U.S. society was in fact so limited that few systematic differences among the men could be discerned.

Cubans

Unlike their Mexican counterparts, most members of the Cuban refugees' immediate families arrived with them in Miami in 1973–1974. Over the following six years, both the size and composition of that family changed very little. The proportion married changed by only 6 percentage points and only a few couples had any additional children. This household stability probably reflects the men's relatively advanced average age. It certainly helps to explain the large difference in their fertility behavior when compared with Mexican immigrants. In the first three years, for instance, only 8 percent of the Cubans, compared with 63 percent of the Mexicans, had an additional child.

For most of these six years, the average number of persons in the immigrants' households was 3.8, virtually the same as the number in average households among all Cubans living in the United States in 1970 (3.7 persons).[6] Seven percent of the men lived alone, while only 10 percent lived with just one other person. More than half the households contained only the husband, wife, and their own children, but both the husband's and wife's parents were also common household members. Distant relatives and close friends were very unlikely to be living with these families.

Both the men and their wives had numerous relatives throughout the Miami area. Three out of every four had at least one relative living in the city: the average was almost three persons. More than half the men (51.7 percent) also had relatives who lived in other cities in the United States.

Like Mexican immigrants, the Cuban men and their wives devoted much of their earlier years to acquiring additional schooling. At the time of arrival, 34 percent of the men planned to continue their education. In the first three years, 43 percent actually received some formal classroom instruction (compared with 36.4 percent of the Mexicans). Between 1976 and 1979, however, the level of participation dropped to just 30 percent. During this latter period, the Cuban men again enrolled at higher rates than the Mexicans but by a much narrower margin: 29.8 percent of the Cubans attended classes compared with 25.0 percent of the Mexicans.

Language instruction was the most popular course in the first three years, but gave way to vocational training after 1976. Table 53 shows that while one in every four attended English-language classes in the earliest

6. Jaffee, Cullen, and Boswell, *The Changing Demography*, p. 249.

Table 53. Formal Education in the United States,
1976 and 1979: Cubans

Education	1976		1979	
	N	%	N	%
None	242	56.8	294	71.2
Language	105	24.6	39	9.4
Vocational	25	5.9	46	11.1
University	8	1.9	15	3.6
Revalidate title	21	4.9	13	3.2
Other	25	5.9	6	1.5
Total	*426*	*100.0*	*413*	*100.0*

years, only one in ten did so after 1976. Those enrolled in vocational courses, on the other hand, increased their share of the total from 6 percent to 11 percent. Unlike the Mexican group, a small but noteworthy group attended classes designed to recertify the professional training they had attained in Cuba.

The duration of these classes followed a similar pattern in the early years as those attended by the Mexicans. Sixty-one percent of the classes lasted six months or less, compared with 66 percent of those taken by the Mexicans. The classes taken after 1976, however, were of longer duration; their average length stretched to more than seven months.

The Cuban refugees' wives were able to enroll in classes much less frequently than their husbands. Between 1976 and 1979, while just less than a third of the men attended classes, only 21 percent (20.6 percent) of the women received similar formal instruction. The women concentrated their classes primarily in vocational training (9.3 percent) and secondarily in English instruction (6.2 percent). Unlike the wives of the Mexican immigrants, however, these Cuban wives were not superior to their husbands in their comprehension or use of English. In 1979, the wives reported their English knowledge as both better and worse than their husbands'. Three percent said they spoke English very well, compared with less than 1 percent of the men. But 33 percent of the wives also said they spoke no English at all, a much greater percentage than the men (21 percent).

Although the men believed their English had improved significantly, their overall level of English comprehension was low after the six years.

Table 54.   Knowledge of English,
1979:   Cubans

Correct Answers	N	%
No knowledge (0-1)	185	44.8
Some knowledge (2-5)	130	31.5
Moderate knowledge (6-7)	62	15.0
Fluent (8-9)	36	8.7
Total	*413*	*100.0*

For instance, in 1973, 62 percent said they knew no English at all; by 1979, that proportion had dropped to 21 percent. Those who felt they were fluent or near fluent climbed from 14 percent to 38 percent. There was, however, a large gap between these self-evaluations and the results obtained in the objective comprehension test (described previously). Table 54 lists the scores on the test. After six years in the United States, 38 percent of the men were unable to answer a single item correctly. If we add to that group those who answered only one item successfully, then almost 45 percent did not understand any English—twice the proportion indicated by their self-reports. With another third demonstrating they had only some knowledge of the language, more than 75 percent answered fewer than half of the items correctly.

Conversation within the household, just as for the Mexicans, was the principal social context for reinforcing the maintenance of Spanish. In 1976, fully 98 percent of the men spoke exclusively Spanish within the private domain of their homes. Only one person interviewed spoke English most of the time. By 1979, the proportion using Spanish was still overwhelming, 91 percent, and those speaking English amounted to only 2 percent.

In more public spheres, the men could also rely successfully on their more familiar Spanish. Table 55, for example, shows that, throughout the six years, the men had access to Spanish-language mass media. Indeed, the striking character of these figures is how little English was actually used. Of course, as was true for the Mexicans, access to television was largely in English. In both 1976 and 1979, about half the Cuban men watched English programs. Roughly one in five watched only Spanish programs, an understandable consequence of the existence of only one Spanish television channel in Miami. When access to alternative Spanish-language media

Table 55. Language of Mass Communication,
1976 and 1979: Cubans

Language	Newspaper				Radio				Television			
	1976		1979		1976		1979		1976		1979	
	N	%	N	%	N	%	N	%	N	%	N	%
English	41	12.0	40	11.2	37	9.9	55	14.0	197	48.4	198	49.1
Spanish	232	67.8	250	69.6	276	73.8	276	70.0	91	22.4	106	26.3
Both	68	19.9	69	19.2	60	16.0	62	15.7	118	29.0	98	24.3
Other	1	0.3	0	0.0	1	0.3	1	0.3	1	0.2	1	0.3
Total	342	100.0	359	100.0	374	100.0	394	100.0	407	100.0	403	100.0

was available, as with newspapers and radio programs, the overwhelming proportion of the men used them. Readers of Spanish newspapers made up 68 percent in 1976 and 70 percent in 1979. Similarly, 70 percent listened exclusively to Spanish radio programs. An additional group, relatively stable over time, read and listened to newspapers and radio in both languages.

Given the large heterogeneous Cuban community into which these men resettled, it is not surprising that the vast majority would have other Cubans as principal social acquaintances. In 1976, 83 percent circulated virtually exclusively in a Cuban social environment, while less than 1 percent mentioned Anglo-Americans as involved in these social relations. By 1979, the same tendency was dominant: nearly three out of every four had only Cuban friends and acquaintances.

The decline in ethnic social concentration, however, did not result in greater participation in exclusively Anglo circles. Rather, the significant increase was in the group whose social relations were ethnically mixed, rising from 13.8 percent to 23.7 percent. The men's wives followed similar tendencies toward completely Cuban social relations: 88 percent in 1976 and 80 percent in 1979. As in the case of Mexicans, a decline in exclusively intraethnic relationships was apparent; still, the dominance of Spanish continued to be cemented by the preference of the vast majority for close social relationships within their own ethnic community.

The Cuban men participated more often in local formal associations than did their Mexican counterparts. In the earlier years, only about a third in each group belonged to these organizations. Yet, while the Mexicans maintained this level, Cubans increased it to more than 50 percent. Thirty-four percent of the Cubans belonged to a local church, 13 percent were

Table 56.   Knowledge of U.S. Society,
1979: Cubans

Correct Answers	N	%
No knowledge (0-1 correct answers)	23	5.6
Some knowledge (2-5 correct answers)	198	48.2
Moderate knowledge (6-7 correct answers)	116	28.2
Extensive knowledge (8-9 correct answers)	74	18.0
Total	*411*	*100.0*

members of professional organizations, 9 percent attended their local PTA meetings, and 5 percent participated in unions. The majority of the members of these associations were Cuban (65.2 percent). In fact, over the entire six years only one in five of the refugees participated in local groups in which they would have the opportunity to socialize with a significant number of Anglo-Americans. Wives participated in these predominantly ethnic organizations about as frequently as their husbands.

Though similar to Mexican immigrants in their patterns of language use and ethnic relationships, Cuban exiles acquired a significantly greater knowledge of American society. As Table 56 shows, in 1979 the distribution of responses to the objective U.S. Information Index indicates that only 6 percent of respondents were virtually ignorant of the society around them. Most of the men demonstrated a moderate to extensive familiarity with the range of political, economic, and practical issues covered by the test.

LABOR-MARKET PARTICIPATION AND INCOME

Mexicans

The large number of sampled immigrants who had lived in the United States before they immigrated legally, plus the extensive social network constructed during these previous moves, meant that from the moment of arrival a close, predictable connection existed between the immigrants' future residences and their places of employment. Table 57 documents what proved to be a striking correspondence. When the men arrived in 1973–1974, a full 79 percent knew where their employers lived. Forty-nine percent named Texas, 17 percent Illinois, and 12 percent California. Six years later, virtually the same proportions lived and worked in each state: overall, 78.2 percent had employers in these three states waiting for them and 82.1 percent lived in the same states in 1979.

The men also seemed remarkably well informed about the types of jobs they would occupy once in the United States. Table 58 compares their expected occupation at the time of arrival with the job actually held in 1976 and 1979. The table also includes the immigrants' last occupations in Mexico and their occupational aspirations as they entered the United States. Columns 2, 3, and 4 show several significant disparities between the immigrants' early expectations and subsequent attainments, but overall the distributions are very similar. And in every occupational category the readjustments that occur after 1976 move the overall distribution closer to the immigrants' original expectations.

Semiskilled laboring jobs are areas of frequent employment for immigrants in most advanced industrial countries because they involve only min-

Table 57. States of Residence in the
United States of Mexican Immigrants
and Their Employers

State	Residence of U.S. Employer, 1973-1974		Current Residence, 1979	
	N	%	N	%
Texas	322	49.4	239	52.5
Illinois	108	16.5	73	16.0
California	80	12.3	62	13.6
New Mexico	32	4.9	19	4.2
Colorado	30	4.6	13	2.9
Arizona	20	3.1	11	2.4
Other	60[a]	9.2	38[b]	8.4
Total	652	100.0	455	100.0

[a]Includes thirty-one U.S. states.

[b]Includes twenty-one U.S. states and two Mexican states (1.1 percent had returned to Chihuahua).

imal on-the-job training and are often indistinguishable from unskilled work except for the character of the machinery they involve.[7] Table 58 shows that a large proportion of our sampled men became semiskilled laborers once in the United States. Only one-fourth (25.2 percent) of the men worked at such jobs in Mexico, but after three years in the United States more than half (51.5 percent) were so employed. And even though the proportion declined by 1979, these men were still much more likely to work as carpenters, bakers, butchers, and machine operatives with some "training" than they had been in Mexico or had expected when they arrived in the United States.

The resulting occupational distribution after six years was also much more concentrated than in Mexico. Roughly 11 percent were agricultural laborers in Mexico, but only 6 percent remained in these jobs by 1979. At the other end of the distribution, there were declines in the proportion who were employed as white-collar and intermediate service workers (clerks,

7. Stephen Castles and Godula Kosack, *Immigrant Workers and Class Structure in Western Europe.*

Table 58. Occupational Expectations and Attainments: Mexicans

Occupational Classification	Last Occupation in Mexico		Expected Occupation 1973-1974		Occupation in 1976		Occupation in 1979		Occupational Aspirations 1973-1974	
	N	%	N	%	N	%	N	%	N	%
Agricultural laborer	82	10.7	69	9.8	40	4.9	24	5.7	23	4.4
Minor urban service worker	73	9.5	77	10.9	25	6.1	43	10.2	10	1.9
Unskilled urban laborer	122	15.9	165	23.4	61	14.9	67	15.9	26	4.9
Small rural proprietor	1	0.1	--	--	--	--	--	--	--	--
Semiskilled urban worker	193	25.2	202	28.6	211	51.5	175	41.5	81	15.4
Skilled urban worker	167	21.8	136	19.3	60	14.6	81	19.2	209	39.7
Intermediate service worker	65	8.5	24	3.4	2	0.5	14	3.3	60	11.4
White-collar worker	51	6.6	20	2.8	23	5.6	13	3.1	43	8.2
Medium or large agricultural proprietor	0	0.0	1	0.2	1	0.2	0	0.0	3	0.6
Manager and owner	4	0.5	6	0.9	5	1.2	3	0.7	30	5.7
University professional	9	1.2	6	0.9	2	0.5	2	0.5	39	7.4
Total	767[a]	100.0	705[b]	100.0	410[c]	100.0	422[d]	100.0	524[e]	100.0

[a]Missing observations: 4; out of the labor force: 51.

[b]117 respondents did not answer or expected to be out of the labor force.

[c]29 respondents did not answer or were not employed at wave 2.

[d]33 respondents did not answer or were not employed at wave 3.

[e]298 respondents had no aspirations or were not employed.

drivers, tailors, barbers, and the like). Skilled urban laborers, mainly craftworkers, suffered an initial decline in the first three years, but by 1979 the proportion had recovered to approximately the same level as in Mexico and in the distribution of early occupational expectations.

Columns 4 and 5 of Table 58 reveal a significant gap between the jobs the men aspired to and those they eventually secured by 1979. Four of every five men aspired to skilled employment; only one in five expected or achieved it. On the other hand, 11 percent were employed in 1979 as unskilled laborers although only 5 percent had initially aspired to such jobs. In general, the immigrants' aspirations went largely unfulfilled: they desired jobs that involved far greater skill and status than they were able to obtain either after three or six years in the United States.

The large differences between the immigrants' 1976 occupations and those they expected upon arrival and later obtained may be due, in part, to the influence of the 1975 recession, but no great shift occurred in the proportion who were unemployed. In 1976, 5 percent were out of work; by 1979 the rate had declined to 4 percent. Still, between 1976 and 1979, roughly 40 percent reported having been unemployed at least once, including 23.1 percent only once, 8.4 percent twice, and 8.1 percent three or more times. When unemployed, the majority went for more than two months until they found other jobs. When the men were interviewed for the last time in 1979, half had been at their current jobs for three years. One in four (27.8 percent), however, had been there for only less than a year.

The top half of Table 59 shows that, in 1976, Mexican immigrants were employed almost completely (95.6 percent) as wage workers in private firms. Only 2 percent were public employees and under 3 percent were self-employed. By 1979 their work had changed only marginally: 91 percent were still private salaried workers, 3 percent worked in public jobs, and the proportion of the self-employed had risen to 6 percent. The men's wives, when they worked outside the home, followed a similar pattern. In 1976, about a third were employed, with the overwhelming proportion (92.7 percent) working as private wage laborers. Another 6 percent were public employees. In 1979, the same proportion had jobs, and the share of private employees had increased to more than 97 percent. Compared with their husbands, however, most of the women had been employed only a short while: two years as opposed to three.

Since most of the men were married, they did not depend solely on their own employment for earnings. Indeed, owing to the household division of labor that developed over these six years, the wage employment of the men's wives contributed substantially to the household income. The wives worked most frequently as semiskilled laborers (30.6 percent). Unlike their hus-

Table 59. Type of Worker, 1976 and 1979: Mexicans

Work Type	1976		1979	
	N	%	N	%
Respondent				
Salaried, private	393	95.6	385	91.0
Salaried, public	8	2.0	14	3.3
Self-employed	10	2.4	23	5.5
Unsalaried	0	0.0	1	0.2
Total	411	100.0	423	100.0
Wife				
Salaried, private	114	92.7	132	97.1
Salaried, public	7	5.7	3	2.2
Self-employed	1	0.8	0	0.0
Unsalaried	1	0.8	1	0.7
Total	123	100.0	136	100.0

bands, however, they also concentrated in white-collar (22.4 percent) and service (23.9 percent) jobs. White-collar jobs, which for many were clerical (secretaries, bookkeepers, keypunch operators, and the like) became more important between 1976 and 1979. Yet the more significant trend during this period was simply an increase in occupational heterogeneity.

Given the size and composition of the households, it is not surprising that few of the other residents worked for wages outside the home. In 1979 only 10 percent (9.6 percent) of the households contained persons other than the husband and wife who worked. Of course, some had more than one additional worker. Many were the immigrants' fathers or sons, followed less frequently by their brothers and daughters. The immigrants' mothers and sisters were the least likely to contribute in this way. The most frequent coresident workers, however, were distant relatives and close friends. Although their presence was infrequent in absolute terms, the potential monetary contribution from all these additional workers was significant. On average they earned $638 a month. Indeed, this amount represents a larger contribution than that made by the immigrants' wives, who, in 1979, averaged roughly $580 a month.

For the men, monthly wages increased significantly during this period, although in real terms the change was relatively modest. In 1976, the average monthly wage was approximately $470; by 1979 it had climbed to $906. A more revealing change, however, occurred in the wage distribution. In 1976 the median exceeded the mean by well over $100: $590 compared with $470, respectively, suggesting a concentration in very low-wage jobs. By 1979, the distribution had shifted in a completely opposite yet more conventional direction. The median in this later year was $800, while the mean surpassed it at $906 a month. This significant increase in the average reflects the "pull" of high wages among a minority of immigrants, which, in turn, indicates an increasing economic differentiation within the sample.

Most of these men worked in small- to medium-sized firms. About 18 percent were employed by relatively large firms that listed more than one thousand total employees. But the majority of the Mexicans worked for firms with only modest labor forces: 20.3 percent had between one hundred and five hundred total employees, 23.9 percent between twenty-one and one hundred, and 20.6 percent between six and twenty. These figures, however, do not capture the precise character of the immigrants' workplace, since almost half (43.5 percent) reported working in only a branch of their firms. Consequently, the size of their local workplaces was much smaller. For example, compared with the 18 percent in large firms of more than a thousand workers, none of the immigrants worked in local shops with that many employees.

Within these smaller, local shops, the immigrants' unskilled and semiskilled jobs typically meant that very few occupied positions with any formal authority over the work process. In 1979, 76 percent of the entire sample said that they supervised no one in their jobs but that instead they were supervised. Among the rest, 8 percent supervised more than five persons, 2 percent more than sixteen, and one person had authority over one hundred workers.

The Mexicans' jobs were also overwhelmingly nonunion. In 1979, a full 73 percent said they were not union members. This figure, however, reveals only part of the story, since 70 percent (70.1 percent) said that no union was available for them to join. Where a local union existed, more than 90 percent (91.2 percent) had joined.

Anglo-Americans employed most of these immigrants. Columns 1 and 2 of Table 60 show that 75 percent (74.5 percent) of the bosses in 1976 were Anglos and that the proportion increased to almost 80 percent by 1979. The proportion employed by other Mexicans remained about the same: 16.2 percent in 1976 and 15.1 percent in 1979. The majority of their co-workers,

THE FIRST SIX YEARS   189

Table 60. Ethnicity of Work Relations,
1976 and 1979: Mexicans

Ethnicity	Owner				Co-workers			
	1976		1979		1976		1979	
	N	%	N	%	N	%	N	%
Anglo	313	74.5	322	79.5	73	17.2	113	27.2
Mexican national and/or Mexican-American	68	16.2	61	15.1	228	53.8	224	54.0
Mixed	--	--	--	--	71	16.7	41	9.9
Other Ethnic	39	9.3	22	5.4	52	12.3	37	8.9
Total	*420*	*100.0*	*405*	*100.0*	*424*	*100.0*	*415*	*100.0*

however, were Mexican. The third and fourth columns of the table demonstrate that more than half of the men worked throughout the six years in firms that employed virtually all Mexican nationals or Mexican-Americans. There was a significant rise in the proportion working primarily among Anglo workers (from 17.2 percent to 27.2 percent), but this shift occurred at the expense of those who had initially found work in firms hiring an ethnically mixed workforce. These figures suggest that, rather than moving toward greater integration, the group again moved in two sharply opposite directions. The majority remained concentrated in jobs employing mostly Mexican workers, while a significant minority gained access to firms with an Anglo workforce.

The ethnic character of the immigrants' economic relations was also evident in their consumption patterns. Table 61 discloses the ethnicity of ownership in stores where immigrants purchased most of their durable goods and smaller items. In 1979, clearly most of the purchases were from Anglo-run stores: 63 percent for small items and 78 percent for durable goods. And, following previous trends, the return immigrants were significantly more active in the Anglo sectors than the first-timers.

Finally, in 1979, one in every five of the men believed that they had many opportunities to advance in their jobs, and almost half (47.9 percent) thought that at least some opportunities were available. More than 25 percent, however, felt that after six years in the United States they had no opportunity for advancement. When asked directly about their job and wage satisfaction, only 4 percent reported dissatisfaction with their jobs and just 11 percent reported dissatisfaction with their salaries.

Table 61. Ethnicity of Ownership of Stores
Used by Immigrants: Mexicans, 1979

Ethnicity	Durable Good 1979		Small Items 1979	
	N	%	N	%
Anglo	346	78.3	276	63.0
Mexican national and/or Mexican-American	68	15.4	121	27.7
Other Hispanic	9	2.0	18	4.1
Black	--	--	1	0.2
Mixed	14	3.2	18	4.1
Other	5	1.1	4	0.9
Total	442[a]	*100.0*	438[b]	*100.0*

[a]Missing observations: 13.

[b]Missing observations: 17.

In sum, the economic activities of the Mexicans represented the dispersal of a wage-labor supply throughout the Southwest labor market. The circulatory character of the flow brought many of these men back to preestablished employers and jobs. As a group, their initial dislocations from the jobs they intended to obtain in the United States were relatively short-lived. Most of the men became semiskilled laborers, which represented an increased occupational concentration in a single job category compared with their jobs in Mexico. In addition, although from the beginning and at each subsequent interview only about 5 percent were unemployed, many experienced temporary spells of unemployment. The group's wages increased throughout the period but most remained low-wage workers. Finally, the majority worked in nonunion shops where most of their co-workers were Mexican nationals or Chicanos, but the owners of the firms were Anglo.

Cubans

Our sampled Cuban men arrived in South Florida with occupational aspirations that well exceeded their past attainments. Six years later, many fell short of the status of even those jobs left behind on the island. But, as

Table 62 demonstrates, the story of these occupational changes is a fairly complex one. Since the proportion of skilled workers in the group remained fairly stable throughout the journey, they form a convenient vantage point from which to interpret the diversity. In Cuba, roughly 22 percent of the men were skilled craftworkers, and upon arrival in the United States a slightly larger proportion aspired to this category. During the first three years, an initial decline occurred in this category among the Cuban subjects, but by 1979 the number of skilled craftworkers had risen again to virtually match the original. And, after those six years, the group had virtually regained the proportion who had aspired to skilled jobs.

The other occupational categories did not experience anything close to the proportional stability of skilled workers. Yet they did share two characteristics. First, between 1973–1974 and 1976 there was a marked overall decline in the level of jobs that these men were accustomed to performing. For example, 7 percent were service laborers (janitors, gardeners, and the like) in 1973; by 1976 the proportion had risen to 13 percent. Similarly, the proportion of unskilled industrial laborers jumped from only 5 percent in Cuba to, in 1976, nearly 10 percent in the United States. By 1979, the picture looked better, at least for the men in these unskilled jobs. The urban service workers had moved to other jobs and the proportion with jobs as laborers had fallen below the corresponding figure in Cuba.

Semiskilled industrial workers showed the most dramatic changes. Only 8 percent of the men held such jobs in Cuba, but by 1976 that share had climbed to 29 percent. Undoubtedly, this increase was a further reflection of the downward shift in the entire group's occupational status. Unlike the unskilled laborers and service workers, however, the proportion of semiskilled workers continued to rise over the entire six years. By 1979, more than one-third of the sample (34.5 percent) were employed in this category.

Conversely, white-collar workers followed a significant decline. In Cuba, white-collar jobs were the modal occupation, comprising 25 percent of the sample. After three years in the United States, the share had plummeted to just 10 percent (10.3 percent). It remained at this level for the next three years.

The second group characteristic, suggested by the skilled workers but experienced by them on a much smaller scale, was the gap between the men's initial occupational aspirations and their subsequent attainments. As a group, the men who aspired to intermediate service work were the most unfortunate, falling short of their goals by a greater percentage than any other group: 31.7 percent aspired to this occupation but only 5.9 percent of the entire sample attained it by 1979. In addition, only a fraction of the men aspiring to become professionals (13.8 percent) were able to reach their goal (6.4 percent).

Since the first interviews were conducted only a short while after

Table 63. Type of Worker, 1976 and 1979, Cubans

Type of Work	1976		1979	
	N	%	N	%
Respondent				
Salaried, private	335	90.5	297	76.0
Salaried, public	4	1.1	11	2.8
Self-employed	28	7.6	83	21.2
Unsalaried	3	0.8	0	0.0
Total	370	100.0	391	100.0
Wife				
Salaried, private	231	95.9	224	92.9
Salaried, public	4	1.6	4	1.7
Self-employed	6	2.5	12	5.0
Unsalaried	0	0.0	1	0.4
Total	241	100.0	241	100.0

arrival, it was very difficult to judge the level of unemployment at that time. By 1976, however, it was clear that a sizable proportion did not have jobs (13.3 percent). This may have been due to the severe 1975 recession. Yet it is instructive that, by 1979, the jobless group had shrunk to well below 4 percent (3.6 percent). And almost all of these men were disabled or retired.

Total unemployment over the entire six years adds support to the impression of strong labor-force participation by the entire sample. A full 75 percent of the men had never been unemployed in the United States and another 15 percent had been out of work only once. When these refugees were out of work, their search for another job lasted, on average, only a few months. This relatively stable employment picture does not mean, however, that most respondents remained with the same employer. In only the last three years, for instance, roughly 40 percent of the men changed their jobs at least once.

The top half of Table 63 shows that the vast majority of the sampled refugees were private-salary workers. Compared with the Mexicans, however, the most significant difference is the proportion who became self-employed: 8 percent of the Cubans versus 2.4 percent of the Mexicans. By 1979, the difference in self-employment had widened considerably. At a time when the self-employed in the Mexican sample increased to just 5 percent, more than one in every five Cuban men (21.2 percent) had come to own and operate his own business or professional office. Correspondingly, the proportion engaged in private-wage employment declined to 76 percent. This pattern corresponds with the expected increasing participation of these immigrants in the expanding Cuban enclave in Miami.

The bottom half of Table 63 reveals the extent and nature of the wives' contributions through work outside the household. With about two-thirds of the wives working, their potential wage contribution was substantial. By 1979, for example. the wives earned an average of $543 a month. Evidently, very few worked as unpaid family labor for the businesses run by their husbands: only less than 1 percent explicitly reported that they did not receive a wage for their work. Fully 92 percent received a wage from a private firm (although this could have been the family business). Outside the home, the wives worked primarily as semiskilled workers (59.9 percent). Both occupations employed a relatively large share of these women, as compared at least with their husbands, and overall indicated a much greater occupational concentration.

Not only did the Cuban men's wives work more frequently than the Mexican immigrants' wives, but also a much larger proportion of their household members were actively engaged in employment outside the home. In 1979, 27 percent of the household members other than the husband and wife held a job (compared with 9.6 percent for the Mexicans). Relationships with those who worked were also very different. The most frequent workers were immediate family members, especially sons and daughters. Other relatives and close friends also participated frequently, while the men's fathers, mothers, brothers, and sisters were virtually unrepresented. And, unlike the Mexicans, these additional workers on average earned less than the wives, roughly $417 a month.

The sampled refugees earned $413 a month in 1973–1974; the comparable median in 1979 was more than double that amount, $869. Taking inflation into account, however, the gain was much less impressive. In 1973 dollars, median earnings in 1979 had not yet exceeded 1.5 times the original figures. The average also obscured an interesting feature of the entire distribution of income for the group. In 1979, median monthly earnings were $869, while the mean had reached $1,068. As in the case of the Mexicans, this reflects the pull of higher earnings among a minority of immigrants. It also adds to both the residential and occupational figures as evidence of increasing internal differentiation within this sample.

Table 64.   Ethnicity of Work Relations,
1976 and 1979, Cubans

Ethnicity	Owners				Co-workers			
	1976		1979		1976		1979	
	N	%	N	%	N	%	N	%
Anglo-American	186	50.1	175	44.4	68	17.7	55	14.9
Cuban	145	39.1	193	49.0	262	68.4	217	58.6
Mixed/Other Latin	40	10.8	26	6.6	50	13.9	98	26.5
Total	*371*	*100.0*	*394*	*100.0*	*383*	*100.0*	*370*	*100.0*

The Cubans worked in firms that were of similar size to those in which the Mexicans were employed. They were, however, somewhat less likely (33.4 percent) to have worked with a firm that had many branches. Medium-sized firms were the largest employers, most frequently having between twenty-one and one hundred workers. Only 12 percent worked alone, which meant that the much larger share who said they were self-employed employed other workers.

The character of most of the Cubans' skilled and semiskilled work was such that few had direct authority over fellow workers. Seventy-one percent in 1979 did not supervise any other workers, and those who did were limited to only a few subordinates. Of course, the substantial percentage of the Cubans who were self-employed gives the group a much different character than the Mexican group in this regard.

Also, the Cubans were even less likely than the Mexicans to be union workers. In 1979, fully 91 percent worked in nonunion jobs. Like the Mexicans, however, this lack of union participation was related strongly to the availability of labor organizations: 87 percent reported that no local union existed. Still, when a union was available, a much smaller proportion of the Cubans became union members (65.4 percent).

Perhaps the largest and most important difference with Mexican immigrants was the ethnicity of the Cubans' work relations. Table 64 shows that a much greater proportion of Cubans than Mexicans worked in firms whose owners were from the same ethnic group. This proportion even increased over time, rising from 39.1 percent in 1976 to fully 49 percent in 1979. Contrary to the Mexican experiences in the labor market, the proportion of

Cubans working for Anglo-Americans decreased with time. In the earlier years, about half the Cubans worked for Anglos, but this proportion dropped to 44 percent in 1979. These results are again consonant with the consolidation of an immigrant enclave economy in Miami, a phenomenon that is explored further in Chapter 6.

Within the Cuban sample, more than half the immigrants worked in places employing mostly Cubans: 68.4 percent in 1976 and 58.6 percent in 1979. The apparent decline in ethnically exclusive work relations did not, however, initiate a corresponding increase in those employed in firms hiring mostly Anglos. Instead, as Table 64 indicates, a shift occurred out of both exclusive categories—either all Cuban or Anglo—and into firms employing both ethnic groups in roughly similar proportions. Over the six years, in fact, the share in these mixed workforces nearly doubled, rising from 14 percent to 27 percent.

The Cubans' consumption activities were involved in the Miami Cuban community as much as their employment and residential experiences were. Unlike the Mexicans, they often made routine purchases at stores owned and operated by other Cubans. Table 65 shows that slightly more of the Cubans shopped for small items at Cuban-owned shops than at those run exclusively by Anglo-Americans or operated by both Anglos and Cubans. This proportion compares to a full 63 percent of the Mexicans who bought smaller items from Anglo-run stores. The Cubans clearly purchased durable goods, however, from stores operated mostly by Anglos (66.3 percent). Yet even here the proportion was significantly less than for the Mexicans (78.3 percent).

Throughout the six years, the Cubans remained fairly optimistic about future employment opportunities. In 1976, 14 percent believed that many opportunities existed to fulfill their occupational aspirations. At the end of the period, 17 percent still believed that these opportunities were available. However, the proportion who felt in 1976 that such chances did not exist (22.1 percent) increased to more than a third of the sample (34.5 percent) by 1979. Nevertheless, even this relatively large number of men who no longer expected to advance further toward their aspirations did not prevent the entire group from reporting overwhelmingly high levels of satisfaction with both their jobs and their earnings.

In sum, Cuban refugees collectively experienced a substantial initial decline in their occupational status. Their rate of unemployment also rose to a significant level during the first three years. Although, by 1979, they had partially recovered their lost status and unemployment among them had declined dramatically, they still had not reached the level of their original occupations in Cuba or their aspirations for life in the United States. Their experiences, however, had two distinctive features that contrasted

Table 65.   Ethnicity of Ownership of Stores
Used by Immigrants: Cubans, 1979

Ethnicity	Small Items		Durable Goods	
	N	%	N	%
Anglo	134	32.7	263	66.3
Black	2	0.5	1	0.2
Cuban	138	33.7	81	20.3
Anglo and black	1	0.2	0	0.0
Anglo and Cuban	131	31.9	45	11.2
Latins	4	1.0	8	2.0
Total	*410*	*100.0*	*400*	*100.0*

with those of the Mexican sample. From the beginning, Cubans were nearly four times as likely as Mexicans to be self-employed, and, by 1979, 20 percent had become employers. More importantly, the majority of the men who were wage workers were employed by owners of firms who belonged to the same ethnic minority. These two factors reflect the pivotal role of the Miami enclave economy in guiding the process of incorporation of recently arrived Cuban immigrants.

DISCUSSION

Obviously, we have not attempted to offer an interpretative account of the many complex trends and comparisons examined in this chapter. Each of the next four chapters will examine in greater detail the topics of employment, social relations, and subjective perceptions and orientations touched on here. Also, we have postponed for our final chapter the theoretical discussion of these results. Nevertheless, a few simple summary observations may be made on the three general areas of focus presented here: residence, social adaptation, and employment.

As is generally the case, the portrait of the experiences of these immigrants does not fit neatly with any prior expectations stemming from different theoretical perspectives. Overall, the two groups exhibited several contradictory and unanticipated traits. The Mexicans dispersed throughout the country on a much greater scale than the Cubans, who concentrated exclusively in South Florida. Yet, within their several principal locations, Mexicans clustered in Mexican *barrios* and, over time, the large majority remained there. Rather than showing an increasing integration of ethnic groups over time, the Mexican pattern suggested a marked polarization: most immigrants held onto their residences in inner-city ethnic neighborhoods, while a smaller group moved away into virtually exclusively Anglo neighborhoods.

Cubans, on the other hand, fully concentrated in the Miami metropolitan area, clustering at the start in the inner-city neighborhood known as Little Havana. Later on, however, there was a significant move out of this and similar areas into mixed ethnic suburbs. The Cubans followed a path of concentrated decentralization or dispersion within relatively well-defined community boundaries.

Both groups sought additional education in the United States in the areas of English-language instruction and vocational training. Yet both groups spoke very little English after six years. One reason was that each group was able to rely on the local ethnic community, which offered a supportive context for the continuing dominance of the mother tongue. These ethnic ties, however, meant different things for the two groups, at least in terms of their knowledge of American society. The filtering of information about the United States through the Spanish-language press and media left Mexicans significantly less informed than Cubans.

Potentially, the principal activities shaping both the immigrants' knowledge of American society and their other experiences and perceptions include the social relations encountered through work, either on the job or as a consequence of the earnings and location of employment. Occupational gains for each group were modest after six years, certainly not fulfilling the immigrants' own aspirations. Their real earnings also increased slowly. Nevertheless, the two groups occupied very different positions in the occupational–class structure of the local areas where they settled.

These contrasting paths of incorporation do not agree with general expectations derived from orthodox economic and social-assimilation theories; nor do they unambiguously coincide with the conflict-based labor-market-segmentation perspectives. We believe that the principal source of factual discrepancy, and the primary difference between the two groups, is that they have entered social contexts that are both structurally diverse and largely unanticipated by past theories. These contexts have been formed by the specific historical development of economic activities and ethnic residential patterns. The Mexican migration, as a whole, represents a wage-labor flow, creating ethnic communities that take on the character of poor inner-city neighborhoods. As with any minority, a fraction will "make it," largely by gaining access to whatever resources are available in the broader Anglo-dominated economy. The apparent polarization of the Mexican sample mirrors this development.

The social context for Cuban refugees is, however, the distinct one of an economic enclave created by earlier exile cohorts.[8] Characteristic of this formation are, first, the growth and visible presence of immigrant enterprises and, second, the fact that the average immigrant does not need to go beyond the physical and social limits of the enclave to carry out many routine activities. The rapid rise in self-employment is an indication of this unique context, as are the substantial numbers of sampled refugees employed by other Cuban exiles.[9]

These divergent paths of incorporation suggest that, despite similar levels of reliance on Spanish and ethnic social relations, various individual traits will have very different effects in terms of promoting labor-market success and structuring the immigrants' social lives, depending on the specific context in which they operate. Finally, in addition to those dimensions distinguishing the process of incorporation of each immigrant group, it is clear that both have become increasingly heterogeneous, economically and socially, over time.

In the next four chapters, we examine determinants of this process and its different manifestations in both samples. In particular, the analysis focuses on the interface between individual-level variables and structurally distinct social contexts as they have affected immigrant economic attainment, social relationships, and cultural orientations over time.

8. Portes, Clark, and Lopez, "Six Years Later," pp. 19–22.
9. Kenneth L. Wilson and Alejandro Portes, "Immigrant Enclaves."

6

THE CUBAN ENCLAVE IN MIAMI

This chapter examines the labor-market experiences of Cuban refugees in Miami. Our aim is to continue the analysis of survey results initiated in Chapter 4, weaving together the themes of class and ethnicity in order to explain economic and social positions of the sampled refugees after six years of resettlement. In contrast to that of the previous two chapters, however, the focus here is more analytical than descriptive and, where appropriate, utilizes relatively complex multivariate techniques.

This analysis of labor-market behavior corresponds to the third theoretical area outlined in Chapter 1—the uses of immigrant labor. In that chapter, we presented four perspectives on this economic theme: orthodox economic theory, internal colonialism, the cultural division of labor, and segmented-labor-market views. The major difference among these theories was their contrasting emphasis on individual attributes as opposed to structural characteristics of the labor market. For this reason, we return now to the discussion in the first chapter to help organize the presentation of survey results. The importance of identifying the dimensions of an ethnic enclave as a viable alternative path of labor-market incorporation provides the rationale for the following sequence of analytical tasks.

MODES OF INCORPORATION

Conventional labor-market theories maintain two distinct assumptions regarding immigrant workers. Immigrants face an openly competitive labor market in the United States and, as a result, the primary determinants of their economic positions and progress are the individual skills they "bring with them" from abroad. If the immigrants face initial disadvantages in the U.S. labor market or find themselves in lower level jobs than expected, the reason lies in the inappropriateness of their personal skills or abilities. Technical skills and education acquired in their home country either are inferior to those possessed by U.S. workers or are geared to a specific type of labor practice no longer available in the United States. In either case, immigrants have difficulty transferring their knowledge and ability to the new economy. To overcome these disadvantages, they must invest in the acquisition of new human capital through retraining in the United States.[1]

We have argued throughout the previous chapters, however, that immigrants do not arrive on the shores of the United States as isolated individuals clutching only their personal resources as tools for resettlement. Rather, in addition to individual capacities, immigrants have access to the resources of the larger social groups of which they are part. The organization of these groups, which we saw in Chapter 4, helps explain both the origins and stability of the migratory flow and establishes the availability and limits of opportunities for the individual immigrant. As before, the organization of this larger group is based upon three sets of stratifying relationships: economic position (class and status), access to social networks, and state-policy reactions. The reorganization of these relationships, as they confront the structure of the American economy, contributes to the formation of a segmented context of resettlement. Complementary but unequal positions in this context constrain immigrants' employment possibilities and create differentiated paths of labor-market incorporation.

Since orthodox labor-market theories provide few insights into this process, we turn first to a review of the various perspectives that propose criteria for identifying the specific dimensions of the structural context in Miami. Following this, we turn to the empirical investigation of paths of incorporation entered by refugees in our survey.

Labor-Market Segments

Most studies of immigrant labor from the structural perspective concentrate on participation in one tier or another of a segmented labor market.[2] Recall from Chapter 1 that these sectors are typically distinguished along dimensions of job stability, opportunities for career advancement, and the monopoly or competitive character of the sector in which the firm is situated—to name only a few dimensions. For our purposes here, one im-

1. See Barry R. Chiswick, *An Analysis of the Economic Progress and Impact of Immigrants.*

2. Stephen Castles and Godula Kosack, *Immigrant Workers and Class Structure in Western Europe*; Saskia Sassen-Koob, "The International Circulation of Resources and Development: The Case of Migrant Labor."

portant distinction between the sectors is that hypothesized experiences of immigrants in the primary labor market tend to match more closely conventional assumptions concerning the economic payoff of individual skills and abilities. Immigrants are employed in the primary sector according to their occupational skills and certification, while ethnicity or other less formal social connections make only a minor contribution to matching immigrants with employers.

Opportunities for job advancement, particularly through well-defined "career ladders," are also expected to be available to immigrants in the primary sector. Consequently, after a sufficient length of time in the United States, primary-sector immigrants should be able to climb the job ladder to reach levels of remuneration and status comparable to those of domestic workers.

Jobs in the primary sector represent, however, a path of economic insertion available only to *certain* groups of newcomers. This path, regarded as the "normal" one by orthodox theories, is actually restricted to immigrants with certifiable professional, managerial, or technical skills. These immigrants are often recruited deliberately in their home countries or are encouraged to emigrate through the various occupational preferences of United States immigration law.

State policies also work with informal social and economic mechanisms to direct other immigrant groups to the secondary labor market. Here, the terms and conditions of employment are hypothesized to be opposite those in the primary sector. Ethnicity, not individual skills, combines with the immigrants' working-class backgrounds to link secondary-sector employers to these new laborers.[3] Employers find in immigrant workers a certain vulnerability that enforces low wages and work conditions unacceptable to the domestic working class. Indeed, the unstable jobs, rapid turnover, and undesirable working conditions of the secondary labor market have become synonymous with the "ethnic" background of its employees. The result is that these jobs are further devalued in the eyes of domestic workers, who then resist accepting them. When native and immigrant laborers find themselves together in this sector, ethnically based antagonisms are frequently exploited to maintain a weak workplace bargaining position for both groups.[4]

As familiar as these divisions into primary and secondary labor markets have become, however, they do not exhaust the variety of sectors into which immigrants can become incorporated. One reason is that research

---

3. See Alejandro Portes, "Modes of Incorporation and Theories of Labor Immigration."
4. See Antonio Jorge and Raul Moncarz, "International Factor Movement and Complementarity."

from this perspective has focused almost exclusively on immigrant work-ers.[5] Another related reason is the tendency to restrict the analysis to only one primary stratifying relationship, economic position. Even ethnicity, for example, which we shall stress below as a crucial dimension of the social networks that organize migrations, has been treated by labor-market stud-ies as simply a trait that defines the worker's economic status. The result is an incomplete portrait of the diversity among current immigration flows and an overemphasis on the economic functions performed by them.[6] Structurally distinct modes of incorporation exist that may alter the applica-bility of these sectoral distinctions.

Ethnic Enclaves

As seen in Chapter 2, ethnic enclaves are a distinctive economic forma-tion, characterized by the spatial concentration of immigrants who orga-nize a variety of enterprises to serve their own ethnic market and the gen-eral population.[7] Two traits of economic enclaves are fundamental: (1) the presence of immigrants with sufficient capital, either brought from abroad or accumulated in the United States, to create new opportunities for eco-nomic growth, and (2) an extensive division of labor. Typically, this division develops through a successful transplantation of an entrepreneurial class from origin to destination during the first waves of the migration. The growth of this class and the expansion and diversification of its activities offer later arrivals from the same group employment opportunities virtu-ally unavailable to immigrants entering other labor-market sectors.

Entrepreneurial activities can thrive in this situation because they are able to reproduce, on a local scale, some of the features of monopolistic control that account for successful firms in the wider economy. For exam-ple, subsequent mass arrivals from the home country provide immigrant entrepreneurs with privileged access to a source of low-wage labor and new consumer markets. As exemplified by the histories of early Jewish and Japa-nese immigration in Chapter 2, there are definite advantages to invoking the principle of ethnic solidarity. Ethnic entrepreneurs have repeatedly used it to inhibit unionization and fight opposition among their workers. Ethnic solidarity also provides the basis for effective forms of capital accu-mulation through pooled savings and rotating credit systems.[8]

The organization of an immigrant enclave economy typically requires recent arrivals to take a tour of duty at the worst jobs. The willingness of

5. For example, see Michael J. Piore, *Birds of Passage.*

6. Michael Burawoy, "The Function and Reproduction of Migrant Labor."

7. Portes, "Modes of Incorporation," 1981.

8. Ivan H. Light, *Ethnic Enterprise in America;* Edna Bonacich and John Modell, *The Economic Basis of Ethnic Solidarity.*

immigrants to remain in this condition rather than move to higher-paid occupations in the open economy has been often explained by such factors as lack of knowledge of the host-country language or inadequate skills. Such explanations fail to take into account the built-in mobility opportunities in this mode of labor-market incorporation.[9] Immigrant workers willingly remain in subordinate jobs because these jobs open paths of mobility unavailable in the outside. These opportunities are connected with the expansion of immigrant firms, which create managerial-level openings for members of the same minority, or with opportunities for self-employment.

The principle of ethnic solidarity, utilized by successful entrepreneurs, also prescribes the promotion of members of the same minority and the support of their economic activities. Skills and contacts acquired in established firms furnish the basis for frequent moves into self-employment. In this way, a class of low wage earners in an ethnic enclave may move up, in a matter of years, to managerial-level jobs or into petty enterprise. The economic rewards reaped from this mode of labor-market incorporation frequently place the enclave workers' standard of living between that of domestic majority workers, who predominate in the primary sector, and that of impoverished minorities long relegated to the secondary labor market.[10]

Although the organizing principles of the ethnic enclave are clear, its boundaries may seem ambiguous for at least two reasons. First, since the enclave is dependent upon successful entrepreneurial activities, its boundaries may fluctuate and be as flexible as the market for consumer goods produced by these ethnic firms. Second, the boundaries of the enclave are dependent upon the fluidity of ethnic-group borders in general. As a form of social affiliation, ethnicity involves special bonds among people of similar origins and, conversely, a separation from those who are different. Clearly, these boundaries change with time and are likely to fluctuate with the success or failure of ethnicity to "pay off" in economic terms.

Finally, we must also distinguish enclaves from immigrant neighborhoods.[11] Most immigrant groups initially resettle in ethnically concentrated communities and generate a few small businesses to serve immediate, specialized consumption needs. Ethnic neighborhoods fulfill important social

9. Bonacich and Modell, *The Economic Basis of Ethnic Solidarity.* See also Illsoo Kim, *New Urban Immigrants;* Kenneth L. Wilson and Alejandro Portes, "Immigrant Enclaves."

10. When this pattern emerges, the immigrant group as a whole is often labelled according to the miraculous performance of the first-wave entrepreneurs. The exceptional individual skills, initiative, and abilities attributed to entrepreneurs by orthodox theorists are then erroneously applied to the entire immigrant group. These misplaced assumptions are used in turn to "explain" the relative economic advantage of enclave workers. The result is an invidious comparison between immigrants and domestic ethnic minorities based on the alleged differential motivations of each group.

11. See Alejandro Portes, "Reply to Rogg."

support functions, but lack the extensive division of labor of the enclave and, especially, its highly differentiated entrepreneurial class. Ethnic neighborhoods have been the norm in the early adaptation patterns of most immigrant minorities; the formation of ethnic enclaves has been, by and large, the exception.

INSERTION IN THE CUBAN ENCLAVE

Type of Employment

Our first task in investigating the Cuban enclave in Miami is to examine the characteristics of those sampled men who have become entrepreneurs. As mentioned in Chapter 5, only 8 percent of the refugees had acquired their own business after three years in the United States. By 1979, however, one in every five (21.2 percent) had established himself as owner and operator of a business or professional service. Clearly, this proportion makes self-employment a significant feature of this group's insertion in the Miami economy. For this reason, in the following three subsections, we examine differences between these entrepreneurs and refugees who remained wage earners in terms of their industrial and occupational locations, background, individual characteristics, and early resettlement experiences.

Industry and Occupation

Table 66 presents the industrial sectors in which both entrepreneurs and wage earners were employed in 1979. The data reveal three characteristics among the self-employed. First, most of these individuals are concentrated in industrial sectors that reflect intermediate positions in the local economy. Four industrial sectors account for more than three out of every four of the self-employed men: retail trade (24.2 percent), business and repair services (24.1 percent), professional services (12.0 percent), and construction (16.9 percent). While the other three sectors are clearly middle-level activities, the 17 percent with firms in the construction industry requires a brief additional comment.

As mentioned in Chapter 3, the construction industry in Miami is particularly well-integrated in the Cuban enclave. In 1977, Cuban-owned construction firms in the Miami metropolitan area grossed more than $43 million. These firms represented 38 percent of the total number in the area.[12] It is unlikely, however, that construction firm owners among our sample of refugees have become the medium- and large-scale contractors upon which this high level of ethnic participation developed. Instead, construc-

12. Antonio Jorge and Raul Moncarz, "The Cuban Entrepreneur and the Economic Development of the Miami SMSA."

Table 66. Industrial Sector by
Type of Employment, 1979

Industrial Sector	Self-employed		Employee	
	N	%	N	%
Agriculture	5	6.0	2	0.6
Mining	0	0.0	2	0.6
Construction	14	16.9	30	9.7
Manufacturing, durable	4	4.8	54	17.5
Manufacturing, nondurable	2	2.4	64	20.8
Transportation, communications, other public utilities	4	4.8	17	5.5
Wholesale trade	3	3.6	18	5.8
Retail trade	20	24.1	38	12.3
Finance, insurance, real estate	0	0.0	11	3.6
Business and repair services	20	24.1	24	7.8
Personal services	1	1.2	14	4.5
Entertainment and recreation services	0	0.0	2	0.6
Professional and related services	10	12.0	28	9.1
Public administration	0	0.0	4	1.3
Total	*83*	*100.0*	*308*[a]	*100.0*

[a] Persons unemployed in 1979: 21; missing observations: 15.

tion is a type of industry that provides, through subcontracting, many opportunities for new arrivals to establish their own smaller-scale operations.

Second, despite the industrial-sector concentration, there is substantial heterogeneity among the self-employed. Types of firms vary widely, even within the same sector, and there are considerable differences in the size and ethnic composition of their workforces. Of those who operated retail stores, the majority owned drinking and eating establishments (a frequent activity for new immigrant entrepreneurs), jewelry stores, gasoline service stations, and apparel stores. (See Appendix Table B for a complete listing of detailed industrial-sector categories by type of employment.)

Taken as a group, a full 77 percent of these owners said the majority of their employees were Cuban. The size of the workforce, however, was relatively small, employing on the average between ten and twenty workers. In retail, the stores were even smaller: they averaged fewer than five workers. One man, however, owned a grocery store with a maximum of twenty employees, while two others owned gasoline stations of similar size. Fifty percent of the small restaurant owners, and all of the other retailers, hired primarily other Cubans as employees.

Business and repair-service enterprises were equally heterogeneous. The largest share of owners in this sector operated automobile repair shops; a second group ran electrical repair stores. Overall, these shops had slightly more employees than did the retail stores. In contrast to those in the retail sector, however, one man in this sector had acquired a firm of considerable size. He owned an automobile service shop that employed more than one hundred workers. The majority of these employees were other Cubans. Several advertising and management consulting firms also employed more than twenty workers.

Not surprisingly, eight out of the ten men engaged in professional services were doctors and dentists. Several had established a small private practice with fewer than five employees, while others owned modest clinics employing up to twenty workers. Two accountants also set up private firms in which fewer than five individuals were employed.

As anticipated, the construction firms run by these refugees were small subcontracting enterprises. Roughly half were general building contractors, while the others concentrated in special trades. Both sets of contractors maintained only a small pool of workers, typically fewer than five. Roughly 90 percent had mostly Cuban workers in their firms at the time of the interview in 1979.

The third characteristic of self-employment shown by the figures in Table 66 involves the contrast between the industrial sectors of these entrepreneurs and those who remained wage earners. While only 7 percent of the entrepreneurs established their firms in manufacturing, where capital requirements are presumably more substantial than in retail or service, a full 38 percent of the wage earners found jobs in these sectors. Many of these manufacturing jobs, however, were in sectors where Cuban entrepreneurs had established themselves earlier. For example, textiles, which we identified in Chapter 3 as an area of concentrated Cuban ownership, employed one out of every four (26.6 percent) of the sampled men who worked in nondurable manufacturing firms. Similarly, nearly 17 percent of those employed in the nondurable manufacturing sector had found employment in furniture and wood products, industries in which Cubans have been frequent entrepreneurs.

Reflecting the character of these manufacturing jobs, the wage earners

in this sample worked in firms that were much larger than those owned by
their fellow refugees. In textiles, for instance, the average firm employing a
Cuban refugee maintained a total workforce of more than one hundred
workers. Frequently, these firms employed as many as five hundred. This
size difference is particularly noticeable within the retail sector, which
ranked third as an employer of these refugees and first as a type of firm with
which to begin one's own business. In the latter case, the total number of
employees was often fewer than five. In contrast, retail stores in which the
refugees found jobs were major employers in general. On the average,
these retail stores hired close to one hundred workers. These larger stores
also employed a majority of Anglo workers.

Wage earners employed in professional services also work in very different firms than self-employed professionals, despite the fact that each
group has nearly an equal proportion in such enterprises. The majority of
the employees worked as salaried hospital and health-service technicians
rather than as physicians who owned their own practices. These professional employees also worked in the larger hospitals, frequently with well
over one thousand other employees. In only 10 percent of the cases were
most of their fellow workers Cuban.

These industrial-sector differences between the self-employed and employees are reflected to a large extent in the contrast between the groups'
occupations in 1979. The data in Table 67 show, for example, the obvious
occupational tasks required of owners and operators of small businesses: 23
percent of the self-employed worked as managers or administrators compared with only 6 percent of the wage earners. Another 16 percent of the
entrepreneurs were professionals or technicians. Equally predictable,
given the disproportionate share of wage earners employed in manufacturing, are the very low percentages of the self-employed engaged in operative
and laboring jobs.

The data in Table 67 also show that the largest proportion of the men in
either group had skills as craftworkers. Even this similarity, however, is
misleading. When we examine in detail the three-digit occupational codes
of the census, it becomes clear that the self-employed are engaged in activities of a very different kind from those of the employees (see Appendix
Table C for a complete listing of these detailed occupations by type of employment). The self-employed have occupations that can be relatively easily organized in private, small-scale operations that provide services to a
limited market. These services include automobile and electrical repair as
well as both general and specialized carpentry. Less frequent than these
skilled tradesmen are watchmakers, photoengravers, plasterers, plumbers,
roofers, sign painters, and tile setters.

In contrast, craftsmen who work for others are most frequently general

Table 67. Occupation by Type
of Employment, 1979

Occupation	Self-employed		Employee	
	N	%	N	%
Professional, technical	13	15.7	26	8.5
Manager, administrator	19	22.9	17	5.6
Sales	7	8.4	7	2.3
Clerical	1	1.2	23	7.5
Craft	30	36.2	90	29.4
Operator, nontransport	0	0.0	71	23.2
Operator, transport	4	4.8	17	5.6
Laborer, nonfarm	7	8.4	27	8.8
Farmers	1	1.2	0	0.0
Farm laborers	0	0.0	0	0.0
Service	1	1.2	28	9.1
Private household	0	0.0	0	0.0
Total	83	100.0	306[a]	100.0

[a] Persons unemployed in 1979: 21; missing observations: 17.

carpenters, radio and television repairmen, and foremen. A small number, however, had crafts that could be transformed in the future into privately operated services; electricians, air conditioning and heating equipment mechanics, and auto mechanics were among this group. This potential for future private enterprise does not seem to be present in the employee's activities in other sectors. As operatives, this latter group is fairly well tied to either larger machinery or industrial production tasks. The group includes solderers, cutting operatives, assemblers, packers and wrappers, and meatcutters. Similarly, among those employed in service jobs, nearly half (46.4 percent) were janitors.

Differences between the two categories of refugee employment that we have analyzed in this section are most sharply reflected in the income data. The development of an ethnic enclave represents, in essence, a mechanism of differentiation of class positions within a previously homogeneous mass of immigrant workers. Among the self-employed, two such positions can be

Table 68.   Income by Type
of Employment, 1979

	Class Position	N	Mean Monthly Earnings	t
I.	Employees	306[a]	$ 974	
II.	Self-employed without workers	44	$1193	1.76* (II-I)
III.	Self-employed with workers	31	$1924	2.14* (III-II)

[a]Totals exclude those unemployed in 1979 and missing observations.

*p < .05 (one-tailed test).

distinguished: full-time owners who employ others, and those who employ only themselves. Average income differences between these positions are presented in Table 68.

Salaried workers have the lowest average income followed by independent entrepreneurs without employees. The income difference between these two groups is statistically significant. Entrepreneurs with hired workers, however, far exceed the income of the other two categories. This latter group includes two owners who hired ten or more workers on a regular basis and whose average income exceeded $3,200 per month. The income difference between entrepreneurs with and without employees is also statistically significant.

In sum, these results show a clear line of differentiation among the men in this sample based on their type of employment. Not only has a significant proportion of the men become self-employed, but the firms they have established appear well situated in intermediate positions in the local economy. Several immigrant entrepreneurs have also generated employment for other Cubans. Unlike the earlier waves of "golden exile" businessmen, doctors, and lawyers, however, these new businessmen have formed relatively small enterprises. Still, their activities have yielded substantial economic returns, especially when the income of employers is compared with those of refugees who remained salaried workers. Results for the wage earners are important too. Although they are concentrated in a few industrial sectors that employ relatively large numbers of other Cubans, their occupations are sufficiently heterogeneous to lead us to anticipate variation in their labor-market locations. This possibility will be examined in detail in a section below.

Individual and Background Characteristics

We turn now to examine whether the men who became self-employed in 1979 started their resettlement experience with background characteristics different from those of the refugees who remained employees. We also ask to what extent their seven years in the United States produced different outcomes. Although the immigrant entrepreneur has been a popular, even folkloric, character of the immigration literature, few attempts have been made to study the process by which only a fraction of some groups of newcomers successfully become established as businessmen.

For this reason, we briefly identify three different sets of expectations about the process of becoming an entrepreneur in the early years after immigration. Expectations of conventional economic theories are that future entrepreneurs will possess specific traits, even drives, that will generate the risk-taking motivations necessary to start a new business venture. A second expectation is a simple reproduction thesis: those who are able to transfer sufficient capital from abroad will be able to reestablish their former class position. A modified version holds that entrepreneurs living abroad may choose to join the migration precisely to take advantage of emerging opportunities in the new immigrant communities.[13]

Finally, a third set of expectations focuses upon the needs of the enclave satisfied through the availability of self-employment as a viable path of incorporation. To a large extent, self-employed "middlemen" play a crucial role in maintaining the level of integration of economic tasks characteristic of this sector. Of course, these three sets of expectations are not mutually exclusive. Even in the latter case, in which self-employment opportunities are collectively reinforced, those who take advantage of the openings are also the ones who successfully draw upon other necessary resources.

Table 69 presents the mean scores for both the self-employed and wage earners on a selected list of background characteristics. Also reported are the probabilities that these mean scores will be equal; the lower the probability, the less likely are the two groups to have similar average characteristics. The selected variables represent three sets of attributes or experiences ordered according to their temporal sequence. The largest group consists of attributes which these men had as they entered the United States. This first set ranges from age at arrival to expected aid from families and friends. The second set includes variables that measure the refugees' experiences during the first three years of resettlement. They include all variables, from months of formal education before 1976, to the proportion with Anglo employers in the same year. Finally, the last three variables in the left-hand column of Table 69 make up the third set, representing attributes acquired throughout all seven years in the United States.

13. Bonacich and Modell, *The Economic Basis of Ethnic Solidarity.*

Table 69. Background Characteristics by Type of Employment, 1979

Variable[a]	Self-employed		Employee		Probability
	X̄	S.D.	X̄	S.D.	
Age at arrival	38.65	6.10	41.21	7.46	0.004
Father's occupational prestige--SEI	31.96	23.00	26.97	19.13	0.046
Father's years of education	6.70	3.97	5.79	2.36	0.008
Respondent's occupation in Cuba--SEI	41.19	24.54	37.64	21.20	0.191
Respondent's years of schooling in Cuba	9.10	4.09	8.52	3.65	0.217
Occupational aspirations at arrival--SEI	39.76	28.59	30.56	27.90	0.008
Salary aspirations at arrival	7.67	1.89	7.12	1.46	0.005
Modernity index	0.10	0.78	0.02	0.83	0.482
Achievement motivation index	0.15	0.79	0.00	0.78	0.135
Knowledge of English at arrival	0.06	0.97	0.01	0.98	0.643
Expected aid from family and friends at arrival	1.68	1.09	1.67	1.03	0.932
Months in courses in U.S. before 1976	4.07	6.34	2.54	4.17	0.009
Knowledge of U.S. society in 1976	3.19	1.74	2.88	1.83	0.192
Occupational prestige in 1976--SEI	41.25	15.73	34.30	13.54	0.001
Salary in 1976 ($)	749.44	444.51	606.19	286.55	0.001
Proportion with Anglo employers in 1976	0.30	0.46	0.50	0.50	0.005
Knowledge of English in 1979	3.24	3.07	2.73	2.92	0.160
Knowledge of U.S. society in 1979	5.40	2.05	5.16	2.27	0.389
Months in courses in U.S. from 1973 to 1979	8.44	13.14	5.88	10.72	0.067

[a]Pairwise deletion of missing data. In 1979, 83 persons (21.2 percent) were self-employed and 308 (78.8 percent) worked as employees for wages.

Results in Table 69 show that self-employed men differ from the group of employees in their backgrounds in several important ways. They are younger, they aspired to greater status and salary, and their fathers were better educated and held higher-status jobs. However, on measures that directly tap social psychological traits claimed to be correlates of entrepreneurial drive—achievement and modern orientations—the two groups show no appreciable differences. In addition, although parental statuses differed, the refugees themselves had similar educational and occupational standings in Cuba. Finally, as they entered the United States, the two groups shared equivalent English language skills and had the same expectations about future aid from family and friends.

Once in the United States, however, the experiences of the two groups soon diverged. Those who later became self-employed spent most of these early years in school. As early as 1976, despite similar levels of general knowledge of United States society, the future entrepreneurs had gained higher status jobs and, on the average, earned $143 more per month than those who would continue to work for someone else. Interestingly, the future entrepreneurs were also significantly less likely than their counterparts to work for Anglo employers in 1976.

These early experiences acquire greater importance as we examine the variables included in the third set. Measuring cumulative experiences throughout the seven years in the United States, these variables show that in 1979 the two groups had no differences in their average level of English knowledge, general knowledge of American society, or length of time enrolled in courses. These results suggest that the principal sources of variation between the two groups lie in their earliest encounters with the American economy.

The bivariate comparisons in Table 69 offer several background traits and experiences as potential predictors of the refugees' type of employment after seven years. Significant contrasts were found for variables that represent each of the three sets of theoretical expectations reviewed previously. For example, the self-employed men's parental-status backgrounds and their younger ages support both the simple reproduction thesis and the risk-taking traits emphasized by orthodox economic theory. Given this promising set of potential predictors, we can estimate a multivariate model using type of employment as the dependent variable and a smaller, more selective list of independent variables.

Table 70 presents the results of a logistic regression of type of employment on a subset of predictors representing background characteristics and experiences. This technique estimates the logarithm of the probability of self-employment in 1979 as a linear function of a constant term and the additive effect of each independent variable.

Table 70. Logit Estimates of Effects of Background Characteristics
and Experiences on the Probability of Self-Employment
and Ethnicity of Employer (Standard Errors in Parentheses)

Predictors	Self-employment in 1979[a]		Ethnicity of Employer in 1976[b]	
	Logit Coefficient	First Derivative[c]	Logit Coefficient	First Derivative[d]
Constant	.382 (1.148)	.064	-.594* (.251)	-.146
Father's years of education	--[†]	--	--	--
Age at arrival	-.081** (.028)	-.014	--	--
Education in Cuba	--	--	--	--
Occupational aspirations-- SEI	--	--	--	--
Expected aid from family and friends	--	--	-.313** (.098)	-.077
Achievement motivations	--	--	--	--
Length of courses in U.S. before 1976--months	.068** (.027)	.011	.042* (.020)	.010
Occupational prestige in 1976--SEI	--	--		
Salary in 1976	.002** (.000)	.0003		
Anglo employer in 1976	-.894** (.356)	-.150		
Self-employed in 1976	4.068** (.809)	.684		
Length of courses in U.S. before 1979--months	--	--		
-2 x log likelihood χ^2	229.43			
Chi square for no effect of variables	76.08 5 df $\rho < .001$		20.51 2 df $\rho < .001$	

[a]Self-employed is coded 1; employee, 0.   [b]Anglo employer is coded 1; Cuban or other ethnic employer, 0.

[c]Computed as $b_i P^* (1-P^*)$, at $P^* = .214$; where b_i is the coefficient of each predictor and P^* is the proportion of the sample that is self-employed.

[d]Same as note 3 except $P^* = .561$.   *Significant at .05.

[†]Insignificant effects, deleted from final estimation.   **Significant at .01.

For ease of presentation, we have also included in Table 70 the first-order partial derivative of each predictor. Each derivative may be interpreted as the effect of a one-unit increase in the independent variable on the actual probability of becoming self-employed. The derivatives are calculated using the sample proportion as the estimate of the true probability of self-employment.[14]

Results in Table 70 clearly indicate the need to integrate contrasting theoretical expectations about the nature of the process of becoming self-employed. As suggested by the bivariate results, relative youthfulness increases the probability of leaving wage employment. Each additional year of age decreases the probability of self-employment by roughly one percent (−.014). This result is not surprising, since it is younger adults who generally adjust more quickly to changes induced by resettlement and who can afford the risks of new ventures. Access to additional schooling in the United States also aids entrepreneurial activity. Each additional month adds to the likelihood of self-employment by about 1 percent.

Perhaps more significant, however, are the variables that do not yield reliable contributions to type of employment. These represent an impressive array of individual resources and propensities, including education, aspirations, expectations, and motivations. The strongest predictors of employment in 1979 are those associated with experiences in the United States. In addition to the retraining noted above, one step towards opening a new business is apparently gaining access to a higher wage. This probably reflects the need to accumulate sufficient capital to cover initial start-up costs. According to these results, however, those costs represent a significant share of monthly earnings. For example, for a person to increase his chances of self-employment by only 3 percent, his monthly wages would have to increase by $100.

Not surprisingly, self-employment in 1976 is the best predictor of independent enterprise three years later. By itself, this merely indicates that a large proportion of these small businessmen were able to maintain their operations for at least the next three years. It is more interesting, however, that self-employment after just three years in the United States was positively associated with only one background characteristic, the man's income in his last job in Cuba. This fact supports the view that some refugees find in self-employment a viable path to starting to reestablish their former wealth.

From the point of view of insertion into the Cuban enclave in Miami, the coefficient corresponding to ethnicity of employer in 1976 is clearly the most important. This result shows that early association with Cuban employers, net of other important individual and experiential factors, plays a strong role

14. Eric Hanushek and John E. Jackson, *Statistical Methods for Social Scientists.*

in promoting self-employment. Indeed, this assistance is so substantial that it increases the probability of self-employment by a full 15 percent.

Since this result is clearly indicative of incorporation into the enclave, we pursued its implications one step further. In Table 70 we also report the logistic regression of ethnicity of employer in 1976 on the same background variables used before. Only two predictors have reliable effects. Each month of schooling in the United States after arrival increases the likelihood by 1 percent that these men will work for Anglo employers. But it is the contribution of expectations of aid from family and friends that adds most to our understanding of the supportive mechanism at work in the enclave. The negative coefficient for expected aid shows that if the refugee expects little or no aid from family and friends in Miami, chances increase that he will find work with an Anglo employer. Conversely, the more aid expected from these social networks, the more likely the refugee is to be hired by a fellow Cuban.

Indirectly, therefore, self-employment in 1979 is related to at least two clear support mechanisms identified with an enclave mode of incorporation. Through contacts with other Cubans in Miami, the newly arrived refugee finds a job with a Cuban employer, from which, after a temporary spell of wage labor, he may move on to establish his own enterprise.

Results of this section clearly substantiate the importance of self-employment as a major characteristic of the insertion of new Cuban refugees into the Miami economy. These entrepreneurs entered intermediate positions in the local economy where they not only provided services to the community but also offered, on a modest scale, employment opportunities to other Cubans. Their achievement of independent economic status was significantly determined by the early support of family and friends and by employment in Cuban-owned firms. Consequently, throughout the first six years of resettlement, the attributes of an ethnic enclave stand out as offering a viable mode of labor-market incorporation; this is reflected in the significant number of immigrants who became entrepreneurs, the types of firms they established, and the process by which they became self-employed.

Sectoral Divisions

Previous research from a structural perspective has identified two contrasting claims concerning the labor-market experiences of immigrants. The first virtually ignores the significance of ethnic enterprises but, when they are acknowledged, emphasizes their exploitative effect on immigrant workers. This claim has been formulated as follows:

New immigrant workers concentrate in the secondary labor market, where they share the characteristics of peripheral employment, including low prestige, low income, job dissatisfaction, and absence of return to past human capital investments. Only a few may gain access to the primary sector.[15]

The second claim focuses upon the distinctness of the enclave:

Immigrant workers are not restricted to the secondary labor market. Those who enter an immigrant enclave are empirically distinguishable from workers in both the primary and secondary labor markets.[16]

Our task in this section is to determine whether the distinctions between the enclave, primary, and secondary labor markets can be empirically identified on the basis of the experiences of these sampled refugees.

The major problem in this part of the analysis is the selection of criteria for assignment of the refugees to one or another labor-market sector. Several sets of criteria have been developed in reference to the American labor force, not all of which are applicable to the local economic structure of the Miami area. Identification of participants in the enclave is straightforward: all men indicating employment in firms owned by Cubans are assigned to the enclave. This group includes the significant number of self-employed businessmen identified previously. A total of 180 cases, or 46 percent of the sample in 1979, are classified as enclave participants.

Criteria for assignment to primary or secondary labor-market sectors pose a greater problem. Several criteria have been used in previous research on this group of refugees, including opportunities for job advancement, size of the firm in which the men are employed, and average wage levels of these firms. In addition, standardized procedures have been developed for the assignment of whole industries to the "core" or the "periphery" of the American economy. A preliminary analysis based on one of these scoring procedures, developed by Tolbert, Horan, and Beck, showed an erratic pattern of differences between refugees assigned to one or another economic sector.[17] In other words, while the industry classification method may reflect the *average* characteristics of industries in the American economy, it does not fit well with the specific characteristics of those in the Miami area.

15. Wilson and Portes, "Immigrant Enclaves," p. 301.

16. Ibid., p. 302.

17. Charles Tolbert, Patrick M. Horan, and E. M. Beck, "The Structure of Economic Segmentation." The Tolbert et al. classification leads, in this case, to contradictory results such as lower average education, lower unionization, and greater job instability among primary-sector workers. Similarly, knowledge of English is lower in the primary sector and there are insignificant differences in earnings and occupational prestige. Clearly, the patterned differences between sectors in the U. S. labor market, shown by Tolbert et al. on the basis of their industry-classification scheme, are not applicable to the local Miami economy or, at least, those enterprises that employ Cuban refugees.

For this reason, we opted for a different approach. Following the rationale of segmented-labor-market theories that characterize the secondary
sector as an "ethnic" labor market, we assigned individuals to sectors depending upon the ethnicity of their co-workers.[18] In this analysis, primary-
sector workers are defined as those hired by Anglo employers and who work
in a predominantly Anglo workforce. Secondary-sector workers are those
employed by Anglos but who labor alongside other Cubans or ethnic minorities. These criteria classify 99 cases, or 25.3 percent, as primary-sector
workers and 112 cases, or 28.7 percent, as secondary-sector employees.
Appendix Tables B and C list the industrial sectors and occupations classified by these criteria into each sector.[19]

Two arguments favor this approach. First, since our interest in this
chapter is to identify the ethnically based organization of the enclave, the
sharpest contrast with the central economy may be gained by using similar
criteria to identify divisions in the "open" labor market. That is, rather than
to identify the enclave as an "ethnic" phenomenon and the primary and
secondary sectors as industrial divisions, we seek to contrast all three labor-
market segments along a similar dimension.

Second, by restricting the classification criteria to ethnicity, we can (1)
identify the structural or demographic attributes that successfully discriminate among the three sectors and (2) measure the relative magnitude of
their importance. That is, we shall use the structural characteristics of occupations and industries as independent variables to examine the extent to
which they help identify different forms of ethnically organized labor market sectors. This approach, however, modifies some of the expectations
about returns to human capital traits in each sector described previously.
We shall leave the rationale for these modifications to a later section, in
which we examine labor-market processes across the three sectors.

Bivariate Analysis

We must first identify a set of variables that can be used to distinguish
empirically the location of these sampled refugees in the three labor-
market sectors. Table 71 initiates this task by presenting the mean scores for
each sector on seventeen selected variables. These variables were chosen
to reflect criteria generally used to distinguish labor-market segments as

18. See David M. Gordon, *Theories of Poverty and Underemployment;* Edna Bonacich,
"A Theory of Ethnic Antagonism"; and Piore, *Birds of Passage.*

19. This classification may overestimate somewhat the number of primary-sector workers, since Anglo firms may not exhibit the characteristics associated with the primary labor
market, while those with an ethnic work force will tend to exhibit those of the secondary. The
effect of this bias is conservative, however, since it would attenuate expected differences between the two sectors.

Table 71. Average Characteristics of Three Labor Markets
for Cuban Refugees in Miami, 1979

Variable	Enclave	Primary	Secondary	Total
Occupational prestige*	34.90	35.32	29.03	33.16
Workplaces since 1976 (N)*	1.70	1.45	1.74	1.64
Total employees in firm**	3.12	4.65	4.39	3.97
Unionized workplace**	0.06	0.21	0.19	0.14
Times unemployed since 1976	0.41	0.27	0.38	0.36
Home ownership	0.46	0.35	0.38	0.40
Relatives in the U.S. (N)	6.92	6.17	7.00	6.72
Social relations with Anglos**	0.19	0.48	0.26	0.28
Ethnic store owner for small-item purchases*	0.37	0.22	0.33	0.32
Ethnic store owner for large-item purchases*	0.26	0.13	0.19	0.21
Ethnic neighborhood*	0.68	0.59	0.77	0.68
Knowledge of U.S. index	5.10	5.42	5.16	5.21
Citizenship	0.87	0.88	0.82	0.86
Opportunities to interact with Anglos**	0.57	0.82	0.57	0.64
Perceived discrimination against Cubans in U.S.**	0.35	0.19	0.24	0.27
Would return to Cuba if political conditions changed*	0.29	0.17	0.19	0.22
Opportunities for job advancement**	0.50	0.59	0.51	0.52

*Probability of equal means < 0.05.

**Probability of equal means < 0.01.

well as others that potentially indicate the specific dimensions of an immigrant enclave. Six variables are objective indicators of economic position:
occupational prestige of the present job, measured in Duncan SEI scores;
home ownership, primarily a measure of economic stability, but also indirectly a measure of type of community; unionized workplace, which refers
to whether or not a union was available in the firm, not necessarily whether

the individual was a member; total number of employees in the firm; the number of unemployment spells between 1976 and 1979; and, the number of workplaces in the last three years.

Five variables measure objective characteristics of the refugees' social relations. The most straightforward indicator is a simple count of the number of relatives currently living in the United States. The other five variables tap the ethnic characteristics of these men's lives outside the workplace. The most general indicator is whether or not the refugee or his wife have any social relationships that involve Anglos. Two variables reflect whether the refugees make purchases within an enclosed ethnic community or enclave rather than outside of it. The indicators are the ethnicity of store owners for small and large purchases. Finally, a direct measure of ethnicity of the neighborhood is included, based upon respondents' reports as to whether most residents in their vicinity are Anglos or not.

The remaining variables in Table 71 focus on subjective perceptions and knowledge of American society. As described in Chapter 3, the U.S. Information Index (USIN) measures the person's recognition of significant political and economic facts about the society. The variables "Citizenship" and "Would return to Cuba if conditions changed" reflect the person's perception about the likelihood of becoming an American citizen and his hypothetical judgment of whether he would return to Cuba under different circumstances. The remaining three variables measure the number of opportunities the refugee believes he has had to interact with Anglos, whether or not he perceives general discrimination against Cubans in the United States, and to what extent he perceives opportunities for job advancement.

The variables in Table 71 are coded in agreement with their labels. For purposes of this analysis, ordinal-level variables were dichotomized to render means (in this case, proportions) interpretable. For example, social relations is coded 1 if most of the refugee's close relationships are with Anglos or exhibit a mixed pattern, and 0 if they are exclusively with Cubans. Variables pertaining to ethnicity of store owners are coded 1 if they are mostly Cuban and 0 if they are mostly Anglo. Ethnicity of neighborhood is 0 if most neighbors are Anglo and 1 if most are Cuban or members of another ethnic minority (blacks, Hispanics). Variables in the third block, with the exception of knowledge of American society, measured by the USIN index, are dichotomies. High scores correspond to the label of each variable.

This relatively extensive list of economic, social, and subjective characteristics should reveal systematic differences between sectors, if any exist, as well as indicate similarities among them. Taking the set of economic variables first, we find that, according to the measure of occupational prestige, not only are the sectors significantly different but, as expected, jobs within the enclave are at an intermediate level between primary- and secondary-sector occupations, but closer to the former. Enclave workers are also intermediate in the number of workplaces in which they have been employed over the past three years. On two of the other three economic dimensions, however, refugees in the enclave do not occupy an intermediate position. Such differences are especially important given the nature of these variables. Refugees employed in the enclave work in much smaller firms, with the total number of employees in enclave businesses significantly lower than those in either the primary or secondary sectors.[20] Not surprisingly, primary-sector firms are the largest. Smaller enclave firms are also less unionized. Workers in the enclave, however, are no different from their counterparts in the outside economy in terms of either their previous unemployment experiences or their frequency of home ownership.

Given the large number of relatives in the United States for everyone in the sample, it is not surprising that there is virtually no difference in the amount of social contacts across the three sectors. On every other dimension of social relations, however, the three groups differ significantly. Clearly reflecting the relatively enclosed borders of the enclave, very few opportunities exist there for the refugees to interact with Anglos. This situation contrasts sharply with the almost 50 percent of the men in the primary sector whose social relationships reflected their greater contact with Anglos in the workplace. Secondary-sector workers had many fewer Anglo contacts than primary-sector employees but still had a greater level of exposure than those in the enclave. These differential social relationships are clearly an important feature of Cuban refugees' early experiences in the United States. For this reason, Chapter 9 will be dedicated to examining them.

Consumption activities and residential locations also reflect this differential participation in the enclave or the outside labor markets. Enclave workers purchased goods more frequently from Cuban-owned stores than did workers in either the primary or secondary sectors. As expected, primary-sector workers made almost all their purchases in Anglo-run stores. Interestingly, however, while refugees in the primary sector again had greater contacts with Anglos through the ethnic mix of their neighborhoods, those in the secondary sector lived in areas with greater proportions of minorities than did members of the enclave. The reason for this greater ethnic concentration is that secondary workers lived in both predominantly Cuban neighborhoods and in those where most residents were other His-

20. The fact that refugees in the enclave are employed in smaller firms is partially an artifact of including the self-employed in this sector. When the self-employed are excluded, however, enclave members are still significantly more likely to work in smaller firms than both primary and secondary workers. The mean is 3.61 for enclave workers on the variable "Total Employees in Firm" when the self-employed are excluded.

panic immigrants. This pattern supports the importance of distinguishing between the concepts of ethnic enclave and ethnic neighborhood, as emphasized previously.

The third set of variables adds to these contrasts by revealing significant differences in the refugees' subjective perceptions. Although no sectoral differences exist in terms of the refugees' general knowledge of American society and their intentions to become U. S. citizens, enclave workers shared with secondary-sector workers the perception of fewer opportunities to interact with Anglos. Enclave workers believed that there is discrimination against Cubans more frequently than did those in the outside economy. If political conditions changed in Cuba, enclave workers would also be more prone to return. Conversely, refugees who found employment in the primary sector reported both less discrimination and less willingness to abandon the United States.

Finally, and contrary to previous expectations, enclave workers shared with secondary employees the perception that few opportunities for advancement existed in their present jobs. This result reflects, in part, the fact that many of those in the enclave had already "advanced" into self-employment and had thus reached their original targets. In agreement with segmented-labor-market theory, primary-sector workers perceived significantly greater opportunities for advancement than those in either ethnic labor market.

Taken as a whole, bivariate comparisons in Table 71 suggest a clear distinction between enclave workers and those in the other sectors. The dimensions of enclave life cover not only particular conditions of employment, but fully extend into community life and personal sentiments and perceptions. Conditions in the enclave also appear supportive of higher-status economic and social positions. On other dimensions, however, especially those involving relationships between Anglos and ethnic minorities, Cubans in the enclave share more similar experiences with secondary-sector workers. Whether these contrasts hold when all dimensions are combined is the question to be examined in the following section.

Multivariate Analysis

We can now test the contrasting hypotheses concerning labor-market segmentation. According to the first theoretical claim outlined previously, there are systematic differences between primary- and secondary-sector workers, particularly in terms of their differential economic conditions. In this case, we would substantiate the expectation that refugees are inserted into a fragmented labor market of the general Miami economy. Support for the second claim would require enclave workers to emerge as an empirically distinct group, in opposition to both the primary and secondary sectors.

To test these expectations, we employ discriminant analysis, a technique that identifies linear combinations of independent variables to distinguish among specified subgroups. The maximum number of these combinations, or discriminant functions, is one less than the number of subgroups. In addition, standardized coefficients permit analysis of the contribution of each variable to defining each particular function.[21]

Table 72 presents results of this analysis, including the standardized discriminant function coefficients, relative percentages for each eigenvalue, canonical correlations and group centroids. Also presented are chi squares and probability levels for each discriminant function. These last statistics indicate whether there are significant differences among subgroups along the measured dimensions of the independent variables. Finally, canonical correlations are included to show the overall association of each discriminant function with the set of variables representing the three labor-market subgroups. The analysis produced two significant discriminant functions, the first with a sizable canonical correlation and the second with a modest but still significant association.

The nature of the two discriminant functions can be gathered from two primary statistics, the standardized coefficients and the group centroids. If we disregard for the moment the direction of the relationships, the first and most important discriminant function is defined by the men's social relations with Anglos, self-employment, the size of the firm, the number of times unemployed since 1976, and perceived discrimination against Cubans. The second function shares two variables with the first function, social relations with Anglos and self-employment. In addition, however, the second function is defined by the opportunities for job advancement, the number of workplaces since 1976, opportunities to interact with Anglos, the ethnicity of the store owner for large-item purchases, and the ethnicity of the men's neighborhood.

The significance of these different discriminating variables is established by the group centroids. These statistics bear directly upon the hypotheses described previously. Group centroids are the average discriminant score for each group on the two functions. The clear strength of the first function, as indicated by the significance of χ^2, is primarily a result of the differences between the enclave and the other two groups. That is, refugees in the enclave are empirically distinguishable, on the basis of this set of variables, from those in the central economy. Primary and secondary workers are virtually indistinguishable for this combination of social and economic characteristics. This result clearly supports the second hypothesis

21. For this analysis, ordinal-level variables are restored to their original multiple coding. The direction of scores is the same as that described previously.

Table 72. Discriminant Analysis of Characteristics of Cuban
Refugees in Three Labor Markets in Miami, 1979

Variables	First Function	Second Function
Occupational prestige	0.09[a]	-0.10
Relatives in United States (N)	0.04	0.14
Home ownership	0.18	0.16
Social relations with Anglos	-0.45	-0.35
Unionized workplace	-0.17	0.13
Opportunities for job advancement	0.11	0.41
Self-employed	0.33	-0.36
Total employees in firm (N)	-0.48	0.18
Times unemployed since 1976 (N)	0.20	-0.13
Workplaces since 1976 (N)	-0.09	0.23
Knowledge of U.S.	-0.16	-0.12
U.S. citizenship	0.15	-0.18
Would return to Cuba if conditions changed	0.14	-0.10
Opportunities to interact with Anglos	-0.11	-0.26
Perceived discrimination against Cubans in U.S.	0.27	-0.06
Ethnic store owner for small-item purchases	0.12	0.07
Ethnic store owner for large-item purchases	0.10	-0.26
Ethnic neighborhood	0.08	0.41
Eigenvalue--relative percentage	80.78	19.22
Canonical correlation	0.57	0.32
χ^2	178.67	38.69
ρ	0.00	0.00
Group Centroids:		
Enclave	0.81	-0.13
Primary labor market	-0.83	-0.35
Secondary labor market	-0.27	0.48

[a]Figures above the dotted line are standardized canonical discriminant functions.

above, confirming the tentative conclusion from the bivariate comparisons. Immigrants in an enclave economy cannot be simply assimilated into the ranks of ethnic minorities in the secondary sector.

Returning to the standardized coefficients, we can interpret both their magnitude and direction in terms of their relationship to enclave sector membership. The strong contributions of self-employment and size of workplace, net of all other attributes, supports the general line of argument presented throughout this section. Self-employed entrepreneurs are clearly prevailing features of the Cuban enclave, but they are not the most important characteristic. Among economic variables, size of the workplace adds most to the identification of enclave employment, as opposed to work in the outside economy. Net of other variables, employment in larger firms is a defining characteristic of economic activity outside the enclave. This difference remains significant even if we exclude from the analysis the private entrepreneurs. Surprisingly, however, enclave employment is also associated with spells of unemployment, a characteristic more commonly attributed to secondary-sector workers.

Outside work relationships, enclave participation is characterized by few social relationships with Anglos and perceived discrimination against Cubans. The fact that these two variables maintain a strong net association with the first discriminant function suggests that the ethnic boundaries of the enclave are drawn fairly tightly. However, they do not completely eliminate opportunities to interact with Anglos.

The second function discriminates among the three groups in a very different manner. In this case, the significant contrast is between secondary-sector workers on the one hand, and enclave and primary-sector workers on the other. This result again supports our initial theoretical claim. Refugees incorporated into the enclave are not only distinct from those in secondary-sector jobs, but their ethnically bounded support mechanisms contribute to advancing their economic position. These results indicate that enclave workers resemble the relatively advanced status commonly associated with employment in the primary sector.

Beginning with economic characteristics, secondary-sector employment is predictably associated with two attributes having little connection to enclave or primary-sector employment: few opportunities for job advancement and a higher rate of job turnover. Job turnover, however, measured by the number of workplaces, does not necessarily involve repeated periods of unemployment. Self-employment also has a strong, but negative relationship to secondary activities.

Secondary-sector work, as defined here, shares with enclave employment a separation from Anglos outside the workplace. Like enclave workers, secondary workers have few social relations with Anglos despite their participation in the central economy. There is some evidence, however, that these ethnic boundaries work in fundamentally different ways across the labor markets. Comparing the two functions, an important defining attribute of the secondary sector is the small number of opportunities available to interact with Anglos. As noted above, in the enclave, those opportunities existed, but were not pursued. In addition, despite their employment by Anglo businessmen, perceived discrimination against Cubans is not a significant item of identification for secondary-sector workers.

A final relationship uncovered in the second function requires special note. In contrast to both the enclave and primary sectors, secondary-sector workers tend to make large-item purchases in stores owned and operated by Anglos. This tendency occurs even though the neighborhoods in which they live are populated by ethnic minorities. This set of results again supports the earlier distinction between the concepts of enclave and ethnic neighborhood: while ethnicity of neighborhood is not important in identifying enclave employment, it is strongly associated with employment in the secondary sector. In the latter case, as these men go outside the ethnic neighborhood to work, their consumption patterns also integrate them into the outside economy.

In synthesis, results presented in Table 72 demonstrate two different sources of labor-market segmentation. The first divides participation in the enclave from employment in the wider central economy. Ethnic divisions combine with entrepreneurial activities and job opportunities in a proliferation of small-scale firms to keep these refugees within a distinguishable labor-market segment. A second source of differentiation shows that the ethnic boundaries of the enclave do not necessarily have a negative economic effect on its members. Instead, enclave employment appears to offer opportunities comparable to the higher status jobs found in the predominantly Anglo sector. This possibility is further examined in the following section.

LABOR-MARKET RETURNS IN THREE SECTORS

Early Occupation and Income

Having established systematic differences in the characteristics of work among the three labor-market sectors, we turn now to the possible effects of this segmentation on occupational status and income. To accomplish this task, we estimate the effects of a limited list of predictors representing both orthodox and structural theories on five dependent variables in each labor-market sector. The selection of independent variables is not intended to set up a final test of competing labor-market theories. Rather, the task here is to assess the extent to which segmentation alters expected relationships among a variety of background and structural characteristics.

As mentioned earlier, we expect significant differences in the occupational- and income-attainment process for immigrants inserted in the three labor markets. In contrast to secondary-sector workers, for example, both enclave and primary-sector employees should receive significant returns on their human capital skills. In the primary sector, these returns should be related to formal training and individual motivations. Enclave workers, on the other hand, should receive substantial rewards from skills that can be employed within the ethnic market. More importantly, however, occupational gains in the enclave should involve support mechanisms such as family and kinship. Secondary-sector workers can be expected to receive fewer rewards for their skills or certification, especially in comparison with those in the primary sector. Since formal training and skills count for less in the secondary labor market, occupations and income in this sector should be less frequently determined by the set of background human-capital variables.

The dependent variables in this analysis are principal occupation in Cuba and occupation and income in the United States in 1976 and 1979. Regressions are based on respondents who were employed in 1979 and thus omit the small percentage who were out of the job market at the time.[22] Occupational variables are coded in Duncan's Socioeconomic Index (SEI) scores. The use of this measure does not assume that it represents the only relevant dimension of occupation. A number of studies have shown, however, that SEI is a statistically well-behaved scale that taps what may be defined as the perceived desirability of occupations. Other studies have provided evidence of the cross-national stability of occupational rankings, as measured by SEI-type scales.[23] This last result is relevant, for it supports our coding of occupations in Cuba and the United States in the same metric. The income variables are the natural logarithm of the sum of a person's monthly wages, salary, business profits, and other income sources at the time of each survey. This metric is adopted to normalize the skewed 1979 income distribution. Its adoption implies that net effects indicate proportional differences in income within each sector rather than absolute income differences.

The analysis is divided in two parts. First, we examine early occupational and income attainment, three years after arrival (1976); second, we consider effects of subsequent United States-acquired skills on the same

22. To avoid the additional loss of cases, the few respondents unemployed in 1976 but employed in 1979 were assigned the mean of the 1976 occupational distributions.

23. Donald J. Treiman, *Occupational Prestige in Comparative Perspective*. For a commentary on the application of the SEI scale to Hispanic samples, see Ross M. Stolzenberg, "Occupational Differences Between Hispanics and Non-Hispanics."

Table 73. Determinants of Early Occupational Status and
Income in Three Labor Markets, 1973-1976

Dependent Variables	Independent Variables			
	Father's Occupation	Work Experience	Education	Income in Cuba
Enclave				
Occupation in Cuba	.180[a]*	.309*	4.478*	--
Occupation in U.S., 1976	-.060	.374*	1.941**	3.785*
Income in U.S., 1976	.150	-1.866**	-1.690	.953
Primary Sector				
Occupation in Cuba	.098	.300*	4.896**	--
Occupation in U.S., 1976	.112	.034	.461	3.431*
Income in U.S., 1976	.001	-.313	1.433	5.109
Secondary Sector				
Occupation in Cuba	.159*	.577**	4.246**	--
Occupation in U.S., 1976	-.007	-.047	0.057	1.679
Income in U.S., 1976	.543*	-.873	-5.258**	10.893*

[a]Metric regression coefficients. Those in the income regressions are taken to the fifth significant digit and multiplied by 100.

dependent variables in 1979. Table 73 presents regressions involving the first three dependent variables: occupation in Cuba and occupation and income in 1976. Following standard human-capital models, all three variables are modelled as functions of father's occupation, work experience, and education. A quadratic term for work experience is also included to capture the possible nonlinear effect of this variable. In addition, 1976 attainments are hypothesized to be dependent upon other individual characteristics uniquely relevant to immigrants. These are knowledge of English at arrival, occupational aspirations at arrival, and the months of formal education acquired in the United States. Finally, income in Cuba and expected aid from

Occupational Aspirations	Knowledge of English, 1973	Expected Aid	Education in the U.S. 1973-1976	Occupation 1976	R^2
Independent Variables					
	Enclave				
--	--	--	--	--	.586
.164**	.365	.588	.276	--	.401
-.302	-2.186	3.707	-.111	2.053**	.305
	Primary Sector				
--	--	--	--	--	.581
.083	4.430**	-.647	.152	--	.432
-.177	3.490	-11.261*	.174	1.064**	.366
	Secondary Sector				
--	--	--	--	--	.558
.166	-.613	.814	.592	--	.222
.179	2.430	.802	-.145	1.356**	.418

*Coefficient exceeds twice its standard error.

**Coefficient exceeds three times its standard error.

family and friends are included as predictors. The first is an indicator of the class origins of the refugee, while the second taps the probable degree of assistance from his social networks during the early years of resettlement.[24]

Table 73 presents regressions of these dependent variables in each

24. Father's occupation and occupational aspirations at arrival are also coded in Duncan's SEI scores. Education is coded in number of years completed. Work experience is defined as age minus education minus 6. Knowledge of English is measured by the KEI scale. Income in Cuba is the natural logarithm of the respondent's average income in the year before arrival in the United States, coded in pesos per month. Expected aid is a four-point scale ranging from "much aid" (coded highest) to "none."

labor-market sector. Figures in the table are unstandardized regression coefficients. Those in the income regressions are taken to the fifth digit and multiplied by 100 to eliminate leading zeros. The quadratic term for work experience failed to have a single significant effect and is thus dropped from all the equations.

Occupation in Cuba is included as a dependent variable to check the possibility that contemporary differences across labor markets are not a result of structural market characteristics in the United States, but rather of individual traits. It is conceivable that systematic differences in causal effects on occupation predated the arrival of immigrants in the United States and account for those found later. Such preexisting differences would virtually eliminate experiences in the Miami economy as a source of differential occupational outcomes.

Results in Table 73 show, however, a fundamental similarity in the determinants of occupation in Cuba for refugees in all three labor-market subsamples. In all three sectors, the equation accounts for more than half of the variance in Cuban occupational status. Education is, by far, the strongest predictor. In each sector, one year of additional education yields a substantial increase of roughly four SEI prestige points. Effects of work experience come next and, though they are more modest, they still reach statistical significance in every sector. The only exception to the similarity of results across sectors is the absence of a reliable effect of father's occupation in the primary subsample. Differences with corresponding coefficients in other sectors are not, however, statistically significant.

Having established that subsequent sectoral differences in the United States do not originate with experiences in Cuba, we examine next the determinants of occupation and income after three years in the country. Differences between the three subsamples illustrate the decisive consequences of incorporation into one or another labor-market sector in the early years. In the enclave, occupational status is again most strongly determined by education, followed by occupational aspirations, income in Cuba, and work experience. One year of Cuban education leads to a two-point gain in occupational prestige in the United States. Though smaller than the original effect on Cuban occupations, the amount is still substantial. All significant effects are in the predicted direction and, together, they explain 40 percent of the variance in 1976 occupations.

These results are congruent with expectations based on human-capital theory. However, such expectations are not supported by results in the secondary sector. In the latter, *not a single* predictor has a reliable effect on occupational status. Explained variance is roughly half the corresponding figure in the enclave, and is not statistically significant. Finally, explained variance in the primary sector is about the same as in the enclave. As in the latter, income in Cuba has a significant positive influence on 1976 occupations. However, the strongest determinant of occupation in this sector is not education but knowledge of English. Each unit increment in the ten-point KEI scale yields a gain of more than four SEI prestige points.

Taken together, these results support the argument of significant structurally conditioned differences on occupational attainment across labor markets. They also offer some telling lessons about opportunities available to newcomers in the United States: when a preexisting economic enclave exists, immigrants can readily make use of their past formal training, material resources, and experience. Motivational factors also contribute significantly to their advancement. Knowledge of the host country language is less important, since mobility opportunities exist within the boundaries of the ethnic economy.

Immigrants who gain access to primary-sector jobs also derive a significant advantage from their past skills and resources, but these are of a different nature. It is not formal education acquired in the home country, but proficiency in English that leads to early occupational advancement in this Anglo-dominated sector. Immigrants employed in the secondary labor market find, however, that neither their education nor their language skills nor any other qualification provides a return in terms of occupational advancement. In the early years at least, their occupational situation is unrelated to their human capital, a fact congruent with the characterization of employment conditions in this sector.

Regressions of income in 1976 also reveal significant differences. In all three sectors, occupational status has a reliable effect on income, but this influence is strongest in the enclave where it exceeds eight times its standard error. Net of occupation, the only other significant coefficient in the enclave sector, corresponds to work experience, but its sign is negative. This apparent anomaly can be readily explained as an age effect. Recall that entrepreneurs have higher incomes and are also younger than refugees in wage employment. As seen in the previous results, work experience in Cuba leads to higher level occupations in the United States. Once this effect is controlled, the remaining influence of work experience on income reflects the negative bearing of age upon independent entrepreneurship. Early income attainment in the enclave is thus a process of translating human capital, material resources, and aspirations brought from the home country into higher occupations, which in turn decisively affect income levels. Approximately one-third of the income variance in 1976 is explained by this process.

Predictors of income in the primary sector account for slightly more variance than in the enclave, but the configuration of effects is different. The influence of occupation on income is significant, though weaker than in the enclave sector. Net of occupation, the only other significant effect, is that of expected aid from family and friends. Among Cuban refugees in the enclave, this effect is positive and significant before the effect of occupational status is considered. Among those in the primary sector, however, expected aid from social networks has a *negative* influence on income. This result strongly suggests the differential use of social resources according to mode of incorporation. In contrast to the enclave, ethnic social ties in the Anglo firms of the primary sector work directly against economic rewards. Adding to this contrast is the role of these social resources in the secondary sector. In this labor market, where ethnic groups are organized on a competitive rather than on a collaborative basis, expected social assistance has an insignificant effect on income.

Finally, the bottom row of Table 74 shows that, over the first three years in the United States, the economic situation of secondary-sector employees continues to be tied to their former positions in Cuba. Net of the effect of occupational status, father's occupation and past income levels in Cuba also have reliable effects on 1976 income.[25] All three coefficients are in the direction predicted by human-capital theory. However, the strongest determinant of 1976 income and that which accounts for the higher explained variance in this sector is education. Surprisingly, this effect is negative. In other words, for refugees in secondary-sector jobs, past educational qualifications not only have no economic payoff, but actually *depress* income levels during the first three years in the United States.

We could only speculate about the mechanisms that produce this unexpectedly strong negative effect. Regardless of its causes, it is clear that this effect does not fit the description of a homogeneous labor market in which past human capital investments are always rewarded. Instead, it is congruent with characterizations of a labor-market sector in which formal qualifications often represent a handicap rather than an asset for new entrants, including recently arrived immigrants.

Occupation and Income after Six Years

To synthesize results up to this point: we have shown that labor-market differences in the United States cannot be attributed to preexisting group selectivity in Cuba, but that they begin to unfold in the earliest years of

25. A plausible explanation of this last result has to do with alternative uses of economic resources brought from Cuba. Those who invested them in independent businesses or used them to gain access to better occupations are in the enclave and in the primary sector. They essentially committed resources to occupations with a higher earnings potential. Those who failed to follow this route may still derive some income from other sources in addition to their salaries. This effect will be reflected directly in total income levels, independent of the influence of occupation.

resettlement. The transfer of Cuban human capital, economic resources, and motivations is readily apparent in the enclave where it translates into different occupational positions, which, in turn, decisively affect income levels. There is also a significant return for past skills in the primary sector but, in this case, the key factor is knowledge of English at arrival. Proficiency in English translates into higher-level occupations, which lead, in turn, to higher income. Another significant effect in this sector indicates that immigrants in Anglo-dominated firms do better economically by lowering expectations of support from their ethnic networks. Finally, neither formal qualifications brought from Cuba nor knowledge of English affect occupational positions in the secondary labor market. Higher-level occupations within this sector also have a positive effect on income, as do variables linked to past class origins in Cuba. However, the strongest and most theoretically significant effect shows that better educated refugees actually fare worse economically, when confined to secondary-sector jobs, than do their less trained co-workers.

We can turn now to the variables of greatest interest, namely occupational status and income after six years in the United States. The predictor variables in these equations are those included in the previous analysis, with several exceptions. Knowledge of English in 1979 substitutes for knowledge of English at arrival. Because of strong collinearity between the two variables, both cannot be included simultaneously. Having examined effects of knowledge of English in 1973 on early occupation and income, we opt for making use here of the more recent indicator.[26] Early education in the United States, which failed to have a single significant effect on 1976 variables, is substituted for months of formal education during the last three years. Finally, occupation and income in 1979 are also regressed on their respective 1976 indicators as a means of examining their stability over time.

During preliminary runs, the large number of variables included in the income regressions led to a substantial loss of cases and, hence, instability in the estimation of slopes.[27] For this reason, we reestimated equations after excluding early (1973) variables that failed to have a single reliable income effect in any sector. Final regressions thus include all post-1973 predictors, plus earlier ones that affect income significantly in at least one subsample. Results are presented in Table 74.

26. Results are not significantly different regardless of which measure of knowledge of English is employed.

27. This is a result of the compounding effect of missing data on predictor variables. Missing data are handled listwise, which means that regression estimates are based only on those cases for which complete information is available. Since the sample is already subdivided, a large number of predictors in the income equations reduces subsample Ns in two sectors to an unacceptably low number.

Table 74. Determinants of Occupation and Income
after Six Years in the United States

Dependent Variables	Independent Variables				
	Father's Occupation	Work Experience	Education	Income in Cuba	Occupational Aspirations
Enclave					
Occupation, 1979	-.091[a]	-.200	3.398**	1.968	.083
Income, 1979	#[b]	-.910*	-1.797	#	.368**
Primary Sector					
Occupation, 1979	-.010	-.266	-1.051	-.353	.138*
Income, 1979	#	.189	3.528*	#	-.241
Secondary Sector					
Occupation, 1979	.162	.012	1.340	7.786**	-.002
Income, 1979	#	-1.130*	-.974	#	.099

[a]Metric regression coefficients. Those in the income regressions are taken to the fifth significant digit and multiplied by 100.

[b]# = variables excluded from the equation.

Roughly half of the total occupational-status variance is explained by the model in each subsample. Explained variance is not significantly different between the primary and secondary sectors or between the secondary and the enclave, but it is different between the latter and the primary sector. The configuration of significant effects on 1979 occupation is also quite different across the three sectors: in the enclave, education continues to be the strongest determinant of occupational status. This effect is greater than in 1976 and approaches the original influence of education on occupation in Cuba. In 1979, one year of Cuban education yielded a reliable gain of three-and-a-half SEI prestige points. The only other significant effect on occupation in this sector is also an educational one. Net of the influence of Cuban education, one month of education acquired in the United States during the last three years produced an increase of an additional one-half

Expected Aid	Occupation, 1976	Income, 1976	Education in the U.S. 1976-1979	Knowledge of English, 1979	Occupation, 1979	R^2
				Independent Variables		

Expected Aid	Occupation, 1976	Income, 1976	Education in the U.S. 1976-1979	Knowledge of English, 1979	Occupation, 1979	R^2
			Enclave			
-.761	.196	#	.460*	-.544	#	.481
#	#	27.094**	.069	.773	.906**	.449
			Primary Sector			
.699	.708**	#	-.367	3.794**	#	.586
#	#	22.548**	.076	.416	.681**	.362
			Secondary Sector			
1.965	.369*	#	.503	1.753*	#	.530
#	#	50.967**	-1.302*	-1.128	.951**	.461

*Coefficient exceeds twice its standard error.

**Coefficient exceeds three times its standard error.

SEI point. Reflecting rapid occupational changes in the enclave and, in particular, the move into self-employment, occupation in 1976 failed to have a significant effect on the same variable three years later.

Primary-sector occupations are far more stable over time. The net causal effect of early occupational attainment on that achieved subsequently is equivalent to almost three-fourths of one SEI prestige point. In contrast to results in the enclave, education in Cuba or in the United States is not a significant predictor in the primary sector. The decisive determinant of occupational status in this sector continues to be knowledge of English. The corresponding coefficient exceeds by four times its standard error. Net of the effects of occupational status and knowledge of English, the only other reliable predictor is occupational aspirations. Since this effect was not present in 1976, it suggests a significant but delayed payoff for early motivational factors in primary-sector occupations.

Occupational attainment in the secondary labor market is affected by a different set of factors. In this sector, the strongest determinant is not formal education or knowledge of English but the refugee's preexile income. Recall that this variable was a significant predictor of income but not occupation in 1976. Thus the transfer of the resources represented by this variable into an occupational return is a delayed process in this sector, whereas the process was already manifest in the enclave and the primary subsamples in 1976. Six years after arrival, knowledge of English also becomes a significant predictor of occupation among secondary-sector workers. The size of this coefficient is, however, half that of the corresponding figure in the primary sector. The differences between knowledge of English effects in these two sectors yields a t-statistic of 1.72, significant at the .05 level in a directional test. Similarly, the transfer of occupational status from 1976 to 1979 is also present in the secondary sector, but is again significantly weaker than in the primary subsample.

Overall, the pattern of occupational attainment after six years suggests that individuals who found employment in the enclave were in the best position to translate formal training into more desirable jobs. The payoff of education brought from Cuba is supplemented by a significant return for additional education in the United States. In the primary labor market, the key to success is knowledge of English, a result congruent with requirements of the large Anglo firms that dominate this sector. There are also sufficient opportunities in this sector for refugees to implement, albeit with some delay, their occupational aspirations. Workers in the secondary labor market receive some returns for their proficiency in English, though these are significantly smaller than in the primary sector. The decisive factor here continues to reflect the influence of past economic position in Cuba, rather than that of formal training or subsequent experiences and aspirations in the United States.

Determinants of income in 1979 are more similar across the three subsamples. In all sectors, the two strongest effects are those of 1979 occupation and of income in 1976. The first effect reproduces the pattern already found in 1976: six years after arrival, occupational status continues to be a major determinant of income in all labor markets. Evaluated at the mean of the respective income distributions, each additional SEI prestige point increases monthly income by slightly more than $10 in the enclave, $9 in the secondary sector, and close to $7 in the primary. Effects of 1976 income reflect the fundamental stability of this variable over time. This inertial effect is, however, stronger in the secondary sector. A comparison of the corresponding coefficient with that in the enclave yields a t-statistic of 1.53, significant at the .10 level in a one-tailed test; the difference with the primary sector is slightly larger.

There are, however, significant differences across the three subsamples. As in 1976, the third reliable effect on income in the enclave is that of work experience, and its sign is negative. Once again, this result reflects the negative impact of age on income-producing activities associated primarily with independent enterprise, once the effect of occupation is taken into account. In the primary sector, education has a reliable positive effect on income. In dollar terms, this influence is sizable: net of other variables, an additional year of education yields an average increase of more than $36 per month.

In contrast with this last result, effects of education and knowledge of English in the secondary sector are all negative, and one is statistically significant: just as in 1976, Cuban education produced a negative economic return, in 1979, additional formal training in the United States led to a net income loss. Each month of United States education during the preceding three years *reduced* average monthly income by $14. It is possible that such additional education may eventually yield an economic payoff, primarily by allowing refugees to leave jobs in this sector. In the short run, however, and in contrast to the experiences of primary-sector workers, those in the secondary labor market found that past investments in education were not only worthless, but actually counterproductive in economic terms.

As in the enclave, there is also a reliable negative effect of secondary-sector work experience on income. This result suggests an adverse age influence on the income-transferring activities—first from Cuba to the United States and then from 1976 to 1979—which appears to lie at the core of the attainment process in this sector.

Thus, despite a certain convergence of the income-attainment process across the three labor markets, significant differences remain. While not all of these differences could be anticipated, the overall pattern is one congruent with our earlier theoretical expectations. Added to the marked differences encountered in occupational attainment, these results support the thesis that incorporation into different economic sectors represents a decisive factor conditioning immigrants' opportunities to use their human-capital resources and implement their aspirations. Results of the above analysis consistently show that such chances are greater among refugees who became part of the Cuban enclave in Miami or those who found employment in the primary sector. Workers confined to the secondary labor market did not find their path of advancement completely blocked, but their occupational and income attainment was determined by a different set of factors. The causal process in their case seemed dominated by the transfer of economic resources associated with former class position in Cuba; this process simultaneously penalized the early transfer of intellectual skills and their subsequent acquisition in the United States.

CONCLUSION

We can now return to the central theme of this chapter to place the results in overall perspective. Our aim was to examine the application of different theories on the uses of immigrant labor to the experiences of Cuban refugees in Miami. At the heart of this task was the goal of examining the tenability of structural theories of labor-market segmentation as alternatives to those widely held in the existing economic and sociological literature. The results, therefore, should be placed in the context of this theoretical controversy.

A central theme throughout the preceding chapters has been the interweaving of class and ethnicity, as manifested in the experiences of different immigrant groups. In reviewing structural theories of labor-market segmentation, we realized that both class and ethnic dimensions were imperfectly explored. The focus of previous studies had been limited to the working class and thus had restricted the scope of ethnically organized economic activities and their consequences. By integrating the concept of ethnic enclave with the analysis offered by segmented-labor-market theory, we expected to obtain a more accurate image of the range of modes of incorporation available to new immigrants and the consequences of participation in each. Our focus then narrowed to examine the process that organized these structural alternatives around ethnic solidarity, competition, and antagonism.

One crucial feature of the class divisions formed as Cuban refugees merged into the Miami economy was the growth of a small-scale entrepreneurial class. Contrary to orthodox expectations, the proliferation of independent business ventures was not a consequence of an inherent entrepreneurial spirit carried by the more adventurous men into their new country. Rather, assistance from established social networks within the Cuban community and, especially, contact with other Cuban entrepreneurs appeared to be the decisive factors propelling many into self-employment. In turn, these new enterprises offered limited employment opportunities to Cuban wage earners. Thus, we witnessed the incorporation of part of this late wave of Cuban refugees into a vertically integrated, ethnically enclosed economy.

As fully expected, however, the enclave sector represented only one mode of incorporation. A slight majority of the total sample entered the outside economy, where they faced the segmented layers of employment opportunities characteristic of the primary and secondary sectors. Continuing with our central theme, we sought to determine how ethnicity contributed to the differentiation of labor markets outside the enclave. The analysis revealed that, although similar in ethnic origins, Cubans employed in the primary and secondary labor markets experienced the influence of ethnicity differently from those who became part of the enclave. For example, although the degree of social separation from Anglos was a shared characteristic of enclave and secondary-sector workers, as opposed to those in the primary sector, this dimension actually served to differentiate the three groups in a multivariate analysis.

Indeed, this discriminant analysis showed that the combination of class and ethnicity used to define the three labor markets represents boundaries of very different sets of economic and social activities. Ethnicity as the organizing principle of a class-differentiated enclave represents primarily a mechanism of economic support. Though the resulting ethnically enclosed labor market is quite different from the Anglo-dominated primary sector, both yield comparable benefits. Ethnicity in the secondary sector, on the other hand, reflects the lower rewards and subordinate social and economic positions characteristically found among immigrant minorities.

Results from the last section support this conclusion, and challenge orthodox theories that assume an homogeneous, openly competitive labor market. It is identifiable sectoral differences that transform those causal processes that determine the influence on income and occupational status of individual skills and experiences. As expected, results in the primary sector conform closely with conventional expectations. For immigrants who work for and alongside Anglos, knowledge of English is a clear asset in competing for higher status occupations. Similarly, prior formal education significantly aids in obtaining a higher income after six years. On the other hand, expectations of support from the immediate ethnic community reduce early income levels in this sector and continue to have an indirect effect afterwards.

For immigrants who work outside the Anglo-dominated sector, a different set of individual skills are important. In the enclave, Cuban education contributes to occupational gains very early in the resettlement experience, with the magnitude of that advantage increasing over time. Enclave workers also benefit initially from their work experience in Cuba and, subsequently, from additional U. S.-acquired education. No such benefits are available, however, to refugees who become part of the secondary sector. Instead, this latter group competes with other ethnic minorities in firms that provide few rewards for individual skills and that tend to penalize past educational achievement. Attainment in this sector appears primarily determined by the inertial effect of economic resources transferred from Cuba and, over time, acquired in the United States.

Overall, results of this chapter establish the importance of distinct modes of structural incorporation as they apply to the experiences of this sample of Cuban refugees. Yet if the insights gained from this analysis are to be useful outside the Miami context, they should contribute to an understanding of the varied experiences of other immigrant groups. For this reason, we turn in the following chapter to a comparison of the labor market experience of Cuban refugees and Mexican immigrants.

7

THE SECONDARY LABOR MARKET:
ECONOMIC AND OCCUPATIONAL
MOBILITY OF MEXICAN IMMIGRANTS

This chapter continues the exploration of the third research area outlined in Chapter 1: the uses of immigrant labor. In this instance, we focus on the experience of Mexican immigrants as they become incorporated in the American (primarily the Southwest) economy. In order to pursue this analysis in parallel fashion to that of Cuban refugees, we examine first that aspect that is most characteristic of the Mexicans' entry into the United States labor market. Just as the central characteristic in the case of the Cubans was the rapid increase in self-employment, that among Mexicans was the substantial number with extensive occupational experience in the United States prior to legal entry.

This last characteristic reflects the circulatory nature of Mexican immigration across the border, marked by multiple returns and reentries. Thus, paralleling the analysis of Cuban self-employment and its correlates in Chapter 6, the first part of this chapter examines the occupational differences associated with prior U. S. residence among Mexican immigrants. This exploration is then followed by an analysis of labor-market segmentation, corresponding to that conducted in the Cuban sample. In the Mexican case, however, the enclave sector does not exist as a viable mode of incorporation. On the contrary, Mexican immigration has been consistently characterized as prototypical of the flow directed to the competitive or secondary sector of the economy.[1] In this analysis, we examine whether this assertion is adequate and, more generally, whether identifiable empirical

---

1. See Michael J. Piore, *Birds of Passage*, and Alejandro Portes and Robert L. Bach, "Immigrant Earnings."

differences can be established between the labor markets hypothesized by dual-economy theory.

The next section presents an analysis of differential economic returns to human capital and other individual attributes for Mexican immigrants employed in each labor-market sector. Paralleling the analysis of Cuban attainment, our focus here is on determinants of occupation and income after three and six years in the country. Finally, the last section brings together findings in this and the preceding chapter by comparing directly the occupational and income attainment of Mexican and Cuban immigrants.

MEXICANS IN THE AMERICAN LABOR MARKET

Prior U. S. Residence and Its Correlates

Chapter 4 identified divisions within the Mexican sample that resulted from differential participation in the circular labor flow across the Southwest border. As reported, close to 70 percent of the sample lived and worked in the United States for at least a year before acquiring the necessary certification to enter as permanent resident aliens. Only 30 percent reported that their entry to the United States in 1973–1974 was the first one.

Prior residents form a distinctive group in this sample. They are younger than first-time arrivals and less educated. Their occupational experiences in Mexico are more deeply rooted in the countryside, where many of their fathers worked in agriculture, and they held unskilled and semiskilled jobs more frequently than the rest of the sample. Previous moves north had also contributed to forging important social connections. For example, compared with first-time arrivals, a greater proportion of prior residents had wives already waiting for them in the United States.

To determine whether prior U. S. residence has a significant relationship to U. S. occupations, this section compares the sectoral distributions of first-time and return immigrants in 1976 and again in 1979. This analysis is followed by a more detailed comparison of other characteristics of jobs held by immigrants in both subsamples.

Industry and Occupation

Table 75 reports the industrial classification of Mexican occupations by prior residence. A more detailed listing by 3-digit census codes is presented in appendix Table D. The figures in Table 75 can be read in two ways. First, the subsample distributions can be compared within each year. For example, in 1976 both subgroups were concentrated in the manufacturing sector. Although significant differences existed between durable and nondurable firms, 40.4 percent of first-time arrivals were employed in this sector

Table 75. Industrial Sector by Previous Residence
in the United States: Mexicans, 1976 and 1979

Industrial Sector	No Previous Residence		Previous Residence	
	1976	1979	1976	1979
Agriculture, forestry, fisheries	6.6	9.7	7.0	5.0
Mining	0.0	1.9	2.1	1.9
Construction	12.6	5.8	13.5	12.6
Manufacturing--durable	12.6	20.4	25.7	24.8
Manufacturing--nondurable	27.8	18.5	15.5	16.4
Transportation, communication, other public utilities	6.6	1.9	7.4	5.7
Wholesale trade	3.3	6.8	1.6	2.8
Retail trade	12.6	13.6	13.9	11.0
Finance, insurance, real estate	0.7	1.9	1.2	0.3
Business and repair services	11.3	13.6	6.5	9.7
Personal services	1.3	3.9	1.6	2.5
Entertainment and recreation services	1.3	0.0	1.6	0.6
Professional and related services	0.7	1.0	1.2	3.2
Public administration	2.6	1.0	1.2	3.5
Total	*100.0*	*100.0*	*100.0*	*100.0*

compared with 41.2 percent of prior residents. The subgroups also shared similar proportions in the other most important sectors of employment, including agriculture, construction, retail trade, and transportation.

In 1979, the subsamples were still employed in similar industrial sectors. As in 1976, virtually the same proportions held jobs in manufacturing firms, and this sector remained the primary locus of employment for the entire group. Retail trade also provided jobs for a similar proportion of each subsample. Only in construction were differences greater in 1979 than in 1976: construction work in 1979 was the third largest source of employment for prior residents, while it ranked sixth among first-time residents.

Second, the distributions of each subsample can be compared over time. A common expectation is that employment disparities between prior

Table 76. Occupation by Previous Residence in the
United States: Mexicans, 1976 and 1979

Occupation	No Previous Residence		Previous Residence	
	1976	1979	1976	1979
Professional, technical	2.0	1.0	2.7	1.9
Managers and administrators	3.3	2.9	2.7	1.3
Sales workers	2.6	1.0	2.0	0.3
Clerical and related workers	2.6	7.7	1.6	1.3
Craftsmen and related workers	23.5	28.8	23.9	25.4
Operatives, nontransport	30.1	30.8	31.4	30.7
Operatives, transport	3.9	1.9	6.7	4.0
Laborers, except farm	22.2	6.7	15.3	20.7
Farmers and farm managers	0.7	0.0	0.4	0.0
Farm laborers and farm foremen	3.9	8.6	4.7	4.7
Service workers, except private household	5.2	10.6	8.6	9.7
Total	*100.0*	*100.0*	*100.0*	*100.0*

residents and first-time arrivals will be greatest in the earlier years. As first-time arrivals move into the receiving labor market, their occupational distribution will naturally converge with that of immigrants who were already there. The data in Table 75 generally support this expectation, especially within the major sectors. Between 1976 and 1979, there was a substantial redeployment of first-time workers between manufacturing firms. While the concentration of prior residents remained stable, the redistribution of first-time immigrants narrowed the gap between the two subgroups: in 1976, a 13-point difference existed between the proportions employed in durable manufacturing; by 1979, the difference was only 4 points.

Similar patterns are reflected in the occupational status distributions, presented in Table 76. The most prominent feature of this table is the remarkable similarity in occupations held by both subgroups in 1976 and 1979. Indeed, the most frequently held jobs, craft and operatives, are virtually the same throughout the period regardless of when the immigrants entered the United States.

The most substantial occupational change occurred in the proportions who worked as laborers. In 1976, nearly one out of every four first-time immigrants (22.2 percent) worked as a laborer. By 1979, the proportion had dropped roughly 70 percent, to fewer than one person in ten (6.7 percent). During the same period, the proportion of prior residents engaged in non-farm labor increased marginally: 15.3 percent in 1976 to 20.7 percent in 1979. Overwhelmingly, these job shifts occurred within the construction sector. Detailed occupational listings in appendix Table E show that, among workers with prior U.S. experience, one in every three laborers in 1979 worked in construction.

Other Job Characteristics

Although broad industrial and occupational differences are not significant, the data in Table 77 suggest that prior residence in the United States has a differentiating effect on other employment characteristics. These figures show that the subsamples have similar occupational prestige levels, as measured by the SEI scale, in 1976 (19.86 and 20.15 SEI points), and in 1979 (21.79 and 19.49). In addition, the subsamples share the same rate of

Table 77. Employment Characteristics in the United States by Previous Residence: Mexicans, 1976 and 1979

Variables	No Previous Residence in the U.S. $\overline{X}$	Previous Residence $\overline{X}$	ρ
1976			
Number of jobs, 1973-1976	2.10	2.20	0.50
Unemployed	0.13	0.05	0.01
Occupational status	19.86	20.15	0.65
Monthly income	518.37	670.03	0.00
1979			
Number of jobs, 1976-1979	2.12	2.02	0.53
Unemployed	0.09	0.04	0.03
Occupational status	21.79	19.49	0.12
Monthly income	823.84	936.15	0.00
Unionized job	0.21	0.33	0.01

job turnover throughout the six years. On the other two dimensions, however, the subgroups differ significantly.

One-third of the prior residents were employed in a job that had union representation, compared with only 21 percent of new arrivals. In addition, the returnees had significantly lower rates of unemployment: 5 percent compared with 13 percent in 1976, and 4 percent compared with 9 percent in 1979. The most important correlate of prior residence is, however, average monthly income. In 1976, the income gap was roughly $150 in favor of the returnees; by 1979, although it had narrowed, the difference remained a highly significant $110.

These last results are of special interest to the analysis of the process of incorporation of Mexicans into the American labor market. Although not too different from the newcomers in the industries where they work or the status of the jobs they hold, prior experience in the United States appears to confer on returnees a significant economic advantage. However, these bivariate results offer only a glimpse of the underlying causal processes. The following sections will clarify the nature of this advantage and the causal linkages leading to it.

Segmented Labor Markets

We turn now to examine (1) whether identifiable labor-market segments exist in the occupational history of this sample, (2) whether a majority concentrates in the secondary sector, and (3) whether the apparent advantages conferred by prior U. S. residence are due to differential entry into one or another sector. Following a major theme of the previous chapter, this analysis considers not only the usual job-related characteristics, but also those variables pertaining to the ethnic characteristics of the places where immigrants work and live. As explained previously, the basic division to be expected in this instance is between entry into primary- versus secondary-sector jobs. Unlike Cuban refugees, Mexicans could not avail themselves of the relative protection offered by an established enclave economy. On the contrary, they had to fend for themselves in the open labor market from the very start.

Bivariate Results

As in the case of Cubans, empirical criteria for establishing sectoral divisions in the Mexican sample pose a certain difficulty. A number of indicators have been employed in previous research, including size of firm, occupational stability, average wage levels, and opportunities for job advancement. In addition, procedures have been developed for assigning entire industries to different sectors of the economy. We performed an analysis of this sample

based on one of these procedures, devised by Tolbert and his associates.[2]
Although results were more plausible than those obtained for Cubans, they
still produced an inconsistent pattern of differences between Mexicans assigned to the "core" and the "periphery" industrial sectors.

In the end, we chose to rely again on the criterion provided by ethnicity
of the labor force. This procedure reflects directly the emphasis placed by
dual-labor-market theories on ethnic divisions and the characterization of
the secondary sector as an "ethnic" one. More important, this sectoral differentiation more faithfully reflects the particular conditions of entry of
Mexicans in the American labor market, mostly in the Southwest. The large
majority of these immigrants find employment in small industrial and service firms with a predominantly ethnic work force; only a minority manage
to gain access to jobs in larger Anglo-owned and -staffed firms. Finally, the
use of the ethnicity criterion permits direct comparison between results for
Mexicans and those obtained for Cubans based on the same indicator.

Predictably, ethnicity of the labor force divides the Mexican sample into
two very uneven segments. Those who gained entry into the Anglo-dominated primary sector represent only 25 percent, or 113 cases; those in the
ethnic or secondary labor market comprise the remaining 75 percent, or
312 cases. As in the case of Cubans, we regard this initial division as tentative and in need of additional empirical confirmation. For this reason, the
remainder of this section examines the extent to which assignment to one or
another segment of the labor market on this basis produces empirical differences corresponding to prior theoretical expectations.

As a first step in this investigation, Table 78 presents average scores in
fourteen selected variables. The latter are subdivided into three sets: five
variables are indicators of job-related characteristics, including occupational status in 1979, size of the workplace, and monthly income;[3] the next
four variables measure characteristics of the immigrant's social relations,
including the ethnicity of his employer, number of relatives in the United
States, and ethnicity of his neighborhood; the last set pertains to subjective
attitudes and skills, including satisfaction with present job, knowledge of
English, and information about American society.

This relatively extensive list of economic, social, and subjective characteristics should reveal systematic differences, if any exist, between the two
hypothesized labor-market segments. First, the set of job-related characteristics yields differences that run consistently in the direction anticipated

2. The classification method used is described in Charles Tolbert, Patrick M. Horan, and
E. M. Beck, "The Structure of Economic Segmentation."
3. The cost-of-living adjustment was based on figures provided for the SMSA in which
the person lived in 1976 or 1979, or on the nearest administrative unit for which there was
available data.

Table 78. Average Characteristics of Mexican Immigrants
in Two Labor Markets, 1979

Variable	Primary	Secondary	Total
Occupation in 1979 (Duncan SEI scores)	20.75	19.81	20.06
Total employees in firm	4.43	4.36	4.36
Unionized workplace	0.36	0.31	0.32
Times unemployed since 1976	0.53	0.62	0.60
Monthly income in 1979 ($)†	1,003.39	880.27	913.42
Anglo employer in 1979[a]†	0.88	0.74	0.78
Number of relatives in the United States	43.81	39.65	40.75
Anglo neighborhood, 1976[a]†	0.31	0.18	0.22
Anglo neighborhood, 1979[a]†	0.41	0.21	0.27
Perceived opportunities to interact with Anglos[a]†	0.68	0.52	0.56
Perceived opportunities for job advancement[a]*	0.75	0.67	0.10
Salary satisfaction[a]**	0.19	0.11	0.13
Knowledge of U.S. index, 1979[b]	3.34	3.00	3.09
Knowledge of English index, 1979[c]**	3.73	2.99	3.18

[a]Dichotomized variables; coded 1 in agreement with their respective labels and 0 otherwise.

[b]USIN scale.   [c]KEI scale.

*Probability of equal means smaller   **Probability of equal means smaller
than .10.   than .05.

†Probability of equal means smaller than .01.

by dual-labor-market theory but that in most cases are not significant. The exception represents, however, a most important aspect for immigrant workers: as expected, those in the primary labor market receive an average income that surpasses the secondary-sector figure by a highly significant $123.12 per month.

Figures pertaining to the other two sets of variables indicate a number of additional sectoral differences. Workers in the primary sector are, for example, more likely to work and live alongside Anglos. Primary-sector workers also live more frequently in predominantly Anglo neighborhoods, both in 1976 and in 1979. Consistent with their concentration in an ethnic work force and in ethnic neighborhoods, Mexican immigrants in the secondary sector believe that they have fewer opportunities to interact with Anglos. They also perceive fewer opportunities for job advancement and are significantly less

satisfied with their present income. Perhaps associated with both their restricted circle of social relations and their perceived occupational limitations,
these immigrants have a level of English-language comprehension significantly below that of their primary-sector counterparts.

As a whole, these bivariate results are consistent with hypothesized differences between segmented labor markets. Most Mexican immigrants are
concentrated in an ethnic work force in which they earn significantly lower
wages; in addition to ethnic co-workers, they live among predominantly
Mexican or Mexican-American neighbors, have a greater chance of working
for a non-Anglo employer, comprehend minimal English, and perceive
their terms of employment as less satisfactory and without as many opportunities as are available to primary-sector employees. Only a relatively
small proportion of the sample managed to gain access to jobs in the Anglo-
dominated primary sector and the associated advantages.

Multivariate Analysis

In contrast to bivariate comparisons above, this section seeks to establish the causal process leading to entry into the primary labor market. In
this instance, we ask which variables discriminate best in giving access to a
minority of immigrants to better-paid jobs alongside Anglo co-workers. For
this purpose, labor-market-sector data in both 1976 and 1979 are regressed
on immigrant characteristics at the moment of arrival and on those acquired during their initial years in the United States.

The first two columns of Table 79 present results of a logistic regression
using sector of employment in 1979 as the dependent variable. In addition
to logit coefficients, which estimate the logarithm of the probability of employment in the primary sector, the first-order partial derivatives are also
included. The latter are interpretable as effects on the probability of gaining access to a primary-sector job of a unit increase in each independent
variable, controlling for the others. Independent variables for this analysis
include father's occupation, in Duncan SEI scores; years of formal schooling
in Mexico; years of prior residence in the United States; knowledge of English; and the immigrants' expected level of aid from family and friends,
coded from a low score for "no aid" to a high for "much aid."

Three variables are derived from the second interview in 1976 and indicate the number of months of formal schooling in the United States from
1973 to 1976, the ethnicity of employers, and the sector of employment in
the latter year. Each variable in the list represents attributes measured
before 1979, thus eliminating the possibility of ambiguous causal relationships with the dependent variable.

Results in Table 79 indicate that individual background variables, including such indicators of human capital as education and knowledge of English, do not significantly affect access to primary-sector employment after six years in the United States. The strongest effects on the dependent variable are the inertial one of employment sector in 1976 and of employer's ethnicity in the same year. After controlling for them, the only other effect that approaches statistical significance is that of expected aid from family and friends. The influence of this variable is noteworthy: the *more* aid expected, the *less* likely are immigrants to obtain access to the Anglo-dominated primary sector.

Results of this first regression show, however, that Mexican immigrants are incorporated into one or another labor market soon after legal entry and tend to stay there. Hence, the next logical step consists of investigating determinants of early employment in either sector. To pursue this issue, the last rows of Table 79 present results of two other logistic regressions, with sector of employment in 1976 and ethnicity of employer in 1976 as dependent variables. In contrast to the preceding run, the first of these regressions shows that the early entry of workers into the primary sector is related to several background characteristics. Although the immigrant's own education has no effect, his father's occupational status and his knowledge of English increase the probability of working among Anglos in 1976. Equally important is the effect of prior U. S. residence: the longer a person has lived previously in the United States, the greater are his chances of primary-sector employment. This last effect begins to bring into focus the causal relationship between prior residence on the one hand and access to better-paid and stable jobs on the other. These results suggest that the economic advantage of returnees over first-time entrants is related to the fact that the latter are able to translate their previous U. S. experience into access to jobs in the primary sector.

Determinants of finding a job with an Anglo employer in 1976 further clarify this causal relationship. The last columns of Table 79 show that, among individual characteristics, only prior residence in the United States again contributes significantly to an explanation of this dependent variable. Thus, the two variables that most powerfully affect current (1979) employment sector are themselves significantly affected by the years that the immigrant had spent in the country. This result again supports the conclusion that the economic advantage of Mexican returnees is due to their superior access to employment in the upper tier of a segmented labor market.

At first glance, this result seems entirely consistent with human-capital theories, which argue that longer residence in the United States gives the immigrant time to learn skills required to obtain good jobs. However, this interpretation would be erroneous. Length of residence in the country is

Table 79. Logit Estimates of Effects of Background Characteristics and Experiences
on the Probability of Sector of Employment and Ethnicity of
Employer: Mexican Immigrants
(Standard Errors in Parentheses)

Predictors	Sector of Employment, 1979[a]		Sector of Employment, 1976[a]		Ethnicity of Employer, 1976[b]	
	Logit Coefficient	First Derivative[c]	Logit Coefficient	First Derivative[c]	Logit Coefficient	First Derivative[c]
Constant	-2.687[+] (.495)	-.524	-2.322[+] (.278)	-.325	.483[+] (.148)	.094
Father's occupation	--[‡]		.016** (.007)	.002	--	
Education	--		--		--	
Prior residence in United States	--		.182** (.082)	.025	.362[+] (.077)	.071
English knowledge at arrival	--		.292* (.121)	.041	--	
Expected aid from family and friends	-.210* (.114)	-.041	--		--	
Length of courses in United States before 1976	--		--		--	

employed, within a human-capital framework, as a proxy for unobserved skills learned through an hypothesized assimilation process. In the present analysis, we have been able to use direct measures of skills acquired before and after entry into the United States as predictors of primary-sector employment. Inclusion of these measures in the equations should effectively reduce the effect of the proxy—length of residence—to insignificance. Results show precisely the opposite, as net effects of this variable are maintained while those of most other individual traits become insignificant in the 1976 regressions.

In addition, perhaps the most relevant skill considered in human-capital analyses of immigrant labor, knowledge of English, has a negative (albeit insignificant) association with employment in an Anglo-owned firm. Evidently, and contrary to conventional expectations, these immigrants are not hired by Anglo employers on the basis of individual skills said to be highly valued in the American labor market.

The relationship between prior U. S. residence and access to primary-sector jobs is not due to the gradual acquisition of skills by immigrants but, apparently, to the social networks established *before* legal entry. As reported in Chapter 5, many of the immigrants who lived and worked in the United States before 1973 were returning to the same cities *and* jobs. The initial link between Mexican worker and Anglo employer and co-workers seemed to have occurred while the immigrant was temporarily north of the border, either as a commuter or as an illegal alien. Upon their reentry into the United States, many of these immigrants simply returned to their old jobs and were rehired irrespective of their "new" human capital.

In synthesis, results in this section show, first, that systematic empirical differences exist between primary and secondary labor markets, as defined by the ethnicity of the labor force; second, that a substantial majority of Mexican immigrants cluster in the secondary labor market, as anticipated by qualitative descriptions of this flow; and third, that the advantage of prior U. S. residents over first-time immigrants in terms of occupational stability and higher wages is due, at least in part, to the more frequent entry of the returnees into the primary sector, where those job advantages are predominant. The relationship between previous U. S. experience and access to better jobs does not depend, however, on the acquisition of superior skills by the returnees. Instead, it appears to reflect the greater ability of prior residents to establish the networks necessary to gain access to firms with a predominantly Anglo workforce. This process accounts for the prompt entry of many returnees into primary employment and the consequent division of the sample along labor-market segments, almost immediately after arrival.

LABOR-MARKET RETURNS IN TWO SECTORS

The present section examines the logical next question, namely whether the process of occupational and income attainment differs for immigrants once they become inserted into one or another labor market. This analysis parallels that conducted for Cubans in the previous chapter. At first glance, this presentation is redundant, since results of being incorporated into the primary, as opposed to the secondary, sector can be easily anticipated on the basis of past research and the pattern established for Cuban refugees. This is not the case, however. Past research on dual labor markets has dealt primarily with the general population, not with specific immigrant groups. It is perfectly possible that immigrants from two different minorities incorporated into the same sector of the economy experience very different outcomes in terms of occupation and income. This is the question to be explored in this analysis.

The dependent variables are occupation and monthly income in the United States in 1976 and 1979. Occupational-status variables are again coded in Duncan SEI scores; income is the natural logarithm of the individual's total monthly earnings plus receipts from other sources, such as rents and interest. In this sample, income is, for all practical purposes, identical with wage earnings. The logarithmic transformation implies that differences in the dependent variable represent *proportional* differences in actual income.

Table 80 presents the regressions of occupation and income in 1976 on the following variables drawn from standard status-attainment models: father's occupation, work experience and its quadratic term, education, and occupational aspirations. In addition, several variables are included that reflect the uniqueness of immigrants' occupational experiences in general and of Mexican immigrants in particular. These are monthly income prior to legal entry, length of prior residence in the United States, knowledge of English at arrival, expected aid from family and friends, and months of formal schooling in the United States.[4]

Figures in Table 80 present a fairly complex pattern. Examined in detail, however, they reveal important aspects of the process of incorporation

---

4. Father's occupation and occupational aspirations are coded in Duncan SEI scores. Work experience is defined as age minus education minus 6. Education at arrival is coded in years, and U.S. education in months completed. Income prior to legal entry is the natural logarithm of the respondent's monthly earnings and other monetary receipts in the year prior to arrival as a permanent resident. Knowledge of English at arrival is measured by the KEI scale. Length of prior residence and expected aid from family and friends are both ordinal scales described previously.

Table 80. Determinants of Early Occupational Status
and Income in Two Labor Markets: 1976

Independent Variables	Dependent Variables			
	Primary Sector		Secondary Sector	
	Occupation, 1976	Income, 1976	Occupation, 1976	Income, 1976
Father's occupation	.108[a]	.473*	.067*	-.192
Work experience	.159	-1.219	.164	.249
(Work experience)^2	-.003	.011	-.007	-.019
Education	-.672	1.765	.088	-.245
Occupational aspirations	.094*	-.034	.012	-.162
Income before entry	3.806*	23.782**	1.454*	10.228**
Prior residence in the U.S.	-9.638**	-4.787	-.749	13.743*
Expected aid	-.246	.783	-.132	.548
Knowledge of English	.843	1.591	1.607*	-1.115
U.S. education	.176	.831*	-.184*	.664
Occupation, 1976	--	.128	--	2.498**
R^2	.199	.438	.099	.254

[a]Metric regression coefficients. Those in the income regressions are taken to the fifth significant digit and multiplied by 100.

*Coefficient exceeds twice its standard error.

**Coefficient exceeds three times its standard error.

of Mexican immigrants. In other words, occupational and income attainment among Mexicans do not mechanically reproduce those of the labor force as a whole or those found among Cubans.

We consider determinants of occupational status first. Indicators of background human capital or that acquired in the United States do not do well as predictors of occupation in either sector. In the primary regression, the only predicted effect that turns out to be significant corresponds to occupational aspirations and is relatively small. An effect of similar magnitude, corresponding to father's occupation, is found in the secondary sector.

In both regressions, a key determinant of early occupational status is the immigrants' income prior to legal arrival. Since prior U. S. residence and work experience are controlled, this income effect cannot be interpreted as a proxy for previous employment in the United States or for longer stays in the labor market. Instead, preimmigration income may represent a facilitational variable, allowing immigrants to select their occupations more carefully or perhaps even buy their way into better jobs.

Education in the United States has a sizable *negative* effect on early occupation among Mexicans in the secondary labor market. This effect, reminiscent of a similar one found for Cuban refugees in the same sector, can be readily interpreted as a result of the reduced opportunities for on-the-job promotion involved in acquiring additional training during the early years.

However, the most significant results in the occupational regressions correspond to prior U. S. residence and knowledge of English. Recall that these were the two major variables determining access of Mexican immigrants to primary-sector employment. Once inside this labor market, however, knowledge of English has no effect on occupations and that of prior residence is strongly negative. This last result suggests that, while longer U. S. residence may be the common path of access to primary-sector jobs, those first-time immigrants whose qualifications allow them to enter this market directly do better in terms of early occupational attainment. In contrast to primary-sector results, immigrants in the secondary labor market experienced a significant positive occupational return on their knowledge of English in 1976.

Regressions of 1976 income follow the same general pattern. As in the occupational regressions, explained variance in the primary subsample is significantly higher. This result is not due, however, to the predicted positive effects of human-capital variables. Neither education nor knowledge of English has a significant effect on income in the primary sector. Surprisingly, not even occupation affects income in the same year. Among human-capital indicators, only father's occupation and U. S. education have the anticipated positive effects. Both are relatively small. The same absence of effects of individual-level skills is apparent in the secondary sector, where the sole predicted effect to reach significance is that of current occupation. In contrast to primary-sector results, however, this effect is quite sizable: an additional SEI status point yields a reliable average gain of $14.70 per month in 1976.

In both regressions, income prior to legal entry plays a pivotal role in determining economic position three years later. These effects are congruent with those of the same variable on 1976 occupation and again partially reproduce those detected in the Cuban analysis. The effect of prior residence in the United States on income in the primary sector is negative, although, in this case, it does not reach statistical significance. In the secondary labor market, however, prior U. S. residence exercises a strong positive influence. Evaluated at the mean, each additional one- to two-year period of residence in the United States yields a net payoff of $80 per month.

This complex set of results suggests that Mexican-immigrant incorporation into the two segments of the labor market yields consequences at variance with those found among the general population and among Cuban refugees. As we saw previously, only a minority of Mexican immigrants managed to gain access to the Anglo segment of the labor force, but those who did received significantly higher incomes. However, Mexicans in primary-sector firms appear confined to the same low-level menial jobs characteristic of secondary employment, as evidenced by the absence of significant occupational-status differences between the two sectors. In 1976 and again in 1979, average SEI scores for immigrants in the two sectors differed by less than one SEI point.

More important, however, is the fact that human-capital variables do not seem to help Mexicans to move out of their uniformly low-level positions in the primary sector. In contrast with the situation for Cubans, knowledge of English does not yield a sizable occupational return for Mexicans; nor does any other individual skill. Occupational status fails, in turn, to affect income, which continues to depend on the inertial effect of preentry resources. Thus, contrary to expectations, Mexican immigrants in primary employment find opportunities for advancement on the basis of personal skills blocked.

Before attempting an interpretation of these surprising results, we must see whether they continue to hold after six years in the United States. The set of predictors for these new regressions is identical to that in Table 80 with the following exceptions: expected aid from family and friends is deleted, since it did not have a single reliable effect; U. S. education in the early years is substituted for months of formal training between 1976 and 1979; knowledge of English in 1979 replaces knowledge of English at arrival, both variables being correlated over .90. Finally, occupational status and income in 1976 are included as predictors of the respective dependent variables in 1979.

Results of the 1979 regressions are presented in Table 81. They show that after six years the pattern of effects on occupation begins to approximate the expectations stemming from dual-labor-market theory. As predicted, explained variance is significantly higher in the primary sector, and in this case the result is a consequence of effects of several human-capital variables. Net of the effect of 1976 occupation, five significant coefficients correspond to father's occupation, education, occupational aspirations at arrival, and the linear and quadratic terms of work experience. However,

Table 81.   Determinants of Occupational Status and
Income in Two Labor Markets: 1979

Independent Variables	Dependent Variables			
	Primary Sector		Secondary Sector	
	Occupation, 1979	Income, 1979	Occupation, 1979	Income, 1979
Father's occupation	.152^{*a}	.348	.089*	.129
Work experience	2.130**	.341	.008	2.213*
(Work experience)^2	-.039**	-.044	.035	-.045*
Education	2.783**	-2.344	1.262**	1.723
Occupational aspirations	.129*	.141	-.013	.190
Income before entry	-1.215	9.537*	-.306	.994
Prior U.S. residence	-4.391	-6.516	-.383	13.124*
Knowledge of English	-.677	2.268	.526	1.919*
U.S. education	-.264	.462	.099	.136
Occupation, 1976	.248*	--	.366**	--
Income, 1976	--	18.227**	--	30.605**
Occupation, 1979	--	.391	--	.364
R^2	.469	.330	.267	.369

^{a}Metric regression coefficients. Those in the income regressions are taken to the fifth significant digit and multiplied by 100.

*Coefficient exceeds twice its standard error.

**Coefficient exceeds three times its standard error.

net effects of knowledge of English and prior U. S. residence are both insignificant and negative.

Also in agreement with dual-labor-market predictions is the fact that the process of occupational attainment in the secondary sector is much less strongly determined. Three reliable effects are also present in the primary subsample, but they are different in magnitude. Education and father's occupation have positive effects on occupational status; the size of these coefficients is, however, smaller than in the primary sector. The difference between the two education coefficients yields a t-statistic of 2.08, significant at the .025 level in a directional test; that between parental occupation effects is significant at the .10 level.

On the other hand, the influence of 1976 occupation is much stronger among secondary-sector workers. This result suggests that the process of reaching occupations in this sector is largely determined in the early years, when it is influenced by such variables as knowledge of English and preentry income. Subsequent occupational attainment reproduces, for the most part, the earlier positions.

However, it is the set of income regressions that provides the conclusive evidence on sectoral differences in the Mexican sample. The primary-sector coefficients follow closely the pattern detected in 1976. In this case, results are still more compelling: not a *single* indicator of human capital affects income directly in this sector. There are no indirect effects of these variables either, since 1979 occupation also fails to affect income. In other words, the pattern of reliable human-capital influences on occupation detected earlier is entirely self-contained, and fails to translate into sizable income differences. In this situation, 1979 income is primarily a function of the same variable three years earlier, which in turn is determined by pre-entry income.

Results in the secondary subsample are equally unambiguous. Income in 1976 also exercises a strong but by no means exclusive influence on the same variable in 1979. In this case, work experience displays the nonlinear effect anticipated by human-capital theory. The more theoretically important results correspond, however, to the other two reliable coefficients in this regression. In contrast to primary-sector results, both knowledge of English and prior residence in the United States significantly increase 1979 income. The magnitude of these effects is substantial: each unit increase in the Knowledge of English Index adds $17.60 per month, on the average; each one- to two-year period of U. S. residence adds a net $115.

An initial interpretation of these results is based on the alternative uses to which certain individual resources can be put: a minority of Mexican immigrants are able to translate their prior experience in the United States and knowledge of English into access to primary-sector firms and better-paid, although dead-end jobs. The majority, confined to the secondary labor market, can still improve their lower absolute incomes through an alternative use of the same resources. In this sector, where most co-workers are fellow ethnics, better English improves the chances of occupational advancement, which translates in turn into higher wages. More important still, prior experience in the country has a decisive effect on income levels, probably by allowing immigrants to identify the more remunerative opportunities available within the secondary labor market.

This interpretation differs, of course, from theoretical characterizations of employment conditions in the dual-labor-market literature. It finds a precedent, however, in a few empirical studies which have identified secondarylike, dead-end jobs within large "core" firms.[5] These studies suggest the existence of a "lower tier" within enterprises in the primary sector, composed of low-level menial occupations such as janitorial services, custodial positions, and the like. Such jobs benefit from the higher wages offered by these firms, but do not form part of their internal ladders of promotion.

The evidence presented in this chapter indicates that this kind of niche is apparently reserved for Mexican immigrants in firms where an Anglo labor force is dominant. Access to these firms confers on the immigrants certain clear advantages in terms of better pay and occupational stability. However, Mexicans remain confined to menial occupations not too different from those in the secondary sector. More important, income level among Mexicans in the primary labor market is indifferent to the immigrants' personal attributes and skills: no matter what level of education immigrants have acquired or how much English they know, their pay remains about the same.

A more basic interpretation of these results is based on the class composition of Mexican immigration. Qualitative descriptions of this flow have noted that, despite somewhat diverse occupational origins in Mexico, immigrants in the United States are directed to the same homogeneous pool of low-wage, menial labor. The characterization of Mexican immigration as being overwhelmingly a source of labor for the secondary sector is not only supported by the above results, but acquires, in their light, a more poignant meaning. Unlike other working-class immigrations, it is not the case that a majority of Mexicans concentrate in low-level jobs, while a few manage to gain full access to the primary sector. Among these immigrants, even those employed in primary-sector firms are confined to secondarylike occupations. This explains why no occupational-status differences exist between Mexicans in the two sectors and why the significant differences between them have to do more with residential and social variables than with actual conditions of employment. The latter are similar in both labor-market segments, reflecting the uniformly subordinate position assigned to these immigrants in the American labor market.

MODES OF STRUCTURAL INCORPORATION: CUBANS AND MEXICANS

We turn now to a direct comparison of the labor-market experiences of the two samples. This task focuses on a comparison of the processes of these groups' occupational and income attainment. The purpose of this exercise

5. See Michael J. Piore, "Notes for a Theory of Labor Market Stratification," and Richard Edwards, *Contested Terrain*, chaps. 9, 10.

is to bring into a coherent whole previously noted differences between the two groups. These results provide the basis for an integrated statement about the occupational and economic impact of different factors.

Clearly, a simple contrast of main effects will not do, since, as repeatedly demonstrated above, the distinct feature of the attainment process in both samples is the interaction of individual with structural variables. To avoid a simple repetition of prior results, this last analysis approaches the issue of occupation and income from a somewhat different perspective. The analysis assumes that the 1979 indicators of these variables are dependent exclusively on variables measured at the same point in time or at the moment of arrival. By eliminating intervening effects, these reduced-form models provide an answer for a somewhat different, albeit significant question: To what extent is the attainment process affected by the original background variables and by traits acquired during the entire postmigration period?

Comparative Processes of
Attainment: Occupation

Predictor variables for this analysis are the same employed in the preceding sections. Knowledge of English in 1979 is used in lieu of knowledge of English at arrival, given the high intercorrelation between both. Prior U. S. residence is employed only in the Mexican regressions, since the variable is close to a zero constant in the Cuban sample. Marital status at arrival (coded 1 for married and 2 for single, separated, divorced, or widowed) is the single variable added to the list of predictors. All other variables in the analysis, including occupational status, are measured as described previously.

Collinearity between additive predictor variables and multiplicative ones measuring the various interactions reduces the explanatory power of the latter and renders interpretation of the actual magnitude of effects problematic. Following Lane, we computed F-ratios to test the significance of differences in explained variance between the additive and additive-plus-multiplicative models.[6] Through use of a stepwise procedure, it was also possible to monitor changes in the magnitude of coefficients as new interactions were added. Results presented below reproduce the basic pattern of main effects and principal interactions found to emerge in each sample after a number of runs. Because of collinearity, the actual magnitude of coefficients must be interpreted, however, with caution.

Table 82 presents the ordinary least squares regressions of 1979 occupational status on independent variables for both samples. All main effects are included, as are those interactions found to be significant in each sample. The first and most obvious result is that occupational attainment among

6. Angela Lane, "Occupational Mobility in Six Cities."

Table 82. Determinants of Occupation in 1979:
Cubans and Mexicans

Predictors	Occupational Status, 1979			
	Cubans		Mexicans	
Father's occupation	.126	(.074)[a]	.203*	(.043)
Education	1.778*	(.623)	.894*	(.317)
Work experience	.355	(.670)	.379	(.291)
(Work experience)^2	-.006	(.011)	-.005	(.006)
Income before legal entry	3.228*	(1.226)	-.047	(.636)
Occupational aspirations	.018	(.085)	.022	(.032)
Expected aid	-1.292	(1.299)	.166	(.560)
Marital status	-.442	(3.667)	.674	(2.083)
Prior U.S. residence	--[d]		-.679	(1.507)
Education in the U.S.	.414*	(.163)	.089	(.070)
Knowledge of English	2.287*	(.881)	.930*	(.285)
Education/PSI[b]	-1.250	(.687)	.982*	(.474)
Work experience/PSI	--[d]		.906*	(.453)
U.S. education/PSI	-.526*	(.228)	--[d]	
Knowledge of English/PSI	2.393*	(1.154)	-1.325*	(.571)
Father's occupation/EI[c]	-.234*	(.106)	--[d]	
Education/EI	2.100*	(.809)	--[d]	
Knowledge of English/EI	-2.292*	(1.149)	--[d]	
R^2	.471		.254	

[a]Standard errors in parentheses.   [b]Primary-sector interaction.

[c]Enclave interaction.   [d]Excluded from the equation
                                          (insufficient variance or
*Coefficient exceeds twice its   tolerance level).
standard error.

Cuban exiles is far better explained than among Mexican immigrants. The model accounts for close to half the occupational-status variance in the Cuban sample, but only one-fourth in the Mexican. As expected, interaction effects contribute significantly to explained variance, accounting for a ten-point net increase in the Cuban regression and close to five points in the Mexican.

After controlling for sectoral interactions, the pattern of main effects continues to display many more differences than similarities across samples. Education and knowledge of English are significant predictors of occupational status in both samples, but their effects are stronger among Cuban refugees. The difference between the knowledge of English effects yields a t-statistic of 1.465, significant at the .08 level in a directional test; the difference between education coefficients is statistically significant at the .12 level.

In addition, education acquired in the United States and income in the year prior to arrival significantly improve occupational status in the Cuban sample, but not in the Mexican. For Cuban refugees, the effect of U. S.-acquired education is quite strong; in this regression, a month of additional training yields almost a half-point net increase in occupational status. Among Mexicans, it is not U. S.-acquired training, but background parental status that continues to have a significant effect on 1979 occupation.

The existence of major differences between the two immigrant groups is confirmed by the interaction effects. What these results indicate is that not only are Mexicans and Cubans different in their modes of labor-market incorporation, but the outcomes of their entry into the *same* sectors also diverge. For example, while education and knowledge of English have positive main effects in both samples, their interaction with primary-sector employment produces effects of opposite sign: reflecting the central role of knowledge of English for primary-sector mobility among Cubans, the corresponding interaction is both positive and significant; reflecting the fact that knowledge of English facilitates access to the primary sector, but has no payoff within it for Mexicans, the same interaction is negative.

A positive education / primary-sector interaction in the Mexican sample corresponds to the status gain after six years reported earlier in this chapter. The sizable negative interactions between primary-sector employment and both education at arrival and U. S. education among Cubans reflect the fact that educational variables have a higher occupational payoff in the enclave. Reinforcing this conclusion, the corresponding enclave / education interaction is positive and significant. Finally, the relative unimportance of knowledge of English for occupational advancement in the enclave, as contrasted with the primary sector, is reflected in the negative enclave / English interaction in the Cuban sample.

Despite difficulties of estimation, results from this analysis provide an adequate summary of the divergent occupational careers of Cubans and Mexicans in the United States. In both samples, occupational attainment is modified by insertion into different labor markets and education and knowledge of English have significant positive effects, but this is as far as similarities go. Because the histories and their employment options upon arrival differ sharply between the groups, the effects of background variables and U. S.-acquired skills diverge even after incorporation into different labor markets is controlled for. Significant interactions emerge in both samples, but they are frequently of opposite signs. The existence of an enclave employment option for Cuban refugees and the characteristic insertion of Mexicans into secondarylike occupations are the major factors underlying these results.

Income

Since monetary rewards are the main focus of interest of labor-market studies, this last analysis addresses the most sharply contested theoretical terrain. Again, our dependent variable is income, defined as the sum total of money wages and salaries, profits, dividends, interest, and rents. We begin this analysis by comparing the average income of both groups in 1976 and 1979.

Table 83. Average Monthly Income: Mexicans and Cubans, 1976 and 1979

Year	Mexicans, $\bar{X}_1$	Cubans, $\bar{X}_2$	$P\ [\bar{X}_1 = \bar{X}_2]$
1976 Income			
Unadjusted	$629.40	$616.73	.546
Adjusted for cost of living[a]	$649.37	$621.71	.216
1979 Income			
Unadjusted	$909.20	$1,042.81	.001
Adjusted for cost of living[a]	$912.40	$1,056.62	.000

[a]Cost of living adjustment based on the respondent's place of residence in each year.

Table 83 shows that in 1976 there was virtually no difference between the average monthly income of these immigrant groups: both received roughly $620 a month or $7,400 a year. Since each group is concentrated in a very different region of the United States where cost-of-living differences may obscure unequal income, we also calculated comparisons among adjusted figures. Each group's income increased as a result of these adjustments, while the gap between them widened. The difference, however, was not statistically significant.

Figures in the table also show that, three years later, Cuban refugees had gained a significant advantage of roughly $135 a month. In 1979, Cubans received an average $12,500 a year, compared with $11,000 for Mexicans, assuming continuous work for all employed respondents throughout the year. Adjusting for cost of living, the income differential was even greater.

The following analysis of income attainment employs as dependent variable the natural logarithm of monthly income in 1979. It is important to emphasize again that absolute differences in this transformed variable represent *proportional* differences in real income. Table 84 presents results of regressing logged income on all predictors and significant interactions in both samples. As in the occupational regressions, the first finding of note is that income attainment is much better explained by this set of predictors in the Cuban than in the Mexican sample. Roughly two-fifths of income variance is accounted for in the Cuban regressions, as opposed to one-fifth in the Mexican. Despite high collinearity, interactions increase explained variance by slightly over 10 percent in each sample.

After controlling for labor-market interactions, the pattern of main effects continues to be different across samples. Results essentially replicate those presented earlier: among Cubans, income attainment is a direct consequence of occupational attainment; in agreement with sectoral regressions presented in Chapter 6, occupational status has the sole significant main effect on income, net of interactions, and accounts by itself for most explained variance. Occupation is also a significant, but much weaker predictor in the Mexican sample. Reliable effects among the latter are also associated with work experience, knowledge of English, and prior legal residence. Linear and quadratic effects of work experience are in agreement with predictions stemming from human-capital theory, as are those of knowledge of English and time spent previously in the country.

Had we confined the analysis to main effects in the total samples, we would have missed, however, the divergent processes underlying these findings. As earlier results demonstrated, knowledge of English and prior U. S. residence are major determinants of the attainment process among Mexicans, but their role varies across labor markets: in the predominantly

Table 84.   Determinants of Income in 1979:
Cubans and Mexicans

Predictors	Income, 1979			
	Cubans		Mexicans	
Father's occupation	.222[a]	(.146)	.203	(.132)
Education	-2.587	(1.682)	1.179	(1.103)
Work experience	.269	(1.968)	2.063*	(.962)
(Work experience)^2	-.028	(.037)	-.045*	(.019)
Income before legal entry	5.536	(3.624)	2.398	(2.455)
Occupational aspirations	.315	(.196)	.157	(.097)
Expected aid	5.405	(3.094)	-.263	(1.736)
Marital status	13.717	(7.870)	2.251	(7.332)
Prior U.S. residence	--[d]		18.063*	(5.365)
Education in the U.S.	-.269	(.267)	-.433	(.313)
Knowledge of English	-.732	(1.450)	2.288*	(.880)
Occupational status, 1979	1.014*	(.157)	.359*	(.177)
Education/PSI[b]	5.165*	(2.201)	-2.345	(1.610)
Work experience^2/PSI	.097*	(.048)	-.029*	(.014)
Prior income/PSI	--[d]		11.358*	(3.980)
Prior residence/PSI	--[d]		-20.808*	(10.350)
Expected aid/EI[c]	10.467*	(4.527)	--[d]	
R^2	.415		.227	

[a]Metric regression coefficients taken to the fifth significant digit and multiplied by 100; standard errors in parentheses.

[b]Primary-sector interaction.

[c]Enclave interaction.

[d]Excluded from the equation. (Insufficient variance or tolerance level.)

*Coefficient exceeds twice its standard error.

ethnic secondary sector, these variables confer a significant advantage; although they also facilitate entry into the Anglo-dominated primary sector, they have no payoff once immigrants are in it. Significant main effects of knowledge of English and prior U. S. residence in the total-sample regression are a consequence of combining both types of influence.

The pattern of interaction effects again reinforces the conclusion of major differences between the two immigrant groups. In agreement with prior findings, interactions with primary-sector employment vary significantly across samples. The education/primary-sector interaction is significant and positive among Cuban refugees, reflecting the higher economic payoff of formal training in this labor market. Among Mexicans, the corresponding coefficient is insignificant and negative. Similar interactions are found with the quadratic term of work experience: among Cubans in the primary sector, this variable has a beneficial effect on income; among Mexicans, the same effect is also reliable, but negative.

It is the remaining interactions, however, that most sharply reflect the contrasting modes of incorporation of these immigrant groups. The sizable interaction of expected aid from family and friends with enclave employment highlights the central role of social networks in promoting economic mobility among refugees in the Miami economy. In contrast, the important, but contradictory influence of prior residence in the United States for Mexican immigrants is revealed again by its large negative interaction with primary-sector employment.

The absence of an economic payoff for human capital among Mexicans in the primary sector is again demonstrated by these results. The differential effects of education and knowledge of English in this sample are insignificant; those of work experience and prior experience in the country are actually negative. In this situation, only preentry income makes a difference in the economic situation of primary-sector employees after six years in the United States.

SUMMARY

Any attempt to integrate the many analytical steps taken in this chapter requires a return to its central theme, the differential use of immigrant labor. More than any other topic, this is one where conventional labor-market theories join popular mythology in defining the economic progress of immigrants in the United States as dependent exclusively upon individual abilities and motivations. Whether this is called "Americanization" in orthodox texts or assimilation in the sociological literature, the analytic emphasis is the same.

In this and the preceding chapters, we have attempted to examine in close detail the processes through which two immigrant groups become incorporated into the American labor market and experience occupational and economic mobility. It is not the case that individual background experiences and skills are unimportant, but that a gross assessment of their effects conceals significant nuances specific to each group. The latter processes, depending on the concrete structures into which immigrants become incorporated, make a decisive difference in their occupational and economic situation. In constructing an alternative account, we have drawn from both human capital and nonorthodox dual-labor-market theories for models of the attainment process. These theoretical guides have been supplemented, however, by a knowledge of relevant factors in the history of each group.

The analysis in the present chapter started with a consideration of historical rather than theoretical differences: those existing between Mexican immigrants with a prior history of undocumented residence in the United States and first-time arrivals. Results confirmed the significance of such differences. Following the guide of dual-labor-market theory, we defined labor-market sectors according to the predominant ethnicity of their labor force. The analysis then moved to demonstrate empirical differences between the Anglo / primary and the ethnic / secondary sectors over a series of economic, social, and social psychological variables. The historical and theoretical notions guiding the analysis converged in results that showed prior U. S. residence to be a decisive facilitator of entry into the primary sector.

Up to that point, results followed closely the pattern predicted by dual-labor-market theory. The next set of findings diverged sharply, however: Mexican immigrants in the primary sector receive higher average incomes by reason of their gaining access to it, but are not rewarded economically for their human capital; economic returns to individual skills and experience are actually higher in the secondary sector. These findings are consistent with the characterization of Mexican immigration as being overwhelmingly a menial labor flow confined to subordinate positions in the U. S. labor market. Not only does the majority of these immigrants cluster in the secondary sector, but those who have gained access to primary employment appear confined to jobs in which individual skills are not translated into economic returns.

Finally, we compared occupational and income attainment between the two immigrant samples. This last analysis summarizes the many but systematic differences in the labor-market experiences of both groups. As a summary statement, such results provide final evidence of the contrasting modes of incorporation of Cubans arriving in a setting dominated by immigrant business networks and Mexicans who perpetuate the fate of earlier

8

AMERICA IN THE EYES
OF THE IMMIGRANTS

In this chapter, we examine the views of immigrants with respect to American society and their place in it. In the first sections, we present the evolution of perceptions and attitudes of immigrants toward a variety of issues. The last part focuses on the development and measurement of a general concept—perceptions of society and discrimination—and an analysis of its determinants.

The study of attitudes and perceptions corresponds to the fourth theoretical focus outlined in Chapter 1—the process of immigrant cultural adaptation. In the past, most scholars' attention has focused on the ways the native population viewed different immigrant minorities and the social distance it chose to keep from them.[1] Clearly, however, the perceptions immigrants have of the receiving country, in particular the extent to which they see themselves fairly treated or discriminated against, are central aspects of the adaptation process. A major difference between competing theoretical perspectives in this area has to do precisely with the evolution of immigrants' attitudes over time.

The assimilation and ethnic-resilience perspectives suggest very different outcomes for the sequence of events through which immigrants come to view their situation in the host society. For this reason, we return here to the theoretical discussion in the first chapter, drawing from it competing hypotheses that can be examined on the basis of our data. The interplay

This chapter was written with the collaboration of Thomas W. Reilly.

1. See, for example, W. Lloyd Warner and Leo Srole, *The Social Systems of American Ethnic Groups*, and Milton Gordon, *Assimilation in American Life*.

between assimilation and ethnic consciousness as alternative paths of the adaptation process will frame the presentation of results from the two immigrant samples below.

PERCEPTIONS AND ATTITUDES: DESCRIPTIVE FINDINGS

Early Expectations

At the time of arrival in the United States, Cubans and Mexicans differed in their views about the kind of society they were entering. Results in the top panel of Table 85 indicate that Mexicans were much more sanguine about opportunities to fulfill their occupational aspirations in the United States. Fewer than half (46 percent) believed that they would have at least sufficient opportunities to attain these goals. Another fourth (27 percent) were unwilling to voice any aspirations. Perhaps reflecting their lack of prior familiarity with American society and correspondingly greater optimism, 66 percent of Cuban refugees believed that they would have sufficient or many opportunities to fulfill their own goals.

Three years after arrival, however, a notable convergence had taken place. Both immigrant samples were now very close in their views of opportunities available to them in the United States. As the bottom panel of Table 85 shows, the general trend was toward a more pessimistic outlook, but the change had occurred at a different pace. Among Mexicans, the proportion believing in at least sufficient opportunities had dropped slightly to 42 percent; among Cubans, however, the decline was precipitous: from two-thirds of the sample in 1973 to only 41 percent in 1976. At the other extreme, the proportions believing that the United States held few or no opportunities for them increased rapidly, reaching about one-fifth of each sample in 1976.[2]

The shift toward less optimistic occupational expectations may reflect a more realistic appraisal of existing conditions, a trend most marked among those immigrants with less prior experience of American society. Our follow-up survey in 1976 coincided with the tail-end of the 1975 recession, which made it more difficult for recent entrants in the labor force to improve or even maintain their positions. The sharp increase in pessimistic assessments

2. These and subsequent figures are based on the full samples drawn at each stage of the study. This is based on evidence, presented in Chapter 3, of the absence of serious mortality bias in the follow-up samples. An alternative strategy would have been to consider only those immigrants interviewed at all three points in time. However, frequency distributions for these subsamples reproduce, with minor variations, those obtained from the full samples of both immigrant groups. To avoid redundancy, only the latter are presented.

Table 85. Perceptions of Opportunities for Attaining
Occupational Aspirations in the United States,
1973-1976

	Little or None, %	Some, %	Sufficient, %	Many, %	No Aspirations (D.K.[a]), %	Totals, %
			1973			
Cubans	4.2	23.9	41.4	24.4	6.1	100.0 (587)
Mexicans	6.6	21.1	29.8	15.0	27.5	100.0 (802)
			1976			
Cubans	20.8	28.9	28.2	13.2	8.9	100.0 (418)
Mexicans	17.9	35.0	31.9	9.7	5.6	100.0 (414)

[a]D.K. = don't know.

[b]In this and subsequent tables, figures in parentheses are the number of cases on which percentages are based.

among both immigrant groups, and especially among Cuban exiles, corresponded to this changing and increasingly difficult economic climate.

Satisfaction, Problems, and Plans

In 1976 and again in 1979, immigrants were asked how satisfied they were with their new lives. Contrary to what may be expected on the basis of the above results, the reported levels of satisfaction were high for both groups on each occasion. Three years after arrival, respondents who reported themselves satisfied with their present lives composed 79 percent of the Mexican sample and 81 percent of the Cuban. At the other extreme, those dissatisfied with their situation were only 1 percent and 3 percent, respectively (Table 86).

Six years after arrival, this result held firm. As Table 86 shows, variations occurred in endorsement of specific categories, but the overwhelming consensus was that life in America had been a positive experience. Again, 79 percent of Mexican immigrants reported themselves satisfied with their

Table 86. Satisfaction with Life in the
United States, 1976-1979

	Very Dissatisfied, %	Dissatisfied, %	In-between, Undecided, %	Moderately Satisfied, %	Very Satisfied, %	Totals, %
1976						
Cubans	0.7	2.3	15.7	42.9	38.4	100.0 (427)
Mexicans	0.2	0.9	19.8	38.3	40.8	100.0 (439)
1979						
Cubans	0.2	0.7	5.3	38.7	55.0	100.0 (413)
Mexicans	0.0	0.4	20.7	52.4	26.4	100.0 (454)

Table 87.   Plans for Residence and
U.S. Citizenship, 1976-1979

Plans to Remain in the United States

Year	Sample	Permanently, %	Temporarily, %	Other (D.K.[a]), %	Totals, %
1976	Cubans	88.5	4.7	6.8	100.0 (427)
1976	Mexicans	85.2	6.8	8.0	100.0 (439)
1979	Cubans	95.9	2.4	1.7	100.0 (411)
1979	Mexicans	88.3	9.5	2.2	100.0 (454)

Plans to Become U.S. Citizen

Year	Sample	Yes, %	No, %	D.K., %	Totals, %
1976	Cubans	77.2	7.3	15.5	100.0 (426)
1976	Mexicans	67.6	14.8	17.6	100.0 (438)
1979	Cubans	85.7	4.9	9.5	100.0 (412)
1979	Mexicans	71.0	11.6	17.4	100.0 (455)

[a]D.K. = don't know.

situation; among Cuban exiles the proportion increased to 95 percent, virtually the entire sample.

These results might be challenged on the grounds that positive responses to this kind of question are normative. In other words, there may be a "desirability bias" leading immigrants to declare themselves more satisfied than they really are. As a check on this possibility, we examined responses to other, more behaviorally oriented measures that should correspond to different levels of satisfaction.

Table 87 presents immigrant reports about the subjects' intentions to remain in the United States and their intentions to become American citizens. In 1976, 85 percent of the Mexicans and 88 percent of the Cubans stated that they intended to stay permanently. By 1979, the figures had increased to 88 and 96 percent, respectively. Similarly, heavy majorities of both samples declared their intentions to become U. S. citizens in 1976 and, in each case, the proportion increased with time. In 1979, 71 percent of the Mexican immigrants and 86 percent of the Cuban exiles indicated plans for citizenship. Included in these figures are 44 immigrants (24 Cubans and 20 Mexicans) who had already become citizens.

The same general trend surfaced when immigrants were asked in 1976 whether, given a chance, they would come again to the United States or opt for remaining in their home country. Almost all indicated that they would come again: 93 percent of Cubans and 96 percent of Mexicans. Thus, we are reassured that high levels of satisfaction voiced by Cuban and Mexican immigrants are not a casual or normative response, but correspond to their actual beliefs and plans for the future.

Finally, Table 88 presents the distribution of major problems that immigrants indicated they had confronted in the United States. Lack of knowledge of the language and economic difficulties were the principal problems afflicting both groups. In 1976 and again in 1979, English was the principal problem among Cuban refugees. Economic complaints dropped in relative importance for both samples over these three years, though in 1979 they continued to be the principal problem for Mexicans. The most noteworthy

Table 88. Principal Problem Confronted
in the United States, 1976-1979

	1976		1979	
	Cubans	Mexicans	Cubans	Mexicans
None, %	26.5	36.5	44.8	59.6
Language, %	31.1	27.9	27.1	11.6
Economic difficulties, %	21.6	19.4	11.1	16.0
Customs, cultural adaptation, %	7.5	7.3	3.4	3.9
Family problems, %	2.2	2.7	1.8	1.9
Health problems, %	7.7	3.9	9.4	3.3
Other, %	3.4	3.3	2.4	3.7
Totals, %	100.0 (427)	100.0 (438)	100.0 (413)	100.0 (455)

finding, however, was that a large proportion of immigrants indicate that they confronted *no* major problem in adapting to American society. In 1976, more than one-third of the Mexican immigrants and one-fourth of the Cuban refugees reported no major difficulties; three years later, these proportions had actually increased to 60 percent and 45 percent, respectively.

Thus, despite lowered expectations concerning occupational opportunities, the two immigrant groups appear quite committed to their new lives. These results support the conclusion of a relatively smooth process of adaptation and correspondingly high levels of satisfaction. Immigrants do not wish to return to their home country and, knowing what they know about the United States, they would come again. Given the opportunity to complain about major problems found in this country, substantial proportions of both samples said that they had encountered none.

Views of American Society

In addition to evaluations concerning their own situation, immigrants were asked for their opinions about other aspects of the receiving country. In general, their views were positive, a result that converges with the high levels of satisfaction noted above. Table 89 presents frequency distributions for three opinion items included in the 1976 and 1979 follow-up surveys.

Asked about the nature of economic opportunities in America, most immigrants indicated such opportunities were available to everyone rather than reserved for those at the top. More than 85 percent of the Mexicans and more than 90 percent of the Cubans in 1976 and again in 1979 endorsed this view. Thus, despite their perception of deteriorating occupational opportunities, these immigrants continued to believe that whatever economic chances remained were still open to all.

There is a common impression that immigrants from Latin America come to the United States for economic reasons, but that they regard American life styles as less fulfilling, in an expressive sense, than their own. In this view, daily life would appear to them regimented and boring, while Americans would be regarded as too aloof and inexpressive to develop warm personal relations.[3] Results in the bottom panels of Table 89 contradict this impression. At two different points in time, heavy majorities of both samples indicated that life in the United States was quite stimulating and that making friends with Anglos was not a particularly difficult task.

Mexicans endorsed these views more frequently than Cubans, the difference in one case exceeding 15 percent. Among the latter, however,

---

3. See, for example, Morris A. Horowitz, *La Emigración de Profesionales y Técnicos Argentinos*; Ramiro Cardona, *El Exodo de Colombianos*; NACLA "Undocumented Immigrant Workers in New York City."

Table 89.   Perceptions of American Society,
1976-1979

---

1.   Economic opportunities in the United States

Sample	Year	a. Are available to all, %	b. Are available to those at the top, %	c. Undecided (D.K.[a]), %	Total, %
Cubans	1976	91.3	6.8	1.9	100.0 (426)
Cubans	1979	90.3	6.8	2.9	100.0 (413)
Mexicans	1976	85.9	9.6	4.5	100.0 (439)
Mexicans	1979	86.3	11.5	2.2	100.0 (454)

---

2.   Quality of life in the United States

Sample	Year	a. Stimulating, %	b. Boring, %	c. Undecided (D.K.[a]), %	Total, %
Cubans	1976	76.8	18.1	5.2	100.0 (426)
Cubans	1979	78.9	12.6	8.5	100.0 (413)
Mexicans	1976	83.4	11.2	5.4	100.0 (439)
Mexicans	1979	85.5	10.6	3.9	100.0 (454)

---

3.   Establishing friendships with Anglo-Americans is

Sample	Year	a. Easy, %	b. Difficult, %	c. Undecided (D.K.[a]), %	Total, %
Cubans	1976	68.9	20.0	11.1	100.0 (425)
Cubans	1979	65.4	23.7	10.9	100.0 (413)
Mexicans	1976	74.5	18.9	6.6	100.0 (439)
Mexicans	1979	81.7	14.3	4.4	100.0 (454)

---

[a]D.K. = don't know.

positive responses never dropped below two-thirds of the sample. Thus, the decision to stay permanently in the United States, reported by most immigrants, appears based not only on the calculation of economic gain, but also on a positive assessment of the new social and cultural setting.

Immigrant opinions are less positive on the way American life styles affect the family. In 1976, about one-third of Mexican immigrants and more than two-fifths of Cuban refugees believed that life in this country did weaken the family. As results in Table 90 show, this opinion was also reflected in their views of how children ought to be raised. Despite commitment by most to a permanent life in the United States, many still preferred to raise children according to their own culture. Among Mexicans, those endorsing the "Mexican way" were almost as numerous as those believing in a shift to American customs. Resistance to acculturation was still stronger among Cubans, half of whom preferred a traditional Cuban education. This number was more than twice that of those who had come to support the American way.

By 1979, negative views about the family in America had weakened somewhat. Proportions believing in the negative effect of the new culture on family life dropped by 6 percent in one sample and by 10 percent in the other (Table 90). Persistent resistance to acculturation was shown, however, in the pattern of response to the second item. The number of immigrants wanting their children raised in the traditions of Mexico or Cuba had declined, but the shift was not in favor of total acculturation. Instead, an increasing proportion of immigrants now favored a "mixed" path, combining cultural elements of their native country and the United States. This result may be interpreted as a pragmatic recognition of the need for children to learn the ways of the new country along with a lingering preference for those of the old.

Perceptions of Discrimination

Perhaps the most important aspect of immigrants' perceptions of the host country is the way in which they see themselves reflected in the eyes of the native majority. Immigrants' views of how they are regarded by the native population, and especially by its dominant groups, is an area that has not received close attention in the past, despite its theoretical significance. For this reason, a series of questions bearing on this issue were included in both follow-up surveys.

Table 91 presents the results of an initial set of questions concerning the perceived quality of relationships between the immigrants' own ethnic group and the white Anglo majority. Immigrants were asked to describe the overall nature of this relationship by endorsing one or another of a series of paired adjectives. Perceptions elicited by this procedure were, without

Table 90. Acculturation and the Family,
1976-1979

1. American way of life weakens family ties

Sample	Year	a. No, %	b. Yes, %	c. Undecided (D.K.[a]), %	Total, %
Cubans	1976	48.6	44.4	7.0	100.0 (426)
Cubans	1979	52.1	38.0	9.9	100.0 (413)
Mexicans	1976	60.7	29.9	9.4	100.0 (438)
Mexicans	1979	76.4	18.3	5.3	100.0 (453)

2. The best way of raising children is[b]

Sample	Year	a. The American way, %	b. The Cuban/Mexican[c] way, %	c. A combination of both, %	d. D.K., %	Total, %
Cubans	1976	22.0	50.7	23.5	3.7	100.0 (353)
Cubans	1979	27.4	35.0	36.4	1.2	100.0 (343)
Mexicans	1976	36.5	35.0	26.8	1.7	100.0 (414)
Mexicans	1979	38.6	27.4	33.8	0.3	100.0 (391)

[a]D.K. = don't know.

[b]Question asked only to respondents who had or planned to have children.

[c]Item phrased according to nationality of respondent.

Table 91. Perceived Relationships between Immigrants
and Anglo-Americans, 1976-1979

Relationships between Cubans/Mexicans
and Anglos are[a]

Sample	Year	Cordial, %	Cold, %	Neither (D.K.), %	Total, %
Cubans	1976	81.3	13.5	5.2	100.0 (422)
Cubans	1979	68.1	19.0	12.9	100.0 (405)
Mexicans	1976	82.2	12.8	5.0	100.0 (438)
Mexicans	1979	79.6	13.2	7.2	100.0 (455)

Sample	Year	Friendly, %	Hostile, %	Neither (D.K.), %	Total, %
Cubans	1976	83.9	5.2	10.9	100.0 (422)
Cubans	1979	81.1	8.0	10.9	100.0 (413)
Mexicans	1976	81.5	11.6	6.9	100.0 (434)
Mexicans	1979	84.2	8.8	7.0	100.0 (455)

Sample	Year	Close, %	Distant, %	Neither (D.K.), %	Total, %
Cubans	1976	70.1	24.9	5.0	100.0 (421)
Cubans	1979	63.8	25.4	10.8	100.0 (413)
Mexicans	1976	68.7	25.8	5.5	100.0 (432)
Mexicans	1979	73.6	20.4	5.9	100.0 (455)

[a]Item phrased according to nationality of respondent.

Table 92.   Perceptions of Discrimination in the
United States, 1973-1979

Is there discrimination against
Cubans/Mexicans in the U.S.?[a]

Sample	Year	Yes, %	No, %	Don't Know, %	Total, %
Cubans	1973	4.6	69.0	26.5	100.0 (590)
Cubans	1976	26.3	67.8	5.9	100.0 (426)
Cubans	1979	26.4	62.5	11.2	100.0 (413)
Mexicans	1973	21.7	61.5	16.8	100.0 (816)
Mexicans	1976	40.0	48.3	11.7	100.0 (437)
Mexicans	1979	36.3	53.8	9.9	100.0 (455)

[a]Item phrased according to nationality of respondent.

exception, positive. Four-fifths of Cuban exiles and Mexican immigrants described relationships with white Americans as "friendly"; similar proportions described them as "cordial." Majorities in both samples also viewed
these relationships as "close," though about one-fourth in each sample
defined them as "distant." The profile of positive interethnic relationships
provided by these results changed remarkably little in the three years between the two follow-ups.

A second series of items was designed to tap directly the immigrant's
perceptions of discrimination in the United States. The first asked whether,
in his opinion, there was racial discrimination in economic opportunities.
Majorities in both samples again indicated that there was not, though the
proportion believing in economic discrimination hovered at about 25 percent of both groups in 1976 and again in 1979.

A second item concerned discrimination against the immigrants' own
ethnic group. This question was asked to every respondent in each of the
three surveys. Hence, it is possible to assess the pattern of change over the
entire follow-up period. Results, presented in Table 92, are based on the full
samples available at each point in time. Since there was significant sample

Table 93. Ethnic Status Perceptions,
1976-1979

In relation to Cubans/Mexicans,[a]
Anglo-Americans consider themselves

Sample	Year	Superior, %	Equal, %	Inferior, %	D.K.,[b] %	Total, %
Cubans	1976	41.8	52.1	0.2	5.9	100.0 (426)
Cubans	1979	50.8	33.7	1.9	13.6	100.0 (413)
Mexicans	1976	56.4	36.1	0.7	6.8	100.0 (438)
Mexicans	1979	49.0	39.6	0.2	11.2	100.0 (455)

In relation to Anglos, Cubans/Mexicans[a]
consider themselves

Sample	Year	Superior, %	Equal, %	Inferior, %	D.K.,[b] %	Total, %
Cubans	1976	17.4	77.5	1.9	3.2	100.0 (426)
Cubans	1979	19.6	72.4	3.1	4.9	100.0 (413)
Mexicans	1976	8.0	71.0	16.8	4.2	100.0 (438)
Mexicans	1979	9.2	62.6	22.0	6.1	100.0 (455)

[a] Item phrased according to nationality of respondent.

[b] D.K. = don't know.

mortality between 1973 and 1976, the analysis was replicated among respondents interviewed in all three surveys. Results did not differ significantly from those presented in the table.

In 1973, practically none of the newly arrived Cuban refugees perceived discrimination against Cubans in the United States, though 26 percent indicated that they did not know. Among Mexicans, however, 22 percent already believed in the existence of discrimination, while an additional 17 percent did not know. The most significant finding in Table 92 is the rapid increase in perceptions of discrimination in the first three years after arrival. Those believing in the existence of discrimination against their own ethnic group doubled among Mexicans, reaching two-fifths of the sample, and quintupled among Cubans. "Don't know" responses decreased accordingly. Perceptions of discrimination remained about the same in the next three years; respondents perceiving no discrimination declined marginally in the Cuban sample and increased in the Mexican.

Two final items attempted to gauge immigrants' perception of their ethnic status vis-à-vis the Anglo-American populations. Results are presented in Table 93. Three years after arrival more than half of the Mexican immigrants believed that Anglos considered themselves superior to Mexicans, while practically no one thought that Anglos regarded themselves as inferior. With slight variations, these proportions held in 1979. Major differences emerged, however, when the question was inverted: more than two-thirds of the Mexican immigrants in 1976 thought that Mexicans considered themselves equal to Anglos, but close to one-fifth believed that Mexicans saw themselves as inferior. The same pattern reappeared, with minor variations, three years later.

Cuban exiles saw themselves in a more positive light. Smaller proportions detected a feeling of superiority among native Anglos and correspondingly greater proportions believed that Anglos regarded Cubans as equal. When the question was inverted, about three-fourths of the respondents indicated that Cubans also viewed themselves as equal. The remainder was distributed in a manner exactly opposite to that for Mexican immigrants: about one-fifth of the sample in 1976 and again in 1979 reported that Cubans actually regarded themselves as superior, while almost no one indicated an inferior self-perception.

Despite these differences, results for the two examples are similar in one basic sense: there is a large gap in perceived equality between native Anglos and members of the immigrants' own ethnic group. Smaller proportions of Cubans and Mexicans reported egalitarian self-perceptions among Anglo-Americans than among their own minority. For half the respondents in each survey, the nature of interethnic relationships, from the Anglo viewpoint, was one marked by social distance and not equality.

PERCEPTIONS OF U. S. SOCIETY
AND DISCRIMINATION

Having examined the immigrants' attitudes and perceptions of American society, we must next ascertain the likely causes of these views. For this purpose, we will consider the simultaneous effect of predictors suggested by different theories of adaptation on a summary measure of immigrant perceptions. This measure consists of the sum of responses to a series of individual items. The resulting Perceptions of Society and Discrimination Index (PSDI) is described below.

PSDI consists of the unit-weighted sum of seven items tapping the immigrants' views on the existence of discrimination in the United States, on how the American way of life affects the family, and on relationships between Anglo-Americans and their own ethnic group. Table 94 presents the seven PSDI items and associated indicators of reliability and validity. Items are described in summary fashion in the table, since they have been examined in the previous section. The actual wording of questions in Spanish balanced the meaning of positive and negative answers in order to avoid a normative positive bias.

Components of PSDI were selected by factor analysis using principal components extraction with iterations. The analysis revealed a clear unidimensional structure for both samples, with the first unrotated factor accounting for most of the common variance and no significant secondary factors. Alpha coefficients indicating a theoretical lower bound of reliability are the same for both samples. Heise and Bohrnstedt's omega coefficients are slightly larger and, again, very similar for Cubans and Mexicans.

As an indicator of construct validity, Table 94 presents correlations between immigrants' reports of actual experiences of discrimination suffered in the United States and their PSDI scores. The assumption underlying this coefficient is that the more frequent the personal confrontations with discrimination, the more negative the immigrants' perceptions should be. As expected, the correlation is positive and significant in both samples.

Results in Table 94 are based on the final 1979 survey. Additional support for the reliability of the PSDI index comes from the 1976 follow-up. Factor analyses conducted on data from this earlier survey produced the same unidimensional structure involving the same items.[4] The fact that the same set of items converged into a single factor for two independent samples at two different points in time increases our confidence in its validity as an indicator of the dimension of interest. Results involving the 1976 measure will be reported, where relevant, below.

CAUSAL HYPOTHESES

The two competing theories on social and cultural adaptation lead to very different predictions concerning changes in immigrants' perceptions. As summarized in Chapter 1, the core of the assimilation perspective is a

---

4. The lone exception is item 5 in Table 95, which was excluded from the 1976 index.

Table 94. The Perceptions of Society and
Discrimination Index

Item	Mexicans		Cubans	
	Loading[a]	r_{it}[b]	Loading[a]	r_{it}[b]
1. There is racial discrimination in economic opportunities in the U.S.	.484	.455	.485	.431
2. American way of life weakens family ties.	.416	.394	.391	.359
3. Relations between Mexicans/Cubans and Anglo-Americans are mostly cold.	.770	.596	.695	.563
4. Relations between Mexicans/Cubans and Anglo-Americans are mostly distant.	.706	.572	.699	.587
5. Relations between Mexicans/Cubans and Anglo-Americans are mostly hostile.	.700	.528	.664	.533
6. Anglo-Americans discriminate against Mexicans/Cubans.	.627	.542	.687	.603
7. In relation to Mexicans/Cubans, Anglo-Americans regard themselves as superior.	.520	.485	.547	.495

First Factor:	Eigenvalue	2.652	2.572
	% of variance explained	76.1	84.1
	α[c]	.782	.782
	Ω UWML[d]	.821	.830
Validity Coefficient[e]:	$r_{PSDI.EXP}$	.324*	.332*

[a]Unrotated first factor loadings. Principal factors extraction with iterations.

[b]Item-to-total correlations corrected for auto-correlation.

[c]Cronbach's alpha.

[d]Heise and Bohrnstedt's omega.

[e]Construct validity:
   Correlation of perceptions of society and discrimination with actual
   experiences of discrimination.

*$p < .01$.

focus on the process of consensus building among dissimilar populations. While much of this literature is devoted to obstacles to assimilation, a common assumption is that the process possesses an "inner logic," whereby a number of variables coalesce along certain patterned lines.[5] For example, it is commonly assumed that immigrants who are or become more educated, more familiar with the language, and more knowledgeable about the ways of the society, will become more rapidly assimilated.

This prediction follows from the assumed operation of two simultaneous processes: first, as immigrants gain greater knowledge of the language and culture, they become more acceptable to the native majority; second, as they gain greater understanding of the receiving society, their acceptance of it also increases. Following this logic, lack of assimilation can be regarded as a consequence of initial mutual ignorance and distrust and the lack of preparedness of immigrants to deal with the cultural requirements of the society.[6]

The study of assimilation has generally focused in the United States on the attitudes of the white majority and the social distance that it keeps from different immigrant and ethnic minorities. Nevertheless, perceptions held by the latter represent a crucial aspect of the assimilation process insofar as they affect the immigrants' willingness to surrender their own culture and accept a new one. From the assimilation standpoint, such perceptions are ultimately governed by the changing levels of education and cultural proficiency among immigrants. Formally stated,

The higher the education, knowledge of English, and information about American society, the more favorable are the attitudes toward it and the less common the perceptions of discrimination.

The contrary hypothesis, associated with the ethnic-resilience perspective, identifies the same factors of education, knowledge of the language, and information as significant determinants of immigrants' perceptions, except that their effects are predicted to run in the opposite direction. From this conflict perspective, greater knowledge of the new language and culture and greater familiarity with members of the dominant group do not necessarily lead to more positive attitudes and more rapid assimilation. They can lead precisely to the opposite, as immigrants come to learn their real social position and are exposed to prejudice and discrimination. Ethnicity is not, after all, a mere consequence of the persistence of traditional cultural traits,

5. See, for example, S. N. Eisenstadt, "The Process of Absorbing New Immigrants in Israel," and J. Heiss, "Factors Related to Immigrant Assimilation."
6. This logic underlies both classic and contemporary studies of immigrant assimilation. See, for example, Oscar Handlin, *Boston Immigrants*, and Eleanor M. Rogg, *The Assimilation of Cuban Exiles.*

but a product created by the host society. Confrontation with the latter's realities has made "ethnics" of groups having no common national identification at arrival.[7]

From this alternative viewpoint, rising ethnic consciousness and the resilience of ethnic culture thus represent important instruments of resistance by subordinate groups. Formally stated,

The higher the education, knowledge of English, and information about American society, the more critical are the attitudes toward it and the more common the perceptions of discrimination.

The data from this study are uniquely suited to examine the above predictions, since they contain reliable measures of all the relevant variables. In addition, it is possible to establish a clear causal order by examining relationships between predictors measured at the time of arrival and perceptions measured six years later.

From the original 1973 survey, we selected the following variables as most pertinent: education, measured in years completed; knowledge of English, measured by the KEI index[8]; psychosocial modernity, measured by Inkeles and Smith's OM-Short Form 5 scale[9]; and length of prior residence in the United States. The modernity scale is included on the assumption that those who score high on it should be more attuned to American-style values and customs. "Empathy"—defined as the ability to assume psychologically the orientations predominant in the advanced countries— has been described as a central characteristic of modernity.[10] Hence, the more modern immigrants should also be the more informed about the culture of the society receiving them.

Length of prior residence in the United States is included on the assumption that those who have lived longer in the country should be more knowledgeable about it. For Cubans, this variable is a quasi constant and, hence, its correlation with PSDI is zero. For this reason, this relationship is only examined for the Mexican sample.

From the 1979 survey, the following variables were selected: knowledge of English, measured by KEI; information about American society, measured by the USIN index[11]; and education acquired after 1976, mea-

7. On this point, see Robert Blauner, *Racial Oppression in America*, and Manuel Castells, "Immigrant Workers and Class Struggles in Advanced Capitalism."

8. See Chapter 3 for a description of this index, and Chapter 5 for an analysis of its frequency distributions.

9. This scale was selected because of its brevity and the fact that it had been standardized in six developing countries, including two in Latin America. The scale is described in Alex Inkeles and David H. Smith, *Becoming Modern*.

10. See, in particular, Daniel Lerner, *The Passing of Traditional Society*.

11. See Chapter 3 for a description of this index, and Chapter 5 for an analysis of its frequency distributions.

Table 95. Correlations of Perceptions of Society and
Discrimination (PSDI) with Selected Predictors: 1973-1979

Variable[a]	PSDI			
	Cubans		Mexicans	
	r^b	$r_1{}^c$	r^b	$r_1{}^c$
Education	.19**	.21**	.09*	.10*
Modernity	.13*	.20**	.27**	.37**
Knowledge of English--1973	.13*	.15**	.09*	.10*
Knowledge of English--1979	.19**	.22**	.20**	.23**
Information about U.S. society--1979	.10*	.13*	.14*	.19**
Education in the U.S., 1976-1979	.15**	.16**	.13*	.14*
Pre-1973 residence in the U.S.	--	--	.17**	.19**

[a]See text for description of variables.

[b]Missing data deleted.

[c]Corrected for attenuation.

*$p < .05$.

**$p < .01$.

sured in months completed. Selection of these variables follows directly
from the wording of both hypotheses above.

Table 95 presents correlations between the above variables and PSDI.
The first column for each sample presents the raw coefficients; the second
presents coefficients corrected for attenuation due to measurement error.
Because of large sample sizes, all correlations in the table are statistically
significant. In substantive terms, however, none is sizable. Still, the central
finding is that all coefficients run consistently in one direction: that predicted by the second (ethnic-resilience) hypothesis.

To fully grasp the significance of this finding, one must remember that
these results were obtained from two independent samples and that about
half the predictors were measured six years before the actual perceptions.
Regardless of whether one considers predictors at the time of arrival or six
years afterwards, coefficients follow the same consistent pattern. Contrary
to the assimilation hypothesis, the more educated, modern, proficient in

Table 96. Correlations of Perceptions of Society and
Discrimination (PSDI) with Selected Predictors: 1973-1976

Variable[a]	PSDI	
	Cubans, r[b]	Mexicans, r[b]
Education	.10*	.09*
Modernity	.13*	.22**
Knowledge of English--1973	.15**	.10*
Knowledge of English--1976	.25**	.12*
Information about U.S. society--1976	.22**	.04
Education in the U.S., 1973-1976	.15**	.13*
Pre-1973 residence in the U.S.	--	.18**

[a]See text for description of variables.

[b]Missing data deleted.

*$p < .05$.

**$p < .01$.

the English language, and informed immigrants are, the more critical their perceptions of the receiving society and the stronger their perceptions of discrimination.

This conclusion is based on results from the first and last surveys. It can be further examined by an analysis of correlations between the same set of predictors and the dependent variable measured in 1976. Results of this analysis are presented in Table 96. Corrections for attenuation are omitted, since they do not significantly alter the size of any correlation. As shown in the table, the same pattern of results detected in 1979 was already present three years earlier. Without exception, all coefficients support the conflict hypothesis.

CAUSAL MODELS

Regressions

Having examined the distribution of individual attitudes and the correlates of perceptions of discrimination, we consider next the possibility of developing models of the process leading to these perceptions. This analysis seeks to identify the most parsimonious combination of predictors hav-

Table 97. Regressions of Perceptions of Society and
Discrimination (PSDI) on Selected Predictors, 1979

Predictor	PSDI[a]					
	Cubans			Mexicans		
	b	SE$_b$	β	b	SE$_b$	β
Education	.070	.031	.12	--	--	--
Modernity	--	--	--	.611	.151	.23
Age	-.049	.014	-.17	--	--	--
Pre-1973 residence in the U.S.	--	--	--	.163	.062	.14
Knowledge of English--1979	--	--	--	.097	.043	.13
Information about U.S. society--1979	--	--	--	--	--	--
Education in the U.S.--1976-1979	.028	.010	.14	--	--	--
R^2			.09			.12

[a]Insignificant effects deleted.

ing a significant effect on the dependent variable. Subsidiary questions are the stability of these effects over time and differences in model structure between the two samples.

As a first step, all independent variables were entered into a stepwise ordinary least squares (OLS) analysis with PSDI as the dependent variable. Missing data were deleted listwise, a procedure that reduced the follow-up samples somewhat. In addition to variables included in the preceding analysis, age was entered as a control variable. Age is a potentially important factor both because of its possible main effect on immigrants' perceptions and because of its possible interaction with other exogenous variables. Because of high collinearity between the two knowledge of English measures, only KEI-1979 was included.

Table 97 presents results of this analysis. It excludes negligible effects so that models presented are the most parsimonious. Coefficients in the table all exceed twice their standard errors. Comparing them across samples, it is evident that causal models of immigrants' perceptions are quite different for Cubans and Mexicans.[12]

12. The two models are not strictly identical, since the variable Length of Prior Residence in the United States is included in the Mexican but not the Cuban regressions. In the Cuban sample, this variable has almost zero variance and is, hence, unrelated to all exogenous and endogenous variables. Its inclusion would leave present results unaltered.

Table 98. Regressions of Perceptions of Society and
Discrimination (PSDI) on Selected Predictors, 1976

| Predictor | PSDI[a] | | | | | |
| | Cubans | | | Mexicans | | |
	b	SE_b	β	b	SE_b	β
Education	--	--	--	--	--	--
Modernity	--	--	--	.597	.149	.25
Age	--	--	--	--	--	--
Pre-1973 residence in the U.S.	--	--	--	--	--	--
Knowledge of English--1973	.213	.108	.11	--	--	--
Information--1976	.095	.048	.11	--	--	--
Education in the U.S.--1973-1976	.041	.020	.11	.032	.014	.10
R^2			.06			.08

[a]Insignificant effects deleted.

The two OLS models do not share a single common predictor. Among Cubans, it is education, both in Cuba and in the United States, plus age that have the significant main effects on PSDI. The age effect is negative, indicating that younger immigrants tend to be more critical of the receiving society and to perceive higher levels of discrimination. Among Mexicans, reliable effects on PSDI are associated with modernity at arrival, prior residence in the United States, and knowledge of English.

Despite these differences, the two models have several aspects in common. First, explained variance is very modest in both cases. Second, the OLS analysis revealed no significant interactions between age and other variables, or, for that matter, between any possible first-order variable combination. Third, with the exception of age, the main effect of which was not predicted by either theory above, the sign of all coefficients again lends support to the ethnic-resilience hypothesis.

It is possible to examine the stability of these models over time by comparing them with similar results obtained three years earlier.[13] Table 98

13. As noted above, the 1976 PSDI includes six rather than seven items as in the 1979 version. This difference makes results not strictly comparable. In practice, replication of the analysis with PSDI-1979 reduced to the six original components leaves unaltered the direction and magnitude of unstandardized coefficients.

presents results of regressing the 1976 PSDI index on the same set of predictors. Given unequal variances, unstandardized regression coefficients are appropriate for comparisons both between samples and over time. Regardless of which coefficients are considered, however, the conclusion is the same: major predictors of perceptions of discrimination vary over time as well as between immigrant groups.

Exceptions to this pattern include (1) modernity, which is, by far, the strongest predictor of perceptions of discrimination in the Mexican sample in 1976 and again in 1979, and (2) education in the United States, which has reliable effects on the endogenous variable among Cubans in both years. Explained variance in the 1976 models is again very modest. Despite differences in the combination of significant predictors, however, the general pattern of results continues to reflect the same conclusion: three years after arriving in the United States, more modern immigrants—those more knowledgeable about the society and language and those who had received more education—saw American society in more critical terms and perceived greater discrimination against their own groups.

Maximum-Likelihood Estimation

The principal difficulty with the models discussed so far is the presence of measurement error. Because several of the variables, including PSDI, are measured imperfectly, the magnitudes of causal effects are unreliable. Recent model-construction techniques make it possible to introduce the fallible measurement structure of variables into the model and adjust the magnitude of causal effects accordingly. The models presented below are estimated with the Full Information Maximum Likelihood (FIML) procedure developed by Jöreskog and Sörbom.[14]

In the revised model, the matrix of coefficients relating the construct Perception of Society and Discrimination (PSD) to its individual indicators is left unconstrained. This allows us to examine directly the measurement structure of this variable. Following the factor analytic model presented above, the initial assumption is that of uncorrelated errors among empirical indicators of the endogenous variable. An important feature of FIML estimation is that it allows relaxation of this assumption.

Among exogenous variables, age, education in the country of origin, education in the United States, and length of prior U. S. residence are assumed to be self-measured and error free. Variances in the modernity and knowledge of English constructs are adjusted according to the known reliability of their observed empirical measures; error terms affecting the respective scales are

14. Karl G. Jöreskog and Dag Sörbom, *LISREL IV*. See also Karl G. Jöreskog and Dag Sörbom, *Advances in Factor Analysis and Structural Equation Models*.

simultaneously fixed at the product of observed scale variance times the unreliability.[15] This procedure corrects for the effect of measurement error,
thus permitting a more accurate assessment of causal effects.

Another substantive shortcoming of the preceding models is the omission of experiences of discrimination as a predictor. This variable was excluded from the earlier analyses, since it was not directly pertinent to the
test of the two competing hypotheses. However, both assimilation and conflict theorists would agree that a most direct way of increasing awareness of
discrimination is to make immigrants experience it. The available indicator
of this variable is the frequency of experiences of discrimination suffered by
the immigrant himself or by a member of his family, ranging from "never"
to "frequently." This measure will be incorporated in the following models
and is defined as both endogenous and causally prior to PSDI.

The estimation of the two recursive models proceeded by successively
freeing restricted parameters, according to the relative magnitude of the
first-order partial derivatives. The final models developed by this procedure
are presented in Figures 5 and 6. In both cases, the assumption of uncorrelated disturbances between exogenous and endogenous variables is preserved,
though not that of uncorrelated error terms among PSD indicators.

Before examining the full final models, we consider their reduced
forms, since they are directly comparable with the OLS estimates above.
Reduced form coefficients are presented in Table 99, and can be directly
compared with those in Table 97. In the Cuban sample, education in the
United States ceases to be a significant predictor, leaving education at arrival and age as the only reliable determinants of immigrants' perceptions.
Older and less educated refugees are significantly less likely to perceive
discrimination after six years in the country. Adjusting for measurement
error in the PSD construct does not improve explained variance, which
remains at 9 percent.

In the Mexican sample, the FIML estimation leads, however, to a sizable increase in explained variance: from 12 to 18 percent. The improvement is totally due to the sharp increase in the effect of modernity, once
measurement error is partialled out. The effect of knowledge of English
drops below significance leaving, as in the Cuban case, only two reliable
determinants of perceptions of discrimination. For both samples, however,
adjustment for an imperfect measurement structure leaves the direction of
effects unchanged: as in the earlier analysis, every effect is in the direction
predicted by the conflict hypothesis.

---

15. Formulas are as follows: $\sigma_T = r_{tt}(\sigma_{T^1})$; $\sigma T_e = (1 - r_{tt})(\sigma_{T^1})$, where σ_T = variance of
unmeasured construct T; σ_{T^1} = observed variance; σT_e = variance of error term; and r_{tt} =
reliability of T^2.

Table 99. Reduced Form Effects on Immigrants'
Perceptions of Society and Discrimination (PSD)
FIML Estimation, 1979

Sample	Educa-tion	Modern-ity	Age	Prior Residence in the U.S.	Knowledge of English	Education in the U.S.	R^2
Cuban	.1486[a]*	--	-.1873*	--	--	.1088	.092
	(.0100)	--	(-.0062)	--	--	(.0025)	[.220]**
Mexican	--	.3462*	--	.1342*	.0918	--	.180
	--	(.1505)	--	(.0200)	(.0093)	--	[.2826]**

[a]Standardized solution; unstandardized coefficients in parentheses.

*Coefficient exceeds twice its standard error.

**R^2, full model.

Comparison of explained variance between these reduced form models and the final ones (bracket-enclosed figures in Table 99) already shows the impact of experiences of discrimination on immigrants' perceptions. Effects of the experience variable (Figures 5 and 6) quintuple their standard errors in both samples and increase explained variance by 13 points in the Cuban sample and 10 in the Mexican. These effects are positive, as expected.

The two models are dissimilar, however, in their fit to the data. The final model for the Cuban sample (Figure 5) does not yield a satisfactory fit (χ^2 = 47.966, $p < .05$). This represents, however, a considerable improvement from the original model with uncorrelated error terms, as reflected in average chi-square point reduction per degree of freedom ($\chi^2/df_6 = 11.18$). Relaxation of other assumptions did not significantly improve the fit of model to data. This result suggests that other variables, omitted from the present model, exercise a significant influence on Cuban-refugee perceptions of U. S. society. A logical possibility is that perceptions of American society are influenced by the labor-market processes explored in the preceding chapters. However, the causal processes leading to different perceptions do not change markedly across labor-market sectors; significant effects are common to the entire sample. Hence, missing predictors must be sought in other characteristics not considered here.

In contrast to Cuban results, the final model estimated for the Mexican sample (Figure 6) fits the data rather well (χ^2 = 25.893 $p > .80$). Average improvement per degree of freedom is also substantial ($\chi^2/df_6 = 30.96$). These final models are not directly comparable because of different causal structures. For the sake of clarity in comparisons internal to each, coefficients from the standardized solution are presented in the figures. Results

Fig. 5. Final Model of Perceptions of Society and Discrimination (PSD)—Cubans, 1979

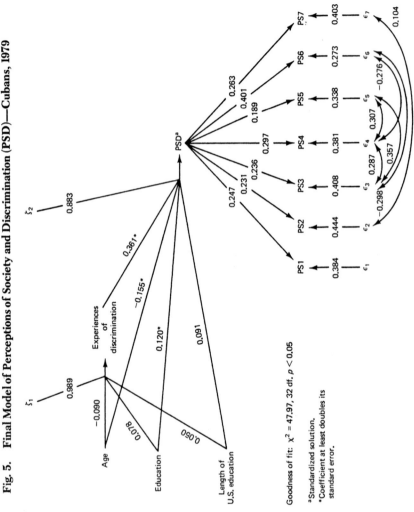

Goodness of fit: $\chi^2 = 47.97$, 32 df. $p < 0.05$

[a]Standardized solution,

*Coefficient at least doubles its standard error.

Fig. 6.   Final Model of Perceptions of Society and Discrimination (PSD)—Mexicans, 1979

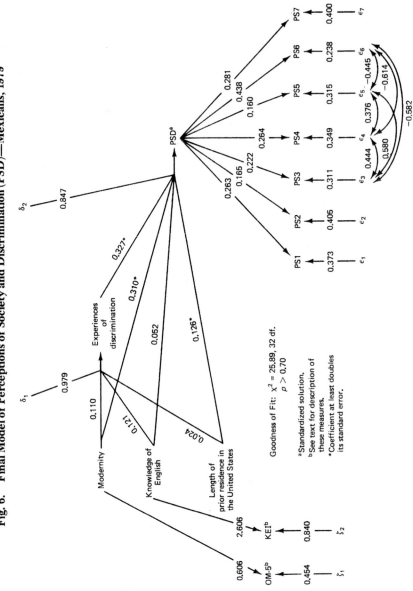

pertaining to the measurement of perceptions of society and discrimination may be considered first.

Lambda coefficients linking PSD to its observed indicators exceed at least six times their respective standard errors in the Cuban sample and at least five times in the Mexican. Despite correlated error terms, the strength of these coefficients lends definite support to the measurement model. Comparison of structural effects with reduced form coefficients in Table 99 shows that experience of discrimination is not a significant intervening variable between other predictors and immigrants' perceptions: effects of exogenous variables on PSD are only slightly reduced by introduction of the experience variable. Further, no single exogenous variable has a significant effect on experiences in either model.

These results suggest that effects of the set of predictors derived from the two hypotheses above and those of experiences of discrimination operate largely independently of each other. The first set of effects follows the logic of the conflict hypothesis; the second effect follows common sense in relating more frequent experiences of discrimination with a more critical stance toward the receiving society. Together these effects succeed in explaining a substantial proportion of the variance in immigrants' perceptions.

CONCLUSION

The findings presented in this chapter can be succinctly summarized as the expression of an apparent contradiction: on the one hand, levels of satisfaction and commitment to the United States are high for both immigrant groups; on the other, perceptions of discrimination against their respective ethnic groups increased markedly during the first years in the country and now make up a sizable percentage of both samples. More importantly, these perceptions are consistently associated with greater education, knowledge of English, modernity, and years of residence in the country. To the extent that these variables can be expected to increase with time, so should the negative perceptions of American society and of the immigrants' own situation in it.

To summarize the causal results: education and age are the most significant determinants of perceptions of society and discrimination in the Cuban sample; their influence holds across the three labor-market sectors in which this group is segmented. Psychosocial modernity and length of prior residence in the United States have a similar role among Mexicans. In both samples, prior experiences of discrimination have a major independent effect on subsequent perceptions, a result congruent with common sense expectations. Of all these effects, the only one that would encourage a prediction of less critical perceptions with the passage of time is that of age.

The fact that multivariate results run consistently in the direction predicted by the ethnic consciousness and not the assimilation hypothesis may suggest the prospect of increasing alienation and interethnic hostility in the communities where these immigrants settle. If effects detected above can be extrapolated into the future, then greater perceptions of discrimination would be the likely consequence of education and increasing knowledge of the language and culture. This would lead, in turn, to greater alienation.

There are several reasons why such a conclusion is not warranted. First, results indicate a consistent trend, but causal effects are relatively weak, thus leaving room for many other possible determinants. Second, there is no guarantee that the direction of these effects can be extrapolated into the future, nor that, if it were, it would automatically be converted into militant action. Third, the conclusion of greater ethnic alienation runs against the body of results above, which indicate widespread satisfaction and commitment to life in this country.

This seeming contradiction represents, perhaps, the most important lesson to be derived from this analysis, for it clarifies the actual nature of adaptation to American society as opposed to conventional idealizations. Refugees and immigrants who say that they are satisfied, intend to stay in the United States, *and* feel discriminated against are not expressing a contradiction. They are voicing instead a realistic assessment of their situation.

The more critical immigrants are probably more integrated than those who continue to adhere to uniform and often highly idealized views. The latter—found among older and less educated immigrants, and those with less knowledge of the language—are often living in American society without yet being a part of it. Heightened perceptions of discrimination among the younger and the more educated can be interpreted as evidence of increasing participation in American society and, hence, greater awareness of how it actually functions.

To act effectively within a new social order, immigrants must first grasp fully the significance of its major cleavages. It is for this reason that increasing perceptions of discrimination are found among the better educated and more informed members of each minority. Such perceptions are inevitably linked with the reinforcement of ethnic boundaries and ethnic solidarity. Far from leading to mass withdrawal, the latter should be interpreted as instruments of collective defense and promotion *within* the existing society.

The sequence of events suggested by this interpretation is certainly different from that portrayed by assimilation theory. Unlike the latter, it does not see adaptation as a gradual movement toward cultural convergence and consensus building, but rather as a complex and frequently contradictory process. This process includes the demise of the original idealized image of the receiving country and the increasing grasp of its social dynamics and problems, including the reality of discrimination. Adaptation to American society does not consist of ignoring its many contradictions and conflicts, as implicity suggested by assimilation theorists. It consists instead of grasping these constraints and reacting to them as part of the struggle for social recognition and ascent.

From this perspective, the satisfaction voiced by most immigrants in our samples and their desire to stay in the United States become readily understandable. These conditions reflect the fact that the immigrants' efforts so far have been successful. Critical perceptions voiced by a substantial and growing minority reflect, in turn, an assessment of the difficulties already experienced and those that lie ahead. Being aware of these problems does not guarantee overcoming them, but represents a first and necessary condition for incorporation into a new social order.

9

REACHING OUT: THE SOCIAL RELATIONSHIPS OF IMMIGRANTS IN THE UNITED STATES

A second element of the process of immigrant adaptation that complements the transformation of values and perceptions is the changing social relationships of the immigrant community. Whom the immigrants see, with whom they interact, and what organizations they join are aspects at least as important as the jobs they hold, the money they make, and the views they hold about the receiving society.

The study of immigrant relationships can be subdivided, in turn, into two aspects, one qualitative and the other quantitative. We want to know, first of all, how frequent these relationships are, both at the level of primary face-to-face interactions and at that of formal secondary associations. We also want to explore the nature of these ties, primarily the extent to which they are confined to the ethnic community or reach out beyond it.

The two competing theoretical perspectives on immigrant adaptation, reviewed in the preceding chapter, do not differ greatly in their predictions of how these processes occur. Both assimilation and ethnic-resilience theories agree in viewing the ethnic community as a source of emotional support, protection against external pressures, and even economic gain. The dense networks of contact within the immigrant community function routinely as sources of employment, information about events in the host and home countries, and social support.[1]

This chapter was written with the collaboration of Thomas W. Reilly.

1. As examples of the first, see Oscar Handlin, *Boston's Immigrants*; and Carl Wittke, "Refugees of Revolution." For the second, see Robert Blauner, *Racial Oppression in America*, chaps. 3 and 4, and the recent analysis of the Japanese in the United States by Edna Bonacich and John Modell, *The Economic Basis of Ethnic Solidarity*.

The main difference between the two perspectives lies in the time dimension associated with changing social relationships. For assimilation theorists, the immigrant community constitutes the original and necessary reception center, the substitute social cradle that protects newcomers until they are able to fend for themselves in the new country. After years or generations, immigrants will be gradually weaned away from the original ethnic bond and absorbed by the population at large or by one of the triple or quadruple melting pots that compose it. For Milton Gordon, the gradual entry of immigrants and their children into social networks of the host society—a process that he labels structural assimilation—represents the critical moment of the adaptation process. More than acculturation, it is the real-world social relationships that immigrants establish that represent the decisive element in their long-term adaptation.[2]

From the ethnic-resilience viewpoint, the early functions that immigrant communities play are undeniable, but the bonds of ethnic solidarity among immigrants extend beyond the early years as a consequence of the process of reactive formation. Precisely as a consequence of socialization into the realities of American society, immigrants are made aware of the convenience of continuing solidarity within their own communities. Having understood that theirs is a disadvantaged position and that this disadvantage is legitimized by an ideology that defines their race or culture as inferior, immigrants will hold on to ethnic ties long after the early days of arrival as a logical protective strategy.[3]

The ethnic-resilience perspective does not predict, however, that immigrant social interactions will always take place exclusively within the ethnic community. Nothing in the logic of the theory prevents immigrants from establishing relationships, both at the formal and informal levels, with others outside their own group. The hypothesis, instead, is that there is no linear decline in intraethnic relationships as a consequence of the adaptation process; relationships within the ethnic community represent an enduring and substantial (but not exclusive) component of immigrant social networks over time.

The temporal scope of our data prevents a clear adjudication between these competing hypotheses. Six years in the United States is not long enough to distinguish between the period of early adaptation, in which both perspectives coincide, and the subsequent period, in which they diverge. Thus, if we were to find a significant decline in intraethnic relationships over time, this result could be interpreted as supporting the assimila-

2. Milton M. Gordon, *Assimilation in American Life.*
3. See Andrew M. Greeley, *Why Can't They Be Like Us?*; William Petersen, *Japanese Americans*; and Gerald D. Suttles, *The Social Order of the Slum.*

tion hypothesis. However, since the opposite hypothesis does not predict exclusively intraethnic relationships, the evidence could not be used against it. Similarly, if intraethnic relations persisted at very high levels, this fact would not provide conclusive support for ethnic resilience, since it could be argued that, after six years, immigrants are still in the early adaptation period and continue to depend heavily on their ethnic communities.

Because of this indeterminacy, it is necessary to focus less on the absolute frequency of intra- or extraethnic relationships and more on the nature of predictors affecting these variables. This analysis will be guided less by specific hypotheses stemming from the assimilation or ethnic-resilience perspectives than from the general "mode" of theorizing that each exemplifies. The characteristic mode of assimilation writings emphasizes individual variables. Personal traits are said to determine both the immigrants' capacity for assimilation and the receptivity of the native population toward them. More educated immigrants, those from higher occupational backgrounds, and those more fluent in the new language should be able to undergo socialization more rapidly and be better prepared to enter into relations with members of the native majority.

Psychosocial characteristics are also important. In the specific context of immigration to the United States, individuals who are more "modern" should be at an advantage in gaining entrance into nonethnic groups. For the dominant Anglo population, individual characteristics of the immigrants are the crucial aspects determining the degree of social distance that it chooses to keep from them. Assimilation theorists have identified four such characteristics: race, religion, language, and status of origin. In the United States, the more the immigrant corresponds to the prototype of the white, Protestant, middle-class, English-speaking American, the faster he will gain admittance into domestic social circles.[4]

The mode of theorizing characteristic of ethnic-resilience writings emphasizes, on the other hand, structural conditions. Aside from the specific prediction of durable intraethnic relationships, the logic of the theory calls attention to those structural factors that promote or discourage associations with members of the native population. Immigrants living in "mixed" areas or working in firms with a multiethnic labor force will tend to establish relationships outside their own group. Those confined to ethnic neighborhoods, employed in enclave enterprises, or working in firms where most of the labor force is of the same group will find their social relationships restricted to the ethnic circle. Obviously, individual characteristics will affect

---

4. Emory S. Bogardus, *Immigration and Race Attitudes*; W. Lloyd Warner and Leo Srole, *The Social Systems of American Ethnic Groups*; and Gordon, *Assimilation in American Life*.

where immigrants live and work, but the emphasis of the structural approach is on those conditions that, independent of personal traits, also determine the character of immigrant relationships.[5]

The theoretical counterpoint between individual characteristics and structural conditions will provide the organizing framework for the data analysis in this chapter. The next section summarizes descriptive findings concerning patterns of immigrant relationships over time. This summary will serve to introduce the analysis of associations between social relationships and variables suggested by the two theoretical approaches. As in the preceding chapter, this analysis will then be followed by an effort to identify major predictors of the dependent variables and a comparison of results across samples. The bearing of these findings on the general issue of immigrant social adaptation will be discussed in the conclusion.

A PROFILE OF RELATIONSHIPS OVER TIME

As reported in Chapter 5, the social world of immigrants in the United States is one thoroughly permeated by kinship and ethnic ties. At the moment of arrival in 1973, Cuban exiles had an average of ten relatives and friends awaiting them. Three years later, they reported an average of four relatives living in the same city and an additional 2.5 living elsewhere in the country. These figures remained unchanged during the following three years. Cuban wives, similarly, had numerous relatives in the city of residence, a pattern that reinforced the dense kinship networks in which Cuban refugees move.

Though much more widely dispersed, Mexican immigrants exhibit similar characteristics. At the moment of arrival, they had an average of four kin and friends expecting them. Six years later, the mean number of relatives living in the same city was the same as for Cubans, and the number of Mexican relatives living elsewhere in the United States doubled the Cuban figure. Mexican wives had even more kinship ties than their husbands, an average of 5.6 in the same city and 6.3 in other U. S. locations.

The role of kinship networks in the process of adaptation is reflected in the respondents' reports of help received from their relatives since arrival. In 1973, one-third of the Cubans and more than half of the Mexicans said that they expected little or no help from their relatives living in the United States. Three years later, those who had in fact received no help were only 13 percent in the Cuban sample and 29 percent in the Mexican, while those reporting some or a great deal of help represented 75 and 50 percent, respectively. Dense kinship networks provide the basis for a pattern of social

5. This argument is developed at greater length in Alejandro Portes, "Modes of Incorporation and Theories of Labor Immigration."

relationships revolving around the ethnic community. In 1976, Cuban refugees reported an average of eight "close" friends living in the same city. Of these, seven were Cuban; moreover, 93 percent had no American friends. Among Mexican immigrants, eight out of an average of ten close friends in the same city were Mexican or Mexican-American. As in the Cuban sample, nine out of ten immigrants had no American friends.

Results presented in Chapter 5 confirm that the overwhelming proportion of immigrants in both samples conducted their social life primarily within their own community. To summarize: 76 percent of Mexican immigrants and 75 percent of their wives maintained social relations with other Mexicans in 1976. Among Cubans, the pattern was even more marked: 83 percent of the immigrants and 89 percent of their wives circulated socially within the Cuban community; fewer than 1 percent mentioned Americans as their primary social attachment.

By 1979, however, there had been a marked decline in this pattern of ethnic concentration, though the mode remained typical of social interaction in both samples: among Mexicans, those whose primary relationships took place exclusively within the ethnic community declined to 56 percent of the immigrants and 59 percent of their wives; among Cubans, the corresponding percentages dropped to 72 and 78 percent, respectively. The shift in both samples was not toward exclusively American relationships, whose incidence remained negligible, but toward a "mixed" pattern combining intra- and interethnic interactions. This category represented about one-third of the Mexican sample and one-fourth of the Cuban in 1979.

For reasons explained above, these results by themselves do not support any particular theoretical perspective on social adaptation. The massive preference for intraethnic relationships in both samples is obviously congruent with predictions based on ethnic-resilience writings, but it is not wholly incompatible with the assimilation viewpoint. Similarly, the shift of a substantial number of immigrants toward a mixed mode of social interaction during the last three years provides evidence in favor of assimilation, but it is not at odds with the continuing resilience of ethnic ties.

Unlike primary social relationships, patterns of formal organizational membership differed markedly between the two samples. As shown in Table 100, about two-thirds of the Cubans and Mexicans did not belong to any organization in 1976. In 1979, the situation remained unchanged for the Mexicans, but more than half of the Cubans now belonged to at least one organization. Churches were the preferred form of organizational membership in both groups. Trade union membership experienced a precipitous decline, especially among Mexicans. Still, the number of Mexican immigrants belonging to trade unions was higher, in absolute and relative terms, than among Cubans. Conversely, about thirty Cuban exiles belonged to professional organizations in 1979, while only one Mexican did.

Table 100. Membership in Organizations, 1976-1979

Variable	Cubans		Mexicans	
	1976, %	1979, %	1976, %	1979, %
1. Membership in Organizations				
None	65.0	47.1	66.9	65.2
One	27.2	39.6	29.0	29.3
Two or more	7.8	13.3	4.1	5.5
Total	*100.0* (427)	*100.0* (412)	*100.0* (438)	*100.0* (454)
2. Type of First Organization[a]				
Religious (churches)	47.9	54.3	37.0	65.8
Trade unions	17.6	8.7	48.2	15.2
Professional associations	11.3	13.3	0.8	.7
Social/recreational	19.0	5.9	11.1	12.0
PTA	--	10.0	--	3.8
Others	4.2	7.8	2.9	2.5
Total	*100.0* (142)	*100.0* (219)	*100.0* (135)	*100.0* (158)
3. Ethnicity of Members of First Organization[a]				
Cuban/Mexican[b]	64.4	65.2	59.9	69.8
Anglo	16.3	19.2	27.0	15.0
Both	11.9	12.8	7.2	11.2
Blacks	0.8	1.0	4.0	2.0
Other	6.6	1.8	1.9	2.0
Total	*100.0* (135)	*100.0* (218)	*100.0* (126)	*100.0* (153)

[a]Percentages based only on respondents belonging to at least one organization minus missing data.

[b]Coded according to nationality of respondent.

Despite these differences, the two groups are similar in the ethnic character of the organizations they join. As shown in Table 100, about two-thirds of the Cubans affiliated with at least one organization belonged to ethnic (Cuban) ones in 1976 and again in 1979. Among Mexican immigrants, intraethnic affiliation actually increased during those years, reaching 70 percent in 1979. Membership in predominantly Anglo organizations increased marginally in the Cuban sample between 1976 and 1979, while among Mexicans, there was a sharp drop in both absolute and relative terms. To summarize, immigrant social relations in both personal and formal organizational contexts involved predominantly members of the same minority.

Some marginal increases occurred in relationships with Anglo-Americans over six years, but the number of these relationships remained, on the whole, very limited. Though suggestive, these preliminary results do not clarify the actual determinants of organizational membership or ethnic affiliation. The next sections carry the analysis further by examining the interrelationships between these variables and predictors suggested by the two theoretical perspectives.

AFFILIATION AND ITS DETERMINANTS

The two dependent variables considered in the following analysis are the organizational affiliation of immigrants and the predominant ethnicity of their social relationships, both formal and informal. This section considers the first question, leaving for the next the more complex analysis required by the second.

As seen above, organizational affiliation is uncommon among both groups of immigrants. Even among Cubans, affiliation, when it occurs, is generally restricted to a single organization. The theoretical literature in this area has located determinants of affiliation in a series of factors held to affect the individual's willingness to spend the time and effort required by organizational membership. The logic of the hypothesis is fairly simple: affiliation will be more frequent among those able to perceive the need and benefits of collective action. Higher education and information, occupational status, and modern orientations will thus lead to higher levels of affiliation. Among immigrants, knowledge of the host-country language may provide an additional indicator of capacity to understand the meaning and goals of associational membership in the United States.[6]

6. Alex Inkeles, "Making Men Modern: On the Causes and Consequences of Individual Change in Six Developing Countries"; H. E. Freeman, E. Novak, and L. G. Reader, "Correlates of Membership in Voluntary Associations"; and Alan Peshkin and Ronald Cohen, "The Values of Modernization."

To examine this hypothesis, we correlated number of organizations to which the immigrant belongs with a series of predictors, including years of education and principal occupation at arrival, education acquired in the United States, present occupation and income, modernity, information about U. S. society, and knowledge of English both at arrival and at the time of the follow-up. Age is also included, though its potential effect on affiliation is not clear from the hypothesis.[7]

Table 101 presents the corresponding bivariate coefficients for both samples in 1976 and 1979. The pattern of associations in the Cuban sample fits the hypothesis quite well. Without exception, all coefficients are in the predicted direction and all are statistically significant. Several of these correlations, such as those involving education, occupation, and knowledge of English, are fairly sizable. Among Cuban exiles, organizational affiliation is thus consistently associated with those factors identified by the above hypothesis as increasing individual commitment to organizations.

Age, included as an additional independent variable, failed to correlate with affiliation in 1979 but had a small significant relationship in 1976. The direction of this coefficient suggests a weak tendency for older refugees to join organizations more frequently.

Results for the Mexican immigrants are quite different. Given the general similarities between Cubans and Mexicans in other aspects of social adaptation, the pattern of coefficients in this table is surprising indeed. Among the Mexican immigrants, organizational affiliation is unrelated to almost everything. Neither education nor occupation, modernity nor information correlate with organizational membership. Knowledge of English and earnings have weak positive associations in one of the follow-up surveys, but have none in the other. Overall, these findings lead to a definite rejection of the hypothesis as it applies to Mexican immigrants.

This unexpected divergence between the two samples requires additional investigation. One possible clue is given by the type of organizations that immigrants join. As shown in Table 100, substantial proportions of immigrants who reported organizational membership belonged to religious ones, mostly churches. Church membership (Catholic for the overwhelm-

---

7. Education is measured in years completed at arrival in the United States. Occupation at arrival and present occupation are coded in Duncan SEI scores; alternative coding schemes, such as the Siegel occupational prestige scale, did not yield significantly different results. Knowledge of English at arrival and at present are scores in the KEI index, described in Chapter 3. Modernity are scores in Inkeles and Smith's OM-short Form 5 scale, referenced in Chapter 8. Education in the United States is total months of completed formal instruction since 1973, regardless of the content of courses. Present earnings is the natural log of respondent's total monthly earnings. Information about the United States is coded in USIN index scores, described in Chapter 3.

Table 101. Organizational Affiliation and
Independent Variables, 1976-1979

| Independent Variable[a] | Affiliation[b] | | | |
| | Cubans | | Mexicans | |
	1976	1979	1976	1979
Education	.29**	.38**	.04	.02
Occupation at arrival	.25**	.34**	.03	.01
Knowledge of English at arrival	.21**	.30**	.10**	.01
Modernity	.07	.16**	.01	.08
Age	.11*	.07	-.01	.02
Education in the U.S.	.17**	.13*	.08	.07
Present occupation	.14**	.34**	.05	.01
Present income	.11*	.22**	.08	.13*
Present knowledge of English	.20**	.33**	.03	.07
Information about the U.S.	.17**	.19**	.02	.05

[a]See footnote 7 for a description of variables.

[b]Zero-order correlations; pairwise deletion of missing data.

*$p < .05$.

**$p < .01$.

ing majority) may not correspond to the type of organization envisioned by the hypothesis above: among Mexican immigrants, it is possible that church affiliation represents a "traditional" response, lacking the characteristics of personal decision and commitment associated with membership in other organizations. In a country where the vast majority of the population is nominally Catholic, saying that one belongs to this church may be a function of habit rather than rational decision making.

If this is the case, church affiliation will be no different, from the standpoint of the hypothesis, from complete lack of affiliation. The available data do not allow us to examine in detail the actual nature of religious participation. It is possible, however, to test indirectly this reinterpretation by identifying respondents whose sole organizational membership is a religious one. A new variable can thus be constructed that divides the sample into those be-

Table 102.   Affiliation to Nonreligious Organizations
and Independent Variables, 1979

Independent Variable	Nonreligious Affiliation[a]	
	Cubans	Mexicans
Education	.37**	.12*
Occupation at arrival	.28**	.10*
Knowledge of English at arrival	.30**	.05
Modernity	.21**	.18**
Age	.01	.04
Education in the U.S.	.15**	.09*
Present occupation	.36**	.02
Present income	.29**	.09*
Present knowledge of English	.34**	.07
Information about the U.S.	.21**	.10*

[a]Zero-order correlations; pairwise deletion of missing data.

*$p < .05$.

**$p < .01$.

longing to no organization at all or to Catholic ones alone (the large majority
in both samples) and those affiliated to at least one other organization.

Table 102 presents zero-order correlations between this new dependent
variable and independent ones for both samples in 1979.[8] The pattern of
results for Mexican immigrants is now closer to theoretical expectations: two-
thirds of the predicted associations are significant and all are of the right sign.
Though coefficients are quite modest, they provide tentative support for the
modified hypothesis.

Results for the Cuban sample are also instructive. Comparing them with
figures in Table 101, we find close similarities in the pattern of correlations.
Predictors identified by the original hypothesis correlate almost equally well
with nonchurch participation as with organizational membership in general.
This result suggests that, among Cubans, nonreligious affiliation better fits

8. Results for 1976 are omitted because they essentially reproduce the pattern of coefficients in the table.

Table 103.   OLS Regressions of Number of Organizations Joined
             on Independent Variables: Cuban Sample

Independent Variable	b	SE_b	β
Constant	-22.959		
Education	.029	.014	.140*
Occupation at arrival	.002	.003	.071
Knowledge of English at arrival	-.018	.058	.023
Modernity	.070	.049	.076
Age	.011	.004	.121*
Education in the U.S.	-.001	.004	-.007
Present occupation	.002	.002	.067
Present income	.204	.091	.134*
Present knowledge of English	.043	.020	.167*
Information about the U.S.	-.016	.020	-.047
R^2			.189

*Significant at the .05 level or higher.

the characteristics of information and commitment said to underlie organizational membership. In the Cuban sample, however, church affiliation cannot be effectively equated with nonparticipation, as is the case among Mexicans.

The next step of the analysis consists in placing these findings in a multivariate framework in order to identify the significant predictors of affiliation. The dependent variable for this analysis varies, however, between samples. Among Cubans, affiliation is an interval-level variable: number of organizations to which the respondent belongs. An ordinary least square analysis is appropriate in this case. Among Mexicans, affiliation is adjusted by subtracting church membership, following the above argument. Once this is done, the dependent variable becomes a highly skewed dichotomy: those who belong to at least one organization (11 percent of the sample) and those who do not. In this case, OLS is inappropriate and we employ instead a logistic regression procedure, eliminating comparability between samples.

Results for the Cuban sample are presented in Table 103. Not surprisingly, variance explained in this case is almost 20 percent. This is due to the

Table 104. Logistic Regression Describing Effects of
Independent Variables on the Log-Odds of Joining a
Nonreligious Organization: Mexican Sample

Independent Variable	Logit Coefficient	Standard Error	First Derivative[a]
Constant	-105.461	55.243	
Education	.157	.084	
Occupation at arrival	-.004	.013	
Knowledge of English at arrival	.133	.250	
Modernity	1.098*	.380	.106
Age	.052	.028	
Education in the U.S.	.037*	.015	.003
Present occupation	-.036	.020	
Present income	.347	.476	
Present knowledge of English	-.142	.112	
Information about the U.S.	.073	.119	
Proportion of affiliation	.108		
Chi square for no effect of variables	25.874	10 df	$p < .01$
Log-likelihood R^2	.132		

[a]Computed as $b_iP(1-P)$ where b_i = independent variable coefficient; P = proportion of the sample affiliated to at least one nonreligious organization.

*Significant at the .05 level or higher.

effect of four predictors: education, knowledge of English, present earnings, and age. The age coefficient is positive, indicating higher net levels of affiliation among older immigrants. All other significant effects are in the predicted direction. While reliable, the substantive impact of these effects on affiliation is relatively small. For example, one additional year of education increases the probability of joining another organization by only 3 percent. In absolute terms, the strongest effect is associated with logged dollar earnings where a unit change increases the probability of affiliation by 20 percent.

Table 104 presents results of the logistic regression for Mexican immigrants. In addition to logit coefficients, the first-order partial derivatives of each independent variable with a significant effect on affiliation are computed. These figures are interpretable as the actual probability of affiliation associated with a one-unit increase in the relevant predictor. As shown in the last two rows, chi square indicates that the set of predictors has a significant effect on the dependent variable and that the log-likelihood analog to R^2 is different from zero. These results are due to the effect of only two predictors—modernity and education acquired in the United States. Though both are reliable, their absolute magnitude is very different. As indicated by the two derivatives, a unit change in the OM-5 modernity scale increases the probability of affiliation by almost 11 percent. On the other hand, one month of additional education in the United States increases this probability by only three-tenths of 1 percent.

Despite the lack of comparability between samples and the fact that only a minority of independent variables plays a significant role in each regression, the overall pattern of results clearly supports the original hypothesis. Higher education, higher income, better knowledge of English, and more modern orientations all increase the likelihood of organizational membership. The fact, however, that this set of predictors explains only one-fifth of the variance in the Cuban sample and even less in the Mexican indicates that other factors, not identified by the theory, exercise a significant effect on this aspect of immigrant social relations.[9]

ETHNICITY OF SOCIAL RELATIONS

Bivariate Results

Having examined determinants of organizational affiliation, we may now consider the more complex question of ethnic preferences in social interaction. This analysis will employ three dependent variables: (1) the ethnicity of the respondent's primary social relations outside the home, (2) the ethnicity of his wife's social relations, and (3) the ethnicity of members of the major organizations to which immigrants belong. Each variable is coded along a three-point scale ranging from "exclusively ethnic" (Cuban or Mexican) to "mixed" to "exclusively Anglo." As seen above, majorities in both samples reported that their personal relations, those of their wives, and the formal organizations to which they belonged were all defined by their own ethnicity.

Despite the apparent similarity among the three dependent variables,

9. A series of other possible predictors of affiliation, including interaction effects between variables in Table 104, were entered into the regression equation without significantly increasing explained variance. We conclude that the only significant predictors of affiliation available in the data are those included in these final regressions.

there is a major difference. The first two dependent variables focus on the more personal and informal relationships maintained by the immigrant and his spouse. Responses to these items can be interpreted as a statement of actual preferences in *face-to-face associations*. The third item involves membership in formally structured organizations. Though immigrants may also select organizations according to their congeniality, other factors clearly influence membership. One of them is the association's willingness to accept immigrants, a variable not governed exclusively by individual preference. In addition, organizational membership entails a more distant social bond than those created by face-to-face personal relations.

Predictors of these dependent variables are derived from the two theoretical perspectives outlined above. For the first, it is the immigrant's individual characteristics, such as social status, value orientations, and proficiency in English, plus certain ascriptive traits, such as religion and race, which should determine the nature of his social relationships in the United States. For the second, it is the structure into which immigrants become incorporated, which selectively facilitates or discourages interaction after controlling for the different individual variables.

Available indicators of individual-level variables include most of those employed in the preceding analysis: education and occupational prestige at arrival, education acquired in the United States, present occupational prestige and income, knowledge of English at arrival and at present, modern orientations, and information about American society. Since the spouse's social relationships are also considered, available indicators of her own social status must be included. These indicators are education, present occupation, and present income.

In addition, indicators of the immigrant's religion and race are also available. Religion is the respondent's 1979 statement of his religious preference. Following the theoretical argument concerning greater acceptability of immigrants whose religion is closer to that of dominant native groups, the variable is dichotomized into "Protestant" and "Catholic." The latter category represents the overwhelming majority of both samples; included in it is a small percentage reporting no particular religious preference.

Interviewers in the original survey were trained to evaluate different racial characteristics. Their observations were combined into a summary measure of race. Among Mexicans, race is essentially a dichotomy between *mestizos* and dark-skinned whites. Among Cubans, it is also a virtual dichotomy between darker- and lighter-skinned whites. There were no *mestizos* in the Cuban sample and, contrary to expectations, the number of blacks and mulattoes was insignificant.

Available indicators of the structural argument include predominant ethnicity of neighborhood and of the labor force in places of employment.

Both are coded as three-point scales according to whether most neighbors and co-workers are of the same group (Cubans or Mexicans, coded highest), mixed, or whether they are mostly Anglo. As seen in Chapter 6, employment in enclave firms is an important structural variable among Cuban refugees. This variable should be negatively associated with social relationships outside the ethnic community. There is no comparable indicator for Mexican immigrants, since no enclavelike economic structure was found among this group. For Mexicans, however, prior residence in the United States represents an additional important structural dimension. Length of prior residence in the country should increase the opportunities for establishing relations with those outside the ethnic circle as a result of time elapsed, independent of individual skills or personal traits.

The structural perspective is ultimately based on the idea of "conduciveness," meaning contexts of interaction that automatically increase opportunities for certain relationships to emerge. Following this logic, respondents were asked directly about their opportunities for meeting native Anglo-Americans during the preceding years. Responses, ranging from "none" to "many," constitute the final structural indicator in the following analysis.

Table 105 presents zero-order correlations between these different independent and dependent variables. Results reveal a fairly clear pattern of associations. Coefficients involving the immigrants' own primary relationships are considered first. In both samples, individual-level predictors fail consistently to correlate with this variable. Out of thirty coefficients, only three are statistically significant. The correlation involving race in the Cuban sample is significant, but in the direction *opposite* from that predicted: lighter-skinned refugees apparently prefer to associate among themselves.

Significant correlations involving immigrant primary relations occur, almost exclusively, with variables identified with the structural perspective. All correlations with these indicators are significant and all run in the expected direction. This pattern includes the predicted negative association between enclave employment and non-Cuban social relationships and the positive one between prior residence in the United States and greater Anglo relations for Mexicans.

Correlations involving wives' social relationships follow a similar pattern. The only noteworthy exceptions are the significant associations involving wives' education in both samples and those with wives' occupations among Mexicans. These three coefficients run in the direction predicted by individualistic theory, although they are small in absolute terms. With this exception, results indicate that the ethnic composition of immigrants' face-to-face relationships has little to do with individual characteristics such as social status, religion, or knowledge of English. Instead, social relations

Table 105. Ethnicity of Immigrant Relationships
and Independent Variables, 1979

Independent Variable	Primary Social Relations-- Respondent		Primary Social Relations-- Wife		Ethnicity of Organiza- tions-- Respondent	
	C[a]	M[b]	C	M	C	M
Education	.01[c]	.00	-.03	.02	.24**	.10
Occupation at arrival	.04	.00	.01	-.03	.18**	.04
Knowledge of English at arrival	.08	.08	.05	.08	.14*	.06
Modernity	-.03	-.07	-.07	.05	.09	.17*
Present occupation	.09*	-.06	.02	.05	.18**	.09
Present income	.06	.12**	-.06	.07	.29**	.11
Present knowledge of English	.04	.08	-.07	.13**	.24**	.15*
Information about the U.S.	-.06	.01	-.08	.00	.07	.08
Education in the U.S.	.11*	.04	-.05	.06	.07	.00
Wife's education	-.03	.03	.13**	.14**	.19**	.10
Wife's present occupation	-.02	.01	.06	.17**	.02	.08
Wife's present income	-.02	.10	.07	.06	.07	.14
Religion	.01	.06	-.02	.07	-.10	-.09
Race	-.13**	.03	-.05	.05	-.03	.22**
Neighborhood	-.11*	-.13**	-.11*	-.17**	-.22**	-.19**
Ethnicity of co-workers	-.25**	-.15**	-.16**	-.10*	-.22**	-.24**
Enclave employment	-.15**	--	-.15**	--	-.11*	--
Prior residence in the U.S.	--	.11**	--	.11*	--	.01
Opportunities to meet Anglos	.28**	.25**	.15**	.18**	.29**	.13*

[a]Cubans.

[b]Mexicans.

[c]Zero-order correlations; pairwise deletion of missing variables.

*p < .05.

**p < .01.

appear to reflect primarily structural conduciveness: where immigrants live and work, how long they have lived in the United States, and how many chances they have had to interact with Anglo-Americans.

Results involving ethnicity of formal organizations are less conclusive. In this case, both individual and structural indicators display significant correlations with the dependent variable. In both samples, correlations with structural variables are all significant and in the expected direction, with the exception of the insignificant association with prior United States residence among Mexicans. Samples differ consistently, however, in the pattern of correlations with individual-level variables. Among Cubans, status indicators—including education, occupation, and earnings—plus knowledge of English correlate significantly with ethnicity of organizations. Neither race nor religion has a significant association with this dependent variable. For Mexican immigrants, the pattern is almost exactly the reverse: not a single status variable has anything to do with the ethnic character of organizations. In this instance, it is race, knowledge of the language, and psychosocial modernity that relate significantly to the dependent variable.

Differences in results involving the three dependent indicators may be attributed directly to their different meaning, as discussed earlier. Summarizing the overall pattern, we may tentatively conclude that informal face-to-face relationships among both immigrant groups correlate almost exclusively with the social contexts into which they have been incorporated and the derived opportunities to interact outside their own ethnic circle. The ethnic character of formal organizational membership correlates also with structural variables, but it does so, in addition, with several individual characteristics. This last result is congruent with the fact that participation in formal associations is not just an exclusive function of individual preference, but also of eligibility and receptivity by their prior membership.

Individual variables relating to ethnicity of organizations are not identical between the two samples, however. Among Cubans, more educated and higher status refugees tend to join Anglo organizations more frequently. Among Mexicans, status levels make little difference; instead, lighter-skinned immigrants, those endorsing modern values, and those able to speak English are more likely to join Anglo organizations. Results thus point to the bifurcation of social relationships along the formal/informal axis, as well as that determined by the specific characteristics of each immigrant group.

Multivariate Analysis

The next step consists of transforming the above relationships into a causal statement about major determinants of immigrants' social relations.

This analysis faces several problems, already suggested by the above results. Readers unfamiliar with multivariate statistics may find the following sections difficult. For their benefit, results will be summarized in the conclusion. The first and major difficulty is the choice of a dependent variable. The three indicators of ethnicity of social relationships above do not reflect the same dimension. However, comparison of three different sets of regressions for two different samples would be excessively cumbersome and would tend to obscure major results in the data.

The alternative strategy, adopted here, is to concentrate on face-to-face relationships and to define the *couple*, not the individual as the appropriate unit of analysis. The primary reason for this choice is the greater incidence of personal relations on immigrants' lives. Almost all respondents reported some kind of primary-level interaction, while substantial proportions did not belong to a single formal organization. Given this situation and the fact that ethnicity of organizations correlates poorly with the other two dependent variables, we opted for eliminating it from this part of the analysis.

The reason for adopting the couple rather than the individual as the unit of analysis is the high intercorrelation and similar pattern of associations involving the immigrants' own social relations and those of their wives. This allows us to define a single composite measure that can be simultaneously related to different predictors. The resulting dependent variable, labelled ETHSOC, is constructed as the unweighted sum of the spouses' social preferences, each coded as indicated above.[10]

A second difficulty consists in the direction of causal effects. Clearly, the immigrants' network of personal relationships can interact with almost any independent variable. In other words, it can be argued that the immigrant's place of employment, his neighborhood, and his time in the country, knowledge of the language, education, and occupation not only affect but are themselves affected by who his friends are. For example, preexisting social relations can influence the immigrants' motivation to learn English and acquire additional education, the occupational opportunities available to them, and the places where they choose to live.

---

10. To avoid a significant loss of cases, we multiplied by 2 single immigrants' scores. The correlation between ethnicity of social relations of married respondents and their wives is .56 in both samples. An alternative procedure would have been to limit the analysis to married subsamples, accepting the loss of about fifty cases in each sample. To examine the extent of bias introduced by our decision, we replicated the analysis on the married immigrants alone. Results are omitted here, since they are identical to those presented below. A stepwise procedure run simultaneously for the married and full (adjusted) samples shows the same significant effects entering the analysis in the same order in both the non-lagged (Table 106) and lagged (Table 107) regressions. Variations in the absolute size of coefficients and variance explained do not justify separate presentations.

Table 106. Regressions of Ethnicity of Social Relations (ETHSOC)
on Individual and Structural Variables, 1979

Predictor	Cubans			Mexicans		
	b	SE_b	β	b	SE_b	β
Knowledge of English at arrival	.154[a]	.065	.173			
Present occupation				-.011	.005	-.123
Present knowledge of English	-.068	.023	-.226			
Information about the U.S.	-.053	.024	-.130	-.071	.037	-.130
Race	-.161	.080	-.106			
Wife's education				.048	.019	.162
Ethnicity of co-workers	-.297	.066	-.245	-.155	.077	-.124
Opportunities to interact with Anglos	.256	.052	.275	.284	.066	.273
R^2			.222			.157

[a]Insignificant effects and predictors omitted; listwise deletion of missing data.

This reciprocal causation is especially likely in the case of the last structural indicator—opportunities to meet with Anglos. The availability of such opportunities should affect the nature of primary social relations, but the opposite is also true: immigrants whose social life revolves around their own ethnic circle reduce, by that very fact, their chances to meet with those outside of it.

Among possible solutions to this problem, we opted for the simplest. First, ETHSOC is regressed on all predictors listed above. This analysis follows the logic of both the individual and structural perspectives in assuming that the main direction of effects is the one they hypothesize. Second, ETHSOC—composed of items measured in 1979—is regressed on predictors measured three and six years earlier. These results make it much more difficult to argue that present social relations affect independent variables measured at an earlier point in time.

Table 106 presents the first set of ordinary least square regressions for both samples. All predictors are included in the equations, though those lacking reliable effects are omitted from the table. This multivariate analysis yields a counterintuitive finding that could not have been anticipated on the basis of the bivariate correlations alone. Before discussing it, we examine the more predictable results: opportunities to interact with Anglos is the single strongest determinant of ethnicity of social relations. This effect quintuples its standard error in the Cuban sample and quadruples it in the Mexican. Ethnicity of co-workers is the second significant structural predictor in each sample, though its effect is stronger among Cubans.

There are four significant individual-level effects in each regression. The novel finding is that all but one are of the *opposite* sign from that predicted. Lighter-skinned Cuban refugees and those with a better command of English are more likely to favor relations within their own ethnic group; the same is true for Mexican immigrants of higher occupational status. In both samples, more information about American society also leads to a preference for intraethnic social relations. Only knowledge of English among Cubans and wives' education among Mexicans have effects congruent with the individualistic argument.

This finding suggests several conclusions. First, it casts doubt on conventional analyses of immigrant social relations, at least as formulated so far. Second, it is compatible with results presented in Chapter 8 concerning immigrants' perceptions of American society. We saw there that better informed immigrants and those with greater knowledge of English were more likely to hold critical opinions and be more aware of the existence of discrimination. The same information and knowledge variables now emerge as increasing the probability of face-to-face relationships within the ethnic community.

Table 107 presents the second set of regressions based on the set of lagged predictors. Results do not perfectly reproduce those obtained earlier, but they follow the same basic pattern.[11] Opportunity to meet with Anglos, measured in 1976, is again the major determinant of social relations outside the ethnic group. Information about the United States also emerges as a significant predictor in both samples, and its effect is once again negative.

Ethnicity of co-workers in 1976 ceases to have a significant net effect on ETHSOC. The two other lagged structural variables emerge, however, as

11. These regressions are not strictly comparable to those in Table 106. Owing to high collinearity between the two knowledge-of-English measures, only the earlier one is included. Second, wives' present occupation and income were ascertained in the final survey but not in the intermediate one. Hence, they are also excluded. Wives' education was also measured in 1979. Given little additional training by wives since 1973, the variable essentially measures educational levels at the time of the respondents' arrival. For this reason the variable is included.

Table 107.   Regressions of Ethnicity of Social Relations (ETHSOC)
on Lagged Predictors,[a] 1973-1979

Predictor[a]	Cubans			Mexicans		
	b	SE_b	β	b	SE_b	β
Wife's education-- 1973				.040	.020	.139
Present occupation-- 1976	.001	.0005	.106			
Information about the U.S.--1976	-.081	.025	-.199	-.110	.039	-.193
Enclave employment-- 1976	-.226	.109	-.126			
Neighborhood--1976				-.267	.094	-.195
Opportunities to interact with Anglos--1976	.199	.055	.226	.186	.075	.172
R^2			.151			.137

[a]Insignificant effects and predictors omitted; listwise deletion of
missing data.

significant predictors. Among Cubans, employment in enclave firms in
1976 reduces the probability of Anglo or mixed social relationships three
years later; among Mexicans, residence in a Mexican neighborhood in 1976
has the same effect.

This last result deserves additional comment, for it again bears on the
alternative modes of incorporation of these two immigrant groups. As seen
in Chapter 6, the emergence of an economic enclave is a significant determinant of Cuban exiles' occupation and income. These results are complemented by present ones, which show that the enclave also plays an important role in determining the character of Cuban social relations. Net of the
effect of enclave membership, residence in a Cuban neighborhood actually
decreases the probability of intraethnic relations, though its effect is not
significant.

Among Mexican immigrants, however, the significant structural variable is not the place of employment, but that of residence. The *barrio* substitutes for the nonexistent economic enclave as the major structural support
of ethnic boundaries. Thus, immigrants living in the *barrio* are significantly

more likely to restrict their friendships to other Mexicans in preference to those on the outside.

Causal Models

The above results do not exhaust a causal analysis, however, nor do they resolve the controversy between the individual and structural arguments. Proponents of the individualistic perspective can argue that personal traits do not relate to ethnicity of immigrant relations directly, but have a significant *indirect* influence through their effect on the social contexts that determine social interaction. This possibility suggests extending the analysis toward a more complex causal structure.

A hypothetical model of immigrant social relations is presented in Figure 7. The model makes use of the longitudinal nature of the data to establish causal direction among exogenous and endogenous variables. The number of predictors is reduced to those which, for theoretical and empirical reasons, appear most important in both samples. For purposes of clarity, straight arrows in the diagram connect blocks of variables rather than individual ones.

Reading from left to right, the model asserts that there are four major exogenous variables—education of self, education of spouse, knowledge of English, and occupation at arrival—and that their effects on ethnicity of social relations are entirely mediated by other variables. The first set of endogenous variables includes occupational status and income in 1976. The model asserts that their effects on ETHSOC are also wholly indirect. Lagged structural variables—ethnicity of neighborhood, co-workers, and enclave employment—compose a second block of endogenous variables with hypothesized direct and indirect negative effects on social relations. Finally, the two immediate predictors of ETHSOC are opportunities to relate with Anglos and information about U. S. society. As suggested by preceding results, their effects are of opposite signs.[12] Double-pointed arrows between sets of endogenous variables measured at the same point in time indicate that the model makes no causal statement as to their interrelationships.

The model is first evaluated in Tables 108 and 109, which present ordinary least square equations for Cubans and Mexicans, respectively. Standardized path coefficients are presented for the sake of clarity and because comparisons across samples on their basis yield results identical to those

12. The fact that immediate predictors are measured in the same survey as ETHSOC indicators creates the possibility of reciprocal causality. We opted for this solution, since lagging them would only reproduce and multiply the problem among 1976 variables. As seen previously, lagged indicators of opportunities for interaction and information about U. S. society also have significant net effects on ETHSOC. This evidence supports the appropriateness of the causal sequence posited by the model.

Fig. 7. A Model of Immigrant Social Relations in the United States

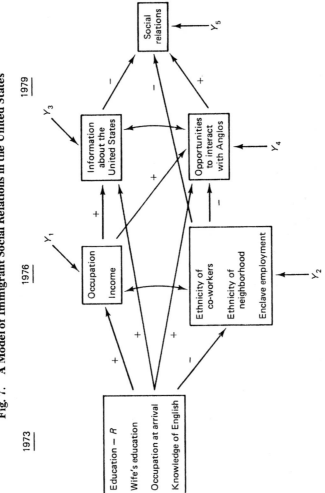

Table 108. Recursive Model of Social Relations: Cubans

Predictor	Occupation--1976	Income--1976	Ethnicity of Neighborhood	Ethnicity of Co-workers	Enclave Employment	Information About U.S.	Opportunities to Interact with Anglos	Social Relations
Education--R	.18[a]*	.06	-.01	.11	.12	.34**	.01	-.20*
Wife's education	.02	.10	-.01	-.04	-.01	.16**	.05	.03
Occupation at arrival	.26**	.08	-.11	-.20**	-.08	.08	.11	.08
Knowledge of English at arrival	.09	.04	.04	-.08	-.04	-.03	.06	.10
Occupation--1976						-.03	-.02	.03
Income--1976						.12	.09	.04
Ethnicity of neighborhood						.07	-.05	.10
Ethnicity of co-workers						.12*	-.13*	-.04
Enclave employment						-.12	-.02	-.13*
Information about the U.S.								-.17**
Opportunity to interact with Anglos								.24**
R^2	.23	.05	.01	.04	.01	.24	.07	.13

[a]Standardized path coefficients.

*Coefficient doubles its standard error.

**Coefficient triples its standard error.

Table 109. Recursive Model of Social Relations: Mexicans

Predictor	Occupation--1976	Income--1976	Ethnicity of Neighborhood	Ethnicity of Co-workers	Enclave Employment	Information About U.S.	Opportunities to Interact with Anglos	Social Relations
Education--R	.00[a]	.00	.09	.01	.03	.25**	.11	-.13*
Wife's education	.01	.04	-.14*	-.02	.01	.01	-.04	.16*
Occupation at arrival	.19**	-.01	.02	.03	.11*	.05	-.16**	.10
Knowledge of English at arrival	.19**	.16*	-.12	-.15*	-.05	.17**	.09	.06
Occupation--1976						.15*	.22**	-.02
Income--1976						.06	.03	.00
Ethnicity of neighborhood						-.08	-.01	-.16*
Ethnicity of co-workers						-.02	-.16**	.02
Enclave employment						.08	-.10	-.03
Information about the U.S.								-.12*
Opportunities to interact with Anglos								.26**
R^2	.08	.03	.03	.02	.01	.22	.14	.14

[a]Standardized solution.

*Coefficient doubles its standard error.

**Coefficient triples its standard error.

based on the unstandardized solution. To maintain strict comparability between samples, the same indicator of enclave employment used in the Cuban sample is also included in the Mexican regression.[13]

Results involving ETHSOC may be considered first. They indicate that the model is parsimonious, accounting for similar amounts of variance in both samples with fewer than two-thirds of the predictors employed in the preceding regressions. An analysis of interaction effects, omitted here, indicates that no first-order interaction significantly increases explained variance in either sample. The causal sequence outlined in Figure 7 is generally supported by these results. Since the set of regressors is not identical to those employed earlier, findings may be briefly summarized.

Opportunities to meet with Anglos is again the major determinant of social relations outside the ethnic community. Information about United States society is also a significant predictor and its effect is again negative. Enclave employment in the Cuban sample and ethnicity of neighborhood in the Mexican sample continue to have comparable negative direct effects on relations outside the ethnic community.

Effects of achieved occupation and income in 1976 as well as knowledge of English at arrival are entirely mediated by subsequent variables. There are, however, three additional direct effects on ETHSOC that were not anticipated by the model. In the Mexican sample, wife's education has a sizable positive effect. In both samples, however, respondent's education has a significant sizable *negative* direct effect. Thus, after controlling for all other predictors, we find that better educated immigrants continue to prefer face-to-face relations within their ethnic group. This truly unexpected result will require additional investigation.

Next, we consider effects on the two immediate predictors of ETHSOC. These path coefficients are generally similar for both samples. Among both Cubans and Mexicans, information about the United States is primarily a function of education at arrival. The relevant coefficient quadruples its standard error in both samples. Thus, the negative effect of education on social relations outside the ethnic group is both direct and indirect through information. Other strong net effects are associated with knowledge of English among Mexicans and with wife's education among Cubans. In the Cuban sample, enclave employment somewhat depresses levels of information, while Anglo co-workers increase it.

The main determinant of opportunities to meet with Anglos in both samples is ethnicity of the labor force in places of employment. This effect

13. Although no Mexican enclave exists, a few Mexican immigrants were self-employed or employed in scattered firms belonging to Mexicans or Mexican-Americans. For the sake of symmetry with the Cuban model, these immigrants are coded as enclave members.

is negative, indicating fewer opportunities among those whose co-workers are of the same ethnicity. This coefficient is the only significant one in the Cuban sample, which accounts for the low proportion of variance explained on this endogenous variable. In the Mexican sample, opportunities for outside interaction are also influenced by occupation in 1976. This effect is positive and quite strong. However, occupation at the moment of arrival has a significant net negative effect. This suggests that higher status immigrants who did not manage to translate their original skills into better occupations are among the most isolated within the ethnic community.

Among remaining effects in the table, the relevant ones for this analysis are those linking exogenous individual-level variables with 1976 structural predictors. These coefficients are the ones that bear on the argument that immigrant social relations are indirectly determined by individual characteristics, since the latter decisively affect the structural contexts into which immigrants can move.

Results in Tables 108 and 109 show, however, that individual occupation, education, and knowledge of English in 1973 had very little to do with the residential and occupational contexts where immigrants were found three years later. There are only four significant effects among the two samples combined, and only one is relatively strong. Variance explained in structural indicators by the exogenous variables does not exceed 4 percent in either sample. Thus, the process of incorporation into different contexts operates with almost complete autonomy of individual characteristics at arrival. Immigrants of very different status origins and knowledge of English have about equal probability of finding themselves in the same social contexts after several years in the country.

More systematic evidence in support of this conclusion is presented in Table 110, which decomposes effects of exogenous variables on ethnicity of social relations.[14] Indirect effects of all exogenous variables through ethnicity of neighborhood, ethnicity of co-workers, and enclave employment are not significantly different from zero in either sample. Apart from spurious effects, due to intercorrelations among the exogenous variables themselves, the only sizable coefficients in the table are the direct effects already examined. Only three indirect paths reach .05, and two of these are negative: both the effect of occupation at arrival on opportunities to meet with Anglos and that of education on information about U. S. society *decrease* the probability of relationships outside the ethnic group. Thus, individual-level variables fail to exercise their predicted influence on immigrant social relations, either directly or indirectly.

14. Kenneth C. Land, "Principles of Path Analysis"; Otis D. Duncan, "Path Analysis: Sociological Examples."

Table 110.   Decomposition of Effects on Ethnicity
of Social Relations (ETHSOC), 1973-1979

Effects	Predictor			
	Education --R	Wife's Education	Occupation at Arrival	Knowledge of English at Arrival
Direct				
Cubans	-.20[a]	.04	.08	.09
Mexicans	-.16	.13	.13	.08
Indirect through 1976 occupation and income				
Cubans	.01	.01	.02	.01
Mexicans	.00	.00	.00	.01
Indirect through ethnicity of neighborhood, co-workers, and enclave employment				
Cubans	-.02	.00	.00	.01
Mexicans	-.01	.01	-.02	.01
Indirect through information about U.S.				
Cubans	-.06	-.03	-.01	.01
Mexicans	-.03	-.01	.00	-.02
Indirect through opportunities to meet Anglos				
Cubans	.00	.01	.02	.01
Mexicans	.04	.00	-.05	.03
Spurious				
Cubans	.18	-.03	-.11	-.10
Mexicans	.10	-.04	-.02	-.04

[a]Standardized solution.

Maximum-Likelihood Estimations

This last section incorporates the third dependent variable, ethnicity of formal organizations, omitted from the preceding analysis. Despite the lack of correlation between this and the other dependent variables, it is possible to consider them simultaneously by defining an unobserved construct—ETHSOC—which directly influences observed scores in each of them. A full-information maximum-likelihood (FIML) procedure makes it possible to reestimate the model on the basis of this endogenous construct and to adjust for imperfect reliability in some of its predictors.[15]

The main purpose of this final analysis is to arrive at a causal statement that provides a reasonable fit to the data on the basis of all the available information concerning measurement structure and relationships among these variables. A second related goal is to check the reliability of findings, especially unexpected ones, stemming from the previous analysis. The FIML procedure starts with the hypothetical model presented in Figure 7 and successively frees initially restricted parameters according to the relative magnitude of the first-order partial derivatives.

Following the model in Figure 7, the initial estimation assumed uncorrelated measurement errors and uncorrelated disturbances. In addition, causal effects were estimated among six unobserved constructs corresponding to the six blocks of variables depicted in the figure, each defined by the corresponding empirical indicators. Our primary concern was to establish whether the variance / covariance matrices of error variables were indeed diagonal, as assumed by the model.

Estimation of this initial model yielded unsatisfactory test statistics for both samples. Successive freeing of restricted parameters did not significantly improve the model's fit. A second model was thus defined under the same causal assumptions but on the basis of self-measured variables, with the exception of the final endogenous construct. Results also indicated that several of the predictors posited in the original model had consistently weak effects on subsequent variables. These were eliminated and the model reestimated on the basis of a simpler causal structure.

In the final models, all exogenous and endogenous predictors are assumed to be self-measured and error free. Exceptions are knowledge of English at arrival and information about U. S. society, measured by the KEI and USIN scales. Variances in these two constructs are adjusted according to the known reliability of their empirical indicators. Corresponding error terms are fixed at the product of observed scale variance times the unreliability, according to the procedure outlined in Chapter 8.

Final models are presented in Figures 8 and 9. The goodness-of-fit test statistics ($\chi^2 = 43.985$, $df = 39$, $p > .26$, Cubans; $\chi^2 = 35.671$, $df = 28$, $p > .15$, Mexicans) indicate an acceptable fit to the data in both samples. The major structural modification in comparison with earlier models is the elimination of achieved occupation and income, which failed to affect subsequent

15. Charles E. Werts, Karl G. Jöreskog, and Robert L. Linn, "Identification and Estimation in Path Analysis with Unmeasured Variables"; Karl G. Jöreskog, "Structural Equation Models in the Social Sciences."

Fig. 8. Final Model of Ethnicity of Social Relations (ETHSOC) Cubans—Standardized Solution

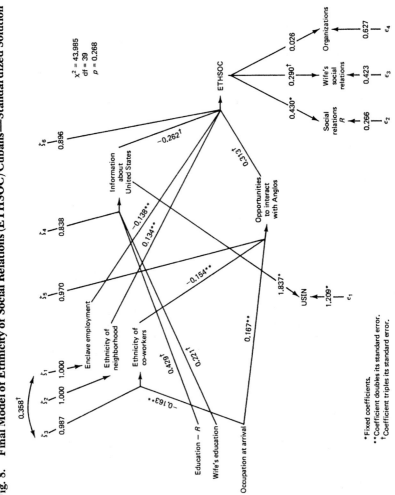

*Fixed coefficients.
**Coefficient doubles its standard error.
†Coefficient triples its standard error.

Fig. 9. Final Model of Ethnicity of Social Relations (ETHSOC) Mexicans—Standardized Solution

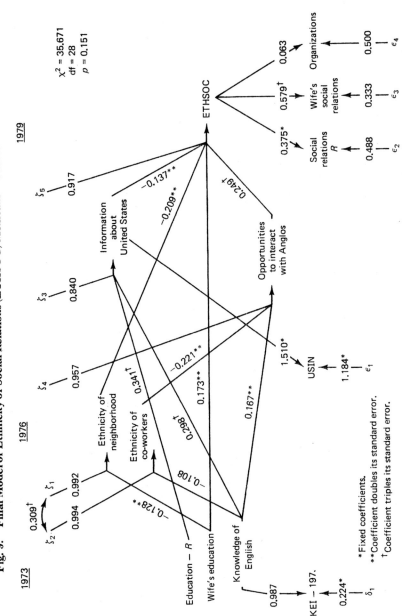

$\chi^2 = 35.671$
$df = 28$
$p = 0.151$

*Fixed coefficients.
**Coefficient doubles its standard error.
†Coefficient triples its standard error.

variables significantly. Predictably, enclave employment is also a poor predictor of later endogenous variables in the Mexican sample, and is also omitted. Among exogenous variables, knowledge of English in the Cuban sample and prior occupation in the Mexican are eliminated for similar reasons. Final models differ as well in the pattern of causal effects. An identical solution for both samples would have produced an unacceptable fit in either model or both. Effects are thus not comparable across samples. For this reason, standardized solutions are presented, since they facilitate internal comparisons within each sample.

To avoid repetition, we omit a detailed review of results in favor of highlighting the most significant differences with those from the OLS analyses. Adjustment for fallible measurement of the final dependent variable improves explained variance in both samples in comparison with earlier regression estimates. Roughly one-fifth of the variance in ETHSOC is accounted for in each sample, despite the fact that the FIML solution retains less than half of the original predictors. For Mexicans, the pattern of effects on ETHSOC is a repetition of the one encountered earlier, with the exception of education, which ceases to have a significant direct effect. The negative influence of education on relations outside the ethnic community is now wholly indirect through information about American society.

Determinants of the next-to-last endogenous variables are again similar to earlier results for the Mexican sample. Opportunities to interact with Anglo-Americans are negatively affected by ethnic co-workers and positively influenced by knowledge of English. Education and knowledge of English lead to significantly higher levels of information. The FIML estimation does not improve explained variance in opportunities for interaction, but accounts for close to one-third of the variance in information about the United States.

For Cubans, there are two significant differences in comparison with least square estimates. First, occupation at arrival joins ethnicity of co-workers as a significant predictor of opportunities for interaction with Anglos. The occupation effect is positive, as predicted. Second, ethnicity of neighborhood has a direct effect on ETHSOC, which effectively cancels that of enclave employment. This result was noted in the OLS analysis, though it did not reach statistical significance. It coincides with those results obtained in Chapter 6 concerning the effect of neighborhood among Cubans. For this sample, participation in an ethnic economy is the decisive factor constraining social relationships with the outside. Refugees who are not part of the enclave, even when living in predominantly Cuban areas, tend to extend their social relationships beyond the ethnic community.

In both samples, lagged structural indicators are essentially independent of individual traits, a result that confirms the prior conclusion that contexts of social interaction incorporate, with about equal probability, individuals with different backgrounds and abilities. Finally, we consider the lambda (Λy) matrix of regression coefficients relating the final dependent variable to its empirical indicators. In both samples, this measure shows that the ethnic character of organizations is different from other items and is a poor empirical indicator of the underlying construct. Thus, ETHSOC continues to be reflected primarily in ethnicity of face-to-face relations of the immigrant and his spouse.

Despite difficulties of estimation introduced by the organizational affiliation item, the analysis as a whole is valuable in providing an integrated statement of major causal relationships in the data.[16] The FIML procedure casts doubt on some effects found earlier and introduces new ones, but leaves intact the basic direction and relative importance of major effects on immigrant social relations. Since the model incorporates all the available information and adjusts for the fallible measurement of the dependent variable, it eliminates objections to the findings stemming from the procedural restrictions of regression analysis.

CONCLUSION

The reader who has followed us through this long journey will have noted a series of statistical anomalies and may be wondering what these numerous results amount to. To understand their overall meaning, we must return to the original theoretical question, namely the nature of social adaptation to American society. Deeply ingrained in scholarly and lay views on the topic is the idea that "successful" adaptation, defined as rapid integration into American social circles and culture, depends on individual traits, abilities, and motivations. This perception, embodied in most sociological writings on assimilation, leads to an almost exclusive concentration on individual characteristics, neglecting the social contexts into which newcomers become incorporated.

In this chapter, we have advanced an alternative interpretation, labelled it "structural," and deliberately contrasted its predictions with those stemming from the more conventional individual perspective. Empirical results relevant to this theoretical counterpoint are fairly consistent in their implications. In summary, structural variables emerge, in every instance, as the most significant predictors of the nature of social relations that immigrants engage in. Reported opportunities to meet with Anglo-Americans is the single most

16. Attempts to estimate a nonrecursive model incorporating a hypothetical causal loop between ethnicity of social relations and opportunities for interaction did not yield a stable solution in either sample. This result may be attributed to the unbalanced measurement structure of ETHSOC, as defined in this analysis.

important determinant of ethnicity of immigrant relations, whether measured at the same time or three years earlier. In turn, opportunities for interaction are significantly determined by the ethnic composition of the labor force in places of employment.

Other structural variables also affect the character of immigrant relations directly, but they vary according to their different modes of incorporation. Employment in Cuban enclave firms in Miami is the significant factor among Cuban refugees; residence in a Mexican *barrio* occupies a comparable place among Mexican immigrants. Among Cubans, ethnic places of residence, net of the effect of enclave employment, tends to increase the probability of external social relations.

To our surprise, individual background variables had only feeble effects on the process by which immigrants became incorporated into different social contexts. Individuals whose educational levels, occupational statuses, and knowledge of English differed markedly found themselves, with about equal probability, in the same neighborhoods and places of employment. This result indicates that the specific process by which immigrants are channelled toward different niches in the social structure depends on variables other than those suggested by an individualistic perspective.

However, this conclusion does not exhaust our significant findings, a second group of which pertains to the actual behavior of individual-level variables. This group contains both expected and unanticipated results. To summarize: education, information about the United States, knowledge of English, modernity, occupation, and income all have positive effects on affiliation to organizations, especially in the Cuban sample. In addition, the same variables correlate positively with a tendency toward joining nonethnic organizations.

These expected results, however, contrast with the remaining ones. A multivariate regression analysis reveals that education, information about U. S. society, present occupation, and present knowledge of English *decrease* the probability of face-to-face relationships outside the ethnic group. After controlling for structural variables, education and information both lead to a preference for keeping informal personal relations within ethnic boundaries. This result holds for both samples; present occupation among Mexicans and present knowledge of English among Cubans have similar effects.

An integrated causal model, estimated with a maximum likelihood / full-information procedure, eliminates several of these effects, most importantly the negative direct influence of education. This model, however, preserves the crucial negative influence of information about U. S. society on extraethnic relationships. Education and knowledge of English also continue to have negative effects through their strong influence on levels of information.

In order to interpret these surprising results, we must relate them to those reported in the previous chapter. That analysis found that variables such as education, information, and knowledge of English increased critical perceptions about American society. In particular, those variables increased the probability of perceptions of discrimination against the respondent's own ethnic minority. Together, those findings and the current ones suggest a rather complex process of social adaptation. While a superficial interpretation would suggest that they point to growing interethnic hostility and withdrawal from the mainstream, this conclusion is negated by the immigrants' high levels of satisfaction and the fact that the more educated and informed join more organizations, in particular nonethnic ones.

Adaptation, as portrayed by these results, is a process whereby gradual entry into American institutions is accomplished through increased awareness of how they actually function and a resilient and even growing attachment to ethnic ties as a source of personal support. Those immigrants more able to relate effectively to various aspects of life in America are often those who most strongly adhere to personal relationships within their own communities. Awareness of barriers and, at times, outright hostility confronting them in the outside has its counterpart in the reaffirmation of primary relations within protected ethnic circles. This interpretation integrates the above complex set of findings into a perspective on the process that is quite different from the unilinear sequence portrayed by the assimilation model.

Early adaptation, according to these results, is not a matter of simply moving *from* the ethnic community *into* the broader society. It is instead a simultaneous and complementary process whereby close ethnic ties are emphasized precisely as individuals attempt to gain entry into institutions of the host society and move up its different social hierarchies. Rather than abandoning personal relationships within their own groups, immigrants who have moved farthest into the outside world seem to rely more heavily on such bonds. Ethnic resilience, not assimilation, is the theoretical perspective more congruent with this interpretation. This resilience is not, however, a force leading to collective withdrawal, but rather a moral resource, an integral part of the process of establishing and defining a place in a new society.

10

CONCLUSION: IMMIGRATION THEORY AND ITS PRACTICAL IMPLICATIONS

In the preceding chapters, we have presented a great deal of information on two recent immigrant groups and their histories after reaching American shores. These final pages are not dedicated to a detailed summary of the findings, since such summaries are found in the concluding sections of each of the preceding seven chapters. The reader unable to read through the entire text is referred to those sections for a synthesis of the major results.

Our goal in this book was to tell the story of Cuban and Mexican immigrants arriving in the United States in recent years, but to do so in a manner organized by existing theory. By using theoretical perspectives as the starting point, we hoped to do two things: first, to generate important questions that would guide our inquiry into the actual situations of the two immigrant groups; second, to examine the extent to which findings coincided with predictions stemming from competing paradigms. This latter strategy corresponds, of course, to the goal of making results relevant to issues that transcend the specific characteristics of the two samples.

This last chapter is intended as a reflection upon major trends extracted from the data, as they bear on both theoretical and practical issues. Regarding the former, there arises the issue of what hypotheses have been left untested and what lines of future inquiry are suggested by our results. Regarding the latter, we will examine the implications of the histories of Cubans and Mexicans for other recent minorities and the policies applied to them.

THEORETICAL CONTROVERSIES

The first chapter was dedicated to a review of theoretical viewpoints and the specific areas that they covered. Table 111 summarizes that discussion

Table 111. Theories of Immigration

Area	Orthodox	Nonorthodox		
		a	b	c
Origins of migration	Push-pull theories	Deliberate labor recruitment	Gradual penetration and imbalancing of peripheral areas	
Stability of immigrant flows	One-way flows toward high-wage areas	Target earning and return migration	Multiple cyclical displacements in pursuit of different economic opportunities	
Uses of immigrant labor	Supply source to counteract domestic shortages (equilibrium theory)	Supply source for permanently subordinate activities benefiting the dominant group (internal colonialism)	Supply source to counteract organizational strength of domestic labor (split labor markets)	Supply source to firms in the competitive sector (dual economy)
Determinants of individual economy mobility	Human-capital theory	Dual-labor-market theory	Multiple segmented labor markets (ethnic enclaves)	
Immigrant social and cultural adaptation	Assimilation theory	Ethnic resilience as an instrument for collective advancement	Ethnic resilience as a reactive formation	

to help clarify the implications of our findings for theory. Although it is possible to identify four different topical areas, as is done in the table, it is clear that there is also an inner coherence among certain sets of hypotheses. For example, the column labelled *orthodox* in Table 111 identifies those views that have dominated social science writings on immigration in the past. These hypotheses have in common a nonconflictual approach to the topic and a view of the society and economy as equilibrium-restoring systems. Within them, chances for individual mobility are determined ultimately by universalistic criteria met through ability, will, and other personal characteristics.

On the other hand, theories labelled *nonorthodox* in the table emphasize positions that are different but not mutually exclusive. What they have in common is their opposition to the orthodoxy based upon a less consensual view of society and a greater emphasis upon class and ethnic cleavages. For these theories, life chances of recent immigrants are as strongly determined by personal traits as by broader structural forces over which individuals have no control.

The evidence presented in the preceding chapters indicates that much in reality corresponds to the portrait of immigration offered by orthodox views. The fact that push and pull forces can be identified in every immigrant flow is almost a truism. Equally undeniable are the facts that *some* immigrant groups leave their countries of origin never to return and that at *certain* historical periods immigrant labor has served mainly as a supplement to a tight domestic supply. Similarly, it is true that many immigrants have been able to translate their skills and motivations into economic returns and that every newly arrived group has undergone some kind of cultural assimilation.

As a whole, however, orthodox theories embody only an imperfect truth. More significantly, the realities that they neglect or conceal are as important for understanding the process of incorporation of specific immigrant groups as those that they emphasize. In Chapter 2, we presented evidence showing the predictive inadequacy of a push–pull approach to the origins of migration. The varying historical origins of population movements—from outright coercion, through deliberate inducement, to the current "spontaneous" outflows from Third World countries—can be more properly attributed to the gradual incorporation of peripheral areas into the world economy, the diffusion of expectations from the centers, and the resulting internal dislocations in these subordinate societies.

Similarly, the historical record of both the pre-World War I era and the post-World War II period leaves no doubt that many immigrant flows fit the target-earning image. Such groups have been characterized by massive rates of return. Still other immigrations, most commonly those not separated by great geographic barriers from their points of destination, have sustained cyclical patterns of migration characterized by periodic returns and multiple displacements. Mexican immigration during this century has been the prototype of this circular flow.

More controversial and more problematic is the issue of how the labor power of immigrants has been utilized. In Chapter 2, we presented data showing that a strong case can be made for the orthodox labor-supplement argument in the 1890–1914 period, but that there is absolutely no support for it after 1945. Instead of varying inversely with domestic unemployment, labor immigration actually accompanied increases in the unemployment rate in these latter years. Various lagged measures of domestic unemployment failed to have any effect upon the size of legal, contract, and apprehended illegal immigration, a result significantly at variance with those obtained for the pre-World War I period.

The data from our longitudinal surveys were used primarily to address the theoretical questions in the last two rows of Table 111. Results indicated that human-capital variables do have significant effects upon the occupation and income of recent immigrants, but that these effects vary both by group and by employment sector. Cubans and Mexicans are prototypical of "political" and "economic" migrants, respectively. Yet the distinct motivations and skills attributed to each of these types of flows could not be identified in the data, much less used to account for subsequent major differences in occupation and income. In terms of personal traits, these groups were more similar than different at the moment of arrival, with both tracing their origins to populations of modest education and economic means in their countries of origin. The factors that differed and that accounted for the manifold differences in their attainment processes were the social contexts the groups encountered in the United States.

The data do not support a structural argument based exclusively upon insertion into the upper or lower tier of a dual labor market. Employment sectors corresponding to the characteristics of a primary and secondary labor market could be identified empirically in both samples, but consequences of incorporation in each sector were not the same. For Cubans, differences between immigrants in primary and secondary employment matched prior theoretical expectations. For Mexicans, the pattern was almost the reverse, especially in terms of income returns on past human capital. This last result is congruent with the overall characterization of Mexican immigration as a circulatory labor flow, filling low-wage positions both in the secondary sector and in the lower tier of the primary labor market.

More importantly, the process of occupational and income attainment among Cuban refugees was significantly influenced by the availability of an ethnically organized enclave. The presence of an economic enclave is reflected in the number of immigrants of modest occupational origins who moved into self-employment after six years and a comparable number employed in firms owned by other Cubans. Self-employment and the economic returns on human capital that the enclave made possible had little to do with the ability and motivation of individual refugees, but depended instead upon the social structures that received them. In contrast, although many Mexicans had greater education and occupational training than their Cuban counterparts, the number of Mexican small businessmen after six years in the United States was almost zero.

As descendents of a long-entrenched system of working-class migration, Mexican immigrants do not have an enclave option. Mexicans do not follow, however, an homogenous path; over time many dimensions of their experiences have stratified them. One such source of internal stratification highlights the need to pursue sectoral divisions in historically defined labor markets. Even after years in the United States, the level of economic rewards for Mexican immigrants continued to depend on whether they participated in the circulatory labor flow or remained in Mexico and entered the United States for the first time as legal immigrants.

Finally, social and cultural adaptation of Cubans and Mexicans proceeded in ways that were, in a superficial sense, unsurprising. Majorities in both samples declared high satisfaction with their present life situations and firm intentions to remain in the United States. Most depended for social support upon relations within the ethnic community, though the incidence of extraethnic ties appeared to increase significantly with time. Variables identified by assimilation theory as the major predictors of immigrants' attitudes and behavior proved to have a significant role. However, the direction of many of these effects was, from the standpoint of that theory, quite unexpected.

The fact that immigrants of greater education, knowledge of English, and information were significantly more critical of American society and more prone to perceive discrimination reflects a very different reality than that conventionally anticipated. These immigrants, at the intellectual forefront of their respective minorities, also preferred to keep their face-to-face relationships within the ethnic community. These basic results are common to both Cubans and Mexicans despite the multiple differences between the groups in residential and occupational histories. Social adaptation, according to these results, is very different from a straightforward path toward cultural integration and consensus building. It involves, rather, a gradual discovery of the realities of the host society, including the actual position of one's group in its ethnic stratification system and the various forms of discrimination. Such adaptation also encompasses the widespread use of intraethnic networks as sources of personal companionship and social support. This function of ethnicity does not diminish but is actually heightened among those immigrants who, by reason of their education and knowledge, have had more exposure to and have gained more awareness of realities in the outside.

In summary, the evidence gathered by this study departs markedly from the set of orthodox theories listed in Table 111. The principal shortcoming of those theories is not that they completely miss empirical reality, but that under broad generalizations they obscure facts that distinguish different immigrant groups. Such facts have less to do with background individual characteristics, both achieved and ascribed, than with the social structures into which immigrants become inserted. Neither do the data lend support to blanket descriptions of immigrants as an unmercifully exploited group. In this regard, results do not accord with the most extreme arguments advanced in opposition to orthodox theories. Throughout the analysis, however, there is the persistent influence of structural factors, channelling immigrants toward different geographic and occupational locations and affecting the character of their social relations. Elements of conflict are present both in the restricted access to positions of economic advantage confronted by many immigrants and in their subjective perceptions of how they are treated by the dominant majority.

ENCLAVES AND MIDDLEMAN MINORITIES

The existence of an ethnic enclave and the empirical demonstration of its multiple effects in the Cuban sample is clearly one of the most important findings of our study. However, the emergence of a network of immigrant small businesses and the presence of an entrepreneurial class among certain groups is by no means a new phenomenon. Similar developments have been noted among other minorities, most notably the Jews and Japanese at the turn of the century and the Koreans at present. Authors such as Ivan Light have written insightfully about the social origins of these groups and the factors propelling them onto an independent business path.[1]

As stated in Chapter 2, among the various explanations advanced for the phenomenon of immigrant enclaves, Frazier's "prior experience in buying and selling"[2] seems the most appropriate. Entrepreneurial experience in the home country plus the existence of the appropriate economic institutions in the immigrant community, such as rotating credit associations, are decisive factors in determining the community's economic future. This effect applies both to the early entrepreneurial waves and to subsequent ones formed by immigrants of lower social origins.

1. Ivan H. Light, *Ethnic Enterprise in America.*
2. E. Franklin Frazier, *The Negro in the United States.*

There is some disagreement, however, about the nature of the economic functions played by entrepreneurial immigrant groups in the host
country. One of the most respected scholars in this area, Edna Bonacich,
has advanced the notion of "middleman minorities" as an appropriate characterization. According to Bonacich and Modell, these groups function as
buffers between elites and masses, "playing the roles of rent collector and
shopkeeper to the subordinated population while distributing the products
of the elites and/or exacting tribute for them."[3] Characteristically, these
groups are not primary producers, but instead "help the flow of goods and
services through the economy."[4] Bonacich cites the Jews in Europe, the
Chinese in Southeast Asia, and the Indians in West Africa as suitable examples. She goes on to apply the concept to the history of the Japanese in the
United States.

There is little doubt that in certain places and periods particular minorities have played the buffer role described by Bonacich. However, the concept of middleman minority fits awkwardly with the experiences of other
immigrant groups. In their study of Japanese small business, Bonacich and
Modell are forced to conclude that no evidence exists to support the hypothesis that local capitalists in California channelled the Japanese into or benefitted from a middleman role. Similarly, the economic history of Jewish immigrants in New York City is not adequately described by portraying them as a
buffer between dominant classes and the mass of the population. Many Jewish merchants and subcontractors may have played something resembling a
"middleman" role, but many others were engaged in direct production for
the general market and commerce with all segments of the population.[5]

In the case of the Cubans in Miami, too, little evidence supports the
middleman hypothesis. First, there are no indications that Cuban businessmen have assumed or have been channelled into the role of intermedi-
aries between Anglo "elites" and other local minorities, such as blacks.[6]
Second, contrary to the description of middleman minorities advanced by
Bonacich, Cuban firms are not exclusively found in commerce and finance
but include a substantial proportion in industry and construction. In addition, the production of these latter firms is not destined exclusively for the
ethnic market. Like produce raised in Japanese farms or garments made in
Jewish factories in Manhattan, Cuban-produced footwear, sugar, cigars,
and furniture are sold in the open market and consumed by the general

3. Edna Bonacich and John Modell, *The Economic Basis of Ethnic Solidarity.*
4. Ibid.
5. Ibid., p. 252. Moses Rischin, *The Promised City.*
6. Antonio Jorge and Raul Moncarz, "The Cuban Entrepreneur and the Economic Development of the Miami SMSA"; Kenneth L. Wilson and W. Allen Martin, "Ethnic Enclaves."

population.[7] As Light noted in the case of the Japanese, the expansion of immigrant enterprises could hardly be sustained if they were limited to supplying their own ethnic market.[8]

The economic histories of Jews and Japanese in the United States, as well as the more recent one of Cubans, are thus imperfectly characterized by the middleman-minority concept. The concept is valuable for describing other historical instances, in Europe and elsewhere, in which foreign groups were indeed inserted between dominant classes and a downtrodden population. In the United States, the activities of entrepreneurial minorities have possessed a strong element of independence that created businesses without explicit directives from above. In each instance, the initiatives of the earlier immigrant waves resulted in a spatially concentrated and dense network of small businesses in industry or agriculture, as well as commerce and services.

Collectively, the economic impact of immigrant businesses has extended well beyond the limits of the ethnic community. Nevertheless, the preservation of primary bonds as the basis of immigrant enterprise has renewed economic opportunities for new arrivals of more modest origins. The existence of such opportunities explains the continuing geographical concentration of these groups and the entry of new immigrants into enclave employment, foregoing higher short-term gains in the outside.

CLASS AND ETHNICITY

Our description of enclaves as places that offer a relatively favorable economic alternative for new immigrants contrasts significantly with other characterizations of ethnic firms. The latter are more commonly portrayed as activities that survive only because of the severe exploitation of new arrivals by their more established conationals. In this sense, labor practices in ethnic enclaves would not differ significantly from those in the secondary sector as a whole; if anything, they would be more unfavorable to workers.[9]

As seen in Chapter 6, this type of description underlies the characterization of immigrant enterprise as part of the secondary labor market. As seen in the same chapter, the evidence consistently contradicts this argument. Thus, the existence of enclaves as distinct social and economic forms runs not only against orthodox theories of individual mobility through human capital, but also against some nonorthodox generalizations about the

7. Wilson and Martin, "Ethnic Enclaves."
8. Light, *Ethnic Enterprise in America*, chap. 2.
9. For a recent statement of this argument as applied to the Cuban case, see L. Arguelles, "Cuban Miami."

structure of advanced capitalism. Proponents of the latter tend to view the process of capitalist accumulation as basically the same everywhere and fragmented only in the more developed economies by the emergence of an oligopolistic sector. Why should immigrant businesses be any different from other small enterprises in the competitive sector?

The answer to that question is implicit in much of the previous discussion. The question is worth additional attention, however, for it lies at the very center of the interface between class and ethnicity, which has been emphasized throughout our analysis. It is neither the case that immigrant capitalists are more generous nor that they bring from their home countries traditions of paternalistic concern for their workers. Those familiar with the economy of prerevolutionary Cuba or that of contemporary Korea can attest to labor practices every bit as harsh, if not more so, than those in competitive firms in the United States.

Hence, the economic opportunities opened to new immigrants by enclave employment derive not from the subjective orientations of the owners, but from the objective fact that they are inserted into a foreign context in a position of relative disadvantage. In the United States in particular, the benefits of state tutelage have consistently gone to domestic enterprises, not to those established by immigrant minorities. State protection can shelter firms from outside competition, subsidize their credit, and ensure the availability and discipline of the labor force. Immigrant small businesses have lacked such protection, especially in their early stages. As seen in Chapter 2, in the extreme case of the Japanese, the state (California) was employed directly as an instrument of landowners to dispossess immigrant farmers and return them to their original condition as laborers.

It is the absence of a privileged relationship with the state that compels immigrant entrepreneurs to rely upon the economic potential of ethnic solidarity. Ethnic bonds can be activated, under circumstances characteristic of each group, to provide initial capital for business ventures. They can also help erect barriers around the community to protect its market from outside competition. More importantly, however, ethnicity modifies the character of the class relationship—capital and labor—within the enclave.

Immigrant capitalism faces an objective dilemma. The viability of its modest firms often depends upon the extraction of long hours of labor for low pay. When labor requirements exceed the level that the owner himself and his immediate family can provide, others must be hired. In the absence of state protection, the requirement of above-average hours for lower wages cannot be simply imposed. Enforcement agencies can readily side with immigrants who defect from such conditions against their politically powerless employers. The objective difficulty then consists in how to extract maximum effort from immigrant workers without encouraging them to leave and join the open labor market; in other words, how to persuade them to accept their own exploitation.

A common national origin is the obvious answer. Ethnic ties suffuse an otherwise "bare" class relationship with a sense of collective purpose in contrast to the outside. But the utilization of ethnic solidarity in lieu of enforced discipline in the workplace also entails reciprocal obligations. If employers can profit from the willing self-exploitation of fellow immigrants, they are also obliged to reserve for them those supervisory positions that open in their firms, to train them in trade skills, and to support their eventual move into self-employment. It is the fact that enclave firms are compelled to rely on ethnic solidarity and that the latter "cuts both ways," which creates opportunities for mobility unavailable in the outside. It is the way in which ethnicity permeates class relations in this situation that distinguishes enclave employment from that in the secondary sector. As seen in Chapter 7, the economic outcome of these alternative modes of incorporation, trivial at the start, becomes quite significant after a few years in the United States.

FUTURE RESEARCH

As noted previously, orthodox theories of immigration share a generalist approach to the process to which they apply. It is not difficult to prove them wrong, less because of their total inaccuracy than because of their failure to take important distinctions into account. Throughout the analysis, we have found numerous differences in the way general predictions apply to the two groups studied. This pattern naturally suggests one kind of investigation required to advance theory in this area.

There are today many immigrant flows and a series of foreign minorities attempting to cope with their new surroundings, both in the United States and elsewhere. Cuban exiles and Mexican immigrants are two major groups, but by no means represent the totality. Thus, the modes of incorporation that they represent and that we have examined in detail do not exhaust possible ones, even in the United States. For example, contemporary professional immigration, originating predominantly in the Asian countries, appears to follow a very different path into the American labor market than those described above. The outflow of professionals and technicians from India, Korea, Taiwan, and other countries—labelled "brain drain" at the points of origin—represents an important variant of contemporary labor immigration. In the United States, university-trained Filipino, Chinese, and Indian professionals enter directly into primary-sector jobs, albeit in subordinate positions, and become geographically dispersed throughout the country.[10]

The classic literature on immigrant assimilation in the United States features studies that focus primarily on the histories of various European groups after their arrival in Eastern ports. A few authors have gone beyond this approach to examine social and economic conditions in the countries of origin, and thus offer a more holistic portrait of the process. Thomas and Znaniecki's *The Polish Peasant* was a pioneer in this respect, providing a model of scholarship seldom attained afterwards.[11]

In Chapter 1, we suggested that a comprehensive approach to the study of immigration would examine not only the conditions at points of origin and destination, but also the global context within which these flows occur. The view of immigrant labor movements as processes *internal* to a changing international system offers the more historically valid hypotheses in such areas as the origins of migration and its shifting directions in time. Further, this perspective facilitates relating labor migrations to other events occurring simultaneously, such as capital and commodity flows.

Finally, results reported above provide evidence of the usefulness of a comparative design. Research that deals simultaneously with two or more groups restrains the tendency to generalize on the basis of findings from a single collectivity. Repeatedly, results that appeared to support conclusively one particular theoretical position were shown to be contingent upon the specific characteristics of one of our samples. A comparative framework can provide novel insights into particular processes that would not emerge from the interplay of past theory and the history of a single minority.

PRACTICAL IMPLICATIONS

Having examined the bearing of results upon theories of immigration, we can now ask what implications these findings have for the situation of the immigrants themselves. As newcomers and noncitizens, immigrants have been generally passive recipients of governmental policies toward them. Although these policies are presented as benign, they are guided by the theoretical orthodoxy, the tenets of which have been proved empirically wrong. For example, one of the goals of United States policy in recent years has been to accelerate the "Americanization" of refugee groups by resettling them throughout the country. The rationale has been that faster cultural assimilation would promote economic mobility among the refugees

10. Rosemary Stevens, Louis W. Goodman, and Stephen Mick, *The Alien Doctors*, chaps. 6, 7, and 10; Alejandro Portes, "Determinants of the Brain Drain."

11. W. I. Thomas and Florian Znaniecki, *The Polish Peasant in Europe and America.*

and work for the benefit of all. Compulsory resettlement programs based on this notion can easily undermine the internal solidarity and organization of newly arrived groups and thus weaken their capacity for mutual assistance and support.[12]

Underlying this and similar policies is a simplified understanding of the fate of immigrants in the United States. The popular and official view amounts, in essence, to an elementary version of queuing theory: recent arrivals are channeled to the bottom of the socioeconomic pyramid, but eventually move up the ladder as still newer groups "push" them from below. Thus a much-advertised book on ethnicity in America states,

> There has also been an historical pattern of one group replacing another in neighborhoods, jobs, leadership, schools, and other institutions. Today's neighborhood changes have been dramatized by such expressions as "white flight" but these patterns existed long before. . . . In nineteenth century neighborhoods where Anglo-Saxons had once fled as the Irish moved in, the middle-class Irish later fled as the Jews and Italians moved in.[13]

These reassuring words, written by a well-known minority scholar, should impress upon blacks and other downtrodden groups the notion that their time will also come. According to the same author, perhaps the most significant characteristic of American ethnic groups has been their "general rise in economic condition with the passage of time."[14] Such statements, asserted and not empirically demonstrated, are flawed in two respects: first, in their historical validity and, second, in their concept of time. Each is worth additional comment.

First, in contrast to the anecdotal evidence marshalled in support of simple queuing theory, serious scholarship has documented the presence of major gaps in the economic advancement of different ethnic minorities. It is not the case that those groups at the bottom of the American labor market are there because they were latest in the queue. Instead, the history of such minorities as blacks and Mexican-Americans has been marked by *reversals* of past economic and social achievements and semipermanent confinement to the bottom rungs of the occupational ladder, while other more recent arrivals have climbed ahead.

Stanley Lieberson has conducted a painstaking empirical analysis of the comparative experiences of blacks and southeastern European immigrants in this century. His conclusion is that the relative stagnation in the

---

12. The resettlement program of Cuban refugees during the 1960s is discussed in Chapter 3. See also John F. Thomas and Earl E. Huyck, "Resettlement of Cuban Refugees in the United States."

13. Thomas Sowell, *Ethnic America*, p. 277.

14. Ibid., p. 275.

position of blacks is a consequence of major setbacks suffered in different areas, from jobs to housing.[15] Similarly, the best studies of the Mexican-American minority in the Southwest, including those of Julian Samora, Leo Grebler, Joan Moore, and Mario Barrera, have documented the major losses experienced by this group, which confined it to a permanently subordinate position. Since the aftermath of the Mexican-American War, such losses have included the mass removal of Mexicans from land ownership, restrictions upon voting rights, and mass expulsion from the country altogether. Government-sponsored campaigns against illegal immigration during the 1930s and 1950s converted U. S.-born Mexican-Americans into a persecuted minority, stripped of civil rights by sole reason of their national origins.[16]

At the other extreme, it is not the case that "successful" immigrant groups have achieved their economic and social prominence by patiently waiting their turn in the ethnic queue. The most representative of these minorities during the twentieth century, such as the Jews and Japanese before World War II, experienced significant progress by moving aggressively into land and business ownership and effectively using bonds of ethnic solidarity for economic advantage. As noted previously, the factor that distinguishes these experiences is that major gains were achieved during the first generation, with the new arrivals often economically surpassing other minorities that had been in the country much longer. Progress made by the immigrants was then consolidated into educational and occupational mobility, within and outside the ethnic enclave, by later generations.

Nor is it the case that entrepreneurial minorities have experienced "ethnic succession." No new ethnic group moved to take over the Japanese farms and produce businesses when the latter were interned during World War II. No identifiable minority replaced the Jews in lower Manhattan as they moved out of small-scale garment production and other industries. Similarly, there is no evidence of a group waiting in the wings for Cubans to depart in order to take over the Miami enclave. The economic histories of these minorities have been unique and thus cannot be adequately subsumed under blanket generalizations about ethnic progress or ethnic succession.

Second, assertions about the gradual advancement and eventual attainment of parity by all ethnic groups are based on an open-ended time framework. From this perspective, the reversals experienced by blacks and Mexican-Americans will eventually be seen as minor, because, in the long run, they too will move ahead as other groups have in the past. The problem

15. Stanley Lieberson, *A Piece of the Pie*.

16. Julian Samora, *Los Mojados*; Leo Grebler, Joan W. Moore, and Ralph C. Guzman, *The Mexican-American People*; Mario Barrera, *Race and Class in the Southwest*.

with this "evolutionary time" perspective is that predictions based on it cannot be falsified since they carry no temporal limit; more importantly, these predictions have no relevance for the present realities of the more downtrodden groups.

An evolutionary approach is more suitable for interpreting remote past events than for analyzing present realities or predicting future ones. It is true that "in the long run" Catholics and Protestants learned to live together in Europe, but this fact did not help victims of countless religious wars. It is also true that eventually slavery was abolished in the Americas, but this outcome gave little relief to the hundreds of thousands chained across the Atlantic and compelled to labor against their will. Similarly, it may be that society will eventually overcome all racial and cultural cleavages, but this happy prediction in no way resolves present inequalities or helps anticipate their course in the future.

Statements about benign ethnic succession and gradual progress have a pleasant ring, but fail to stand up to empirical scrutiny. It is not surprising, however, that they continue to be voiced, even by individuals from the most disadvantaged minorities. Reasons for this persistence have to do less with their historical validity than with their ideological usefulness as instruments of legitimation.

Recent immigrant groups should approach such optimistic statements and the policies that they justify with caution, for they do not often coincide with their own interests. The evidence presented in the preceding chapters clearly shows that neither geographic dispersion nor uncritical acceptance of the values and views of the host society accompanies occupational and economic advancement. Nor is knowledge of the language an indispensable tool for material progress in the first generation.

As a whole, the experiences of Cuban and Mexican immigrants are congruent with historical accounts of earlier arrivals in supporting a basic practical lesson: for foreign minorities, entering at a disadvantage into the labor market and social institutions of the receiving country, preservation of their culture and internal solidarity represent crucial instruments of adaptation. Individual skills and dreams are important, but their effects can be easily blunted outside the appropriate context. As seen above, "success" stories among immigrant minorities have not been those characterized by very rapid cultural assimilation and geographic dispersal. The opposite has more often been the case, as these groups struggled to preserve their identity and cohesiveness well beyond the first generation. Adaptation to American society has always taken place and will continue to do so, but its direction and pace and the manner in which subsequent generations become integrated into the mainstream depend on the modes of incorporation and economic accomplishments of the earlier immigrants.

APPENDIX

Table A.   Item Components of the
U.S. Information Index (USIN)

Questionnaire Item	Translation
1. ¿Conoce Ud. el nombre del actual vice-presidente de Estados Unidos?	Do you know the name of the current vice-president of the United States?
2. ¿Conoce Ud. el nombre del actual gobernador de este estado?	Do you know the name of the current governor of this state?
3. ¿A qué se le llama "Social Security" en Estados Unidos?	What is known as Social Security in the United States?
4. ¿Puede decirme lo que significa "inflación"?	Can you tell me the meaning of inflation?
5. Si Ud. compra una casa a plazos, ¿qué efectos tiene esto sobre lo que Ud. paga en impuesto a la renta?	If you buy a house in installments, what effect does this have on your income tax?
6. ¿Cual es la organización que se identifica como AFL-CIO?	Which organization identifies itself as AFL-CIO?
7. Como Ud. sabe, en Estados Unidos existen tarjetas como "Master Charge" y "Visa" que sirven para comprar a crédito. ¿Conoce Ud. cual es el interés anual que esas tarjetas cobran?	As you know, there are cards such as "Master Charge" and "Visa" which serve for buying on credit in the United States. Do you know the annual interest charged by these cards?
8. ¿Este interés es mayor o menor que lo que le cobraría un banco?	Is that interest higher or lower than what a bank would charge you?
9. ¿V el interés anual que cobran las tarjetas es mayor o menor que lo que cobran las compañías de préstamo?	And the annual interest charged by cards is higher or lower than what finance companies charge?

Table B. Detailed Industrial Sector by Type of Employment and
Labor-Market Sector, Cubans, 1979

Industry[a]	Self-employed, N	Employees			
		Total, N	Enclave, N	Primary, N	Secondary, N
Agriculture	5	2	2	0	0
Agricultural production		1	1		
Agricultural services	1	1	1		
Horticultural services	4				
Mining	0	2	0	1	1
Nonmetallic mining and quarrying		2		1	1
Construction	14	30	17	5	8
General building contractors	6	17	11	4	2
General contractors, except building		1			1
Special trade contractors	8	11	5	1	5
Not specified construction		1	1		
Manufacturing--durable	4	54	11	11	32
Miscellaneous wood products		4	2		2
Furniture and fixtures	2	5	3	1	1
Glass and glass products		1			1
Cement, concrete, plaster		1			1
Blast furnaces, steel mill		1			1
Primary aluminum		3			3
Fabricated structural metal	1	1		1	
Miscellaneous fabricated metal		4	1	1	2
Not specified metal		1		1	
Engines and turbines		2			2
Farm machinery		1	1		
Household appliances	1				
Radio, T.V.		1			1
Electrical supplies		8		4	4
Motor vehicles and equipment		1	1		
Aircraft and parts		1		1	
Ship and boat building repair		11	1	1	9
Not specified professional equipment		2	1	1	
Ordinance		1			1
Miscellaneous manufacturing		5	1		4

[a]Industrial titles are taken from the 1970 U.S. Census.

Table B--Continued

Industry[a]	Self-employed, N	Employees			
		Total, N	Enclave, N	Primary, N	Secondary, N
Manufacturing--nondurable	2	64	18	13	33
Meat products		7	2	1	4
Dairy products		2	2		
Canning and preserving fruits		1	1		
Bakery products		3		3	
Confectionary and related products		1			1
Beverage industry		4		2	2
Miscellaneous food preparation		1	1		
Not specified food industries		5		2	3
Knitting mills		3			3
Yarn, thread, fabric mills		1			1
Apparel and accessories	1	12	2	2	8
Miscellaneous fabricated textile products		1			1
Miscellaneous paper and pulp products	1				
Paper board containers, boxes		2			2
Printing, publishing		5	1	1	3
Plastics, synthetics, resins		2		1	1
Paints, varnishes		1			1
Rubber products		5	2	1	2
Tanned, finished leather		1			1
Footwear, except rubber		7	7		
Transportation, Communication, Public Utilities	4	17	6	8	3
Taxicab service		1			1
Trucking service	3	7	4	3	
Water transportation		1	1		
Air transportation		2		1	1
Services incidental to transport	1	4	1	2	1
Telephone, wire, radio		1		1	
Water supply		1		1	
Wholesale Trade	3	18	8	6	4
Motor vehicle and equipment		2		1	1
Dry goods and apparel		2	1		1
Food and related products	1	2	1	1	
Farm products--raw materials		1	1		
Electrical goods	1	1	1		
Machinery equipment and supplies		2	2		
Wholesalers (not elsewhere classified)	1	6	2	4	
Not specified wholesale trade		2			2

Table B--Continued

Industry[a]	Self-employed, N	Employees			
		Total, N	Enclave, N	Primary, N	Secondary, N
Retail Trade	20	38	17	11	10
Lumber and building material		1	1		
Direct selling establishments	2	1			1
Miscellaneous general merchandising stores		2	1	1	
Grocery stores	1	10	5	4	1
Dairy products stores		1	1		
Food stores (not elsewhere classified)		3		2	1
Motor vehicle dealers		3		2	1
Tire, battery, accessory dealers	1	1			1
Gasoline service stations	2	3	1		2
Miscellaneous vehicle dealers	1				
Apparel and accessory store, except shoe	2	1	1		
Shoe stores		1	1		
Furniture and home furnishings		1			1
Household appliances, T.V., radio		2	2		
Eating and drinking establishments	6	6	4	1	1
Jewelry stores	5				
Miscellaneous retail stores		1			1
Not specified retail trade		1		1	
Finance, Insurance, and Real Estate	0	11	2	6	3
Banking		6	1	3	2
Security, commodity brokerage		1	1		
Insurance		1		1	
Real estate		3		2	1
Business and Repair Services	20	24	6	11	7
Advertising	2				
Services to buildings and dwellings		7	1	5	1
Commercial research, development, testing labs		1		1	
Business management and consulting services	1				
Detective and protective services		1		1	
Business services (not elsewhere classified)	1	2		2	
Auto services, except repair	1				
Auto repair and related services	8	7	2		5
Electrical repair shops	5	1		1	
Miscellaneous repair services	2	5	3	1	1

Table B--Continued

Industry[a]	Self-employed, N	Employees			
		Total, N	Enclave, N	Primary, N	Secondary, N
Personal Services	1	14	1	10	3
Hotels and motels		11	1	7	3
Lodging places, except hotels and motels		2		2	
Miscellaneous personal services	1	1		1	
Entertainment and Recreation Services	0	2	0	2	0
Theater and motion pictures		1		1	
Miscellaneous services		1		1	
Professional and Related Services	10	28	8	13	7
Offices of physicians	7	2	1		1
Offices of dentists	1	1		1	
Hospitals		10	1	8	1
Health services (not elsewhere classified)		5	3	2	
Elementary and secondary schools		1			1
Colleges and universities		3		1	2
Educational services (not elsewhere classified)		1			1
Religious organizations		1		1	
Nonprofit membership organizations		1			1
Engineers and architects		2	2		
Accounting, auditing, bookkeeping services	2	1	1		
Public Administration	0	4	1	2	1
Federal public administration		1		1	
Local public administration		3	1	1	1
Total[b]	83	308	97	99	112

[b]Totals exclude 21 persons unemployed in 1979 and 15 missing observations.

Table C. Detailed Occupation by Type of Employment and
Labor-Market Sector, Cubans, 1979

Occupation[a]	Self-employed, N	Employees			
		Total, N	Enclave, N	Primary, N	Secondary, N
Professional, Technical	13	26	7	14	5
Accountant	2	6	1	2	3
Architect		1		1	
Computer specialist		1		1	
Mechanical engineer		1	1		
Dentist	1				
Physician	7	7	2	3	2
Health technologist--clinical laboratory		2		2	
Health technologist (not elsewhere classified)		3	1	2	
Teachers, except college and university	1				
Draftsmen		2	2		
Surveyor		1		1	
Technicians (not elsewhere classified)		1		1	
Musician and composer		1		1	
Photographer	1				
Public relations and publicity workers	1				
Manager, Administrator	19	17	4	6	7
Assessor, controller, treasurer		1		1	
Bank officer, financial manager		2		1	1
Buyers, wholesale and retail trade	1				
Office manager (not elsewhere classified)		4	1		3
Restaurant, cafeteria, bar manager	2				
Sales manager and department head		3		2	1
Sales manager, except trade		3		2	1
Manager, administrator (not elsewhere classified)	16	4	3		1
Sales	7	7	5	0	2
Salesmen and sales clerk (not elsewhere classified)	7	5	3		2
Sales representative, wholesale		1	1		
Sales representative, retail		1	1		

[a]Occupational titles are taken from the 1970 U.S. Census.

Table C--Continued

Occupation[a]	Self-employed, N	Employees			
		Total, N	Enclave, N	Primary, N	Secondary, N
Clerical	1	23	5	13	5
Bank teller		1		1	
Billing clerk		1		1	
Bookkeeper	1	2	2		
Clerical assistant, social welfare		1			1
Clerical supervisor (not elsewhere classified)		2		1	1
Mail carriers, post office		1		1	
Meter readers, utilities		1		1	
Bookkeeping		1	1		
Computer equipment operators		1		1	
Shipping and receiving clerks		8	1	5	2
Stock clerks and storekeepers		2	1	1	
Not specified clerical workers		2		1	1
Craftworker	30	90	33	22	35
Bakers		1	1		
Brickmason, stoneman	1	1			1
Bulldozer operator		1			1
Cabinet maker		3	3		
Carpenter	4	16	5	3	8
Carpenter apprentice		3	3		
Cement and concrete finisher		1			1
Cranemen, derrickmen		1		1	
Dental lab technician		1		1	
Electrician	2	7	1		6
Electrician apprentice		1	1		
Foremen (not elsewhere classified)		8	4	1	3
Furniture and wood finisher		1			1
Inspector (not elsewhere classified)		1		1	
Jewelers, watchmakers	2	1	1		
Mechanic, repairmen--air conditioning, heating	1	5	3	2	
Mechanic, repairmen--aircraft		1		1	
Auto body repairmen	1				
Auto repairmen--mechanic	7	7	2	1	4
Auto repairmen--mechanic apprentice		1	1		
Auto repairmen--heavy equipment mechanic	1	7	1	2	4
Radio and television repairmen	4				
Mechanic, except auto		1		1	
Mechanic, miscellaneous		8	2	4	2
Mechanic, not specified		2		1	1
Molders, metal		1	1		
Painters, construction, maintenance		2	2		
Photoengravers and lithographers		2		1	1
Plasters	1				

Table C--Continued

Occupation[a]	Self-employed, N	Total, N	Enclave, N	Primary, N	Secondary, N
			Employees		
Plumbers, pipe fitters	1	2		1	1
Pressmen, plate printers		1	1		
Roofers and slaters	1				
Sign painters	1				
Structural metal craftsmen	1				
Tile setters	2	1	1		
Upholsterers		1		1	
Craftsmen (not elsewhere classified)		1			1
Operative, Nontransport	0	71	17	15	39
Assemblers		5		2	3
Bottling and canning operatives		1		1	
Checkers, examiners, manufacturing		1			1
Clothing ironers and pressers		1			1
Cutting operatives (not elsewhere classified)		8	2		6
Dry wall installers		1	1		
Filers, polishers, sanders		2			2
Garage workers, gas station attendants		3			3
Graders and sorters, manufacturing		1			1
Laundry and dry cleaning operatives		1		1	
Meat cutters and butchers, except manufacturing		2	2		
Meat cutters and butchers, manufacturing		5	2	1	2
Metal platers		1			1
Mine operatives		1			1
Packers and wrappers, except meat and produce		5	1	2	2
Lathe machine operatives		2		1	1
Precision machine operatives		1		1	
Shoemaking machine operatives		3	2	1	
Solderers		9	4	2	3
Knitters, loopers, toppers--textile		1			1
Weavers		1			1
Textile operatives (not elsewhere classified)		2			2
Welders and flame cutter		3	1	1	1
Machine operatives, miscellaneous		5			5
Machine operatives, not specified		2		1	1
Miscellaneous operatives		3	2		1
Not specified operatives		1		1	
Operative, Transport	4	17	8	6	3
Deliverymen and routemen	1	5	3	1	1
Forklift and motor operative		3	1		2
Parking attendants		1		1	
Taxicab drivers and chauffeurs		2	2		
Truck drivers	3	6	2	4	

Table C--Continued

Occupation[a]	Self-employed, N	Employees			
		Total, N	Enclave, N	Primary, N	Secondary, N
Laborers, Except Farm	7	27	10	10	7
Animal caretaker		1			1
Construction laborer	1	6	3	1	2
Freight and material handlers		3	2	1	
Gardeners and groundskeepers	4	1		1	
Stock handlers		7	3	3	1
Warehousemen		2	1	1	
Miscellaneous laborers	2	6		3	3
Not specified laborers		1	1		
Farmers and Farm Managers	1	0	0	0	0
Farmers (owners and tenants)	1				
Farm Laborers and Farm Foremen	0	2	2	0	0
Farm laborers, wage workers		2	2		
Service Workers, Except Private Households	1	28	6	13	9
Chamber maids and maids		1	1		
Janitors		13		6	7
Busboys		2		1	1
Cooks		4	2	2	
Food counter and fountain workers		1	1		
Writers		3	2	1	
Food service worker	1				
Attendants, recreation and amusement		1		1	
Housekeepers		2	1	1	1
Guards and watchmen		1		1	
Total[b]	83	308	97	99	112

[b]Totals exclude 21 persons unemployed in 1979 and 15 missing observations.

Table D. Detailed Industrial Sector by Previous
Residence in the United States, Mexicans, 1979

Industrial Sector[a]	No Previous Residence		Previous Residence		Total	
	N	%	N	%	N	%
Agriculture, Forestry, *Fisheries*	10	9.7	16	5.0	26	6.2
Agricultural production	4		10		14	
Agricultural services	5		5		10	
Horticultural services	1		0		1	
Forestry	0		1		1	
Mining	2	1.9	6	1.9	8	1.9
Metal mining	1		2		3	
Crude petroleum and natural gas extractions	1		3		4	
Nonmetallic mining, quarrying	0		1		1	
Construction	6	5.8	40	12.6	46	10.9
General building contractors	4		23		27	
General contractors, except building	0		4		4	
Special trade contractors	2		8		10	
Not specified construction	0		5		5	
Manufacturing--Durable	21	20.4	79	24.8	100	23.7
Sawmills, planing mills, mill work	0		2		2	
Miscellaneous wood products	0		2		2	
Furniture and fixtures	3		6		9	
Glass and glass products	0		1		1	
Cement, concrete, gypsum, plaster products	1		1		2	
Structural clay products	0		1		1	
Miscellaneous nonmetallic mineral and stone products	0		1		1	
Blast furnaces, steel works, rolling and finishing mills	3		4		7	
Other primary iron and steel industries	1		2		3	
Primary aluminum industries	1		1		2	
Fabricated structural metal products	1		8		9	
Screw machine products	0		1		1	
Miscellaneous fabricated metal products	0		10		10	
Not specified metal industries	3		0		3	
Farm machinery and equipment	1		0		1	
Construction and material handling machines	1		2		3	

[a]Industrial titles are taken from the 1970 U.S. Census.

Table D--Continued

Industrial Sector[a]	No Previous Residence		Previous Residence		Total	
	N	%	N	%	N	%
Metal working machinery	0		1		1	
Office and accounting machines	0		2		2	
Electronic computing equipment	0		2		2	
Machinery, except electrical	1		4		5	
Household appliances	0		1		1	
Radio, TV and communication equipment	0		2		2	
Electrical machinery, equipment, supplies	0		6		6	
Motor vehicles and motor vehicle equipment	4		7		11	
Aircraft and parts	0		3		3	
Ship and boat building	0		1		1	
Railroad locomotives and equipment	0		3		3	
Mobile dwellers and campers	0		2		2	
Cycles and miscellaneous transport equipment	0		1		1	
Optical and health services supplies	0		1		1	
Miscellaneous manufacturing industries	1		1		2	
Manufacturing--Nondurable	19	18.5	52	16.4	71	16.9
Meat products	3		9		12	
Dairy products	0		2		2	
Canning, preserving fruits, vegetables, sea foods	1		3		4	
Grain mill products	1		2		3	
Bakery products	1		5		6	
Confectionery and related products	1		1		2	
Beverage industries	1		1		2	
Miscellaneous food preparation	1		1		2	
Miscellaneous textile mill products	0		1		1	
Apparel and accessories	5		11		16	
Paperboard containers, boxes	0		3		3	
Plastics, synthetics, resins	0		3		3	
Synthetic fibers	0		2		2	
Soaps and cosmetics	0		1		1	
Paints, varnishes and related products	0		1		1	
Miscellaneous petroleum and coal products	0		2		2	
Footwear, except rubber	2		2		4	
Leather products, except footwear	1		0		1	
Not specified manufacturing industries	2		2		4	
Transportation, Communication, Other Public Utilities	2	1.9	18	5.7	20	4.7
Railroads and railway express service	1		2		3	

Table D--Continued

Industrial Sector[a]	No Previous Residence		Previous Residence		Total	
	N	%	N	%	N	%
Street railways, bus lines	0		1		1	
Taxicab service	0		1		1	
Trucking service	0		5		5	
Warehousing and storage	1		1		2	
Water transportation	0		2		2	
Services incidental to trans- portation	0		1		1	
Radio broadcasting, television	0		1		1	
Electric light and power	0		1		1	
Gas and steam supply systems	0		3		3	
Wholesale Trade	7	*6.8*	9	*2.8*	16	*3.8*
Food and related products	2		1		3	
Farm products--raw material	0		2		2	
Metals and minerals (not else- where classified)	1		1		2	
Scrap and waste materials	1		0		1	
Alcoholic beverages	0		1		1	
Wholesalers (not elsewhere classified)	2		2		4	
Not specified wholesale trade	1		2		3	
Retail Trade	14	*13.6*	35	*11.0*	49	*11.6*
Lumber and building material	1		0		1	
Department and mail order establishments	2		0		2	
Miscellaneous general merchandise stores	1		0		1	
Grocery stores	0		3		3	
Food stores (not elsewhere classified)	0		1		1	
Motor vehicle dealers	2		5		7	
Gasoline service stations	0		3		3	
Apparel, accessories stores, except shoe stores	1		2		3	
Furniture and home furnishings stores	0		1		1	
Eating and drinking places	6		12		18	
Farm and garden supply stores	0		1		1	
Jewelry stores	0		4		4	
Fuel and ice dealers	0		1		1	
Retail florists	0		1		1	
Miscellaneous retail stores	1		0		1	
Not specified retail trade	0		1		1	
Finance, Insurance, Real Estate	2	*1.9*	1	*0.3*	3	*0.7*
Banking	1		0		1	
Credit agencies	1		0		1	
Insurance	0		1		1	

Table D--Continued

Industrial Sector[a]	No Previous Residence		Previous Residence		Total	
	N	%	N	%	N	%
Business and Repair Services	14	13.6	31	9.7	45	10.7
Advertising	0		1		1	
Services to dwellings and other buildings	2		9		11	
Computer programming services	1		1		2	
Business services (not elsewhere classified)	1		7		8	
Automobile repair and related services	7		7		14	
Electrical repair shops	0		2		2	
Miscellaneous repair services	3		4		7	
Personal Services	4	3.9	8	2.5	12	2.9
Hotels and motels	3		2		5	
Lodging places, except hotels and motels	1		3		4	
Laundering, cleaning, other garment services	0		3		3	
Entertainment and Recreation Services	0	0.0	2	0.6	2	0.5
Miscellaneous entertainment and recreation services	0		2		2	
Professional and Related Services	1	1.0	10	3.2	11	2.6
Hospitals	0		3		3	
Convalescent institutions	0		1		1	
Elementary and secondary schools	0		3		3	
Colleges and universities	0		1		1	
Not specified educational services	0		1		1	
Religious organizations	0		1		1	
Welfare services	1		0		1	
Public Administration	1	1.0	11	3.5	12	2.9
Federal public administration	1		0		1	
Local public administration	0		11		11	
Total[b]	103	100.0	318	100.0	421	100.0

[b]Totals exclude 29 persons unemployed in 1979 and 5 missing observations.

Table E. Detailed Occupation by Previous Residence
in the United States, Mexicans, 1979

Occupation[a]	No Previous Residence		Previous Residence		Total	
	N	%	N	%	N	%
Professional, Technical	1	1.0	6	1.9	7	1.7
Computer programmer	1		0		1	
Engineers (not elsewhere classified)	0		1		1	
Health technologist--radiology	0		1		1	
Clergymen	0		1		1	
Electrical engineering technician	0		1		1	
Vocational, educational counselor	0		1		1	
Radio, TV announcer	0		1		1	
Manager and Administrator	3	2.9	4	1.3	7	1.7
Buyers, wholesale and retail trade	1		1		2	
Restaurant, cafeteria, bar managers	1		0		1	
Sales managers and department heads	0		1		1	
Manager and administrator (not elsewhere classified)	1		2		3	
Sales Workers	1	1.0	1	0.3	2	0.5
Insurance agents, brokers, underwriters	0		1		1	
Salesmen and salesclerk (not elsewhere classified)	1		0		1	
Clerical and Kindred Workers	8	7.7	4	1.3	12	2.8
Clerical supervisors (not elsewhere classified)	2		0		2	
Expediters and production controllers	1		0		1	
File clerks	1		1		2	
Office machine operator--computer	1		0		1	
Secretaries (not elsewhere classified)	1		0		1	
Shipping and receiving clerks	1		2		3	
Miscellaneous clerical workers	0		1		1	
Not specified clerical workers	1		0		1	
Craftsmen and Kindred Workers	30	28.8	81	25.4	111	26.2
Bakers	1		3		4	
Brickmasons and stone masons	0		3		3	
Cabinet makers	2		2		4	
Carpenters	3		6		9	

[a]Occupational titles are taken from the 1970 U.S. Census.

Table E--Continued

Occupation[a]	No Previous Residence		Previous Residence		Total	
	N	%	N	%	N	%
Carpenter apprentices	0		2		2	
Cement and concrete finishers	2		2		4	
Cranemen, derrickmen and hoistmen	1		4		5	
Electricians	0		1		1	
Foremen (not elsewhere classified)	1		6		7	
Furniture and wood finishers	0		1		1	
Glaziers	1		0		1	
Jewelers and watchmakers	0		4		4	
Machinists	2		2		4	
Machinist apprentice	0		1		1	
Mechanics--air conditioning, heating, refrigeration	1		4		5	
Mechanics--automobile body repairmen	3		2		5	
Automobile mechanics	4		8		12	
Automobile mechanic apprentice	0		1		1	
Data processing machine repairmen	0		3		3	
Mechanics--farm implement	2		0		2	
Mechanic--heavy equipment	0		1		1	
Mechanic--loom fixers	1		1		2	
Mechanic--except auto, apprentices	1		0		1	
Miscellaneous mechanics and repairmen	0		3		3	
Molders, metal	2		4		6	
Painters, construction and maintenance	0		6		6	
Plumbers and pipe fitters	1		1		2	
Pressmen and plateprinters	0		1		1	
Rollers and finishers, metal	0		1		1	
Roofers and slaters	0		3		3	
Structural metal craftsmen	1		1		2	
Tailors	0		1		1	
Tile setters	1		0		1	
Upholsterers	0		2		2	
Specified craft apprentices (not elsewhere classified)	0		1		1	
Operatives--Nontransport	32	30.8	98	30.7	130	30.7
Assemblers	0		4		4	
Blasters and powder men	0		1		1	
Bottling and canning operative	1		2		3	
Checkers, examiners, inspectors, manufacturing	1		0		1	
Clothing ironers, pressers	0		3		3	
Cutting operatives (not elsewhere classified)	3		5		8	
Dry wall installers and lathers	0		4		4	
Filers, polishers, sanders, buffers	3		2		5	
Furnacemen, smeltermen, pourers	1		0		1	
Garage workers, gas station attendants	0		1		1	
Produce graders, packers, except factory and farm	0		2		2	

Table E--Continued

Occupation[a]	No Previous Residence		Previous Residence		Total	
	N	%	N	%	N	%
Laundry, dry cleaning operatives	0		1		1	
Meatcutters, butchers, except manufacturing	0		1		1	
Meatcutters, butchers, manufacturing	2		4		6	
Meat wrappers, retail trade	1		1		2	
Metal platers	0		2		2	
Mine operatives	1		1		2	
Mixing operatives	0		1		1	
Oilers and greasers, except auto	0		1		1	
Packers and wrappers, except meat	1		2		3	
Painters, manufactured articles	1		0		1	
Drill press operative	0		2		2	
Precision machine operative	1		1		2	
Punch and stamping press operative	2		0		2	
Sewers and stitchers	1		4		5	
Shoemaking machine operative	1		1		2	
Solderers	5		10		15	
Welders and flame cutters	2		11		13	
Machine operative, miscellaneous specified	2		13		15	
Machine operative, not specified.	2		8		10	
Miscellaneous operatives	1		4		5	
Not specified operative	0		6		6	
Operative--Transport	2	1.9	13	4.0	15	3.5
Bus driver	0		1		1	
Conductors, motormen, urban rail transit	0		1		1	
Deliverymen, routemen	0		1		1	
Forklift and tow motor operative	1		3		4	
Motormen; mine, factory, logging camp	0		2		2	
Taxicab drivers and chauffeurs	0		2		2	
Truck drivers	1		3		4	
Laborers, Except Farm	7	6.7	66	20.7	73	17.3
Animal caretaker	0		1		1	
Construction laborer	1		22		23	
Freight and material handlers	2		7		9	
Gardeners, groundskeepers	0		8		8	
Longshoremen, stevedores	0		1		1	
Stock handlers	2		5		7	
Vehicle washer, equipment cleaner	0		3		3	
Warehousemen (not elsewhere classified)	1		1		2	
Miscellaneous laborers	1		13		14	
Not specified laborers	0		5		5	
Farmers and Farm Managers	0	0.0	0	0.0	0	0.0

Table E--Continued

Occupation[a]	No Previous Residence		Previous Residence		Total	
	N	%	N	%	N	%
Farm Laborers and Farm Foremen	9	8.6	15	4.7	24	5.7
Farm laborers, wage workers	9		15		24	
Service Workers, Except Private Household	11	10.6	31	9.7	42	9.9
Janitors and sextons	2		13		15	
Bartenders	1		0		1	
Busboys	2		0		2	
Cooks	2		9		11	
Dishwashers	1		1		2	
Waiters	1		2		3	
Food service workers	2		0		2	
Health aides, except nurse	0		1		1	
Nursing aides, orderlies, attendants	0		1		1	
Attendants, recreation, amusement	0		1		1	
Guards and watchmen	0		2		2	
Service worker, allocated	0		1		1	
Total[b]	104	100.0	319	100.0	423	100.0

[b]Totals exclude 29 persons unemployed in 1979 and 3 missing observations.

BIBLIOGRAPHY

Acosta, Maruja, and Jorge E. Hardoy
   1973   *Urban Reform in Revolutionary Cuba*. Occasional Papers 1. New Haven: Antilles Research Program, Yale University.
Alba, Francisco
   1976   "Exodo Silencioso: La Emigración de Trabajadores Mexicanos a Estados Unidos." *Foro Internacional* 17 (October–December): 152–79.
   1977   *La Población de México: Evolución y Dilemas*. México D. F.: El Colegio de México.
   1978   "Mexico's International Migration as a Manifestation of Its Development Pattern." *International Migration Review* 12 (Winter): 502–13.
Anderson, Grace M.
   1974   *Networks of Contact: The Portuguese and Toronto*. Ontario: Wilfrid Laurier University Press.
Arguelles, L.
   1982   "Cuban Miami: The Roots, Development and Everyday Life of an Emigré Enclave in the U.S. National Security State." In M. Dixon and S. Jonas (eds.), *The New Nomads* (San Francisco: Synthesis Publications), pp. 27–43.
Arizpe, Lourdes
   1978   *Migración, Etnicismo y Cambio Económico*. México D. F.: El Colegio de México.
   1984   "The Rural Exodus in Mexico and Mexican Migration to the United States." In P. G. Brown and H. Shue (eds.), *The Border That Joins*. Vol. 1. Totowa, N.J.: Rowman and Littlefield. Forthcoming.
Astin, A. and R. J. Panos
   1969   "The Educational and Vocational Development of College Students." Washington, D.C.: American Council on Education. Mimeographed report.
Azicri, Max
   1980   "The Politics of Exile: Trends and Dynamics of Political Change Among Cuban-Americans." Paper presented at the Annual Meeting of the Latin American Studies Association, Bloomington, Indiana (October).

Bach, Robert L.
    1978   "Mexican Immigration and the American State." *International Migration Review* 12 (Winter): 536–58.
Bach, Robert L., Jennifer B. Bach, and Timothy Triplett
    1981   "The Flotilla 'Entrants': Latest and Most Controversial." *Cuban Studies* 11 (July): 29–48.
Badillo-Veiga, Americo, Josh DeWind, and Julia Preston
    1979   "Undocumented Immigrant Workers in New York City." *NACLA Report on the Americas* 13 (November–December): 2–46.
Balan, Jorge, Harley L. Browning, and Elizabeth Jelin
    1973   *Men in a Developing Society: Geographic and Social Mobility in Monterrey, Mexico.* Austin, Tex.: University of Texas Press.
Barkin, David
    1972   "Cuban Agriculture: A Strategy of Economic Development." *Studies in Comparative International Development* 7 (Spring): 19–38.
    1972   "The Redistribution of Consumption in Cuba." *The Review of Radical Political Economics* 4 (5 / Fall): 80–102.
Barrera, Mario
    1980   *Race and Class in the Southwest: A Theory of Racial Inequality.* Notre Dame, Ind.: Notre Dame University Press.
Blauner, Robert
    1972   *Radical Oppression in America.* New York: Harper & Row.
Blegen, Theodore
    1940   *Norwegian Migration to America.* Vols. 1 and 2. Northfield, Minn.: Norwegian-American Historical Association.
Bogardus, Emory S.
    1928   *Immigration and Race Attitudes.* Boston: Heath.
Bonacich, Edna
    1972   "A Theory of Ethnic Antagonism: The Split Labor Market." *American Sociological Review* 37 (October): 547–49.
    1976   "Advanced Capitalism and Black/White Relations: A Split Labor Market Interpretation." *American Sociological Review* 41 (February): 34–51.
    1978   "U.S. Capitalism and Korean Immigrant Small Business." Department of Sociology, University of California, Riverside. Mimeographed.
Bonacich, Edna, and John Modell
    1980   *The Economic Basis of Ethnic Solidarity: Small Business in the Japanese-American Community.* Berkeley, Calif.: University of California Press.
Borjas, George
    1980   "The Earnings of Male Hispanic Immigrants in the United States." Department of Economics, University of California, Santa Barbara. Mimeographed.
Boswell, Thomas D.
    1984   "Cuban Americans." In J. O. McKee (ed.), *Ethnic Minorities in the United States* (Dubuque, Iowa: Kendall / Hunt). Forthcoming.

Burawoy, Michael
    1976   "The Function and Reproduction of Migrant Labor: Comparative Material from Southern Africa and the United States." *American Journal of Sociology* 81 (March): 1050–87.

Bustamante, Jorge A.
    1973   "The Historical Context of Undocumented Mexican Immigration to the United States." *Aztlan* 3: 257–81.
    1976   "Espaldas Mojadas: Materia Prima para la Expansión del Capital Norteamericano." *Cuadernos del CES* 9: 3–6.

Bustamante, Jorge A., and Geronimo G. Martinez
    1979   "Undocumented Immigration from Mexico: Beyond Borders but Within Systems." *Journal of International Affairs* 33 (Fall/Winter): 265–84.
    1980   "La Emigración a la Frontera Norte del País y a Estados Unidos." In M. Kritz (ed.), *Migraciones Internacionales en las Américas* (Caracas: CEPAM), pp. 196–218.

Cardona, Ramiro
    1980   *El Exodo de Colombianos.* Part II. Bogotá: Ediciones Tercer Mundo.

Casal, Lourdes, and Andres R. Hernandez
    1975   "Cubans in the U.S.: A Survey of the Literature." *Cuban Studies* 5 (July): 25–51.

Castellanos, Sylvia
    1980   "The Cuban Refugee Problem in Perspective, 1959–1980." In *The Backgrounder* #124 (Washington, D.C.: The Heritage Foundation).

Castells, Manuel
    1975   "Immigrant Workers and Class Struggles in Advanced Capitalism: The Western European Experience." *Politics and Society* 5: 33–66.

Castles, Stephen, and Godula Kosack
    1973   *Immigrant Workers and Class Structure in Western Europe.* New York: Oxford University Press.

Child, Irving L.
    1943   *Italian or American? The Second Generation in Conflict.* New Haven: Yale University Press.

Chiswick, Barry R.
    1980   *An Analysis of the Economic Progress and Impact of Immigrants.* Final Report to the U.S. Department of Labor, Employment and Training Administration. (Chicago Circle: Department of Economics, University of Illinois). Mimeographed.

Clark, Juan M.
    1970   "Selected Types of Cuban Exiles Used as a Sample of the Cuban Population." Paper presented at the Annual Meetings of the Rural Sociological Society, Washington, D.C. (August).
    1973   "Los Cubanos de Miami: Cuántos Son y de Donde Provienen." *Ideal* 2 (January): 17–19.
    1977   *The Cuban Exodus: Why?* Miami: Cuban Exile Union.

Clark, Juan M., José I. Lasaga, and Rose S. Reque
    1981   *The 1980 Mariel Exodus: An Assessment and Prospect.* Washington,
            D.C.: Council for Inter-American Security.
Cornelius, Wayne A.
    1976   "Mexican Migration to the United States: The View from Rural Send-
            ing Communities." Working paper, Center for International Studies,
            M.I.T.
    1977   "Illegal Immigration to the United States: Recent Research Findings,
            Policy Implications and Research Priorities." Working paper, Center for
            International Studies, M.I.T.
    1978   "Mexican Migration to the United States: Causes, Consequences, and
            U.S. Responses." Working paper, Center for International Studies,
            M.I.T.
    1979   "Mexican and Caribbean Migration to the United States: The State of
            Current Knowledge and Recommendations for Future Research."
            Working Papers in U.S.–Mexican Studies #2, University of California,
            San Diego.
    1981   "Immigration, Mexican Development Policy, and the Future of U.S.–
            Mexican Relations." In R. H. McBride (ed.), *American Assembly of
            Mexico and the United States* (Englewood Cliffs, N. J.: Prentice-Hall),
            pp. 104–27.
Cox, Oliver C.
    1948   *Caste, Class, and Race: A Study in Social Dynamics.* New York:
            Doubleday.
Cue, Reynaldo
    1975   "Men From an Underdeveloped Society: The Socioeconomic and Spa-
            tial Origins and Initial Destination of Documented Mexican Immi-
            grants." Master's thesis, University of Texas, Austin.
Cumberland, Charles
    1968   *Mexico: The Struggle for Modernity.* New York: Oxford University
            Press.
Daniels, Roger
    1977   "The Japanese-American Experience: 1890–1940." In L. Dinnerstein
            and F. C. Jaher (eds.), *Uncertain Americans: Readings in Ethnic History*
            (New York: Oxford University Press), pp. 250–67.
DeWind, Josh, Tom Seidl, and Janet Shenk
    1977   "Contract Labor in U.S. Agriculture." *NACLA Report on the Americas*
            11 (November–December): 4–37.
Diaz-Briquets, Sergio, and Lisandro Perez
    1981   "Cuba: The Demography of Revolution." *Population Bulletin* 36
            (April): 2–41.
Dinerman, Ina R.
    1978   "Patterns of Adaptation Among Households of U.S.-Bound Migrants
            from Michoacan, Mexico." *International Migration Review* 12 (Winter):
            485–501.

Dinnerstein, Leonard
    1977   "The East European Jewish Migration." In L. Dinnerstein and F. C. Jaher (eds.), *Uncertain Americans: Readings in Ethnic History* (New York: Oxford University Press), pp. 216–31.

Dinnerstein, Leonard, and Frederick Cole Jaher
    1977   *Uncertain Americans: Readings in Ethnic History.* New York: Oxford University Press.

Duncan, Otis D.
    1966   "Path Analysis: Sociological Examples." *American Journal of Sociology* 72 (July): 1–16.

Eckstein, Susan
    1977   *The Poverty of Revolution: The State and the Urban Poor in Mexico.* Princeton, N.J.: Princeton University Press.

Edwards, Richard C.
    1975   "The Social Relations of Production in the Firm and Labor Market Structure." In R. C. Edwards, M. Reich, and D. M. Gordon (eds.), *Labor Market Segmentation* (Lexington, Mass.: D. C. Heath), pp. 3–26.
    1979   *Contested Terrain: The Transformation of the Workplace in the Twentieth Century.* New York: Harper Torchbooks.

Eisenstadt, S. N.
    1970   "The Process of Absorbing New Immigrants in Israel." In S. N. Eisenstadt, RivKah Bar Yosef, and Chaim Adler (eds.), *Integration and Development in Israel* (Jerusalem: Israel University Press), pp. 341–67.

Fagen, Richard R.
    1969   *The Transformation of Political Culture in Cuba.* Palo Alto, Calif.: Stanford University Press.

Fagen, Richard R., Richard A. Brody, and Thomas J. O'Leary
    1968   *Cubans in Exile: Disaffection and the Revolution.* Palo Alto, Calif.: Stanford University Press.

Frazier, E. Franklin
    1949   *The Negro in the United States.* New York: Macmillan.

Freeman, H. E., E. Novak, and L. G. Reader
    1957   "Correlates of Membership in Voluntary Associations." *American Sociological Review* 22 (October): 528–33.

Gaertner, Miriam L.
    1955   "A Comparison of Refugee and Non-refugee Immigrants to New York City." In H. B. Murphy (ed.), *Flight and Resettlement* (Lucerne: UNESCO), pp. 99–112.

Galarza, Ernesto
    1977   *Farm Workers and Agri-business in California, 1947–1960.* Notre Dame, Ind.: Notre Dame University Press.

Gamio, Manuel
    1930   *Mexican Immigration to the United States.* Chicago: University of Chicago Press.

Garcia, Mario
   1975   "Obreros: The Mexican Workers of El Paso." Ph. D. dissertation, University of California, San Diego.
Geschwender, James A.
   1978   *Racial Stratification in America.* Dubuque, Iowa: William C. Brown.
Glaser, William A., and Christopher Habers
   1974   "The Migration and Return of Professionals." *International Migration Review* 8 (Summer): 227–44.
Glazer, Nathan, and Daniel P. Moynihan
   1970   *Beyond the Melting Pot: The Negroes, Puerto Ricans, Jews, Italians and Irish of New York City.* Cambridge, Mass.: The M. I.T. Press.
Gordon, David M.
   1972   *Theories of Poverty and Underemployment: Orthodox, Radical, and Dual Labor Market Perspectives.* Lexington, Mass.: D. C. Heath.
Gordon, Milton M.
   1964   *Assimilation in American Life: The Role of Race, Religion, and National Origins.* New York: Oxford University Press.
Grasmuck, Sherri
   1981   "International Stair-Step Migration: Dominican Labor in the U. S. and Haitian Labor in the Dominican Republic." Department of Sociology, Temple University. Mimeographed.
Grasmuck, Sherri, and Patricia Pessar
   1982   "Undocumented Dominican Migration to the United States." Research project, Center for International Studies, Duke University.
Grebler, Leo, Joan W. Moore, and Ralph C. Guzman
   1970   *The Mexican-American People: The Nation's Second Largest Minority.* New York: The Free Press.
Greeley, Andrew
   1971   *Why Can't They Be Like Us? America's White Ethnic Groups.* New York: E. P. Dutton.
Guhleman, Patricia, Marta Tienda, and Marion Bowman
   1981   "An Employment and Earnings Profile of Hispanic Origin Workers in the U. S." In Marta Tienda (ed.), *Hispanic Origin Workers in the U. S. Labor Market: Comparative Analyses of Employment Earnings,* Final Report to the U. S. Department of Labor (Department of Rural Sociology, University of Wisconsin–Madison), pp. 1–91. Mimeographed.
Handlin, Oscar
   1941   *Boston's Immigrants: A Study of Acculturation.* Cambridge: Harvard University Press.
   1951   *The Uprooted: The Epic Story of the Great Migrations that Made the American People.* Boston: Little, Brown.
Hanushek, Eric, and John E. Jackson
   1977   *Statistical Methods for Social Scientists.* New York: Academic Press.
Hardoy, Jorge E.
   1973   "Spatial Structure and Society in Revolutionary Cuba." Warner Modular Publications, Module #265.

Hechter, Michael
1977   *Internal Colonialism: The Celtic Fringe in British National Development, 1536–1966.* Berkeley, Calif.: University of California Press.
Heise, David R., and George W. Bohrnstedt
1970   "Validity, Invalidity, and Reliability." In E. F. Borgatta and G. W. Bohrnstedt (eds.), *Sociological Methodology 1970* (San Francisco: Jossey-Bass), pp. 104–29.
Heiss, J.
1969   "Factors Related to Immigrant Assimilation: Pre-migration Traits." *Social Forces* 4 (June): 422–28.
Hendricks, G. L.
1974   *The Dominican Diaspora: From the Dominican Republic to New York City—Villages in Transition.* New York: Columbia University Teachers College Press.
Horowitz, Morris A.
1962   *La Emigración de Profesionales y Técnicos Argentinos.* Buenos Aires: Editorial del Instituto.
Immigration Commission
1911   *Reports of the Immigration Commission.* Vol. 1. U.S. Senate, 61st Congress. Washington, D.C.: U.S. Government Printing Office.
Inkeles, Alex
1969   "Making Men Modern: On the Causes and Consequences of Individual Change in Six Developing Countries." *American Journal of Sociology* 75 (September): 208–55.
Inkeles, Alex, and David H. Smith
1974   *Becoming Modern: Individual Change in Six Developing Countries.* Cambridge: Harvard University Press.
Iwata, Masakuzu
1962   "The Japanese Immigrants in California Agriculture." *Agricultural History* 36: 25–37.
Jaffe, A. J., Ruth M. Cullen, and Thomas D. Boswell
1980   *The Changing Demography of Spanish Americans.* New York: Academic Press.
Jöreskog, Karl G.
1977   "Structural Equation Models in the Social Sciences: Specification, Estimation and Testing." In P. Krisnaiah (ed.), *Applications of Statistics* (New York: North Holland), pp. 265–87.
Jöreskog, Karl G., and Dag Sörbom
1978   *LISREL IV: Estimation of Linear Structural Equations by Maximum Likelihood Methods.* Chicago: National Educational Resources.
1979   *Advances in Factor Analysis and Structural Equation Models.* Cambridge: Abt Books.
Jorge, Antonio, and Raul Moncarz
1980   "Cubans in South Florida: A Social Science Approach." *Metas* 1 (Fall): 37–87.
1981   "International Factor Movement and Complementarity: Growth and

Entrepreneurship Under Conditions of Cultural Variation." *REMP Bulletin*, Supplement 14 (September).

1982   "The Cuban Entrepreneur and the Economic Development of the Miami SMSA." Department of Economics, Florida International University. Manuscript.

Kahl, Joseph A.
1968   *The Measurement of Modernism.* Austin, Tex.: University of Texas Press.

Kim, Illsoo
1981   *New Urban Immigrants: The Korean Community in New York.* Princeton, N.J.: Princeton University Press.

Kinzer, Robert H., and Edward Sagarin
1950   *The Negro in American Business: The Conflict between Separation and Integration.* New York: Greensburg.

Land, Kenneth C.
1969   "Principles of Path Analysis." In Edgar F. Borgatta and George Bohrnstedt (eds.), *Sociological Methodology 1969* (San Francisco: Jossey-Bass), pp. 3–37.

Lane, Angela
1968   "Occupational Mobility in Six Cities." *American Sociological Review* 33 (October): 556–64.

Lebergott, Stanley
1964   *Manpower in Economic Growth: The American Record Since 1800.* New York: McGraw-Hill.

Lerner, Daniel
1965   *The Passing of Traditional Society: Modernizing the Middle East.* New York: The Free Press.

Levy, Marion J.
1966   *Modernization and the Structure of Societies.* Princeton, N.J.: Princeton University Press.

1972   *Modernization: Latecomers and Survivors.* New York: Basic Books.

Lieberson, Stanley
1980   *A Piece of the Pie: Blacks and White Immigrants Since 1880.* Berkeley, Calif.: University of California Press.

Light, Ivan H.
1972   *Ethnic Enterprise in America: Business and Welfare Among Chinese, Japanese, and Blacks.* Berkeley, Calif.: University of California Press.

Lomnitz, Larissa
1977   *Networks and Marginality: Life in a Mexican Shantytown.* New York: Academic Press.

MacDonald, John S., and Leatrice D. MacDonald
1974   "Chain Migration, Ethnic Neighborhood Formation, and Social Networks." In Charles Tilly (ed.), *An Urban World* (Boston: Little, Brown), pp. 226–36.

Manitzas, Nita R.
1973   "The Setting of the Cuban Revolution." Warner Modular Publications, Module #260.

Mazur, Jay
    1979   "The Return of the Sweatshop." *The New Leader* (August): 7–10.
Mill, John Stuart
    1909   *Principles of Political Economy*. London: Longmans.
Mines, Richard
    1981   *Developing a Community Tradition of Migration: A Field Study in Ru-ral Zacatecas, Mexico, and California Settlement Areas*. Monograph in U. S.-Mexican Studies 3. Program in U. S.-Mexican Studies, University of California, San Diego.
NACLA
    1979   "Undocumented Immigrant Workers in New York City." *North American Congress on Latin America (NACLA) Report on the Americas* 13 (November-December): 2–46.
Nagel, John S.
    1978   "Mexico's Population Policy Turnaround." *Population Bulletin* 33 (3 / December): 1–40.
National Commission for Manpower Policy
    1978   *Manpower and Immigration Policies in the United States*. Special Report #20. Washington, D. C.: National Commission for Manpower Policy.
North, David S.
    1981   "The Impact of Illegal and Refugee Migrations on U. S. Social Service Programs." Paper presented at the Immigration and Refugee Workshop, sponsored by the Ford, Rockefeller, and Johnson Foundations at Wingspread, Wisconsin (August).
North, David S., and Marion F. Houstoun
    1976   *The Characteristics and Role of Illegal Aliens in the U. S. Labor Market: An Exploratory Study*. Washington, D. C.: Linton and Co.
O'Connor, James
    1973   *The Fiscal Crisis of the State*. New York: St. Martin's Press.
Oshima, H. T.
    1961   "A New Estimate of the National Income and Product of Cuba in 1953." *Food Research Institute Studies* 2 (November): 213–27.
Oteiza, Enrique
    1971   "Emigración de Profesionales, Técnicos y Obreros Calificados Argentinos a los Estados Unidos." *Desarrollo Económico* 10 (January–March): 429–54.
Pedraza-Bailey, Silvia
    1981   "Cubans and Mexicans in the United States: The Functions of Political and Economic Migration." *Cuban Studies* 11 (July): 79–97.
Peshkin, Alan, and Ronald Cohen
    1967   "The Values of Modernization." *Journal of Developing Areas* 2 (October): 7–21.
Petersen, William
    1971   *Japanese Americans: Oppression and Success*. New York: Random House.

Piore, Michael J.
    1975   "Notes for a Theory of Labor Market Stratification." In Richard C. Ed-
            wards, Michael Reich, and David M. Gordon (eds.), *Labor Market Seg-
            mentation* (Lexington, Mass.: D. C. Heath), pp. 125–71.
    1979   *Birds of Passage: Migrant Labor and Industrial Societies.* New York:
            Cambridge University Press.

Portes, Alejandro
    1969   "Dilemmas of a Golden Exile: Integration of Cuban Refugee Families
            in Milwaukee." *American Sociological Review* 34 (August): 505–18.
    1974   "Return of the Wetback." *Society* 11 (March–April): 40–49.
    1976   "Determinants of the Brain Drain." *International Migration Review* 10
            (Winter): 489–508.
    1978   "Migration and Underdevelopment." *Politics and Society* 8: 1–48.
    1978   "Toward a Structural Analysis of Illegal (Undocumented) Immigration."
            International Migration Review 12 (Winter): 469–84.
    1979   "Illegal Immigration and the International System: Lessons from
            Recent Legal Immigrants from Mexico." *Social Problems* 26 (April):
            425–38.
    1981   "Modes of Incorporation and Theories of Labor Immigration." In Mary
            M. Kritz, Charles B. Keely, and Silvano M. Tomasi (eds.), *Global Trends
            in Migration: Theory and Research on International Population Move-
            ments* (New York: Center for Migration Studies), pp. 279–97.
    1981   "Reply to Rogg." *Cuban Studies / Estudios Cubanos* 11 (July): 213–15.

Portes, Alejandro, and Robert L. Bach
    1980   "Immigrant Earnings: Cuban and Mexican Immigrants in the United
            States." *International Migration Review* 14 (Fall): 315–41.

Portes, Alejandro, Juan M. Clark, and Robert L. Bach
    1977   "The New Wave: A Statistical Profile of Recent Cuban Exiles in the
            United States." *Cuban Studies* 7 (January): 1–32.

Portes, Alejandro, Juan M. Clark, and Manuel M. Lopez
    1981   "Six Years Later: A Profile of the Process of Incorporation of Cuban
            Exiles in the United States: 1973–1979." *Cuban Studies* 11 (July): 1–24.

Portes, Alejandro, Robert N. Parker, and Jose A. Cobas
    1980   "Assimilation or Consciousness: Perceptions of U. S. Society Among Re-
            cent Latin American Immigrants to the United States." *Social Forces* 59
            (September): 200–24.

Ralph, John H., and Richard Rubinson
    1980   "Immigration and the Expansion of Schooling: 1890–1970." *American
            Sociological Review* 45 (December): 943–54.

Reichert, Joshua S.
    1981   "The Migrant Syndrome: Seasonal U. S. Wage Labor and Rural Devel-
            opment in Central Mexico." *Human Organization* 40 (Spring): 59–66.

Reichert, Joshua, and Douglas Massey

n.d. "Guestworker Programs: Evidence from Europe and the United States and Some Implications for U. S. Policy." Working Papers of the Program in Population Research, University of California, Berkeley.

1979 "Patterns of U. S. Migration from a Mexican Sending Community: A Comparison of Legal and Illegal Migrants." *International Migration Review* 13 (Winter): 599–623.

1980 "History and Trends in U. S. Bound Migration from a Mexican Town." *International Migration Review* 14 (Winter): 475–91.

Rhoades, Robert E.

1978 "Intra-European Return Migration and Rural Development: Lessons from the Spanish Case." *Human Organization* 37 (Summer): 136–47.

Rischin, Moses

1962 *The Promised City: New York Jews, 1870–1914.* Cambridge, Mass.: Harvard University Press.

Roberts, Bryan R.

1976 "The Provincial Urban System and the Process of Dependency." In Alejandro Portes and Harley H. Browning (eds.), *Current Perspectives in Latin American Urban Research* (Austin, Tex.: Institute of Latin American Studies of the University of Texas), pp. 91–131.

Rogg, Eleanor Meyer

1974 *The Assimilation of Cuban Exiles: The Role of Community and Class.* New York: Aberdeen Press.

Rosenblum, Gerald

1973 *Immigrant Workers: Their Impact on American Radicalism.* New York: Basic Books.

Samora, Julian

1971 *Los Mojados: The Wetback Story.* Notre Dame, Ind.: Notre Dame University Press.

Santibañez, Enrique

1930 *Ensayo acerca de la Inmigración Mexicana en los Estados Unidos.* San Antonio, Tex.: Clegg.

Sassen-Koob, Saskia

1978 "The International Circulation of Resources and Development: The Case of Migrant Labor." *Development and Change* 9 (4/October): 509–45.

1979 "Formal and Informal Associations: Dominicans and Colombians in New York." *International Migration Review* 13 (Summer): 314–32.

1980 "Immigrant and Minority Workers in the Organization of the Labor Process." *Journal of Ethnic Studies* 1 (Spring): 1–34.

Seers, Dudley (ed.)

1964 *Cuba: The Economic and Social Revolution.* Chapel Hill, N. C.: University of North Carolina Press.

Silverman, Bertram
    1973   "Economic Organization and Social Conscience: Some Dilemmas of
            Cuban Socialism." In J. Ann Zammit (ed.), *The Chilean Road to Social-
            ism* (Sussex, England: Institute of Development Studies), pp. 391–418.
Sombart, Werner
    1913   *The Jews and Modern Capitalism.* London: T. F. Unwin.
Sowell, Thomas
    1981   *Ethnic America: A History.* New York: Basic Books.
Stevens, Rosemary, Louis W. Goodman, and Stephen Mick
    1978   *The Alien Doctors: Foreign Medical Graduates in American Hospitals.*
            New York: Wiley.
Stolzenberg, Ross M.
    1982   *Occupational Differences Between Hispanics and Non-Hispanics.* Re-
            port to the National Commission for Employment Policy. Santa Mon-
            ica, Calif.: The Rand Corporation.
Stone, Katherine
    1975   "The Origins of Job Structure in the Steel Industry." In R. C. Edwards,
            M. Reich, and D. M. Gordon (eds.), *Labor Market Segmentation* (Lex-
            ington, Mass.: D. C. Heath), pp. 27–84.
Subcommittee on Migratory Labor, U. S. Senate
    1970   "Migrant and Seasonal Farmworker Powerlessness: Who Is Responsi-
            ble?" Hearings before the subcommittee, U. S. Senate, 91st Congress,
            Part 8A (July 20), Part 8B (July 21), and Part 8C (July 24). Washington,
            D. C.: U. S. Government Printing Office.
Suhrke, Astri
    1982   "Global Refugee Movements and Strategies of Response." In Mary
            Kritz (ed.), *U. S. Immigration and Refugee Policy* (Lexington, Mass.:
            D. C. Heath), pp. 157–73.
Suttles, Gerald D.
    1968   *The Social Order of the Slum: Ethnicity and Territory in the Inner City.*
            Chicago: University of Chicago Press.
Tabori, Paul
    1972   *The Anatomy of Exile: A Semantic and Historical Study.* London:
            George Harrap and Co.
Thomas, Brinley
    1973   *Migration and Economic Growth: A Study of Great Britain and the
            Atlantic Economy.* London: Cambridge University Press.
Thomas, John F., and Earl E. Huyck
    1967   "Resettlement of Cuban Refugees in the United States." Paper pre-
            sented at the Meetings of the American Sociological Association, San
            Francisco (August).
Thomas, William I., and Florian Znaniecki
    1927   *The Polish Peasant in Europe and America.* Vol. 2. New York: Knopf.

Thompson, Edgar
   1939   "The Plantation: The Physical Basis for Traditional Race Relations." In
           E. T. Thompson (ed.), *Race Relations and the Race Problem: A Definition
           and an Analysis* (Durham, N. C.: Duke University Press), pp. 180–218.
Tienda, Marta
   1980   "Familism and Structural Assimilation of Mexican Immigrants in the
           United States." *International Migration Review* 14 (Fall): 383–408.
Tilly, Charles
   1978   "Migration in Modern European History." In William S. McNeill and
           Ruth Adams (eds.), *Human Migration, Patterns and Policies* (Blooming-
           ton, Ind.: Indiana University Press), pp. 48–72.
Time
   1978   "Spanish Americans: Soon the Biggest Minority." *Time* (October 16):
           48–61.
Tolbert, Charles, Patrick M. Horan, and E. M. Beck
   1980   "The Structure of Economic Segmentation: A Dual Economy Ap-
           proach." *American Journal of Sociology* 85 (March): 1095–116.
Treiman, Donald J.
   1977   *Occupational Prestige in Comparative Perspective*. New York: Aca-
           demic Press.
Ugalde, Antonio, Frank D. Bean, and Gilbert Cardenas
   1979   "International Migration from the Dominican Republic: Findings from
           a National Survey." *International Migration Review* 13 (Summer):
           235–54.
Unikel, Luis
   1968   "El Proceso de Urbanización en México: Distribución y Crecimiento
           de la Población Urbana." *Demografía y Economía* 2: 139–82.
Urquidi, Victor L.
   1974   "Empleo y Explosión Demográfica." *Demografía y Economía* 8: 141–53.
U. S. Bureau of the Census
   1975   *Current Population Reports—Persons of Spanish Origin in the U. S.*
           Series P-20, #280. Washington, D. C.: U. S. Government Printing
           Office.
   1976   *Historical Statistics of the United States—Colonial Times to 1970.*
           Vol. 2, Bicentennial Edition. Washington, D. C.: U. S. Government
           Printing Office.
   1981   *Statistical Abstract of the United States, 1978.* Washington, D. C.: U. S.
           Government Printing Office.
   1982   *U. S. A. Statistics in Brief, 1981.* Washington, D. C.: U. S. Government
           Printing Office.
U. S. Government
   1980   *Economic Report of the President, 1980.* Washington, D. C.: U. S. Gov-
           ernment Printing Office. Tables B27, B29.

BIBLIOGRAPHY

U. S. Immigration and Naturalization Service
   1974   *Annual Report*. Washington, D. C.: U. S. Government Printing Office.
   1976   *Annual Report*. Washington, D. C.: U. S. Government Printing Office.
   1977   *Annual Report*. Washington, D. C.: U. S. Government Printing Office.
   1978   *Annual Report*. Washington, D. C.: U. S. Government Printing Office.
   1979   *Annual Report*. Washington, D. C.: U. S. Government Printing Office.
   1980   "Cubans Arrived in the United States by Class of Admission: January 1,
           1959–September 30, 1980." Washington, D. C. Internal document,
           mimeographed.
   1982   *1979 Statistical Yearbook*. Washington, D. C.: U. S. Government Print-
           ing Office.
Van Ginneken, Wouter
   1980   *Socio-economic Groups and Income Distribution in Mexico*. New York:
           St. Martin's Press.
Vecoli, Rudolph
   1977   "The Italian Americans." In L. Dinnerstein and F. C. Jaher (eds.), *Un-
           certain Americans: Readings in Ethnic History* (New York: Oxford Uni-
           versity Press), pp. 201–15.
Villalpando, Vic
   1977   *A Study of the Socioeconomic Impact of Illegal Aliens on the County
           of San Diego*. San Diego, Calif.: Human Resources Agency of San
           Diego County.
Warner, W. Lloyd and Leo Srole
   1945   *The Social Systems of American Ethnic Groups*. New Haven: Yale Uni-
           versity Press.
Weber, Max
   1950   *The Protestant Ethic and the Spirit of Capitalism*. New York: Scribners.
   1951   *The Religion of China*. Glencoe, Ill.: The Free Press.
Werts, Charles E., Karl G. Jöreskog, and Robert L. Linn
   1973   "Identification and Estimation in Path Analysis with Unmeasured Vari-
           ables." *American Journal of Sociology* 78 (May): 1469–84.
Wilson, James A.
   1969   "Motivations Underlying the Brain Drain." In K. Baier and N. Rescher
           (eds.), *Values and the Future* (New York: The Free Press), pp. 431–52.
Wilson, Kenneth, and W. Allen Martin
   1982   "Ethnic Enclaves: A Comparison of the Cuban and Black Economies in
           Miami." *American Journal of Sociology* 88 (July): 135–60.
Wilson, Kenneth L., and Alejandro Portes
   1980   "Immigrant Enclaves: An Analysis of the Labor Market Experiences
           of Cubans in Miami." *American Journal of Sociology* 86 (September):
           295–319.
Wittke, Carl
   1952   *Refugees of Revolution: The German Forty-eighters in America*. Phila-
           delphia: University of Pennsylvania Press.
Womack, John, Jr.
   1968   *Zapata and the Mexican Revolution*. New York: Vintage Books.

INDEX